BEHIND THE MAGIC CURTAIN

BEHIND THE
MAGIC CURTAIN

*Secrets, Spies, and Unsung White Allies
of Birmingham's Civil Rights Days*

T. K. THORNE

*Reviewed for Alabama Writers
Forum - Jeanie Thompson.*

NewSouth Books
Montgomery

NewSouth Books
105 S. Court Street
Montgomery, AL 36104

Publisher's Cataloging-in-Publication Data

Names: Thorne, T. K., author.
Title: Behind the magic curtain: Secrets, spies, and unsung white allies of Birmingham's
civil rights days / T. K. Thorne.
Description: Montgomery : NewSouth Books [2021]. | Includes bibliographical
references and index.
Identifiers: LCCN 2021930748 | ISBN 9781588384409 (hardcover) | ISBN
9781588384430 (ebook).
Subjects: Journalists and editors—Civil rights movement—Biography. | Law
enforcement—Civil rights movement—Biography. | Civil rights movement—History—
United States. | 20th century—History—United States. | South—History—United
States. | Alabama—History—United States. I. Title.

Design by Randall Williams
Printed in the United States of America by Sheridan

*The Black Belt, defined by its dark, rich soil, stretches across central
Alabama. It was the heart of the cotton belt. It was and is a place of great
beauty, of extreme wealth and grinding poverty, of pain and joy. Here we
take our stand, listening to the past, looking to the future.*

To my family,
who provided the air of civil and human rights
I breathed in my youth, and to those who loved and love
Birmingham with all her scars, tragedies, and triumphs.

Blessed are the peacemakers, for they shall catch hell from all sides.
SIGN IN THE OFFICE OF BURKE MARSHALL, HEAD OF
ROBERT KENNEDY'S CIVIL RIGHTS DIVISION

Its reputation as a bastion of hard-line segregation notwithstanding, Birmingham's social and political atmosphere was complex.
SOL KIMERLING, BIRMINGHAM HISTORIAN

There were a lot of white people who were with us. Everybody white is not bad and everybody black is not good.
NIMS "DADDY" GAY, CIVIL RIGHTS MOVEMENT LEADER

Events in Birmingham changed the world.
BILL BAXLEY, FORMER ALABAMA ATTORNEY
GENERAL AND LIEUTENANT GOVERNOR

Contents

Eight pages of photos follow page 180

Preface

This book has been the better part of a decade in the making. I was asked to write it by four men who loved Birmingham and wanted to pull aside the Magic City's curtain to tell the untold or forgotten stories of those who worked for peace and racial progress under extraordinary circumstances in extraordinary times. The four were Bill Thomason, Karl Friedman, Doug Carpenter, and Tom Lankford. I was hesitant, but after reading some of Tom Lankford's memoir notes about his whirlwind newspaper career in the heart of historic happenings in the city, I agreed. Lankford and Friedman, in particular, were generous with their time and sharing their experiences and memories. Without their input, this book would not have been possible. I have preserved many of their turns of phrase.

It is a great sadness to me that Friedman, Thomason, and Lankford passed away before seeing the published book. I hope I have done some justice to their vision.

Although this work is based on interviews, personal memos, video recordings, and historical documentation, a dominant narrative voice follows the perspective of Lankford. As a young reporter for the *Birmingham News* embedded with law enforcement by assignment and his own initiative, Lankford was on the scene and behind the scenes on almost all major civil rights happenings in Alabama during the era. Driven by a desire to "get the scoop" and provide information needed in an extraordinary time, he had his hand in some capers of questionable ethics. He didn't question them at the time and is disclosing them now in the name of telling truths about what happened. His unique perspective and stories reveal an untold layer to historical events. That I have relied extensively on his memories and notes does not mean that I endorse all his methods or actions.

Acknowledgments

A sincere thank-you to those who have read the manuscript, multiple times for some, and offered invaluable assistance over the years—Earl Tilford, author and historian; Stephen Edmondson, lore-keeper extraordinaire; Sol Kimerling, local historian, writer, and early mentor; Dan Waterman at the University of Alabama Press, also a mentor and champion of this story; the Reverend Doug Carpenter, son of Bishop C. C. J. Carpenter; Anthony Grooms, author and professor of creative writing at Kennesaw State University; Captains Juanita Eaton and Jennifer Kilburn; Donna Dukes, for tireless efforts to connect me with civil rights icons; and Dana Thomas and Jennifer Buettner at the Birmingham Bar Association. Thanks also to readers who shared their thoughts and support—Odessa Woolfolk, educator and community activist; Jack Drake, civil rights attorney and advocate; Dr. Terry Barr, author and director of creative writing at Presbyterian College; Debra Goldstein, author and retired federal judge; Richard Friedman, community leader; and community volunteer and leader Fran Godchaux.

Also, my sincere appreciation to all who helped on my hunt for photographs and those who gave me their time for personal interviews. The latter are too numerous to mention here but appear in the bibliography. A special thanks, as well, to Pam Powell, for access to raw footage of her video interviews for a film series on this subject; Mark Kelley for his video interview footage on Karl Friedman and Betty Loeb; Jeanne Weaver, for access to her manuscript, now a book, on the history of the Unitarian Church in Birmingham; Janet Griffin, Virginia Volker, Elaine Hobson Miller, Sol Kimerling, Shannon Webster, Sam Rumore, Harriet Schaffer, Chervis Isom, and Robert Vance Jr. for sharing their priceless papers; Alice Westerly for digging up old documents on the Community Affairs Committee; Wayne Coleman, archives director, and Laura Anderson, former archives director at the Birmingham Civil Rights Institute; James L. Baggett and Don Veasey and Catherine Oseas of the Birmingham Public Library; Monika Singletary of Temple Emanu-El; my wonderful agent, Kimberley Cameron, who kept believing in this story; Joe Taylor of Livingston Press at the University of West Alabama who took the book under his wing; and, of course, the amazing shepherds at NewSouth Books, Suzanne La Rosa and Randall Williams.

Most of all, I thank my husband, friend, and first-editor Roger Thorne for his love and support and putting up with the time and attention required for such a project.

Introduction

Much of the truth of Birmingham in the civil rights era is ugly, plain and simple. This book is not an attempt to revise that truth. The darkness, however, is always what allows the light. And in Birmingham's darkness, individual lights grew—some from shades of gray that bloomed into sparks, some lanterns of courage. Painfully and slowly, in tandem with economic forces, judicial justice, labor law reform, and street demonstrations, they led the way out. These stories about the darkness and the shades of light in a city that literally brought change to the world are needed, perhaps now more than ever.

Birmingham's meteoric rise from a cornfield valley after the Civil War to a boomtown in the late 1800s and early 1900s earned it the nickname of the "Magic City." An industrial mining town built on the backs of convict labor, Birmingham was controlled in large part by outsiders. In a unique happenstance of nature, all the ingredients for making steel—coal, iron ore, and limestone—lay under and near the city, ripe for the plucking. And it hadn't taken long for corporate interests from the North to set up shop and pluck it. Those interests supported and encouraged the status quo of racial divide formed with slavery and afterwards encoded into law as a backlash against Reconstruction.

Birmingham would become a major canvas for the civil rights struggles of the 1950s and '60s, and the world's memory has painted the city in indelible ink with the images of firehoses and snarling police dogs. Reality was far more multihued. For Whites in Birmingham, positions on race and segregation existed on a continuum that stretched from strident white supremacists who wielded bombs and murder to those who risked social and financial ostracism, even their lives, to meet in secret with Black friends and activists and take unpopular public stands. In between were varying degrees of segregationists. The majority of Whites disapproved of Klan violence but stood against desegregation.

Shades of progressives also existed—liberal, moderate, paternalistic, and reluctant. Many stayed in the "progressive closet," kept there by the extreme social pressures and intimidation; fear of change; apathy or comfort in the status quo; resentment toward "outside agitators"; a belief that their religion was about "worship," not influencing social change; a perception that Blacks were "happy" in their status; the mindset of powerlessness; fear of losing their sources of income; or fear of physical violence to themselves and their families. In Birmingham, "even talking about race could lead to social rejection. Suspicious glares. Whispered conversations. Backs turned. Anonymous threats. Potential violence."[1]

The city's residents were born into or stepped into the world of Jim Crow, the codified and social laws relegating Blacks to second-class citizenship. Some refused to accept change, but many evolved. A White barber in Birmingham expressed the conflicted nature of that evolution. "I'm a segregationist, but I'm also a realist. There are some things we can't fight and some things we morally shouldn't fight."[2] As Birmingham-born Thom Gossom Jr., the first Black athlete to graduate from Auburn University, reflected, "In the Deep South, change moved in ironic and confusing patterns."[3]

By far, the issue that created the most angst during the civil rights period was the integration of schools, which took nine long years and courageous students, parents, and judges to begin to implement in Alabama, even after the U.S. Supreme Court mandated it. The people of Birmingham, Black and White, shared concerns about the costs and risks of school integration in a razor-edged environment. Many Whites, believing in the moral righteousness of segregation and fearing the mixing of the races, fled the city's school system. But concerns about violence and a poorer learning environment for their children also contributed, as, sadly, it does even today. Not all White parents concerned about their children's education and safety were racists, and many Black parents, although they wanted change, did not want their children to march in demonstrations or to be the ones integrating all-White schools. Historian Jonathan Bass noted, "In Birmingham, opinions concerning the racial crisis varied widely in the Black and White communities."[4]

The same complexity existed for the South's Jewish community, who lived in the shadow of Hitler and WWII and whose members were often the victims of discrimination or viewed as not fully White or as communist agitators behind Black discontent. The Black community remembers Jews from a different but equally confusing mixture of perspectives. As *Southern Jewish Life* editor/publisher Larry Brook puts it, despite "shorthand notions that 'Jews marched with blacks in the South' on one hand, or 'Jews in the South didn't do anything to help' on the other, the reality is much more of a gray area."[5]

Also caught in the middle were many lawmen of the day—sworn to uphold the law and maintain peace in a time when the legitimacy of the law itself was being challenged. Abuses by local police occurred with enough frequency to burn that image into the collective memory of the Black community, but law enforcement beliefs and behaviors also existed on a spectrum. Birmingham's police chief didn't hesitate to jail those who broke the law, but he was torn between his personal values and the ardent segregationist commands of his superior, the infamous City Commissioner Eugene "Bull" Connor. The county sheriff also walked a fine line, as did reporter Tom Lankford with the *Birmingham News*. Assigned to the "police beat," Lankford worked with law enforcement on covert missions. Protection of the community in the charged atmosphere of the times required ensuring timely information and that, in turn, sometimes resulted in dicey choices in gray areas of the law and at times crossing the line of legality and constitutionality, an issue that resonates today.

For some Whites—particularly a group of moderate ministers who would come to be known as "the peacemakers"—the road to equal justice and treatment required preparation to prevent chaos and violence. Progress had to begin with opening a dialogue between the races and needed to proceed slowly for peaceful change in a system of beliefs ingrained for generations. Others believed the moral obligation to right the wrongs of Jim Crow without delay outweighed the risks to societal order. The Black community's views reflected the same dichotomy.

Looking back, the direct nonviolent action of the civil rights movement—and the violence against it—galvanized the nation toward important changes in law and custom. Those who headed in the same direction but took a slower, more deliberate path received little credit and almost as much harsh judgment as that given to segregationist ideologues. Some moderates were considered stumbling blocks for civil rights progress. Some moved the pendulum significantly. Some who appealed to the community to accept desegregation "because it was the law" have been dismissed as only trying to make the best of a situation they would never have chosen. That may be, but a few took on surprising leadership roles and led the community forward in a turbulent time. Others publicly denounced the wrongs of segregation and pressed for civil, educational, and economic equality, but even those brave souls have faded against the backdrop of the movement's street drama. Their acts of courage were important and necessary. History should not be allowed to dismiss their efforts, even as it remembers and honors the Black leaders and foot soldiers that challenged the stifling status quo.

Why tell these stories? As human beings, we are hardwired to simplify and categorize, but we lose important perspectives if we look back from our time or our cultural evolution—such as it may be—to put history in simplistic boxes. Only pieces of the complete truth of anything can ever be told, but we must tell all that we can.

In today's polarized and changing environment, it is helpful to learn from the real and complex people who lived during the mid-twentieth century time of turbulence in the South and understand both their silence and complicity, as well as their courage in the face of hate, fear, and the greed that clings to status quo when it is slanted in one's favor. Hate, fear, and greed are not done. We must remember, so we can have the discernment and courage to speak out when they reemerge in all their guises.

During the civil rights era, Birmingham represented "a real Deep South defiance," declared a press release for the progressive interracial Southern Regional Council. "If it is changing—and I think it is . . . that is quite a story. Whatever happens, the people of Birmingham are quite a story."[6] This book is an attempt to tell forgotten or never-told pieces of that story, to dip more than one brush into the multifaceted palette of a city and a time that played a momentous role in changing the world.

BEHIND THE MAGIC CURTAIN

Abbreviations

ACHR	Alabama Council on Human Relations
ACMHR	Alabama Christian Movement for Human Rights
AAUW	American Association of University Women
ACLU	American Civil Liberties Union
ADL	Anti-Defamation League of B'nai Brith
AIC	Anti-Injustice Committee (of Miles College)
AJC	American Jewish Committee
AP	Associated Press
BCHR	Birmingham Council on Human Relations
CAC	Community Affairs Committee
CFP	Citizens for Progress
CORE	Congress of Racial Equality
CWCA	Concerned White Citizens of Alabama
DIA	Downtown Improvement Association
FBI	Federal Bureau of Investigation
FOR	Fellowship of Reconciliation
JCCEO	Jefferson County Committee for Economic Opportunity
KKK	Ku Klux Klan
NAACP	National Association for the Advancement of Colored People
NCCJ	National Conference of Christians and Jews
NCJW	National Council of Jewish Women
NSRP	National States' Rights Party
SCHW	Southern Conference for Human Welfare
SCLC	Southern Christian Leadership Conference
SNCC	Student Nonviolent Coordinating Committee
WCC	White Citizens' Councils
USW	United Steel Workers
YMBC	Young Men's Business Club

Prologue

Fall 1962: Birmingham, Alabama

Bleary-eyed from an all-night stakeout with the Birmingham vice squad, reporter Tom Lankford pushed through the second-floor doors of the *Birmingham News* into the sprawling newsroom. To his weary ears what was normally a familiar background noise sounded more like the pepper of gunfire—the syncopated clacking from the battalion of manual typewriters and the Associated Press (AP) teletypes that on occasion punctuated their own clatter with bells to alert the copy boy of a "news flash."

He wound his way between the crowded desks, past the newsroom's heart—the city editor who sat in the inside curve of the centrally located horseshoe-shaped city news desk, yelling out assignments, editing stories, and laying out copy. Near the news desk, one of the switchboard operators, perched on a high stool and wearing a headset, waved to get Lankford's attention. He ignored her. He had gone home only long enough to shower and change clothes. Coffee was priority one. An intravenous injection would have been welcome, but all he had was the to-go cup he had picked up on the way in.

With an impatient sweep to make room for the cup, he displaced the stack of unreturned pink phone-message slips on his desk, pried off the lid and downed half of the tepid coffee before acknowledging the switchboard operator's now frantic gestures. She pointed to his phone and mouthed in exaggerated mime, "He's on the phone!"

There was no doubt who "he" was.

Lankford snatched the phone from its cradle, but before he could bring it to his ear, much less say "Hello," Vincent Townsend's voice barked through the receiver, "Lankford! Get in here. My office. Got something I need to talk to you about."

Mississippi-born Vincent Townsend Sr. ruled the *Birmingham News*—from the presses in the basement, the advertising department on the mezzanine, the news department on the second floor, and on up to the production department on the top floor. As Lankford later recalled, "Almost no Jefferson County or Birmingham politician was elected to office without his support. J. Edgar Hoover reportedly had a standing order that any new agent-in-charge of the FBI office in Birmingham was to make his first call to Vincent Townsend. As a sign of his staunch support of law enforcement, Townsend never turned down a request by the FBI or local authorities. To do so would have been un-American."[7]

Townsend's official title was general manager and assistant to the publisher, but he was arguably one of the most powerful men in the southeastern United States, and certainly in the Magic City.

Lankford took a breath to answer his boss just as Townsend changed his command.

"Wait. You had breakfast yet? Julia's out of town, and I'm damned well about to starve to death. Meet me downstairs in five minutes."

For forty years Townsend had lived and preached the motto, "Deadline. Deadline. Deadline." With five daily editions of the *News* to produce, it was not his habit to wait for grass to grow, and he didn't expect his reporters to either. Lankford sighed. At least it was a chance for a *hot* cup of coffee.

Five minutes later, he and Townsend sat at the usual front table in the newspaper's crowded first-floor snack bar. Sleeves rolled to his elbows and tie already askew, Townsend unfurled his napkin with a flourish and laid it in his lap. He was not a physically imposing man. His hairline receded in twin orbs, leaving a thin wave of black in the center. The balding emphasized a high forehead and intense eyes that missed little. Townsend was always in motion, a swirl of energy that pulled everyone into his orbit, even at breakfast.

"Tom, you know we've got a crisis on our hands," he said, blanketing his eggs under a layer of black pepper.

It was the fall of 1962. John F. Kennedy was president. His brother Robert F. "Bobby" Kennedy, was the attorney general. J. Edgar Hoover ruled the FBI with an iron fist, believing communism to be the gravest threat to America and Dr. Martin Luther King Jr. to be a communist sympathizer. Joe Namath played football for the Alabama Crimson Tide. George Corley Wallace, as the Democratic Party's candidate, was guaranteed the governorship. And Birmingham teetered on the cusp of a historic vote that could turn the city upside down.

But the crisis Townsend referred to was one man—Theophilus Eugene "Bull" Connor, the short, strutting, loud, and often likeable Birmingham police and fire commissioner who had risen to political fame as a radio announcer for the Birmingham Barons semipro baseball team. A staunch segregationist, Connor had served a term in the state legislature and had been in his current position (with a one-term gap) for almost twenty-five years. Under his rule, few Blacks registered to vote and no Blacks were on the police or fire department or city hall payrolls save the three elevator operators and the cook and cashier in the basement dining room.

Connor and the Reverend Fred Lee Shuttlesworth, the fiery Black preacher, were mortal enemies who catapulted the city into a spiral of tension—yet offstage Connor called Shuttlesworth "Freddie Lee" in seeming affection as sometimes occurs between old but respected combatants. In civil rights circles, Shuttlesworth was known as "the Wild Man of Birmingham." Arrested at least thirty times, he was as stubborn as Connor. "We're going to kill segregation or be killed by it," he said. Perhaps the police commissioner privately acknowledged him a worthy opponent, but one he would go to great lengths to be rid of.

It seemed to Lankford that the spiral of events bringing him and the city to this point had begun four years ago when, as a young student reporter at the University of Alabama, he chased a story on the Ku Klux Klan—a militant wing of white supremacy responsible for acts of violence and many of the thousands of lynchings that had taken place from 1877 to 1950. But for the Magic City, the crisis had spun out of control only a year ago on Mother's Day, when Connor gave the Klan free rein to beat Freedom Riders at the local Trailways bus terminal. Lankford had been on the scene that infamous day. Photographer Tommy Langston of the rival *Post-Herald* snapped the only surviving picture of the attack, a brutal image of Birmingham that played around the world. That photo, along with boycotts of downtown businesses, the closing of public parks and recreational facilities to avoid desegregating them, not to mention a declining economy, became triggers for sweeping change. As usual, Vincent Townsend was in the middle of the action behind the scenes.

Townsend was accustomed to making decisions. His word was law on what the paper printed and how editorials presented issues. He shaped public opinion. Over the years Lankford had observed that Townsend used such power with one purpose in mind—the good of the city he loved. Of course, Townsend decided what was "good." But that was all right with Lankford. There was no one he respected and admired more.

When Lankford wasn't working, he was likely at Townsend's Southside home, watching him wield influence among the steady stream of power players who called late into the night, huddled around the maps and drawings scattered about, as he pushed for a new freeway, an international airport, or donations for a charity function. He judged a man, Black or White, by his actions. He and others knew the status quo had to change, that Blacks needed the same rights and opportunities as Whites, but to gain them through peaceful means that wouldn't tear the city apart would take time and patience. Townsend had a long view down the road, and Lankford was glad to be a passenger on the journey.

"Tom," Townsend said, shaking even more pepper onto his eggs, "we've got a bunch of guys at city hall who couldn't find their ass with both hands, and this paper is going to do everything it can to get them out of office." He looked up, his piercing eyes fixing on Lankford. "I want your help on it. You and Marcus."

To Lankford, Townsend emanated "strength, confidence, and calm unless 'his' Birmingham was threatened. He was kind to everyone; quick to praise or to correct his staff of editors and reporters; loved sports; loved law enforcement with a passion; was loyal to his employees, city merchants, the Chamber of Commerce crowd and friends; a man you could turn your back on; fearless."

Lankford had been in awe of Townsend from the first day he had met him four years earlier in the offices of the University of Alabama's school newspaper, the *Crimson-White*. Townsend's offer of a job at the *Birmingham News* after graduation had made Lankford feel ten feet tall. His life had taken him on a few detours after completing his master's degree in journalism, but from the moment he arrived at the *News*, Townsend and his wife, Julia, had taken him under their wings. There was no way in hell he was going to disappoint Townsend.

"What do we do, Vincent?" Lankford asked, watching wide-eyed as

Townsend poured half a bottle of hot sauce on the blackened surface of his eggs.

Townsend fixed his gaze on Lankford. "I know Bull trusts you, Tom, and lets you make up his quotes and all, but put that aside. We've got something important that has to be done. Understand?"

Lankford nodded. It is said that those living history are rarely aware at the time of significant moments of change, but only a blind idiot could fail to see that the road Connor and the other two city commissioners were leading them down was paved with self-destruction . . . and blood.

"It's a shame and a disgrace that this city doesn't have a single freeway and there's not even one on the drawing board," Townsend grumbled, sliding into a familiar rant. "I talked to a Shriner potentate yesterday. He's moving his quarry operation to Texas. That's just the beginning. There's gonna be a whole parade of jobs leaving town if we can't make this change in government structure happen." With a scowl, he added, "Just like when we lost the airport expansion to Atlanta."

Although that had happened long before Lankford's time, he knew Townsend was referring to the decision not to move the local airport from its current location ten minutes from downtown. Delta Airlines had offered to make Birmingham their hub if the city would move the airport. Controlled by the Big Mules—Governor Bibb Graves's term for the steel and mining power brokers of Birmingham who did not want labor competition—city leaders declined. In 1940, Delta's move of its headquarters to Atlanta ignited a flurry of growth for that city. Seven years later, the same thing happened with Ford Motor Company. Townsend stabbed at the now unrecognizable eggs. "Hell, we could have had Delta *here!*"

The other major issue holding back the city was its isolation from the surrounding neighborhoods. In 1959, the year Lankford joined the *News*, the suburban municipalities voted down a merger with the city. Townsend and Chamber of Commerce leaders realized Birmingham's future was much brighter as a unified metropolitan area, but the suburban communities wanted no part of Birmingham's outdated governmental structure, too removed from its constituents and incapable of "coping with affairs of an enlarged metropolis."[8] Something had to be done to change their minds.

Birmingham's lack of vision pained Townsend, but he saw Bull Connor as the biggest and most immediate threat to the city. And Connor was not a lone wolf. His supporters included the mining and steel production interests who saw segregation and racial tensions as insurance against communist-supported unionizing; blue-collar Whites living from paycheck to paycheck who feared Blacks would take their jobs; uneducated, impoverished "rednecks" desperate to be superior to somebody; and people who held no particular animosity against Blacks but simply accepted segregation. Connor was a sterling representative of those who held that segregation was the rightful heritage of the South, legally and morally. He wasn't against Blacks rising to their capabilities (however limited those might be, in his view) as long as they maintained separation from the superior White race. He fought to keep Birmingham's strict Jim Crow segregation laws in place, refusing to give an inch of ground.

Though known as "Bull's boy," Lankford was not. He was Townsend's man. He considered Townsend not just his employer, but his close friend and mentor. Townsend expected him to get scoops, and the way to do that was to get close to the people close to what was happening. Connor approved of how Lankford wrote news articles about his policies and gave him latitude to represent him. "Hell, you know what I want to say," the police and fire commissioner would quip, giving Lankford permission to make up a quote.

Like many of his era, Connor never completed high school, but he had successfully run for the state legislature. He understood the power of the press. As an elected official, his job depended on his popularity, and he was not reticent in giving out news releases on police arrests or anti-crime campaigns. He understood too that his constituency was not the business owners who lived in adjacent, wealthier, "over the mountain" suburbs, that is, on the south side of Red Mountain, the Appalachian ridge that bisected the city northeast to southwest. His constituency was the working class within the city limits. Despite his friendliness toward Lankford, Connor did not feel the same way about the newspaper, which had been lobbying to overturn the at-large three-commissioner form of city government. These editorials prompted Connor to rant about the "Jewish-owned, nigger-loving *Birmingham News*." [9]

Lankford worked the police beat, and his effectiveness depended on being trusted by top officials and street-level cops. He knew the value of staying in Commissioner Connor's good graces, but he had just blown all that away with a single daring stunt, an incident that was to help turn the upcoming election and change history and which seemed to have given Townsend the idea that Lankford could be key in providing him with information.

"Okay," Townsend said, seeing that Lankford understood the gravity of the situation. "Get with Marcus and find out where you can order some bugging equipment. Find out what that whole city commission is up to."

Lankford blinked. This was Townsend's way of saying the information Lankford had put in his hands impressed him. Now he wanted more. Timely information was a commodity worth more than gold in navigating the current complex political waters. Knowledge was power, power to lift Birmingham out of the mire of racial strife that was choking the city.

"How am I supposed to pay for it?" Lankford asked, knowing his $100 weekly reporter's salary wouldn't cover the cost of an iced tea tumbler to hold up against a wall.

"Turn it in on your expense report. The *News* will pay for it."

Now Lankford was excited, eager to get to a phone to call his close friend and housemate, Detective Sergeant Marcus A. Jones Sr., who was the only city detective assigned to investigate extremist groups. Jones coordinated with two FBI special agents similarly assigned and reported directly to Birmingham Police Chief Jamie Moore. Unless Moore passed it to him, Bull Connor was not privy to his information.

Jones was a loner. Only after many nights working side by side and keeping his confidences had Lankford earned his trust. Lankford attacked the rest of his breakfast. Marcus would love Lankford's new assignment and the opportunity to expand his arsenal of equipment.

"Look, Tom, I know this is risky," Townsend said. "But you've got law enforcement contacts enough not to get caught . . . especially since you're acting as one of them. You and Marcus call it a police operation if you want, but I've got to know who those guys [Connor and the other commissioners] are promising what." Townsend tapped the table in emphasis. "I want to know every word they're saying ten minutes after they've said it."

Lankford stood. "Let me get with Marcus and some of our friends with the Bureau," he said. "I'll get back with you tonight."

That was how the taping campaign started. Before it was over, the "Unit" was listening with impunity to conversations of practically every source of influence in the city, including Martin Luther King, the Klan, and even local brothels, not to mention Connor and his city hall cronies. It was a deep secret that paralleled and impacted the story of the civil rights struggle and the course of history, a secret that was to last for decades.

As Lankford headed out of the snack bar, leaving the check for Townsend to pick up, he realized he wasn't tired anymore. He was twenty-five years old, a crime reporter for the state's largest circulating newspaper, working for the best newspaperman in the country, and was about to risk his neck big time.

What more could a reporter want?

PART
One

❧

1

Close Encounter with the Klan

As a journalism student at the University of Alabama in 1958, Tom Lankford kept up with events, including in a town just sixty miles up the road, Birmingham, but could not know how his life would one day intersect and entwine with the fate of that city. He had found his element in Tuscaloosa. Being selected as Student of the Month with his photo plastered on a banner above University Boulevard was quite a boost of confidence for a shy country boy who grew up poor on a farm in north Alabama. In high school, he had graduated at the top of his class, but this was a much wider world with tougher competition. Lankford, however, was not afraid of hard work. It was all he had ever known, and all he would accept from himself.

A reporter for the school newspaper and a freelance "stringer" for the *Birmingham Post-Herald*, Lankford was always on the lookout for material. When he smelled a story, he headed straight for it. Rumors had flown across campus that students were making a sport of throwing paint on a Klan sign on the eastern end of University Boulevard. Lankford and a friend and fellow journalism student, Frank Helderman Jr., headed out to find it. Neither paused to consider the wisdom of pursuing a story involving a radical, racist organization whose historical tool was terror.

It would not be the first time the Klan had made itself part of UA student affairs. They had shown they were willing to bring violence to the campus two years earlier in 1956—a year when the state was reeling from major blows to the status quo and the "Southern way of life." Autherine Lucy wanted to complete her college education at a better facility and attempted to become the first Black to enroll in an Alabama state-supported college. Lucy was greeted with a Klan-spurred riot and eventually forced to withdraw from the university.

No one had tried to desegregate the University of Alabama since Lucy, but racial tensions continued to build across the South in resistance to desegregation rulings. Bombings, floggings, and cross burnings proliferated across the state. The Klan erected signs on the outskirts of several cities.[10] The one at the outskirts of Tuscaloosa was a warning, and the fact that students were throwing paint on the warning was a story Lankford was not going to ignore.

He was one year from finishing his journalism degree when he and Helderman headed east down University Boulevard in Lankford's car, a maroon 1950 V8 Ford Custom Deluxe, straight shift with twin exhausts, which he had bought used for $750. It was a lot of money for him.

Dusk had settled before Lankford and Helderman found what they were looking for. The glaring metal sign with splattered paint was easy to see even in the growing darkness, and Lankford snapped several photos before driving off, unaware that Klansmen, angered by the recent vandalism, were lying in wait.

Without warning, a car struck them from behind. Lankford realized at once that it wasn't an accident. The attacking vehicle sported a long whiplash antenna for a CB (citizens band) radio. He was certain it belonged to a Klansman and stepped on the gas, but another car with a similar antenna pulled alongside and swung into him. His first reaction was despair at the damage to his precious car, and he wove desperately, trying to avoid another blow. Fear for his vehicle morphed into fear for their safety as he entered the small town of Alberta City and had to slam on brakes to keep from plowing into a vehicle stopped before him at a green traffic light. That car was in on the assault, he realized, as the driver jerked his car into reverse and slammed into the front of Lankford's Ford.

Shadowy figures piled out of the three cars, yanking Lankford out onto the deserted street and cursing him. Helderman sat in the car, wisely keeping quiet. Lankford's first instinct was to fight, but the assailants rained expletives rather than blows on him, and his concern turned to his camera. His mailroom job paid minimum wages. Even with his new wife's salary as a secretary to the dean of admissions, it would be a real difficulty to replace it, not to mention repairing the damage to his car. He and his wife barely afforded campus housing in a former Army barracks while Lankford worked his way through school.

The sudden appearance of a man with an air of authority quieted his accusers. Lankford later learned that he was none other than Robert M. Shelton, who was to become the Imperial Wizard of the United Klans of America. By day, Shelton worked at a gas station selling tires on the outskirts of Tuscaloosa. By night, he wore the white hood.

Shelton took Lankford's camera, which still hung over his shoulder, renewing his anxiety for his equipment. But Shelton only removed the roll of black-and-white film, handing Lankford a dollar bill. "Tell your student friends we are protecting their future, their heritage," Shelton said, turning to leave. Over his shoulder he added, "And tell them to quit throwing paint on our sign."

Lankford drove straight to his desk at the school's newspaper, the *Crimson-White,* and called in the story to the *Post-Herald* state desk. Although he knew an editor would shorten any piece he submitted, he always wrote with as much detail as he could—stringers were paid by the word, and Lankford needed every penny for every word.

His story ran the next morning, and Helderman was waiting for him in the majestic Woods Hall, home of the journalism department. Lankford could see at a glance that his friend was upset. "Dad called me about that Klan story from last night," Helderman said. "You've got to write a retraction."

Stunned, Lankford stared at him. Helderman had heard Professor Charles W. Scarritt stress many times the importance of getting accurate facts. What did Helderman mean? Lankford always assumed that Helderman, an excellent student, would one day succeed Frank Helderman Sr. as publisher of the *Gadsden Times.* "A Klansman paid my father a visit at the newspaper office," Helderman said.

Lankford listened while his friend explained that the Klansman had threatened his father and demanded Lankford retract the "Tuscaloosa Klan story," which had now made the AP wires and spread across the country.

"Sorry, Frank. I can't do that." Lankford said. Leaving his friend, he headed to Professor Scarritt's classroom on the building's second floor and told his mentor what had happened the previous night.

WHEN LANKFORD HAD GRADUATED from high school in the small, rural community of Hokes Bluff, Alabama, he accepted that life offered him two alternatives to working a farm—enlist in the military, following his older brother's footsteps, or join the other boys his age in migrating to Detroit to work in the car factories. He was surprised when an older high school friend suggested a third choice, encouraging Lankford to join him at Berry College in Rome, Georgia, where he could work his way through school and run on the track team. Lankford jumped at the opportunity, becoming one of just five students from his high school class to attend college.

His first year at Berry, he drove a truck to collect limestone, laid the rock into sidewalks, and washed dishes in the college kitchen. On his entrance papers, he'd listed "high school football coach" as his career goal. A career in journalism had never occurred to him. But when he turned in a book report on Victor Hugo's *Les Misérables* to his English professor, she called him into her office and planted the idea in his head.

After brief stints at other schools, he transferred in 1956 to a real journalism school—the University of Alabama. He loved everything about it. Walking across "The Quad" in the shadow of the Denny Chimes bell tower, surrounded by the stately old buildings constructed after Union troops burned the university at the end of the Civil War, Lankford felt at home for the first time. He had found his calling and his "place."

He found a mentor in Professor Scarritt, an old Kansas City crime reporter. A lanky, frail figure with thin gray hair and heavy black spectacles, Scarritt was often at his desk, spooning Gerber's baby food straight out of the jar for lunch. He had a bad case of acid reflux, not atypical for a newsman stressed with meeting deadlines every day for most of his life.

Scarritt hammered into his students the importance of accurate reporting and taking nothing for granted, even spelling. "That's why so much time is spent on editing copy and proofreading. Spell a name wrong, and you've got an angry subscriber to deal with. You gotta get your facts right. A misspelled name is not factually correct."

Scarritt foresaw the approaching demise of old-school factual reporting and the rise of "PR-style, opinionated, often fabricated news." He fought against it with the tenacity of Don Quixote tilting at windmills, his lance being the drumming of principle into his students, most of whom would leave for jobs in public relations and communications, not newspapers.

With a slight, wry smile, Scarritt listened to Lankford and Helderman's escapades, but when he heard about the Klansman's threat, his brow furrowed. He looked up the sheriff's phone number and invited him to the classroom for a visit, where he threatened media repercussions if the Klan didn't back off.

"I won't tolerate the Klan intimidating my students," he said later, looking up at Lankford through his dark-rimmed glasses.

Soon afterward, the KKK removed its sign from University Boulevard.

2

Power Connections

In his senior year at Alabama, Lankford was elected editor of the *Crimson-White*. Later, the school's yearbook, *The Corolla*, chose him as "Most Outstanding Graduate Student." During his student years, he was also elected president of Sigma Delta Chi, the Society of Professional Journalists, and selected to the Omicron Delta Kappa (ODK) national leadership honor society. Lankford did not have the money to join a fraternity, but "the Machine" recruited him. A secret organization made up of select fraternity males, "the Machine" dominated politics and student life at the University of Alabama, and numerous state and national leaders arose from it. At the initiation and meetings in a gravel pit just off campus, Lankford met students and alumni headed for positions of power—Cecil Jackson, destined to be Governor George Wallace's top aide; Charles "Chuck" Morgan Jr., to rise with the ACLU as one of the leading voices for racial equality in the country; Bill Baxley, future Alabama attorney general, and Julian Butler, a key factor in Baxley's victories; and Max Pope, Ben Reeves, and others who would one day be at the forefront of the Alabama Democratic Party. Outside "the Machine," he met many others, including Morris Dees, an entrepreneurial wunderkind as a UA undergraduate and law student and later a founder of the Southern Poverty Law Center. All these individuals would play various roles in the civil rights movement in Alabama and beyond. Lankford was told he was the first non-fraternity member to be backed by "the Machine."

As editor of the *Crimson-White*, Lankford didn't hesitate to express his opinions, including endorsing for governor that year the feisty, moderate candidate, George C. Wallace. Journalist Wayne Greenhaw reported that Wallace supported segregation in public but in a private conversation with new UA President Frank A. Rose had confided that "the time had come to desegregate the university."[11]

As a delegate to the Democratic National Convention in 1948, Wallace had not walked out with other Dixiecrats in protest of Harry S. Truman's civil rights platform. Instead, Wallace had aligned himself with Alabama's progressive governor, "Big Jim" Folsom. In December 1949, Folsom spoke to a statewide radio audience. "'As long as the Negroes are held down by deprivation and lack of opportunity, the other poor people will be held down alongside them. Let's start talking fellowship and brotherly love and doing unto others. Let's do more than talking about it. Let's start living it.' Wallace applauded that speech as one of the most courageous he had heard from an Alabama politician."[12]

Wallace had been an Alabama circuit judge for six years when he got into the 1958 gubernatorial race. Both the *Birmingham News* and the NAACP endorsed him. As a young lawyer, famed Black civil rights attorney Fred Gray tried cases before Wallace and called him "a moderate, decent, fair-minded person."

Wallace lost the 1958 Democratic gubernatorial nomination to State Attorney General John Patterson. Mobsters had assassinated Patterson's father, attorney general-nominee Albert Patterson in Phenix City, Alabama, in 1954. The son was appointed by the Democratic Party to run in his late father's place and won. In Lankford's opinion, John Patterson rode his father's coattails into the state's highest law enforcement office. As AG, he got the state courts to ban the NAACP from Alabama, calling it a "foreign" organization and demanding its membership list.

Wallace, meanwhile, didn't forget the *Crimson-White* endorsement. That fall, at an annual university pep rally bonfire, he told Lankford, "Tom, I will run again . . . and win. But I will never run again on my personal beliefs. I will tell the voters what they want to hear." He was famously reported to have sworn to others that he would never be "out-niggered" again.

Patterson was inaugurated governor in January 1959. He also had not forgotten the Lankford endorsement of Wallace. When the state legislature took up an appropriations request by the university, Patterson suggested that if school officials wanted their funds they should remove Lankford as editor of the student paper. As a state institution, the university's policy forbade political endorsements by its employees, and Lankford, who received a small stipend as editor of the *CW*, might technically have been a school employee. The *Birmingham News* quoted Lankford protesting that the endorsement had been his own personal choice and that ousting him would violate his constitutional rights. Newspapers all over the state reported the university's crackdown on Lankford's endorsement.[13]

Members of the school's administration met to make a decision. From his seat in the hall, Lankford could hear the voices in the meeting room. Dean John Blackburn seemed to take the governor's threat seriously, and Lankford's heart sank until a voice arose above the clamor. A newcomer to the university let his thoughts be known.

"A student has every right to get involved in politics," Coach Paul William "Bear" Bryant bellowed. "Tell the governor to go to hell!"

The issue was dropped, and the no-endorsements policy for the *Crimson-White* was eventually withdrawn.[14]

UNIVERSITY LIFE WAS A heady time for Lankford. In the offices of the *Crimson-White,* he met a visitor who would have the greatest influence on his life—Vincent Townsend Sr., who immediately struck Lankford as intense, with focused energy, a man who commanded respect. Lankford would learn that his first impression was more than correct.

While pursuing a master's degree in journalism, Lankford sent a proposal to Townsend about expanding the student Sigma Delta Chi journalism society into a statewide organization. The idea impressed Townsend, who agreed to support it and offered to underwrite a "Journalism Day" at the university, climaxed with an initiation of the state's premier journalistic talent, picked by Townsend.

In fact, Townsend was impressed enough to offer Lankford a job after he graduated, a job at the *Birmingham News,* one of the top newspapers in the Southeast. Though honored, Lankford had already accepted a promised job at the rival *Birmingham Post-Herald.*

A day before graduation Professor Scarritt called him into his office. Lankford found his teacher sitting at his desk, eating his usual baby food lunch, the only thing agreeable to his cantankerous stomach.

"Tom, I know you have accepted a job with the *Birmingham Post-Herald,*" Scarritt said, as Lankford pulled up a rickety chair, "but I am not sure that's best for you. They'll put you on a state desk or writing obits. What you need is all-around newspaper experience. Why don't you contact the *Ledger-Enquirer* over in Columbus, Georgia, and see what they might offer? Then, after a while, you'll be ready to join Vincent at the *Birmingham News*."

Lankford followed Scarritt's advice. When he received his master's degree in 1959, the *Ledger-Enquirer* hired him. Before moving to Georgia, he drove to Birmingham to tell *Post-Herald* editor James E. Mills face-to-face that he had changed his mind. Mills was furious. He tailed Lankford down the elevator, letting him know that he would see Lankford never got a job at a Birmingham newspaper. Lankford left the building deflated, feeling he deserved the tongue-lashing for going back on his word.

With his wife and new baby daughter ensconced in Columbus, however, he started work at the *Ledger-Enquirer*. Although assigned to the Phenix City beat, the paper used him on photo features, Sunday pieces, and other projects as needed. The staff was close-knit. Each day, the editor picked him up at his apartment, giving him a ride to work, and Lankford had the use of a company car at work. He was getting the all-around experience that Scarritt had recommended.

In July 1959 he was assigned to document vandalism in Columbus, Georgia. An eighteen-year-old Nazi sympathizer had painted swastikas on two synagogues and burned thousands of dollars' worth of paintings in the Museum of Art and Crafts. The deed angered Lankford. It felt unreal that such a thing could happen in America.

When he returned to the *Ledger-Enquirer* newsroom, the switchboard operator motioned that he had a call and could take it at the vacant slot on the city desk. The call was from Fletcher Moore, who had been Lankford's chief photographer at the *Crimson-White*. Moore was now a photographer at the *Atlanta Journal-Constitution*.

"Drop what you're doing, and get on up here to Atlanta," Moore said. "The city editor wants to hire you."

LANKFORD HAD NEVER DREAMED that working for the *Journal-Constitution* was a possibility, but he told Moore he'd be there. So, after typing the story about the swastikas on his Underwood typewriter, he headed to Atlanta.

Although Atlanta was small compared to big cities in the northeast, its tall buildings, traffic jams, and sidewalk pedestrian bustle overwhelmed Lankford's "country boy" senses. Upstairs in the *Journal-Constitution* building, the news editor was gracious in his praise and offered a reporter's job, which Lankford accepted. But a part of him felt swept on a tide that was moving too fast. The editor saw him to the elevator.

Stepping out on the street at Atlanta's busiest time of day, horns blaring, workers scurrying to their cars for the trip home, and long shadows falling, Lankford retraced his steps to the newsroom and told the city editor, "Thanks, but Atlanta's too big for me; I'm going to Birmingham."

The memory of the job offer from Vincent Townsend that day in the *Crimson-White* office felt like a lifeline, and Lankford was ready to see if it was still good. As soon as he returned to Columbus, he wrote Townsend asking if he still had a position. A few days later, Clancy Lake, the renowned journalist who would bring big-time news reporting to television in Alabama, was on the phone.

"Townsend says get on over here," Lake said.

"When?"

"What about tomorrow?"

3

Police Beat

1959

The next day, Lankford stepped through the doors of the *Birmingham News* for the first time. He was directed to the office of Leroy Simms, managing editor of the *News,* who invited him in. Cigar in hand, Simms pontificated to his captive audience about the history of railroads in Alabama. An old AP newsman, Simms was passionate about railroads. After a while, he picked up Lankford's half-page resume and tilted his head back to survey it, reading glasses perched on the end of his nose.

Chewing on his cigar, he said, "Tom, right now we're looking for a more experienced reporter. But I tell you what. Go back to Columbus for a while and write me a letter about what you'd like to accomplish in life."

He looked up to see the stunned look on Lankford's freckled face, and Lankford could feel his cheeks flushing. Simms had been standing right beside Townsend that day in the *Crimson-White* and heard the job offer, but now he was turning him away as if it had never happened.

Simms fished a pair of scissors from his desk and snipped off the end of his cigar, which he poked into a vest pocket. "But before you go," he drawled, "let's go see Townsend, so he can say hello."

Townsend sat at his sturdy oak desk. He looked up and nodded at Lankford, then fixed Simms in the eye and barked, "Did you hire him, Leroy?"

"Well, no," Simms said. "You see—"

"Dammit, Leroy, hire him!" Townsend shouted.

Through the glass that separated Townsend's office from the newsroom, Lankford could see heads turning to listen.

"I told that boy he had a job here any time he wanted it, so hire him. Now!"

Lankford, recognizing Townsend as a man of his word, knew he had made the right decision about him and guessed that life would never be dull working for him. He had no idea just how right he was.

"We want him on the police beat, Leroy, but first turn him over to Clancy."

Under Clancy Lake's supervision, Lankford took a desk near the city desk, the center of newsroom activity. For weeks following, he wrote or rewrote obit after obit and articles by others, including those brought in by famous sports journalist Zip Newman and aging society columnist Lily May Caldwell—inevitably accompanied by her poodle, which she addressed as Tony Curtis and talked to throughout the day.

One day, police reporter Bud Gordon walked up to Lankford's desk and said, "Come with me, Tom. Townsend wants me to show you the ropes in the police department, and you're taking my place. I'm going to the city hall beat."

Over the next two years on the police beat, Lankford was poised to witness a clash of ideas that would upend Birmingham's foundations and send shock waves across the country, transforming the way of life for both Black and White America.

Lankford's boyhood hero sported two silver-plated .45 Colt pistols, a black mask to protect his identity, and a white hat pulled low. He and his faithful Indian companion Tonto acted without the approval of others in their mission to seek justice. As a boy, Lankford read all *The Lone Ranger* comics, and on Saturdays—cotton picking being suspended at noon—he rode into town in the back of a pickup truck to see the Lone Ranger's movies. He was also a fan of Gene Autry, Roy Rogers, and Johnny Mack Brown, all white-hatted cowboys—the bad guys wore black hats. Life was simple. Just check out the hats.

As Lankford grew older, library books introduced him to a broader world. The clear lines of good and evil blurred. He read about racial prejudice, but there were no Blacks in his hometown of Hokes Bluff, Alabama, and no chance to be prejudiced even if he had wanted to be. His mother and father would not have allowed it. They taught him that everyone was made in the image of God and had the same rights.

His first encounter with racial animosity had occurred not in the South, but in the North. Needing to save money for college, Lankford stayed with his uncle's family over a summer while he worked days at a machine shop and nights and weekends at Geauga Lake Amusement Park in Aurora, Ohio.

A group of Black youths went swimming in the amusement park pool. They were run off, and the pool was drained to keep from "contaminating" White swimmers. The incident left a sour taste in his mouth and stayed with him the rest of his life, yet as a young reporter he didn't equate prejudice with Blacks having to sit at the back of the bus or having separate restrooms and drinking fountains or being unable to sit at lunch counters. Those social injustices were Southern custom, obviously not fair, but life itself wasn't fair. He didn't feel guilty about how things were. He treated everyone the same, did his job, and took one day at a time. As author Chervis Isom reflected, "When you grow up in a culture you don't really rethink it. You simply grew up in it and become a part of it."[15]

As a crime reporter, however, Lankford ran head on into conditions he did see as manifestations of prejudice and evil—people living in squalor; an entire family sleeping in one room with a common "rag pile" of clothes in the middle of the room; children with no "Daddy," only male visitors. He saw it in the derelicts, Black and White, who haunted vacated warehouses, ruining their brains with drinking cheap alcohol, hair tonic, or paint thinner.

Lankford was not blind to the systematic prejudice and corruption he sometimes observed in law enforcement. It grated him, for example, to watch officers haul Negroes out of shot houses, forcing them to pay "the man" to keep from being loaded into the paddy wagon. One such house in Birmingham belonged to a Black man called "Rat Killer" who made regular payments to the "po'-lice" to avoid getting raided, or, at least, to be informed when a raid was imminent. He also gifted officers with a bottle of liquor or some of his famous barbecue cooked outside in a fifty-five-gallon drum.

Lankford suspected Birmingham's top officials helped themselves to that kind of graft. Officer Wallace E. "Wally" Chilcoat recalled being turned away by Public Safety Commissioner Connor's executive secretary when he sought permission to work an extra job and told not to return unless he brought whiskey.[16] Many in the Black community suspected the same. Their opinion of Birmingham's police was not high. Frank Dukes, a Black civil rights trailblazer, later reflected, "Most police had limited education. Ignorance was bliss. Their job was to keep Negroes in line."

Before Rat Killer moved to West End, he sold alcohol out of his shoeshine shop downtown. Policemen came to get their shoes shined. Some paid for the service; some did not. "Big-time pool hustling took place in the backroom billiard parlor, along with other types of wagering. Shots of untaxed whiskey were available. Romantic encounters were sold and purchased. Various illegal pharmaceuticals were dispensed."[17]

A White man who owned a store that legally sold beer and wine across the street took his complaints to Bull Connor about Rat Killer's illegal business and was told "right quick" to leave Rat Killer alone. Word of that hit the streets in the Black neighborhoods, enhancing the view that Connor was on the take.[18]

Lankford occasionally accompanied detectives to their free eating places and drove them on Fridays to hotels and restaurants where they picked up a bottle at each place for the weekend and to their free dry cleaning establishments and movies. Officers had an unspoken code not to overburden the businessmen who offered perks. Lankford saw this in action when he accompanied the chief to lunch one day. Chief Moore, who parked in the rear, entered through the back door and conversed with the cooks, then proceeded to the front and sat at his favorite table. Lankford noticed a detective eating by himself in a corner. Moore didn't give him a look, but after returning to headquarters, he had the detective come in and chewed him out for eating at "his" place, telling him to never go there again. Then he turned to Lankford and explained, "You don't touch these people [business owners] for more than they can stand."

Lankford never wrote a word about any of this. He followed the same code of silence as the officers, regardless of whether they approved of the behaviors of their fellows, because he knew that was the only way to win and keep their trust, and because he understood the officers' daily pressures and the difficulty of feeding their families on small salaries.

The Birmingham Police Department also had a reputation for brutality, much of which was culturally acceptable within the organization and often overlooked by superior officers or, at the least, not easily proven. Houston Brown, who eventually would become the first Black presiding judge of the Tenth Judicial Circuit, said, "Policing was a joke. They gave tickets to those they didn't like and charged people with crimes they didn't commit."[19]

Lankford, who rode almost nightly with the police, had a different opinion. The majority of policemen, deputies, and highway patrolmen were "dedicated, decent professionals." They were hired, he observed, "into an imperfect occupation, with many inadequacies, and they worked tirelessly to make things better."

In the course of his reporting, Lankford often interacted with Bull Connor, who ruled city government with two like-minded commissioners—Arthur "Art" Hanes and James T. "Jabo" Waggoner. All three commissioners rejected "outsider" influences, determined to preserve the Southern culture they considered their heritage, a culture where Blacks and Whites lived in their own spheres and knew their "places."

"Bull," Lankford observed, "was outgoing and loud, a constantly in motion sort of man, who could be friendly if he liked you." Connor got along with Lankford, who listened well. Although Lankford was inexperienced, the first stories he wrote quoting Connor pleased the commissioner. After a while, Connor would tell him to "write him a story" on this or that topic. It wasn't long until Lankford wrote a story about Connor being a strong "law and order" man, declaring war on the slaughter on city streets.

"Okay, son, you got me right, now." Connor told him. "Just go ahead and write what you want. No need to wait around for me anymore."

Pragmatism outweighed Professor Scarritt's journalism teaching to report only the facts, and it became a morning routine for Sergeant John Preddy, Connor's executive assistant, to watch out the window at city hall for the arrival of the *News'* state edition at the rack in front of the Greyhound Bus Station. He'd walk across the street, buy a paper, and return to his desk to see what words Lankford had put into Bull's mouth. Sometimes he would call a news conference and give newsmen the facts from the article.

In April 1960, a reporter from the *New York Times* made a visit that was to upend the city. Harrison E. Salisbury came to Birmingham to write a story. A Pulitzer prize-winning journalist who had extensive experience on international fronts, Salisbury had obtained recent notoriety by writing on Johannesburg, South Africa, where hundreds of rioters were killed and thousands wounded when the government turned the military loose against demonstrators.

After clandestine meetings with Birmingham citizens, Salisbury's article, "Fear Stalks the Streets of Birmingham," appeared in the *New York Times*. In that damning piece, Salisbury noted, "Some Negroes have nicknamed Birmingham the Johannesburg of America. The difference between Johannesburg and Birmingham is that here they have not yet opened fire with the tanks and cannons." He alleged that lawlessness and racial oppression consumed Birmingham; that the city was "fragmented by the emotional dynamite of racism, reinforced by the whip, the razor, the gun, the bomb, the torch, the club, the knife, the mob, the police, and many branches of the state's apparatus."

This allegation incensed many in the White community, including Lankford's boss, Townsend. The inflamed imagery seemed blatantly wrong and unfair. Police didn't use whips or razors, and there were no mobs in the city streets. Klansmen did use whips and not just on Black people. Barbara Espy, a White woman kidnapped and whipped for allegedly having a Black boyfriend, could testify to it. That kind of work by the Klan was done under cover of night and the anonymity of white robes.

From the businessmen's perspective, their city was peaceful and orderly, and Salisbury's article was a terrible, "shoddy, vicious" exaggeration that put them in the worst light possible. White people looked around and saw none of what Salisbury described. His was clearly an "outsider" reporter's dramatization at the expense of the city. Backs stiffened into defensive mode.

Some in the Black community would also have been surprised at Salisbury's portrayal—those in the upper and professional class for whom the system worked, or those who gave no "trouble" to authorities, who taught their children never to look at a White person directly; to give way to them on the sidewalk; to say, "Yes, sir" and "No, ma'am," and always address Whites respectfully, as "Mr. or Miss or Mrs." but expect to be called by their first name or a derogatory "boy"; those who had come to accept the inequities—the fact they had to enter and exit at separate doors; take lower-paying or menial jobs; drink from separate water fountains; refrain from using White-only restrooms or sitting down in public where Whites sat; who had their laundry and their dead carried in "For Colored" vehicles. Many in the Black and the White community accepted this status quo because society had taught it to them from birth. Others chafed and might have agreed with Salisbury's analysis. Judge Houston Brown, who grew up in the city, recalled, "Birmingham was a vicious and violent place."[20]

Deepening the perceived insult, the *Times* also printed a full-page advertisement containing several falsehoods critical of Alabama officials. Connor and fellow commissioner Jabo Waggoner Sr. demanded a retraction. Connor, along with the other two commissioners, a police detective, and commissioners in Bessemer (fifteen miles southwest of Birmingham) sued the *New York Times,* which several years later admitted that some of its journalists "whispered [that] the famed [Salisbury] had 'sometimes exaggerated his reporting.'"[21]

One White person caught in the controversy's aftermath was the Reverend Robert E. Hughes, the director of the Alabama Council on Human Relations (ACHR). This interracial statewide organization was a branch of the Southern Regional Council, born of an interracial organization created in 1918 to counter the influence of the Klan and the violence of lynchings. After working behind the scenes to support the Montgomery Bus Boycott, the ACHR had been forced out of Montgomery, and Hughes moved its headquarters to Birmingham.

Investigators obtained Salisbury's hotel phone logs indicating that he had contacted Hughes while in Birmingham. Hughes then became the victim of hate circulars, threatening calls, and a cross burning; he was subpoenaed when a grand jury convened in Bessemer to determine whether Salisbury had defamed officials. The grand jury also subpoenaed Hughes's list of ACHR members. No one believed for a minute that the list wouldn't be leaked to the Klan. If that happened, many people would be exposed to harassment and violent retribution.

Attorney David Johnson Vann, a future mayor of Birmingham as well as a fellow student with Hughes at the University of Alabama, was a member of the Young Men's Business Club (YMBC), formed in 1946 by progressive, aged-out Jaycees who wanted to lead the city forward. The club was "regarded as a 'maverick' among business organizations because it supported positions that the traditional Chamber of Commerce either opposed or avoided as being too controversial."[22] Some saw YMBC members as communists, dangerous radicals, or worse.[23]

Vann and Roger Hanson, president of the Birmingham chapter of the Council on Human Relations, had taken note of young attorney Charles "Chuck" Morgan, another UA graduate, who had moved to Birmingham to practice law. Morgan had defended a controversial, outspoken Methodist seminarian a few years earlier. Hanson and Dr. Frederick Kraus talked Morgan into providing legal defense for Bob Hughes.[24]

Chuck Morgan had the appearance "of a rural Alabama sheriff, because he was overweight, smoked two packs of cigarettes a day, and his voice carried the sound of the Deep South," but he was the man for the job.[25] Civil rights attorney Jack Drake said Morgan had "the quickest mind of any lawyer I ever knew. He was a very fast thinker, told great stories, and had enormous courage, although he loved the spotlight . . . perhaps too much."[26]

Hughes appeared before the Bessemer court, but refused to give up the names of his organization's membership, and a judge threw him in jail for contempt. Morgan got him out and stopped the prosecutors from receiving the list.

Salisbury, however, was indicted by the Bessemer grand jury. To avoid being served, the *Times* forbade their journalists from stepping foot in Alabama for two-and-a-half years. For six years, the case dragged on until *Connor et al.* lost it on appeal. Meanwhile, the United Methodist Church forced Hughes to resign from his post at the ACHR by assigning him to Africa as a missionary.

4

A Black Hand

While Lankford learned the business of "street" journalism in 1961 and worked his way into law enforcement confidences, freedom whispered to the city's youth. Despite the harsh Jim Crow laws, many young people made their own decisions. In particular, White teens found their way to Black nightclubs to dance and enjoy the music. Birmingham had six Black radio stations. Popular deejays, such as Paul "Tall Paul" Dudley White and Shelley "The Playboy" Stewart, developed a White youth fan base. Bull Connor denounced what Stewart played on the airways as "jungle bunny" music and referred to him as Shelley "The Plowboy" Stewart.

Ironically, though he despised Stewart, Connor once might have saved his life. Segregationist White Citizens' Councils had spread across the South in the wake of the landmark 1954 Supreme Court decision, *Brown v. Board of Education*, which found unconstitutional "separate but equal" education. At a meeting of the north Birmingham WCC, members railed against Stewart's "corrupting influence" over White youth. Their agitation focused on White girls who hung out near Stewart's downtown office on Fourth Avenue North. Clamors for Stewart's death resounded among the WCC members. At length, Connor stood up and agreed with everything that had been said but added that trying to kill the popular deejay would backfire. "Let me handle Shelley 'The Plowboy' Stewart," he said.[27]

College students pushed back against racism in other ways. In particular, Birmingham-Southern College, a White private Methodist-supported liberal arts school in west Birmingham, became a hotbed of hope for those with liberal leanings—or, seen from the other end of the political spectrum, a hotbed of communists.

In 1951, a police detective had caught Connor—who considered himself the arbitrator and enforcer of the city's morals—in the downtown Tutwiler Hotel with his secretary. The incident sidelined Connor and for the next several years he had to watch politics while running his service station. Jimmy Morgan, Robert Lindbergh, and Wade Bradley served as commissioners, and under them the city experienced a brief opportunity to explore race relations.

Into that opening stepped three businessmen, Mervyn Sterne, Jim Head, and Charles Zukoski, leaders of the Interracial Committee, a part of a larger consortium set up to examine and address community challenges. Despite the growing backlash from the *Brown* decision, they organized a 1955 "Educational Institute on Race Relations" hosted by Birmingham-Southern College.

The integrated conference of eight hundred persons met to discuss racial community issues. At the request of the Interracial Committee, the commissioners allowed racially mixed seating, unheard of at the time. The conference received widespread public support. Fifty-three local organizations were listed in the official program.[28]

The liberal arts college was also the site of several other forums organized by Dorah Heyman Sterne and the League of Women Voters to discuss school desegregation. Dorah Sterne found "countless teachers and parents supportive of integration," but the [Birmingham city] school superintendent stood adamantly against any desegregation.[29]

Not all that was going on at the college was in the public view. In the library's basement, Edward Harris brought together a small group of fellow students to discuss race and politics. One Tuesday night he invited Black attorney Arthur Shores to speak. Shores made a deep impression on young Harris. "This was the first time, I guess, that I had really been up close to a [Black] man who was educated, who was powerful in his mentality."[30]

The White Citizens' Council and the Klan mounted a campaign against the Interracial Committee. Segregationist groups threatened the donations of the committee's funding organization, the Community Chest. Caving to fears of losing funding for their work, the executive committee agreed to shut down the Interracial Committee in 1956. Zukoski lamented that its demise was "a very sad day in the life of this community." It left the small Birmingham Council on Human Relations as the city's only integrated group.[31]

The pressures of the Klan and the WCC, however, did not silence everyone. Another Birmingham-Southern student took a public stand in the spring of 1959. Segregationists in the local Highlands Methodist Church, unhappy at the national denomination's support for integration, formed a Methodist

Laymen's Union to resist. More than 1,800 Methodists attended a meeting at Highlands. "A lone seminarian from Birmingham-Southern College stood to denounce the racism of 'The Pronouncement.'" The crowd shouted him down. "Laymen tailed the student back to the school and led an entourage of fifteen horn-honking cars around the campus. These Christians convinced Thomas Reeves's congregation to bar him from the pulpit."[32]

That same year, another Birmingham-Southern student made his position known when Bull Connor came to speak at a chapel service. Connor complained about a newspaper story that said Black inmates died at a higher rate than Whites in the Birmingham jail. "Jack Zylman jumped up and shouted, 'You're a murderer!'" Throughout his life, Zylman often took unpopular stands on issues of racism and fairness. According to immigration activist Helen Rivas, he "did not care who he offended."[33]

Students from across the city again showed their mettle when Klansmen decided they would wait no longer for Connor to handle the charismatic deejay Shelley "The Playboy" Stewart. Stewart's early life had been extraordinary—his father killed his mother with a hatchet in front of him. He had to live with relatives who abused him and forced him to feed himself and his siblings out of garbage cans. He ran away and was homeless when a White man named Clyde Smith took him in. At a critical time in Stewart's young life, "Papa Clyde" taught him the same lesson that Martin Luther King Jr. tried to impart—that one's character was far more important than one's color. But Stewart understood that barriers needed to come down for his people to have a chance. Surviving his brutal childhood had imparted an understanding that the system of racism could stifle the development of character and talent.[34]

On July 14, 1960, Stewart was playing music at a weekly record hop at Teen Town in Bessemer when about eighty Klansmen surrounded the building and sent word to the manager to send Stewart outside. Instead, the manager told the crowd of several hundred White teenagers about the threat to Stewart, and they poured out of the building, confronting the Klansmen. As Stewart and two others ran for his car, several Kluxers spotted him, but three White girls "rushed over and surrounded the three black men, protecting Stewart and his friends. The girls informed the Klansmen they would have to hit them to get to their targets." Lowering "chains and clubs," the Klansmen backed off, and Stewart escaped.[35]

That same day, a thousand Blacks marched peacefully in Montgomery, returning afterward to the Alabama State College campus. Governor Patterson and the state Board of Education pressured the college to expel nine of the students considered leaders of the march. In Birmingham, ninety-seven White students at Birmingham-Southern College protested that infringement of academic freedom by signing a petition objecting to the state's "interference in the affairs of the college."

Thomas Reeves—the twenty-two-year-old student who had stood up at the Highlands Methodist segregation rally—reached out to Miles College and Daniel Payne College to organize meetings between Black and White students. In response, police arrested the pre-ministerial student, and the Klan threatened his life.

Birmingham-Southern President Dr. Henry King Stanford defended his student's right to freedom of speech, refusing to yield to pressure from the community, the alumni, or the supremacists who burned a cross on the school campus. Unyielding, Stanford remained stalwart in Reeves's support. Attorney Chuck Morgan took on the dubious task of representing Reeves. Reeves eventually graduated Phi Beta Kappa and moved to Tennessee.[36]

SPRING 1961 FOUND TOM Lankford in the middle of an intense political battle. Full of energy and commitment to his job, he had no personal interest in politics, but the *Birmingham News* did not believe in coming in second and neither did he. The lesson that survival depended on hard work and grasping opportunities was born and nourished by his early life in Hokes Bluff where he helped on his father's small farm, planting corn, hay, and sorghum. When he and his brother finished with their own farm work, they hired out to neighboring farmers and gathered peanuts or picked cotton. They also worked land their father rented for his boys to plant cotton, giving them the proceeds of their labor. If it rained and was too wet to plow, his father—believing boys shouldn't be idle—"set them to pulling up grass and weeds by hand."

Lankford was grateful to the *News* and particularly to Townsend, who had given him a job in his field of study and an opportunity to support his pregnant wife and young daughter. Assigned to learn what was going on behind the scenes at city hall, he figured the best strategy was to become "one of the boys." To do that, he had to "make quick decisions, do favors, and be trustworthy."

An opportunity to do just that arose in the spring of 1961. At that time, the mayor was one of the three commissioners who ran the city. Mayor Jimmy Morgan had ceremonial duties representing the city and an equal vote in municipal affairs with the two other commissioners, who were now the reelected Eugene "Bull" Connor, over police and fire, and Jabo Waggoner Sr., over streets and sanitation. Clint Bishop, Morgan's executive secretary, made a trip upstairs to the pressroom at city hall, one floor above the mayor's offices. Bishop sat down in a metal folding chair across from Lankford and leaned forward. "Tom, we badly need your help."

Lankford listened intently. This sounded like a perfect chance to do a favor that might be reciprocated, an opportunity to establish himself as trustworthy.

Bishop paused, "Now the mayor isn't in on this, but I'll engage Preddy (executive secretary to Connor) to help, as the party we're interested in will call on Bull soon. You're to do as you think best, but I'm thinking a photograph of 'our man' shaking hands with a black individual is what we need. I can put you on the trail, and you improvise from there."

"Who's to help me?" Lankford asked.

"Anybody you want."

Lankford didn't hesitate. "Jimmy Hale."

Sergeant Jimmy Hale was the toughest, most reliable policeman he knew. Though not a big man, not an ounce of his 150 pounds was fat. Hale was once shot five or six times while confronting criminals but still managed to return fire. He was that kind of man—one you could trust at your back.

Bishop's "our man" turned out to be Tom King, the son of Judge Alta King.

Lankford knew that King was a candidate for mayor and that Bishop liked his position as the mayor's secretary and intended to stay put, though his boss, Jimmy Morgan, was retiring. Bishop must have calculated that his chances of staying employed in city hall were better with Tom King's opponent, Art Hanes, a WWII veteran and former FBI agent.

Lankford agreed to try to get the photo shot, and Bishop, satisfied, stood and shook his hand hard. On the way out the door, Bishop gave Lankford a thumb's up.

It wasn't much longer before the phone in the pressroom rang. Lankford recognized Connor's executive secretary. Excitement brimmed in Preddy's voice. "Tom King will be in Bull's office in fifteen minutes!"

Normally, Lankford rode the elevators, but he didn't have time for that now. Grasping the rail, he vaulted down the stairwell six steps at a time to the basement coffee shop where Sergeant Jimmy Hale waited.

"He's coming, Jimmy!" Lankford shouted. "We better go now!"

Sprinting to the police "run-around"—a semicircular drive on the north side of city hall that curved underneath the small parking lot for the mayor, city council, and police cars—they both jumped into Hale's marked unit. Police lights flashing, Hale headed a few blocks north to a Black neighborhood of dilapidated shotgun houses. Hopping the curb, Hale drove right up into the dusty yard of a house, jumped out of the car and headed up the porch steps, Lankford on his heels.

Inside, four men squatted in a circle on the floor, rolling dice. Hale yanked a raggedly dressed man, who outweighed him by twenty pounds, onto his feet.

"Joe, you're coming with us," Hale snapped, and to keep from wasting time, he tucked Joe under one arm and carried him to the car.

As he drove, Hale told Joe, "You know I have enough on you to put you in jail for the rest of your natural life. You do what Mr. Lankford here tells you to do, and if you mess up, it's back to jail for you." Hale gave Joe $20, which Lankford later learned Connor's executive secretary repaid to Hale.

At the corner of Fourth Avenue and Twenty-first Street North, the home of the *Birmingham News*, Hale stopped. Lankford dashed up to the second floor to the newsroom to grab a telephoto lens.

"We're out of time," Hale said as Lankford jumped back into the patrol car. Lankford knew what that meant—*Hang on*! Heavy traffic, however, mired them down. For the second time that day, Hale jumped the car off the street, this time onto the sidewalk, lights flashing and siren blasting in an unauthorized "emergency run" back to city hall to make sure Tom King did not replace Mayor Jimmy Morgan. It was a surreal scene, with pedestrians jumping out of the way, but Hale didn't blink or take his foot off the gas pedal.

Woodrow Wilson Park (currently Linn Park) sat between city hall and the county courthouse. Hale screeched to a stop at the city hall entrance facing the park. Lankford pulled Joe out of the car and pushed him up the first flight of marble steps where he left him.

In keeping with the movie-chase-scene madness that had ensued since receiving the alert call from Preddy, Lankford dashed up the stairs to the fourth-floor pressroom. The moment he had the window facing the park open, the phone on his desk rang.

"Tom King's on his way out," Preddy said, slamming down the receiver.

What Lankford did not know at the time was that Tom King's visit to Connor's office was "to pay his respects." He knew Connor wouldn't support him for mayor, but he was hoping "at least to get him not to come out for my opponent."[37]

Lankford knew nothing about the exchange, only focusing on getting a photo. He rolled the window farther open, spotting Joe standing below where he had left him on the steps. Steadying the camera, he tried to calm down after all the adrenaline rush.

Joe's instructions were to approach Tom King and say, "Mr. King, us blacks are all gonna vote for you."

"He won't take your hand," Lankford had predicted to Joe, "so you need to grab his and hang on for dear life."

Lankford was wrong. Tom King willingly shook Joe's hand, and Lankford clicked away.

"I got them," he told the mayor's assistant over the phone.

Clint Bishop was up the flight of stairs from the third floor in seconds, snatching the roll of black-and-white film from Lankford's hand.

"You get back to your police beat duties and leave everything to me," Bishop said.

The next morning when Lankford stopped by the *News* before making the morning police roll call at city hall, he found a beehive of activity. During the night, smear sheets of mayoral candidate Tom King shaking hands with a Black man on the steps of city hall had circulated all over town.

What Lankford had not realized was that the *News* had endorsed Tom King, but that was not of much interest to him at the time. He left the politics to the editorial staff and the politicians. What was important was that from now on, he could count on having the inside scoop on anything coming out of the mayor's office and whatever background info he might need. To Lankford's way of thinking, those were long-term advantages that would benefit him, the *News*, and most importantly, Townsend.

The *News* staff scurried to produce a double-page spread, blaming the smear on the City Hall Machine and asking voters not to be hoodwinked.

As far as Lankford could see, that was only going to spread the fact to more White voters that Tom King had shaken a Black man's hand. Only a few thousand Blacks were registered to vote. Although the Fifteenth Amendment of the Constitution gave African American men the right to vote, and the Nineteenth Amendment gave women the right to vote, literacy tests and poll taxes in Birmingham kept all but a small percentage from voting.

The handshake was only part of the "Black Hand" strategy used against King, who had carried the primary with a strong showing by organized labor and the Black voters, the latter measured primarily by the poll near Legion Field on the western side of the city. In Birmingham, the general election had, like so many other conversations, deteriorated to one about race.

The progressive YMBC members saw Tom King as the best choice to lead the city forward. According to Chuck Morgan, who worked on King's campaign, King "was not an integrationist by any means," but he was not satisfied with the status quo regarding Birmingham's stagnation and lack of economic progress.[38] "Tom King threatened the Consensus [mining and big banking] interests with his desire for economic growth at any cost and his willingness to sacrifice segregation in order to dismantle the colonial economy with its regionally discriminatory race wage."[39]

During the campaign, however, King's racial views seemed "not much different from those of Hanes." Near the campaign's end—advised to "fight fire with fire"—King "sunk into the politics of 'seg.'" But the opposition bought ads in the papers and distributed fliers with the image of a Black hand placing a ballot in a box with bold headlines warning, "Defeat the NAACP Bloc Vote." It was a standard technique for alienating voters from a candidate.[40]

Tom King lost to Art Hanes. Joe, the Black man who shook his hand, was not sent back to jail.

A FEW DAYS BEFORE Mother's Day in May 1961, Connor directed Lankford to accompany Detective Sergeant Thomas Cook—Connor's man on racial matters—to a Klan meeting in nearby Midfield, a small town to the west of Birmingham.

"Take your camera," Connor said. "You'll find these guys eager for publicity."

Lankford rode with Cook and two detectives to an open field, lit only by the headlights of pickups and cars and an electrically lighted white cross on a pickup truck bed. About thirty white-robed Klansmen, heads uncovered in the heat, gathered near their pickup trucks and old cars. Knotted around a central figure, they listened intently to a man Lankford recognized—Robert Shelton, the Imperial Wizard of the United Klans of America—the same man who had taken Lankford's film after he photographed the Klan's sign near the University of Alabama.

The Klansmen seemed to expect the group of Birmingham policemen, waving as they approached. Shelton was working hard to liven up the crowd, his high forehead slick with sweat. His difficulty might have been that his "euphemisms, half-truths, and hackneyed phrases from the days of slavery" were spoken in a drawling monotone. A former B. F. Goodrich tire plant worker from Tuscaloosa, Shelton spoke on the level of the men gathered at his feet and gave "honest to God" examples of how the Klan was saving Americans from the "niggers" and all their sympathizers.

Lankford found that Connor had been correct about the Klan's desire for publicity. After the meeting, Shelton agreed to a photograph. Climbing into the bed of a pickup truck, Lankford grabbed onto the battery-powered cross with one hand to hoist himself and his equipment over the edge. Then he motioned the Klansmen into a semicircle, instructing them to drop their pointed hoods over their faces. Bringing up his camera, he adjusted the focus and pressed the shutter to take the first photo. The attached "Mighty Lite" strobe flashed on the surreal scene of the robed Klansmen lined up before him.

Back in the newsroom, Lankford's developed pictures had turned out well. It wasn't every day one could get a photograph of the Klan in full regalia. The city editor didn't agree. "We're not going to give publicity to the god-damn Klan," he said, tossing Lankford's photo into the wastebasket.

Lankford never knew if Townsend nixed the photo or it was the city editor's idea. "Townsend was too busy to make decisions daily on photos and stories. While he could pull or edit any article or photo, he rarely did."[41]

Fellow staff reporter Donald Brown later explained that the *News* management made decisions to put some articles on back pages. "The paper at that time was many pages every day, and a lot of what [we] wrote [on protests and civil rights issues] . . . ended up in the back of the paper just kind of buried among a lot of other news. We would cover certain events photographically, but very few of those photographs were ever published. The *News* at one time had an outstanding archive of many civil rights pictures. Very few ever saw the light of day in the newspaper. I would not say that it kept the news from the community; it just made sure that in its own mind that the news we published wasn't—in the terminology of some of the editors—overplayed and given too much prominence."[42]

The media's response to the early unrest and demonstrations drew criticism of under-representation of racial events both from locals and the outside media. Citizens later claimed they didn't know what was happening in their own city.

On the other hand, the national media used stereotypes in presenting stories. "In Birmingham and other areas of the South, national reporters used a simple formula to cover the racial crises. 'We wrote our stories like western movie scenarios,' remembered one veteran reporter, and Birmingham emerged as the 1960s version of the O. K. Corral. Birmingham Commissioner of Public Safety Bull Connor was cast as the 'big, fat, sloppy sheriff with his cigar, dogs, and cow prods' (the bad guy), and Martin Luther King was the good guy. . . . 'Just change the names and the name of the town, and the story was already written because this had become a ritual kind of reporting.'"[43]

Lankford rescued his Klan photo from the trash and sent it over to the AP, whose desk was in the same newsroom. That day it appeared in most member papers across the nation. Although the image never made print in his own *Birmingham News*, the photo session with the Klan may have saved his life.

5

Birmingham's Bloody Mother's Day, 1961

Connor sat in his office among a retinue of handpicked local reporters, chomping his cigar. "As if that *New York Times* trash wasn't enough," he growled, referring to reporters from CBS who were in Birmingham, "now, we've got [James Peck, a White Freedom Rider] and his niggers on a convoy here to stir up more trouble."

Connor, reflecting the feelings of many Birmingham Whites, did not relish Northerners coming down to tell Southerners what they should be doing or "stirring up trouble." He had taken action to stop it before, even when the troublemakers included Eleanor Roosevelt, the First Lady of the United States. In 1938 she came to Birmingham as a featured speaker for a symposium to address economic problems in the South amid the Great Depression.

For twenty-four hours, the commissioner-approved conference had operated as an integrated body. Then the Big Mules heard about what was happening; these steel and mining industrialists fought integration because they feared a united workers' union would drive up labor costs, and they convinced Connor to enforce the city's segregation ordinances at the conference. Connor got the message. He barged into the ongoing conference and demanded adherence to the segregation law, declaring that Blacks and Whites could not "segregate together." He required Blacks to sit on one side of the auditorium and Whites on the other. The crowd obeyed, but Mrs. Roosevelt planted her chair between the black and white sections and sat in the aisle.[44]

The conference had come to the city in part because Birmingham's Joe Gelders (later kidnapped and beaten by anti-unionist private police) helped persuade President Franklin Roosevelt to support the concept of a Southern Conference for Human Welfare (SCHW) to bring the president's New Deal reforms to the South. Gelders was a "lanky, soft-voiced, academic-looking man with an odd dancing gait . . . a product of bourgeois upbringing, but suffered the kind of social ostracism that came with being a Southern Jew."[45]

Gelders left school to serve in World War I, returning to marry and earn a master's degree in physics from the University of Alabama. Disillusionment with capitalism during the crushing poverty of the Depression led him to embrace communism. The Communist Party wanted him to keep his affiliation secret and use his influence among Southern liberals.

Roosevelt was then unaware of Gelders's communist beliefs. The president read the economic study Gelders presented and gave his support to the symposium in Birmingham. White attendees included Governor Bibb Graves and Supreme Court Justice Hugo L. Black—both, ironically, endorsed by the Klan in their early careers. Graves had become a progressive reformer, abolishing the corrupt and brutal convict leasing system. Black would prove to be progressive on the bench, notably on racial issues.

Other symposium attendees included Aubrey Williams of the Works Progress Administration and Birmingham's own Virginia Durr, a staunch activist for civil and women's rights and a co-founder of SCHW (Durr was also Hugo Black's sister-in-law). For ten years (1938–1948) the Southern Conference on Human Welfare persisted in the region beyond the Birmingham symposium, trying to repeal the poll tax and to improve social justice and civil rights. "The SCHW folded because of funding problems and charges of harboring communist sympathies, but it laid the groundwork for future civil rights activism."[46]

Connor had railed since 1938 against the SCHW alleged communist infiltrators. Now, this morning in 1961, another "communist-inspired group," the Congress of Racial Equality (CORE), was invading his city. CORE member James "Jim" Peck was one of the Freedom Riders on an incoming bus. Peck had a reputation as a civil rights "professional agitator," just the sort to push Connor's buttons. Turning to Sergeant Tom Cook, Connor barked, "Keep me updated. I gotta know what's going on."

Lankford chafed at the wait. Connor had instructed him to show up bright and early this Sunday morning in his office on the third floor of city hall. The police commissioner hadn't had to say why, because every reporter worth his salt had been reading the AP dispatches about the Freedom Riders headed to Birmingham on two interstate buses.

Unbeknownst to Lankford, when Tom King—the subject of the "handshaking with a Black man" photo—had been about to leave Connor's office a few days earlier, the candidate mentioned the Freedom Riders upcoming arrival on Mother's Day. With a smirk, Connor had said, "We will be ready for them too."[47]

The Freedom Riders, Blacks and Whites committed to a strategy of nonviolence, were testing the Supreme Court ruling, *Boynton v. Virginia*, and federal anti-discrimination laws regarding the integration of interstate bus travel and bus station waiting areas and restaurants. CORE knew the laws in the South were not enforced and wanted to bring that to national attention with an integrated bus trip from Washington to New Orleans. It seemed a foolhardy mission. Even activist Fred Shuttlesworth feared for their safety, sending a telegram to Connor asking for police protection for them and warning the Riders that coming to Birmingham was dangerous.

Knowing the risk, the Riders still insisted on completing their journey. But Connor was not about to let "out-of-town meddlers" come to his city and flaunt their disregard for the right of Alabama to make her own laws and protect her "way of life." He shrugged off court rulings—Supreme Court or no, staking his reputation on fighting desegregation. Others might give in, but not Theophilus Eugene "Bull" Connor.

All morning on the bright, sunny Sunday of May 14, 1961, Lankford sat in Commissioner Connor's third-floor office, listening as people telephoned in reports of the buses' progress—one Trailways and one Greyhound. John Preddy sat at his desk outside the office, occasionally bringing in coffee for Connor. Bud Gordon, the *News'* city hall beat reporter, was present, along with a handful of Connor's compatriots, including, of course, Sergeant Cook who came in and out updating Connor.

Lankford always found Cook to be quiet and affable and responsive to inquiries. Like Marcus Jones, he was a loner. Lankford considered him a friend. On several occasions he observed Cook speaking to FBI agents and assumed Cook shared information with them.[48] It made sense, because everyone knew Cook was at the center of information concerning local racial matters. In Lankford's mind, it would have been derelict not to consult with him.

Normally, Lankford would have spent Mother's Day with his mother, Asalee, at the farm in Hokes Bluff. Asalee had taught him more about life and survival than any teacher or university class. When her own mother died in the flu pandemic of 1919, she quit school during sixth grade to care for her eleven brothers and sisters. Lankford was born near the end of the Depression in an old house set back in the woods off a dirt road. They were poor, as were all their neighbors, but they didn't feel deprived. All the children he knew went barefoot until winter, when their mothers bought shoes. Asalee made all their clothes from feed sacks, except for the blue jeans, which were handed down to each younger child as the older one outgrew them. His mother picked cotton to buy those shoes and their schoolbooks each autumn.

After his father got a job at the cotton mill, the family moved up in living conditions to a dog-trot house with rooms sprouting off a central hallway and a well in the backyard. Every day after school, Tom sat at the dinner table while his mother did her chores and helped him with his homework. Asalee insisted the children attend Sunday school and church, pressing a stick of chewing gum into his hand with a penny for the collection plate.

Lankford wanted to be with her on Mother's Day, but this year he sat in Bull's office while the two buses left Atlanta an hour apart, the Greyhound first, with a few regular passengers, the Freedom Riders, two journalists, and two undercover highway patrolmen, Corporals E. L. Cowling and Harry Sims. The latter wore concealed microphones, both to gather information and because State Highway Patrol Director Floyd Mann did not trust local law enforcement, well aware that some had connections to the Klan.[49]

From his office chair, Connor continued receiving frequent reports about the progress of the Freedom Riders—information the FBI supplied Sergeant Cook.[50] Tension grew as the day wore on. Reporters at city hall grabbed lunch out of the basement vending machines, not daring to leave the building. Lankford hated waiting, but there was nothing else he could do until it was time to act. He fingered his 35mm Canon, which he kept on a sling concealed under his left arm for quick action. It was smaller than his Yashica, easier to hide, and pre-focused at a high shutter speed so he wouldn't have to worry about movement blurring a shot.

Several times Connor called his attorney, James Simpson, who repre-sented many of the "Big Mules" mining and steel companies and was also a segregationist. Simpson had mentored Connor early in his political career. In the 1930s they had served together in the state legislature, and Simpson was thought to have pulled Connor's strings behind the scenes.

"They're in Alabama now," Connor reported to the group gathered in his office. One ear to the phone, he updated them a few minutes later. "They've stopped the bus."

While tense minutes passed in Connor's office, the Greyhound bus stopped in Anniston, about seventy miles east of Birmingham. At the station, a White mob rushed it, but the two undercover patrolmen kept the attackers from dragging anyone out. Hastily, the bus pulled out. Just outside the city, however, slashed tires forced the bus to a halt. Waiting Klansmen attacked. The vigilantes broke the windows and threw in a firebomb.

Connor swiveled his chair around to face the listeners, his right hand gripping the mouthpiece. "They're burning the bus!"

Silence descended on the room. Everyone was riveted on a drama miles away. On the lonely stretch of highway, smoke billowed through the bus. Klansmen jumped up into the doorway, blocking the exit and trapping the choking passengers.

Corporal Cowling pushed his way to the front of the bus and drew his gun. He could have simply escaped himself, but he demanded that everyone be let out. Without his intervention, the Riders might have been burned alive. Even escaping that horror, beatings at the Klansmen's hands awaited them as they fled the bus. Cowling and Sims stood over the fallen, trying to protect them. An ambulance pulled up but at first refused to take the Black injured. Encouragement by Cowling, along with the fact that the injured White Riders refused to leave without their compatriots, convinced the driver to take them all to a hospital.

Meanwhile, the Trailways bus continued toward Birmingham. Connor updated the group in his office again. "Another bus will be here in an hour or so."

In Birmingham, a CBS cameraman in a bright red convertible aimed his camera toward the Greyhound bus station. A waiting contingent of reporters included two from CBS, young Dan Rather from Texas and Louisiana-born Howard K. Smith. In an attempt to undo some of the bad publicity of the *Times*' Salisbury article, Townsend had helped persuade CBS to send reporters to see the city for themselves. Smith intended to produce a documentary, "Who Speaks for Birmingham?"[51] Unfortunately for Birmingham public relations, Smith had been tipped off to hang around the bus terminals on Sunday if he wanted "to see some action."

The National States' Rights Party (NSRP), an extreme right wing, anti-Semitic, neo-Nazi organization associated with Georgia attorney J. B. Stoner was also planning to be in on the action at the bus station. According to an FBI report, the NSRP's Edward Fields listed his occupation on his military draft registration as "Anti-Jewish Crusader." The report said that Fields "carries a firearm on his person . . . [and] has warned that he would shoot any FBI agent surveying (sic) him."[52] The NSRP had moved its offices to Birmingham in 1960 in the wake of the Salisbury article uproar. Along with their anti-Catholic and anti-Black hate campaign, Fields launched "an Adolf Eichmann Trial Facts Committee to defend Hitler's architect of genocide."[53]

The Klan was not keen on having the NSRP show up at the bus station. Although the two organizations shared values, the Klansmen claimed they didn't want to have to worry about controlling Fields's thugs. Gary Thomas Rowe, a paid FBI informant, called Detective Cook to complain about the NSRP presence. Cook told him, "Relax, you boys should work together."[54]

Lankford, along with every newsman in Birmingham and the oncoming Riders themselves expected trouble from the Klan. What they didn't know was that Connor's plan to "be ready" included a Klan reception for fifteen minutes before law enforcement would arrive.[55] Connor counted on that sending an unequivocal message about what to expect if Freedom Riders set foot again in Birmingham. Unconcerned about what national media might make of such a confrontation, he, like the to-be Governor George C. Wallace, had made his career by standing up against the federal government. He credited his hard stance on integration for the reason Birmingham had been free of major race riots. Besides, the "progressives" lived in over-the-mountain suburbs and did not vote in Birmingham. His voters had supported him overwhelmingly in his last election—and they were the only ones he cared about.

Chief Moore, who knew the Freedom Riders would be coming through, was visiting his mother in his hometown of Albertville and attending the town's annual Decoration Day, honoring dead family members by sprucing up the cemetery. Connor had encouraged him to go.[56] Lankford doubted that Connor had shared his plans for the Freedom Riders with Moore. Nor had Connor revealed his plans to Lankford or the other newsmen in his office.

Klansmen in regular clothes—not robes—along with CBS newsmen Rather and Smith, not knowing the Greyhound bus had been burned, waited for the Freedom Riders' arrival at the Greyhound bus terminal, located just across the street from city hall. Gary Thomas Rowe, playing his Klansman role with equal enthusiasm as his role of FBI informant, received a phone call that the bus of Freedom Riders was arriving, but at the Trailways station, a little over two blocks away. He passed the word to his fellow Klansmen. A group of White men then ran down the almost deserted streets carrying chains and iron pipes.[57] The CBS newsmen followed in their vehicle.

Only then did Connor tell the reporters in his office that the bus was coming into the Trailways terminal instead of the Greyhound. "So, you," he said, pointing at Lankford, "and Bud [Gordon] get on down there."

Before the newsmen could get there, the big dusty bus arrived. Klansmen rushed onto it, attacking the Black Riders sitting in the White section. White Riders Jim Peck and Professor Walter Bergman intervened, trying to protect their fellows, taking severe beatings. Bergman, a veteran of WWI and WWII, suffered a stroke and permanent brain damage.[58]

Howard K. Smith reported from the scene:

> Toughs grabbed the passengers into alleys and corridors, pounding them with pipes, with key rings, and with fists. One passenger was knocked down at my feet by twelve of the hoodlums, and his face was beaten and kicked until it was a bloody pulp.[59]

That face belonged to Jim Peck, a "frail, middle-aged man at the time."[60] He required thirty-four stitches.

Birmingham Post-Herald photographer Tommy Langston arrived before Lankford. As he snapped a shot of the chaos inside the bus terminal, Klansmen saw his camera flash, grabbed his camera, and attacked him with a bat, chains, and iron pipes. Miraculously, he escaped with only cuts and bruises.[61]

Clancy Lake, the reporter who had befriended Lankford at the *News,* now news director for WAPI radio, was broadcasting an account of the riot from his car when Klansmen smashed the car's windows, destroyed his equipment, and dragged him out of the car. Lake managed to escape. A true newsman, he found a telephone and resumed his broadcast.

Neither Langston nor Lake was in sight by the time Lankford, Gordon, and the other reporters who had been in Connor's office arrived. Though they were less than three blocks from city hall, no uniformed officers were in sight. Lankford's heart raced as he snapped pictures. He knew he was on his own, but that didn't bother him. He was where he belonged—in the middle of the action.

Later, he would struggle to give justice to what he saw:

> . . . smashing fists and pipes and blood . . . a giant of a man, bloody from slugging individuals while his gang held them, led the attacks, crazily swinging blackjacks and lengths of pipe, about eight of them pounded a white man and a Negro to the concrete floor of the bus station.[62]

Klansmen jumped on a CBS reporter and soundman, smashing their cameras and sound gear. Spotting Lankford, several Klansmen grabbed him. Faces flushed with rage, the thugs dragged him down the alley, brandishing bloodstained bicycle chains. One held a lead pipe. Just before the first blow was to fall, he caught a glint of recognition on the face of a burly Klansman he later learned was none other than the infamous Gary Thomas Rowe, who journalist Alvin Benn described as a "fat thug with red hair and a quick temper."[63] Rowe was a wild card. No one knew for sure where his loyalties lay. He held Lankford's left wrist, immobilizing the hand that clutched his camera containing film of the savage beatings he had just witnessed.

To Lankford's great relief, Rowe—recognizing him from the Klan photo shoot in the field a few days before—yelled to his accomplices, "Stop! That's Bull's boy." The Kluxers dragged Lankford across the alley to a more sequestered spot in the rear of the Trailways bus station.

With a nervous look over his shoulder, Rowe said, "We'll have to take your film, Tom."

Lankford didn't argue.

After unloading the film from the camera, Rowe reached into his pocket and tossed Lankford a wadded dollar bill as payment for the film, a surreal replay of the scene in Tuscaloosa from Lankford's student encounter with the Klan Grand Wizard.

6

A Midnight Roundup
& More Blood in Montgomery

Shaken but undeterred, Lankford talked his way into the emergency room at Carraway Hospital. He was often granted special access because of his connections, and it didn't hurt that a director of nurses, Ann Ruth Jones, was Marcus Jones's wife. Inside, nurses shaved the heads of the injured Freedom Riders and treated their ugly wounds. Lankford shot a picture of Jim Peck that depicted the violence done to him, making a copy for investigators.[64]

Attorney Chuck Morgan worked with local Black lawyers Peter Hall and Orzell Billingsley to free the jailed Riders. Several of the wounded showed up at the bus station the following day but could not find a bus willing to take them to Montgomery, their next stop. While they waited at the station, another White mob formed, but this time the police stepped in to protect them, possibly because Shuttlesworth had notified U.S. Attorney General Robert Kennedy of the situation. Kennedy called the police department and got assurances that law enforcement would prevent another incident.

After two canceled flights and another police intervention to forestall a mob at the airport, the Riders flew by plane to New Orleans.[65] Kennedy had sent aide John Seigenthaler to Birmingham "where he joined the Riders at the airport, boarded their flight, and accompanied them to New Orleans."[66]

The violence in Birmingham spurred not only national outrage but also a local front-page protest the following morning from the *Birmingham News*. In the last election that had resulted in Connor's reelection to office, the *News* had tepidly endorsed Connor's recent landslide election, cautioning that "he has not always handled himself well . . . and has been irritating to some citizens."[67]

But now Vincent Townsend, a stalwart supporter of law enforcement, was furious about the bus station assault. The *News* ran an editorial above the front-page headline:

The newspaper supported Eugene Connor for police commissioner . . . because it believed Connor meant what he said when he outlined his policy: that Negro or white, the city of Birmingham would not tolerate violence, disorder, breaking of the law. The Birmingham Police Department under Connor did not do what could have been done Sunday. . . . People are asking: Where were the police?

Noting several times the presence of marked and plainclothes police in the area prior to the attack at Trailways and Connor's knowledge of the arriving bus, the question implied that Connor held back officers. Although the piece was clear in considering the Freedom Riders troublemakers, it also reflected on the irony:

Harrison Salisbury of the *New York Times* last year came to Birmingham and wrote two articles about us which said, in substance, that "fear and hatred" stalked our streets. The *Birmingham News* and others challenged this assertion. The *News* knows Birmingham people, as others know them, and they didn't fit this definition. But yesterday, Sunday, May 14, was a day which [*sic*] ought to be burned into Birmingham's conscience. Fear and hatred did stalk Birmingham's streets yesterday.[68]

Later that week, Howard K. Smith's documentary "Who Speaks for Birmingham?" aired on CBS and included footage from the Klan attack on the Freedom Riders. Connor, however, blamed everything on "out-of-town meddlers"—both those "who got whipped and the ones who did the whipping." He creatively explained the absence of police presence as a result of a shortage of manpower due to the holiday. "We try to let off as many of our policemen as possible so they can spend Mother's Day at home with their families."[69]

Three days after the Mother's Day fiasco, another group of CORE Freedom Riders, including two of the original group, wrote out their wills and showed up in Birmingham. John Lewis, a future U.S. Congressman, was one of them.

On May 17, Connor walked into the bus station where the Riders were waiting for the bus to Montgomery. Lewis recalled recognizing him, though he had never seen him. "He was short, heavy, with big ears and a fleshy face.

He wore a suit, his white hair was slicked straight back above his forehead, and his eyes were framed by a pair of black, horn-rimmed glasses."[70]

Connor announced he was arresting them "for their own protection." They were taken to the city's jail on Sixth Avenue South while he pondered what to do with them. Connor latched onto advice to take them to the Tennessee state line and dump them off on the roadside, believing that would be the end of it all. He called the FBI and invited them to go along, but they turned down his offer and warned that if he crossed the state line with the Riders, he could be charged with kidnapping. Highway Patrol officials also declined. Connor decided he would take the Riders himself and drop them off just inside Alabama at the Tennessee line.

"Okay, Tom," he said to Lankford. "You and Bud be back here at 7 p.m. We're going to rid ourselves of a problem."

Connor arranged for the airport limousine service to loan him a stretch limo for the trip. Connor rode in the lead car, a Birmingham police vehicle. Lankford rode in the limousine that followed. Outside the jail, members of the Klan gathered, keeping a vigil. Inside, the Freedom Riders had been separated by gender and spent several hours in a sparse cell "that looked like a dungeon. It had no mattresses or beds, nothing to sit on at all, just a concrete floor." The Riders refused food and spent the hours singing, to their jailers' annoyance. [71]

When Connor arrived, he introduced himself, Lankford, and Bud Gordon. The Riders, fearful of what awaited them outside in the dark, refused to budge. Jailers had to pick them up like firewood, tossing them headfirst into the limousine. One skidded across the carpeted floor, hitting his head with a sharp smack on the far door.

"At the stroke of midnight," Lankford wrote, "the Nashville college students were loaded into a black limousine and driven from the jail in a three-car caravan."[72]

The vehicles pulled away from the jail. Though Connor had alerted the Klansmen of his plan and "arranged" for safe passage, he was nervous they would attack anyway. The *Selma-Times Journal* reported that a train momentarily blocked the way.[73] Lankford added that the train was moving at a snail's pace through a crossing. Angered at the obstruction, Connor "bulled out of the police car." Lankford knew Connor had been drinking and watched in astonishment as the police commissioner took up a bellicose stance in front of the lead car, "his white mane of hair back-lit by the headlights." He shook his fist at the sky, shouting for the train engineer to stop.

Amazingly, the engineer screeched the train to a halt. A switchman jumped out and uncoupled the boxcars in front of the police convoy. The engine pulled forward, clearing the crossing, and they passed through, headed to the Alabama-Tennessee line.

En route, the detective riding with Lankford in the limo debated with the students over what was termed "nigger rights" or "civil rights," depending on the speaker. Lankford listened with growing embarrassment at the detective's unschooled defense of segregation, a stark contrast to the students' intelligent and articulate expressions of their position.

In a matter of hours, the cars reached the Alabama-Tennessee line but missed the sign. Driving almost a mile into Tennessee before discovering the error, they put out the Freedom Riders inside the Volunteer State, instead of in Alabama as planned, although Lankford wrote it this way:

> Four hours and ten minutes later, the four Negro men and two Negro women were left bag and baggage a few feet from the Tennessee line . . . "There is the Tennessee line," Connor told the Negroes, "cross it and save this state and yourselves a lot of trouble."[74]

Connor dusted his hands of them . . . but the drama was far from over. The next morning, Saturday, May 20, 1961, Lankford looked out the pressroom window at city hall and saw that the Freedom Riders they had dropped off in the middle of the night were sitting at the Greyhound station waiting for a bus. Befriended in Tennessee by an elderly Black couple, they had notified fellow activists in Nashville and a car was dispatched to drive them through the night back to Birmingham. They arrived only a short time after Commissioner Connor's contingent pulled into the police lot just across the street. Lankford blinked at the implausible, farcical outcome of Connor's attempt to rid Birmingham of the Riders' unwelcome presence in his city.

For hours, the Riders tried to get a bus to take them onward, but bus drivers refused to carry them. Cloistered inside the station without food or phone service, they nervously watched the growing crowd of angry Whites. As John Lewis recalled,

With darkness the mob grew bolder and more violent. We could see them through the glass doors and street side windows, gesturing at us and shouting. Every now and then a rock or a brick would crash through one of the windows up near the ceiling. The police brought in dogs and we could see them outside, pulling at their leashes to keep the crowd back.[75]

After some drama with the reluctant bus drivers in Birmingham, Attorney General Robert Kennedy pressured Greyhound to carry the Riders on. Connor was ready to see them out of his city, or perhaps he knew something about what awaited them in Montgomery.

In Birmingham, as the Riders loaded up, Fred Shuttlesworth tried to board the bus, putting his foot on the second step before feeling a hand on the back of his collar. Turning, he saw the hand belonged to Chief Jamie Moore. Though Shuttlesworth waved his ticket in Moore's face, Moore firmly guided Shuttlesworth away from the bus. "There was something about him that was more fatherly than officerly [sic]," Shuttlesworth later said, concluding, in light of the fate of the Riders, that had Moore not kept him off the bus, he could have been killed in Montgomery.[76]

As the bus pulled away with the lights and sirens of a police escort, Lankford jumped into his 1959 Chevrolet Impala and fell in behind, following the bus south down U.S. Highway 31, the main highway to Alabama's capital city. Lankford knew Connor would be enraged at the Riders for foiling his elaborate night efforts, and he feared the commissioner would contact like-minded Montgomery officials and suggest a welcome similar to the one the Riders had received in Birmingham on Mother's Day. Pieces of conversation on his police scanner between the highway patrol units reinforced Lankford's foreboding.

Indeed, an angry mob of white supremacist men and women were waiting for the bus in Montgomery. Lankford found himself in the middle of that bloody attack as well, and wrote, "Mob rule swept horror through the city Saturday, and I was an eyewitness to men mad with hate." The mob also attacked reporters and cameramen. Lankford whipped off his tie to blend in better with the crowd. He witnessed the ironic juxtaposition of a policeman turning his back on the horrific beatings to direct traffic. In contrast, he also saw his friend Floyd Mann—head of the Alabama Department of Public Safety and the Alabama Highway Patrol—wading into the attack, saving the life of "a television newsman and a Negro" and single-handedly stopping the madness by threatening to shoot one of the assailants.[77]

The Riders, at length, made it to Mississippi, where Governor Ross Barnett thought he was teaching a lesson to the Freedom Riders and anyone who tried to follow in their footsteps by putting them in prison. But his harshness backfired. Hundreds of people—Black and White—rode public transport to Jackson, Mississippi, in support of the arrested Riders, resulting in new federal rules ending discrimination.

Delores Boyd, a Black Montgomery resident, reflected on the effects:

> The Freedom Riders introduced the notion that there were fair-minded white persons who were willing to sacrifice themselves, their bodies and their lives, because they too believed that the country had an obligation to uphold its constitutional mandate of liberty and justice for all. And I think it opened our eyes, so we didn't paint white people with the same broad brush.[78]

7

The Damned Spot and the Quilt

The blood of Mother's Day 1961 stained Birmingham with a "damned spot" it could not wash out. On Election Day, Connor appeared in federal court, charged with ordering his officers to delay responding to the beating of the Freedom Riders. The case was being heard in Montgomery by U.S. Middle District of Alabama Judge Frank M. Johnson Jr. because the Justice Department had sued the Montgomery and Birmingham police departments and the Klan in connection with the assaults on Freedom Riders in Anniston, Birmingham, and Montgomery.

In the Montgomery trial, a Birmingham police dispatch tape recording indicated that officers took five minutes to respond to the Trailways terminal after the first report came in of trouble there.[79] While this evidence appears exculpatory for the police, it really only meant that from the time the incident was reported to the dispatcher to the arrival of an officer on the scene was five minutes, however, at least one plainclothes officer was known to have already been at the station prior to the arrival of the bus carrying the Riders. So the question remains whether there was an intentional delay in calling in the incident to police dispatch. Although FBI Klan informant Gary Thomas Rowe later revealed that Connor and the Klan had a deal to delay police intervention at the bus station, that was not known in the Montgomery trial, and Judge Johnson thus did not find that Connor had withheld police protection.

The Freedom Riders' tragedy cost Tom King in his bid to become Birmingham's mayor. Although he led the race in the primary, he lost by a large majority to Art Hanes who saw "no distinction between communists, blacks, liberals, gradualists, integrationists, and Jews."[80]

The Klansmen who smashed the reporter's camera that Sunday morning when the Klan "welcomed" the first group of Freedom Riders had not thought to remove the film. Tommy Langston at the *Post-Herald* had snapped the shot. Injured, he had made his way back to the *Post-Herald*, collapsed into the arms of a colleague and been taken to the hospital. After hearing his story, another *Post-Herald* reporter returned to the scene and recovered the broken camera in a trash can in the alley. To everyone's surprise, the smashed camera held film that produced the assault's only surviving photo. It ran on the front pages of both the *Birmingham News* and *Post-Herald*.

The AP picked up the photo and it made newspaper front pages across the country. It traveled across the ocean to Japan where it was seen by Sidney "Sid" Smyer of Birmingham's powerful Birmingham Realty Co. Smyer, the new chairman of the local Chamber of Commerce, was attending a Rotary International meeting at the time, and the reactions of his fellow Rotarians, including the foreign members, embarrassed him. He was a conservative, segregationist businessman—a Dixiecrat who had parted ways over an integration platform with the traditional Democratic Party in 1948 and had fought integration efforts of the Methodist Church. According to Wayne Greenhaw in *Fighting the Devil in Dixie*, Smyer was at one time even a "guru" of the National States' Rights Party. But he differed from Connor and his ilk in one major way: He recognized that change was inevitable, and that Birmingham's refusal to change was crippling the city, as well as limiting his own real estate business.

On his return to Birmingham, Smyer told the *Wall Street Journal*, "'These racial incidents have given us a black eye we'll be a long time trying to forget.' . . . Unlike the Big Mules who remained mired in the colonial economy, Smyer understood that diversified economic growth was the key to the postwar boom."[81]

The theory of bad publicity affecting economics had confirmed itself after demonstrations in Little Rock, Arkansas, and now it was happening in Birmingham. As historian Sol Kimerling noted, "racial unrest, the faltering of the steel industry, the increasing transition of the national economy from manufacturing to service industries, and the international media spotlight were all taking their toll on the economic health of Birmingham."[82]

Most historical accounts claim that the Freedom Rider assault spurred Smyer to change his mind, but his mind had already been churning in that direction, and he may have just astutely realized in the assault aftermath an opportunity to sway public opinion. A year or two earlier, Smyer's company had hired an economist to study why sales were declining in a rock quarry owned by Smyer's real estate business and what could be done about it.

Sheldon Schaffer was that economist, a "Yankee/Jew/liberal" who had settled in Birmingham in 1959 and observed the changes in the city's economy brought about by the decline in demand for steel. Schaffer's analysis of the quarry situation "dealt with the absolutely terrible social, economic, political, and legal circumstances surrounding African American life" in Birmingham. Smyer read the report and asked Sheldon to discuss with him the findings, which they did for several hours. Schaffer recalled that Smyer "asked many sober, penetrating questions. . . . His search for profits somehow helped to open his eyes to grim reality."[83]

Also, in February before the May attack on the Freedom Riders, Smyer had called Douglas Arant of the Birmingham Bar Association to discuss researching a change to Birmingham's form of government. In response, the Birmingham Bar created a fifteen-member study committee led by Abe Berkowitz, a progressive Jewish attorney who often spoke up publicly, even confronting Bull Connor. Karl Friedman, an attorney and influential congregant of Temple Beth-El, called Berkowitz a "courageous community citizen" who "attacked evil wherever he saw it." Jeff Drew, the son of Black activists John and Deenie Drew, remembered that Berkowitz and his wife Estelle were often guests in their home and donated funds for jail bonds during the movement. When "Uncle Abe" was in the house, young Drew knew that "help was coming."

Berkowitz had never flinched from acting on his convictions. In the 1940s, he convinced the Alabama legislature to pass a resolution supporting the creation of a Jewish state and led Zionist efforts in Birmingham at a time when it was a disputed concept in the Jewish community. Many feared that supporting Israel would call into question their loyalty to America. But Berkowitz did not just articulate his support for the Jewish state, he worked to raise funds and even to smuggle weapons to Israel to prepare for the war that many expected would occur and in fact did. As soon as the fledgling Israel declared independence, it was attacked.

A leader in civil rights issues, Berkowitz represented Black clients and took on the city and the state. One early issue occurred in 1948 when robed Klansmen, infuriated that two White counselors were conducting training at a Black Girl Scout chapter just outside Birmingham, barged into the women's tent in the middle of the night, terrifying them. The name of one of the night-raiding Klansmen would "emerge again and again over the years of racial turmoil—Robert 'Dynamite Bob' Chambliss."[84]

In protest of the Girl Scout camp debacle, Berkowitz wrote a scathing letter to the *Birmingham News* demanding "Alabama Attorney General Albert A. Carmichael take steps to revoke the Klan's state charter. He also offered his legal services free of charge to 'the young ladies who were so threatened, maltreated and abused.' And he added he was 'further confident that any member of the Bar will, on request, gladly render to any citizen of this community, Negro or white, Jew, Protestant or Catholic, his services as an attorney and his aid as a private citizen in connection with any threat or intimidation by the Klan.'"[85] It was a grand and generous gesture, although there is no evidence the Bar honored it or was asked to do so.

Berkowitz had Sid Smyer's respect, although they had previously disagreed on desegregation. Smyer saw the situation through economic eyes, while Berkowitz saw it as a moral issue. Smyer, however, was now persuaded that the issue had to be addressed. In addition to Schaffer's analysis of economics, Smyer's "enlightenment" was also a product of many discussions with fellow businessman and former Chamber of Commerce president, Jim Head, a founding member of the Alabama Chapter of the National Conference of Christians and Jews (NCCJ), an organization that fought bias against Jews and Catholics.

Brigadier General Edward Friend Jr. was also a member of the NCCJ, a president of Temple Emanu-El, the Birmingham Jewish Federation, the Rotary Club, and founding partner of Sirote & Permutt law firm. Friend founded Birmingham's Legal Aid Society in 1954 to provide legal services to Whites or Blacks unable to afford legal fees and expenses.

Sirote & Permutt was also home for Karl Friedman of Temple Beth-El. He began practicing law with the three-man firm in offices on First Avenue North and became the managing partner. As a youth, he had never envisioned himself as a lawyer. His father was an engraver and an artisan and his mother a "hell raiser" who once ran away with a band of Gypsies passing through Berlin. His paternal grandfather, a Reform rabbi, brought his children to Birmingham in 1918. Friedman's first exposure to discrimination occurred at his own birthday party. His mother included Black children in the invitation. Many of the neighborhood mothers refused to allow their children to attend. "Didn't bother my mother," Friedman recalled. She often asked the Black minister from a nearby church for Sunday lunch, inviting curious stares from the neighborhood, especially as the minister shockingly came and went through the front door. "My mother raised us not to go out into the world, but to have the world come into the house. And we, as little children, learned about crippled people, black people, Catholic people, homosexual people—all walks of life." When WWII erupted, Friedman served his country as a fighter pilot. Assigned as a trial judge advocate, he got a taste of law that whetted his appetite for the field.[86] Back home after the war, he attended and graduated from the University of Alabama's law school.

From his early days in law practice, one of Friedman's treasured friendships was with a young Black civil rights attorney, J. Mason Davis. The state of Alabama in the Jim Crow period denied Blacks professional degrees from the state's segregated universities. Instead it gave Black applicants financial support to attend non-segregated universities out of state. This gave lip service to the "separate but equal" doctrine and kept Blacks from attending Alabama schools. In Davis's case, he had been allocated a stipend to attend law school in New York. In 1959, Alabama was slow in sending tuition payment, and Davis was required to borrow money against the state's pledge. When he asked for his tuition money, the state pled proration and lack of funds. Davis said, fine, he'd "pass the hat" for funds and be right down to register at the University of Alabama School of Law. His funds miraculously appeared soon after.

When he graduated in 1960 from the University at Buffalo School of Law, Davis returned to Birmingham. Although he opened his own practice, over the years he would work on civil rights cases with other Black attorneys, including Orzell Billingsley and Peter Hall, who had been among those handling legal issues arising from the Montgomery Bus Boycott. But on his first day walking into the courtroom in Birmingham, he recognized two White men, Jack E. Held and Karl Friedman. Davis was a Talladega College alumnus and Held was from Talladega. And Davis's uncle was a good friend of Friedman. Mason sat with them, and they explained court procedures to him.

A popular spot for downtown lawyers was the Chinese restaurant, Joy Young, but it served "Whites Only," so Friedman, Held, and Davis often ate lunch together from the vending machine in the courthouse basement, establishing a lasting friendship. All three eventually became partners at Sirote & Permutt.

Another deep friendship for Friedman also grew from his early days at the law firm. His job overseeing the actual operations included handling personnel matters, negotiating leases, and purchasing office supplies. In pursuit of such supplies, Friedman often walked down the street to Jim Head's business supply store on First Avenue North. Head was a Baptist, but they became lifelong friends. Friedman described him as a man "whose bright eyes and ready smile reflected the vitality of his spirit." Friedman and Head often ate lunch together at a downtown restaurant a few blocks away. "Everyone who knew Jim respected him," Friedman recalled. "He was honest and decent and forthcoming and interested. He was way ahead of his time."[87]

Although he never finished high school, Head was a powerful influence on the business community and unflagging in expressing his sentiments supporting racial equality. Both Friedman and Kimerling credit Head for, in Friedman's words, causing Smyer to "change horses" on segregation. After the Freedom Rider assault, Head set up a meeting between Smyer and Black businessman A. G. Gaston. That became the genesis of periodic but secret meetings of biracial business and civic leaders chosen by Smyer.[88] For Smyer, progress in race relations needed to be brokered between local parties and not troublemaking "outsiders."[89]

By August 1961, Smyer told Alabama Human Relations Council president Norman C. "Jim" Jimerson that he was willing to "take the bull by the horns" in reducing racial violence and intimidation. Smyer's motivation was two-fold. He recognized the obvious, that the three city commissioners were inflexible in their stand against any change. They were not only holding Birmingham back, they were responsible for the city's violent image. Stagnation threatened the Magic City, which was falling behind Atlanta, Memphis, and New Orleans. Like Vincent Townsend and others, Smyer grated at this. The city had just voted Bull Connor into office by the largest electoral majority in his career. He would remain in office for four more years. The only way to remove him and the other commissioners was to change the form of city government itself, as allowed by a 1955 state law—a bold idea and a daunting task.

Rather than put forward the removal of Connor and the other commissioners as the primary motivation for changing the government, Smyer focused the public purpose of the effort on another goal—transforming the three-commissioner at-large form of government to a more representative mayor-council form, with council members elected by districts. This would give the suburbs a reason to consider coming into the city's fold by offering them more voice in Birmingham's government. Bringing the successful suburbs into the corporate limits of the city was still—as when tried in 1959—"a worthy and important goal in and of itself."[90] The reformers predicted that failing to accomplish this goal—leaving Birmingham isolated from the southern suburbs—would only exacerbate White flight from the city, leaving Birmingham as a majority-Black city.

The previous 1959 effort to consolidate the over-the-mountain suburbs into Birmingham had failed. Nestled in the wooded hills south of Birmingham just over Red Mountain, the cities of Homewood and Mountain Brook were havens for White flight from Birmingham. Mountain Brook, in particular, as Sheila Blair described it, was "civility personified—at least among the whites, and except for maids and yardmen, that's all there were." That earlier campaign, though it included movers-and-shakers, had "problems with petition stealing, falsified signatures and wobbly political support," but in the end had broken down over the issue of race with the erroneous notion that if the over-the-mountain municipalities remained separate from Birmingham, then any court rulings dealing with integration of schools would not affect them.[91]

Perhaps with that lesson in mind, it is clear from the media reports of the day that representatives of Citizens for Progress—the group championing the change in government—were careful not to engage in debates about deposing Connor or attempts to bring other municipalities into the city's fold. They kept the campaign's public focus on the position that the referendum vote was only about instituting a "better" form of government. Sid Smyer and David Vann led the new crusade to change the city's form of government, their efforts endorsed by people long interested in racial justice and new economic avenues. Several were Jewish civic leaders who were members of the progressive YMBC—William P. Engel, Abe Berkowitz, Ferdinand "Ferd" Weil, Emil Hess, and Edward M. Friend Jr. Other YMBC members, including Fred Sington, Jim Head, and Erskine Smith supported the campaign. Vincent Townsend and his mentee, Tom Lankford, would also play important, unforeseen roles.

IN ADDITION TO ATTORNEYS and business leaders, other White supporters of civil rights worked in their own ways, creating a patchwork quilt throughout the city. Religious and civic institutions, organizations, and individuals contributed threads of progressive thought that stitched through the community.

Joseph Ellwanger was a twenty-eight-year-old White Lutheran minister in Birmingham. He shepherded the Black congregation of St. Paul's. A few other White ministers across Alabama did the same—Robert Graetz and Julian L. McPhillips Sr. (Lutheran and Episcopalian, respectively) in Montgomery and Father Maurice Ouellet in Selma, but they were anomalies in the strictly segregated churches in the South. Rarer still was the offer extended by a White Lutheran church in Tuscaloosa.

James Fackler, the minister of University Lutheran Church, issued an open invitation for Black high school youths at Birmingham's St. Paul's to join the White youths of his church for a fellowship night to share stories and experiences. Two Black fifteen-year-old girls from St. Paul's, Carolyn Freeman and Betty Wells, volunteered to accompany church members to the Tuscaloosa church. According to Ellwanger, "black and white youth [were for the first time] talking, singing, praying, and eating together, as though the cultural wall of segregation did not exist."

Three days later, Ellwanger read in the Birmingham papers the story of the Klan's capture and beating of Fackler and "his harrowing experience of being [kidnapped and] forced to walk back to Tuscaloosa on the railroad tracks in the wee hours of the morning."

While Ellwanger was still trying to absorb this, his phone rang with a warning, "Well, you and the two girls are next." When Ellwanger told the girls and their parents about the threat, he asked Carolyn, one of the two who had gone to Tuscaloosa, whether she was afraid. Her answer mystified him and inspired him for the rest of his life.

"No," she said, "I am not so much afraid as I am ashamed."

"What do you mean?" he asked.

"I'm ashamed that others have suffered so much for the freedom of our people, of all people, and I have suffered so little."[92]

Fortunately, the Klan never followed up on its threat.

The Jewish community's involvement in civil rights stretched back across the city's history, perhaps beginning with Samuel Ullman, president and lay rabbi for Temple Emanu-El, who served on Birmingham's first Board of Education in

1884 and advocated for equal educational benefits for Black children, building the first brick and mortar school for Blacks at the site that later became the Jimmy Hale Mission on First Avenue North. His wife, Emma Mayer Ullman, joined with like-minded reformers in the Catholic and Protestant community and founded the Hospital of United Charity, later named Hillman Hospital (ultimately incorporated into the University of Alabama at Birmingham).[93] Although segregated, the Hospital of United Charity served Black and White indigents. The women managed the hospital, keeping it going over the years through difficulties from financial to fire, determined to make health care available to the public, regardless of racial, social, or economic standing.[94]

In the spirit of the Ullmans, Dorah Sterne, wife of philanthropist and financier Mervyn Sterne, led educational, cultural, and poverty initiatives that included the establishment of a summer camp for Black Girl Scouts. "Encouraged by Rabbi [Morris] Newfield to unite forces with the Protestants to better the community, she and other Jewish women became active in the League of Women Voters and the American Association of University Women (AAUW)." A newspaper article reported on the brutal beatings of female prisoners, most of whom were Black, awakening the AAUW to the issue. The women educated themselves about the prison system, talking with experts and visiting prisons, witnessing firsthand the horrifying conditions the prisoners endured. They recommended the state parole board adopt fair and equitable policies for prisoner treatment, and they "established a citizen board to watch over prison guideline enforcement and hiring practices. In March 1939, Sterne successfully linked local and state politicians and officials of the Alabama Department of Corrections for the first time at Temple Emanu-El at a meeting endorsed by the AAUW."[95]

Betty Loeb made the "rogue's gallery" list in Klansman Asa Carter's racist publication, *The Southerner*. She led the local chapter of the National Council of Jewish Women, focusing its efforts on improving laws and voting rights, "social welfare, relief and health work, promotion of peace and world understanding." By 1956 Betty and her husband, Robert Loeb, a member of YMBC, also worked to establish a Birmingham chapter of the American Jewish Committee (AJC), a longtime proponent for Jewish religious issues and for civil rights.

Betty Loeb recalled receiving terrible threats in the middle of the night. The callers threatened to burn the Loebs' house. Robert lightheartedly reminded Betty that family and friends often joked they could not find their home because the Loebs lived "down a dirt road behind someplace." If their friends could not find the house, how could the Klan? Furthermore, Robert, through sources, discovered the identity of the late-night callers. Betty remembered that Robert turned the table on their stalkers one evening, calling them in the middle of the night.[96]

One of the most strident segregationist voices was that of Klansman Asa "Ace" Carter. In 1955, on his radio broadcast on station WILD, he railed against the National Conference of Christians and Jews (NCCJ), linking the group with communism and accusing them of mixing the races. The Loebs and others "blackballed the radio station and sponsors, and the station subsequently fired Carter."

Recognizing the critical importance of education, the Loebs, with other AJC volunteers, visited "any school that would have us." Welcomed at Black and White schools, the women mentored teachers and students and provided books, supplies, and free eye exams. "Any child, black or white, who exhibited a problem would be treated by a local Jewish ophthalmologist, Dr. Ed Miles,[97] free of charge." [98]

Robert Loeb took on Bull Connor when police invaded the home of Fred Shuttlesworth in October 1958 to arrest three visiting Black Montgomery ministers. The ministers had come to advise on and support efforts to desegregate Birmingham buses during Birmingham's bus boycott, a little-known effort that the media, led by the *Birmingham News,* suppressed. The arrests of the ministers were clearly unconstitutional, but Connor cared little for rulings of the Supreme Court, declaring he would arrest any "outside agitators coming to our city and dabbling in our affairs."[99] Loeb was so incensed he took the matter to the Birmingham Bar Association. The Bar, however, did not intervene or speak out, frustrating Loeb's attempts to see justice done.

When the White Methodist church snatched away the director of the Alabama Council on Human Relations after the Salisbury turmoil, sending Robert Hughes to Africa as a missionary, the Council found another man willing to take on the arguably more dangerous work of leading the struggling biracial organization in Alabama. During the oppressive heat of August 1961, the Reverend Jim Jimerson hauled his reluctant family from Virginia to take the position. At that time, the statewide membership was about 450.

Jimerson met other progressive souls in Birmingham, including attorneys Chuck Morgan and David Vann. The latter Jimerson described as "friendly, warm . . . a young white lawyer, probably late twenties. He works for a large, very conservative law firm.[100] He's 'liberal' on race but hides it as much as he can from his colleagues. Kind of a closet liberal."[101] Jack Drake described Vann as being "like an eccentric professor who always had an idea but mostly wanted somebody else to do the work on that idea. He had a hard time practicing law because he was always having ideas about government stuff and not so much with what was on his desk."[102]

Vann introduced Jimerson to a real estate agent who showed his family a house they liked, and Jimerson put down a deposit. At first, the agent said their loan didn't go through, but later he admitted he wasn't about to sell a house to a communist.

Jimerson also found it difficult to find a church home in Birmingham, although he was heartened by the Reverend Al Henry who preached integration at the Pilgrim Congregational Church in Mountain Brook and the Reverend James Pape of the Lutheran Church of Vestavia Hills, who said that if his church asked Jimerson to leave, *he* would leave. And Jimerson learned that Birmingham was also home to a small group of progressive Whites, Blacks, Catholics, Protestants, Unitarians, and Jews who had formed a local branch of his Alabama Council on Human Relations—the Greater Birmingham Council on Human Relations (BCHR). Both organizations shared the mission to promote peaceful race relations, not an easy task and one that would become more difficult as conflicts over race intensified.

The BCHR provided a forum for communication across racial lines, inviting Blacks to share their personal experiences with Jim Crow laws, prejudice, and police and Klan brutality. The small organization spent most of its funds financing legal challenges to segregation, but the members also surveyed the hospitals' racial policies and canvassed neighborhoods, speaking to citizens about school desegregation.

Jim Crow laws allowed Blacks and Whites to meet together as long as they sat separately. According to Peggy Horne Rupp, an Episcopalian and early member of the BCHR, the group ignored that law and practiced mixed seating. For the most part, law enforcement turned a blind eye, although there were many nights when she saw police in the parking lot taking down license plate numbers so the owners could be identified.[103] John Fuller recalled the meetings "were raided a couple of times, and [once] we had to climb out of a window."[104] Vann believed police or FBI informants were present or watching the meetings because often stories appeared in the Klan newspaper naming a particular person who was at a meeting.[105] Members received late-night phone calls. After a week of harassing night calls, Rupp asked another tenant on her party line if she would mind if Rupp took the phone off the hook to get some sleep. Her neighbor agreed.[106]

Jewish members of the BCHR included Abraham and Florence Siegel, "who attended demonstrations and supported the integration of the Medical Center (University of Alabama School of Medicine), where Abraham worked as a biochemist." Florence Siegel said her husband's tenured position allowed her to speak out without fear of affecting his employment.[107] Other Jewish members included Betty and Robert Loeb, Dorah and Mervyn Sterne, Fred and Gertrude Goldstein, and Frederick and Anny Kraus (who were members of the Unitarian Church).

The Krauses had narrowly escaped Nazi Germany and came to the United States expecting to find freedom and equality. Not long in Birmingham, Anny Kraus's first encounter with segregated society came when she took a seat on a city bus. The driver required the Black woman next to her to move. Pregnant and tired, Kraus protested and was forced to get off the bus. The experience seared with the wrongs of Jim Crow laws, and she did what she could to fight. The Krauses helped found the Birmingham Council on Human Relations. Anny took a leadership role in fostering relationships and providing social support to the women in the small community who shared their convictions. She and her husband hosted groups of like-minded academicians and physicians in the Kraus home. Awareness that they were being watched was a constant stress. At one point they discovered that someone had rifled through Kraus's filing cabinet in his home office.[108]

Jimerson reported that Bull Connor sent "police spies" to meetings of the BCHR, and the issues discussed quickly circulated throughout the city. "The Klan and other segregationist groups obtained names, addresses, and phone numbers of council members. Even financial details about [Jimerson's] . . . business in Pennsylvania showed up in reports attacking the Council and alleging its connections to communist organizations and individuals." At one point the Legislative Reference Service of the Library of Congress sent Jimerson a letter requesting information on the organization—its history, materials, and a list of the board of directors. Jimerson, suspicious, declined to respond.[109]

Lankford noted that any harassment and monitoring of the Council on Human Relations was, to his knowledge, strictly under Connor's orders. Neither Marcus Jones nor the operations of Lieutenant Maurice House, head of Birmingham's homicide squad and the criminal intelligence operation, were involved.[110]

MANY BCHR MEMBERS FOUND a haven with other liberal thinkers in the Unitarian Church founded in 1952 by Dr. Joseph F. Volker. Volker would later lead the University of Alabama School of Medicine and the institute that it would become, the University of Alabama at Birmingham (UAB), and would guide the integration of its facilities, faculty, and personnel. Although cautious, he was a progressive administrator "attacked and harassed . . . for his racial liberalism."[111] Some in the community linked his progressiveness to communism and called him "Pink Joe."[112] Volker's supporters included Roger Hanson (BCHR), Dr. Abraham "Abe" Russakoff, and Birmingham-Southern College President Dr. Henry Stanford.

Under the leadership of the Reverend Alfred Walters Hobart, Birmingham's Unitarian Church promoted racial understanding, opened to Black membership, invited Black ministers to exchange pulpits, and hosted biracial forums. Phyllis Benington and Alice Brown were among Unitarians who participated in interracial meetings and activities. For Jackie and Vincent Mazzara, "[the Unitarian Church] was more than an oasis in a situation that would otherwise have been completely a desert."[113]

Hobart, who established an integrated ministerial group, also served as president of the Birmingham Council on Human Relations. He spoke out in support of *Brown* and wrote letters to the editor and articles for the church "in defense of equal and just treatment of Negroes, not only in education but also in voting, criminal justice, and in opposition to all forms of social discrimination."[114]

In addition to his ministerial duties, Hobart served as an officer of the board of the Mental Health Association (now the Crisis Center). One of his parishioners, Ethel M. Gorman, was the program director for the organization. She "took on Commissioner Bull Connor, appointed Negroes as leaders to important committees, and sponsored discussions on topics such as racism and its effect on society." Gorman later led the integrated Head Start program, seeing its successful implementation in Birmingham.[115]

Like other prominent White figures supporting integration and equality for Blacks, Hobart and members of his congregation endured public scorn, threatening phone calls, and stalking by the Klan. According to church member Jackie Mazzara, the Hobarts moved their bedroom from the front of the house to the back because of threats.

One day, the pastor's wife, Mary Aymer Hobart, tired of having a car sitting out on their street watching her house, confronted the vehicle's occupant, asking, 'May I help you? Are you looking for someone?' . . . very innocent but very helpful and ladylike in this thick Southern accent." He politely thanked her and left.[116]

The minister and members were threatened and attacked in race-hate smear sheets. Among the Unitarian membership, "three lawyers, two teachers and a newspaper man lost their professional connections, and another newspaper man was warned to stay in line or else. A high officer in one of the banks [Zukoski] was forced to retire early. A number of others lived in fear of reprisal."[117]

Men of the church rotated the job of sweeping the premises for bombs. Threats were so numerous that "church secretary Eve Gerard told one caller with a bomb threat, 'You'll have to take a number and wait in line. There are already a few people ahead of you.'"[118]

8

The Webs We Weave . . .

It was generally assumed that Bull Connor had been an "under-the-sheet" member of the Klan in the early days of his political career, although he told President Roosevelt in a letter dated August 7, 1942, that he "never joined." According to Lankford, Sergeant Cook infiltrated the Klan to provide information to Connor and carry out his directions and also was not a "card-carrying" member.

Despite assertions by some and popular assumptions that a large percentage of the Birmingham police officers were Klansmen, Lankford believed otherwise: "I feel I can say with certainty, even though . . . other writers paint a different picture, there were less than a half dozen Klansmen in the uniformed and detective divisions of the Birmingham Police Department. There may have been sympathy for segregation, but that's a long way from being in the Klan."[119]

That said, numerous anecdotal incidents of abuse and misuse of power by police during this time were reported to the Council on Human Relations by the Reverend Herbert Oliver, who took affidavits from the people involved. David Vann, as a member of the BCHR, would reproduce them. Copies were sent to "about fifty top businesspeople in Birmingham. . . . The thinking was [that] people who lived . . . over-the-mountain would come to work and go [straight] home, and they really didn't know much about segregation. They didn't know what was going on in this city, and we wanted to make sure they knew what was going on."[120]

The police culture of correcting "on the street" misbehavior, perceived misbehavior, or even attitudes was slow to change. Houston Brown recalled an incident when as a ten-year-old Black youth when he strayed too far afield on his bicycle. Police stopped him and beat him, being careful not to leave marks on his head and face. "Every Black parent had a conversation with their children about the police."[121]

Bull Connor's leadership set a tone that allowed this kind of behavior; he used the officers he commanded, as well as the Klan (and vice versa) to forward goals of maintaining segregation and "keeping Negroes in their place." While Connor was out of office from 1953 to 1957, his replacement was a progressive reformer. Commissioner Robert H. Lindbergh made it known he would "not tolerate an officer insulting any Negro citizen by calling him 'nigger' or 'boy' and had promised a reprimand and disciplinary action if such offenses continued." Ironically, in 1954, the same year as the *Brown v. Board of Education* decision, Lindbergh and the other two city commissioners repealed a city ordinance forbidding Blacks and Whites from participating in the same sporting event. Later that year, when White policemen beat a Black prisoner in the city jail, Lindbergh and his chief of police, G. L. Pattie, promptly investigated and fired the responsible officers. (The other two commissioners, Jimmy Morgan and Wade Bradley, reinstated the officers, giving them only thirty-day suspensions.)

Many in the community reacted in outrage and wrote letters to the papers, which not only published them, but added their own editorials questioning the light punishment and warning of the example it set. The YMBC "denounced the police brutality and lack of safety for prisoners in jail while commending Lindbergh and Pattie." Union attorney Jerome "Buddy" Cooper praised the reformers' "dignity, honesty, and fairness." On the radio program "The People Speak," Mrs. J. E. Hall reported "four to one telephone calls against reinstatement [of the officers.]" She said, "I felt myself growing prouder every minute at the justice and lack of prejudice of those Southern people on that broadcast."[122] Fred Shuttlesworth called Lindbergh a "man of high morals," praise that helped doom Lindbergh's campaign for reelection.[123]

Before losing his commissioner spot back to Connor, Lindbergh hired Jamie Moore as the Birmingham police chief. When he regained office, Connor did not see eye-to-eye with Moore. According to Lankford, "Bull was like General Patton—out front leading the charge, highly visible, vocal, etc. Chief Moore was his 'own man,' an administrator adhering to a chain of command principle. Moore was not a racist and got along fine with Shuttlesworth."[124]

Connor tried to fire Moore by drumming up forty-seven charges of alleged misconduct, including engaging in political activity and wasting city property. To Connor's dismay, the Personnel Merit Board dropped all of the charges. "Merit is what I say it is," Connor snapped in disapproval, an ironic turnabout considering he had been a force as a state representative behind the creation of the merit system and the Personnel Board.[125]

When his efforts to fire Moore proved unsuccessful, Connor picked his "favorites" in the police department, primarily Sergeant Tom Cook, and relied on his own intelligence network to stay in touch with the Klan and to provide information on the activities of the Birmingham and Alabama Council on Human Relations and other "communist-leaning organizations."

Connor and Shuttlesworth were at frequent odds. The commissioner's men kept tabs on Shuttlesworth's organization, the Alabama Christian Movement for Human Rights (ACMHR). Connor sent officers to tape record weekly "mass meetings" in the Black churches. Congregants spotted the White policemen, of course, and the officers made no pretense at being undercover. In fact, part of their presence may have been intended to intimidate, a tactic that did not work.

In contrast, Moore recognized that the city needed long-term solutions. It was critical to maintain the peace long enough to allow the community to move toward those goals at its own pace. That, in turn, required staying on top of situations. He didn't want another incident like the beating of the Freedom Riders. But the city was a tinderbox waiting to be ignited. By November 1961, "reports began to circulate that the Klan was becoming more active in the community than at any time since the Freedom Riders attacks in May."[126] Moore needed to know what was being planned by the white supremacists, the civil rights activists, and by city hall.

To get that information, Moore deployed a talented detective, fellow Zamora Shriner Marcus Jones. An unlikely looking detective, Jones was white-haired, short, and portly. He seemed more a professor or preacher, especially when he peered over his glasses. When his adrenaline flowed, his voice rose into a high-pitched squeak, earning him the nickname in the police department of "Two-toned Jones."

Life had given him enough knocks that Jones trusted very few people. Moore was on that short list, and, after many hours on surveillance assignments watching his back, Lankford earned a place there as well. For a brief time, while he was having marriage difficulties, Lankford lived in a room in his friend's basement. A nearby door led to an electronics equipment lab where Marcus "hoarded batteries, tapes, and stuff we didn't really need, 'just in case.'" It gave him a sense of security to have spare parts at hand, as did the several drawers of new white dress shirts still in their original plastic wrappings.

Many of the Black citizens Jones got to know over the years came to him for advice on subjects ranging from domestic quarrels or money worries, to a "hex" placed on them by an enemy or rejected lover. On one occasion, a Black minister of a Birmingham Methodist church approached Jones with a domestic problem. A large Detroit church had called the minister, but the elders would not allow him a divorce unless he could prove adultery. The minister asked Jones to help prove his case by putting a bug on his phone. Lankford joined in that side escapade, capturing enough evidence from the minister's straying wife to get him the divorce.

Jones's primary business was to compile daily intelligence reports on racial developments. From a law enforcement perspective, preventing violence required adequate police on the scene of a tense situation. History provided clear examples such as Connor's orders for officers to stay away from the bus station, which allowed the severe beatings of the Freedom Riders.

Similarly, no police were stationed at the bus station when Shuttlesworth challenged Jim Crow laws there, resulting in the assault of Presbyterian minister Lamar Weaver. Weaver grew up in the South. During his youth, he formed a close friendship with a Black youth and witnessed a brutal murder of a Black man by a White mob, events that shaped his anti-segregation views. Weaver and two students from Birmingham's Southeastern Bible College traveled across the state, encouraging Blacks to register to vote. He ran for a seat on the Birmingham City Commission against Bull Connor on a platform that supported hiring Black firemen and police officers and giving them a raise. "Let's have a slow integration," Weaver said. "Let's do it because the Supreme Court is going to eventually say that it has to be done, should be done, so let's . . . show some good faith and do it gradually."[127] He came in third, garnering 3,500 votes. But Connor rode the White backlash from the *Brown* decision to win the election.

On a spring night in 1957, following a landslide election that put Connor back in office, Shuttlesworth called Weaver and told him that tomorrow he was going to test the ordinance forbidding Blacks to sit in the White section at the bus station. Weaver met Shuttlesworth at the station and shook the Black minister's hand. The seemingly trivial act made him a target for the White mob waiting outside. Once again, Klansman "Dynamite Bob" Chambliss was part of the violence. As Weaver tried to leave the station, the Klansmen knocked him down and kicked him. Terrified, he somehow escaped and made it to his car. The mob broke his windshield and tried to overturn his car.

Weaver sped off, fleeing for his life. He headed for the police station where he was arrested for reckless driving, running a red light, and endangering a pedestrian. Connor warned him, "Leave Birmingham as soon as possible. Your life is in danger. They are going to try and kill you."[128]

John and Ernest Poole, owners of the Black Poole Funeral Home, bailed Weaver out of jail and hid him in an empty casket while Klansmen searched for him. A. G. Gaston, the Poole brothers, and others in the Black community raised money for an airline ticket to Washington, D.C., where Weaver was to testify before the Senate Judiciary Sub-Committee on Civil Rights, a committee that was considering a civil rights bill. Weaver was not going to miss that plane, and his friends saw to it he didn't.

Another example of the consequences of inadequate police presence occurred in September 1957, when Shuttlesworth tried to register his children at Phillips High School. Klansmen awaited him with brass knuckles and fists, sending him to the hospital. Shuttlesworth had alerted Connor that he was going to be at the school, but Connor failed to station officers to protect him. According to *Birmingham Post-Herald* reporter Edward Harris, an eyewitness, only a few police were dispatched and they arrived late. No arrests were made, even though film footage of the assault existed.

Unable to trust Connor to share information, Moore relied on the intelligence that Jones and Lieutenant House gathered, though House's team principally focused on criminal intelligence. Lankford assisted Jones almost nightly and considered himself a close friend, but Jones understood that Lankford was also Vincent Townsend's eyes and ears.

Townsend's vision and goals encompassed more than reporting the happenings in his city. He meant to help shape its destiny. At the least, he wanted information in advance on what was planned on the civil rights and political fronts. It required a grueling schedule. Lankford's workday started a half hour before the police detectives' morning roll call, a daily meeting to discuss cases, news, and strategies. After roll call, he wrote up the crime news and then spent some time with county sheriff's deputies before joining Jones in the evening to gather intelligence. He worked at least six days a week, long hours each day. He lived, breathed and ate his job.

At night, he typed notes to Townsend and slipped them under his boss's door. If something was important and after hours, he reported directly to Townsend's home. Writing was not Marcus's forte, so Lankford often helped him write his reports, which were then typed by Inspector Bill Haley's daughter, who worked in the secretarial pool. Moore was cautious, not wanting anything to reflect badly on him or the department, and he did not want the commissioners to know about sensitive information. To disguise any intelligence resulting from surveillance, Jones would simply attribute the information to "a source." Still, much of the real information reported to the police chief by Jones and House was given verbally.

9

The Jewish Connection

Jews and Catholics were on the Klan's hate list, but prior to the *Brown* decision, anti-Semitism, though present, was not a critical issue for Birmingham's Jewish citizens. Karl Friedman attributed this to a relationship with one man—Joe Denaburg, who had moved to Birmingham in 1922 after serving in WWI. He married into the Levy family, which owned Levy's Pawn Shop in downtown Birmingham. Denaburg ran the store. "Everyone called him Cousin Joe." Klan members frequented his shop as customers. Perhaps because of his military service, they developed a respectful relationship with him. Friedman recalled that if a Klansman "found a grief with something a Jewish person was doing, or about to do, they would go see Joe. Joe would get it settled. If a Jewish person complained that they were being bothered by Klansmen, Joe would get it solved."

Regardless of whether Cousin Joe single-handedly kept the relationship between the Klan and Birmingham's Jews on tolerant ground, the Klan focused on keeping African Americans—in particular, WWII veterans who returned with a broader view of the world and a desire to have a piece of it—from crossing the invisible but real lines separating them from White society.

Nevertheless, Southern Jews—though they had worked hard to become part of the weave of the community—were always aware that they straddled those lines. Lest they forget, examples of anti-Semitism arose to keep them on edge. One such was that of Leo Frank, a Southern Jew wrongly convicted for the rape and murder of a young White girl and lynched by an angry mob in Marietta, Georgia, in 1915. Three years later, Henry Ford purchased the *Dearborn Independent* and published ninety-one issues with articles claiming a vast Jewish conspiracy was infecting America. He attributed all evil to Jews and Jewish capitalists. He bound all the articles and distributed half a million copies to his extensive network of dealerships, to be handed out to customers. He also republished *The Protocols of the Elders of Zion*, a notorious forgery that claimed the existence of an international Jewish conspiracy to control the world. Ford printed it as fact in his paper. As one of the most famous men in America, Ford legitimized anti-Semitism.

During the Depression and lead-up to WWII, American Catholic priest Charles Coughlin spewed anti-Semitic rhetoric in a weekly broadcast that reached an estimated thirty million Americans. Coughlin blamed his listeners' economic hardship on Jewish bankers. His words were an echo of Adolf Hitler's rhetoric.

In the 1930s, when unions were unable to gain ground in the mining and steel industry in Birmingham, members of the U.S. Communist Party, several of whom were Jews, came to help break down that wall, part of a stated goal to combat racial discrimination and encourage interracial cooperation, as well as a largely unsuccessful effort to recruit Black members. In fact, Birmingham was selected as the Southern headquarters for the party, which did play an important role in establishing the successful but short-lived unions. Southerners thus linked Jews with America's great enemy—communism. Then in 1931, the Scottsboro Boys trials in Alabama triggered a wave of anti-Semitism when nine teenaged Blacks falsely accused of raping two White women were represented by a Northern Jewish lawyer, Samuel Lebowitz, hired by the Communist Party and the NAACP.

LOOMING OVER ALL WAS the shadow of what happened to the Jews in Hitler's Nazi regime, how one of the world's most cultured and progressive nations where Jews had flourished for centuries turned on them, blamed them for the country's woes, and sought to exterminate them.

Karl Friedman's maternal grandparents, wealthy owners of a brewery, had remained in Germany, certain of their status and safety, but in the mid-1930s their letters stopped coming, and the ones written to them from the United States were returned. "That," Friedman said, "was the end of that family." This stark, poignant observation reflected an acute awareness shared by the entire community. American Jews listened with growing fear, as the same rhetoric and hate built in the United States. After the creation of the state of Israel in 1948, Jews were often suspected of dual loyalties. Catholics were likewise suspect as having primary allegiance to the Pope, rather than the U.S.

Jews were caught in the sweeping backlash of the Supreme Court's *Brown* decision. From that point smoldering anti-Semitism "began to blaze in the form of a crusade against the Jewish community . . . nasty calls, letters, and threats against community leaders." Friedman received such calls, as did "all the Jews involved in any aspect of supporting the civil rights of blacks, including some who weren't even Jewish, but had Jewish [sounding] names."[129]

In addition to personal phone calls, the distribution of anti-Semitic printed matter in the South increased by 400 percent in the five years after *Brown*. Jews faced outbursts of anti-Semitic rhetoric, death threats, and dynamite attacks.[130] As the notion of a communist-Jewish conspiracy theory behind the civil and human rights movement became more and more accepted, "the relative paradise that Jews believed they'd found in the South . . . began to unravel."[131]

Random acts of racial violence on non-Jewish members of the community also fed this fear—the bombings over the years of Black homes were so numerous they gave rise to the city's nickname as "Bombingham"; the 1948 Klan raid on the Girl Scout camp; an attack on Nat "King" Cole on an auditorium stage in 1956; the 1957 random kidnapping and castrating of local Black veteran Judge Edward Aaron; and the kidnapping and beating of Barbara Espy in 1960.

Asa Carter's White Citizens' Council designated Jewish bankers who "control the Negro" as a threat to segregated society and called out the local Jewish merchants as "members of the NAACP."[132] When Judge Hugh A. Locke was asked if Jews were or could be members of Birmingham's WCC, he replied, "No, . . . It's the Americans strictly."[133]

Other WCCs allowed Jewish participation but warned that whoever encouraged school desegregation would be "marked by the people of these communities to be an enemy of the white people and a traitor to the . . . heritage of the white people."[134]

The pressure from both the WCCs and the Klan was immense, and the Jewish Committee recommended that in small towns with few Jews to support each other, the merchants should remain where they were and join the WCC if asked. "That may have been cowardice," Friedman reflected, "but it also avoided a lot of unpleasant clashes."

Despite the danger, pressure, and fears, some members of the Jewish community spoke out publicly against racism and segregation, among them in particular, Abe Berkowitz, William P. Engel, Edward Friend, Emil Hess, Dorah Sterne, Betty Loeb, and other members of the Birmingham Branch of the National Council of Jewish Women. Some contributed financially to the NAACP, which supported legal challenges to Alabama's segregated educational system. A few attorneys, including Friedman, silently assisted the NAACP's battles to protect their membership list after Attorney General John Patterson had the organization banned from the state in 1956. Much of the donated monies for that effort passed through Friedman to Black attorney Arthur Shores.[135] To protect its few White members, the NAACP dropped them from the rolls.[136]

Others took quieter, more personal action. Sol Kimerling's family business, Alabama Oxygen Company, sold industrial oxygen, nitrogen, acetylene, and welding supplies. One day Kimerling sent a Black employee to deliver an order of oxygen tanks to a customer. The supervisor told him not to "send a nigger" again. Kimerling replied he would not be sending anyone and refused to do business with him again.[137]

For the most part, the Jewish community attempted to stay out of the civil rights fray, but what had happened on the night of April 28, 1958, exposed the tactic's fragility. A canvas satchel with fifty-four sticks of dynamite was planted at Temple Beth-El. The following day a janitor found the dynamite, with its fuse apparently doused by overnight rain about one minute from detonation.

The near-miss bombing shook the Jewish community. Threats were made that the reform temple, Emanu-El, was next.[138] It drove some more deeply into the "lay low" philosophy. Others, like Betty Loeb, observed that "additional Jewish motivation for [progressive] change stemmed from the attempted bombing."[139]

Bull Connor subsequently called for the death penalty for persons convicted of bombing any unoccupied house, school, or church.[140] Considering Connor's connections to the Klan, whether that declaration was sincere or disingenuous is a matter of speculation. But the pressure was not on the Klan. Several other bombings of synagogues occurred around the South, and circumstantial evidence pointed to a man Connor considered an "outsider," the National States' Rights Party chairman J. B. Stoner.

Jewish leaders asked the FBI for help in solving the Temple Beth-El case. FBI Director J. Edgar Hoover responded that the FBI would not get involved because it was a local jurisdiction matter. Not only did Hoover not want local organizations to "dump these cases on us," he forbade any meeting of the FBI with non-law enforcement members of the community. At the same time, he acknowledged Stoner's probable involvement, stating in an internal memo that the local FBI should "keep pressing on Stoner's participation in order to get a federal violation against him if we possibly can."[141]

Despite Connor's posturing, the attempted bombing had shattered any Jewish delusion of protection by assimilation, civic involvement, or civic leadership. The threat they thought had been left behind in Europe was real here, too. Haunted in the U.S. by the scapegoating rhetoric that gave rise to Europe's Holocaust, American Jews were aware that nothing guaranteed their safety.

REFLECTING THE SEPARATE IMMIGRATIONS of first German and then Slavic Jews, Jewish life in Birmingham was divided among orthodox, conservative, and reform factions—they worshiped in different synagogues, socialized in different country clubs, and even lived in different areas of the city. But that rainy night when dynamite was set outside Temple Beth-El brought the Birmingham Jewish community together in common cause.

One outcome was the creation of a secret "defense committee," called simply the "Jewish Committee" internally. Its chair was granted a position on the larger organization's board.[142] Karl Friedman, the first chair, called together several interested people who met frequently at his home, drafting a document listing anticipated operations. To collect information, the committee members used contacts with the FBI, the police department, the Justice Department, and a few helpful politicians.

"We were vigilant," Friedman observed. "We monitored and attended all the local activities by hate groups and had constant dialogues with sympathetic groups." Information gathering often required attending meetings where Jews were not welcome. In those instances, non-Jewish friends attended and reported back.[143]

One source of information was Leroy Gaylord, whom Karl had met when young Friedman had a paper route through the older black man's neighborhood. They became friends. Gaylord's father owned a small construction and repair business. After Friedman graduated from law school, Gaylord persuaded his father to hire Friedman as the company attorney. The younger Gaylord grew the construction business, specializing in building churches. He had standing credit with the prestigious First National Bank and the Birmingham Trust National Bank. When Gaylord became active in civil rights and was discovered to be a leader among the vigilantes guarding the homes of the Black community at night, his credit suddenly "blew up." The White banks refused to make new or renew old loans. "All of his creditors abandoned him except two Jewish suppliers, Louis Meer and his wife and Bernard Louis," who gave Gaylord whatever he needed to finish his projects, "not charging him a dime."[144]

Birmingham police, meanwhile, conducted sweeps through the Black neighborhoods where the vigilantes patrolled and arrested the participants on whatever charges they could generate. The Jewish Committee provided bond money as well as equipment for the vigilantes, including "baseball bats and loudspeakers" [bullhorns]—items probably "borrowed" from the stores gathered to help support local police athletic teams. Serious risk attached to this "aiding and abetting," and the assistance was kept quiet.[145]

The Jewish Committee met with Black leaders. "Pressure was on us to step forward and represent [publicly speak up for] the black community," Friedman recalled. Jews had a long history in Birmingham of being quiet allies. Even as far back as the 1920s and 1930s, "We helped file a lawsuit that we were behind. We raised money to do things."[146] The committee evaluated the pros and cons and decided they would be more effective staying offstage, helping with financial and legal assistance. With a couple of exceptions, Jewish lawyers, particularly in the Sirote & Permutt and the Berkowitz & Lefkovits firms, actively supported the committee's activities.

"That's why you see historically so few Jewish people up front," Friedman said. Not only was open support of the Reverend Shuttlesworth's efforts risky, but the Jewish community would not have been doing the civil rights movement any favors to declare an open partnership. Local Whites already considered Shuttlesworth's direct action campaign to be a "Jewish-communist plot."

Another avenue of information to the Jewish Committee came circuitously from a law enforcement source. Police Chief Jamie Moore was aware that Marcus Jones shared his findings with the FBI, but Lankford doubted that the chief knew about Jones's relationship with someone entirely outside of law enforcement—Rabbi Milton Grafman of Temple Emanu-El, or the rabbi's confidant, the synagogue's education director, Margaret Lasakow, to whom Jones was covertly delivering a copy of the daily intelligence reports only hours after they had been transcribed "For [Chief's] Eyes Only."

It was Lankford's understanding that Lasakow was not Jewish but had married a Jewish man who later died in a car accident. She became a member of the "Jewish family, a brilliant woman," Lankford recalled. He did not know how Jones had developed a relationship with Grafman or Lasakow, but he knew it was a strong bond. According to Lankford, Jones, though not Jewish himself, "thought more of the rabbi than any other friend."

The informational flow from the police, according to Lankford, originated with Lasakow. She learned from Jones that his bright but troublesome son, Henry "Slug" Clay Jones, was having difficulty in public school. Lankford arranged for Slug's parents to have a personal interview with Frank Rose, president of the University of Alabama. Lankford accompanied them. Dr. Rose recommended that Slug attend a private military academy, but Jones could not afford to send him. Lasakow conveyed this to Grafman, who told Jones "the Jewish community would gladly provide a scholarship to Marion for his son. They wanted nothing in return." But it "would be greatly appreciated if Marcus would let him and friends with the Anti-Defamation League (ADL) take a look at his hand-written notes to Police Chief Jamie Moore each day, especially the ones concerning the hate groups such as the Nazi-inspired, anti-Semitic National State Rights Party."

Slug went on to graduate from Marion Military Institute. Meanwhile, Rabbi Grafman received daily intelligence updates, and when Vincent Townsend told Grafman the city or county Intelligence Units needed funds to purchase surveillance equipment, the rabbi raised and donated the money. Townsend also shared information with and relied on Grafman.

Friedman knew that Grafman had connections and received intelligence from the police department that was fed to the Jewish Committee, but he did not know the background. Grafman understood the importance of keeping confidences and did not reveal, even to Friedman, the source of any information he passed along.[147]

10

Unsung Heroes & Cement Golf Holes

Shortly after the attack on the Freedom Riders, in late May 1961, the Chamber of Commerce, the Committee of 100 (formed in 1950 to attract new industry), and the Birmingham Downtown Improvement Association, which Vincent Townsend chaired, resolved to open an existing Joint Study Committee to include Black representatives, despite the Jim Crow laws forbidding it. One of the committee's duties was to investigate means of creating better relations between the races.[148]

Meanwhile, a confrontation brewed over the city commissioners' stubbornness in resisting Justice Department orders to desegregate local public parks, swimming pools, golf courses, and other recreational facilities. Mayor Art Hanes and Commissioner Jabo Waggoner Sr. had even flown to Washington to discuss the matter with Attorney General Robert Kennedy. Connor refused to go. Hanes and Waggoner warned Kennedy that integration would "fill those pools with blood" and the city would fill them with dirt if Kennedy didn't back off. Kennedy gave them a chilly reception. Feet propped on his desk, he informed them they needed to change how they dealt with Blacks in the South.[149]

In August 1961, activist Fred Shuttlesworth moved his family from Birmingham to Cincinnati, Ohio, where Lamar Weaver, the White minister assaulted by Klansmen for shaking Shuttlesworth's hand at the bus station, had helped arrange a pulpit for him. But Shuttlesworth returned regularly to Birmingham to continue his work on civil rights.

During this time, attorneys in the YMBC formed the idea for a lawsuit with the aim of electing more progressive representation. The ramifications would unintentionally affect future efforts to rid Birmingham of Connor.

YMBC attorney members Chuck Morgan and George "Peach" Taylor, joined later by David Vann and Robert "Bob" Vance Sr., filed a lawsuit in August that would become a landmark voting rights case, *Reynolds v. Sims*.

The suit was filed in the name of labor leader M. O. Sims on behalf of voters. Labor unions helped fund the suit. Jerome "Buddy" Cooper's firm, along with the ACLU, helped litigate the case, which was based on the fact that the 1901 Alabama Constitution was designed to keep power in the hands of the White inheritors of the Black Belt, the rich land of the cotton plantations that had been the preindustrial economic backbone and shaper of the South's cultural mores. The resulting legislative apportionment was based on the number of counties and senatorial "regions," not on population. The effect was keeping state control out of the hands of populists in the (relatively) more progressive large cities, including the most populated area of the state—Birmingham. Eventually, when *Reynolds v. Sims* lost in the lower courts but was appealed, the U.S. Supreme Court affirmed that state legislative districts should be based on voting population, establishing the "one person, one vote" doctrine. Chief Justice Earl Warren wrote, "Legislators represent people, not trees or acres. Legislators are elected by voters, not farms or cities or economic interests."

WHILE *Reynolds v. Sims* wound its way through the courts, a lawsuit filed by Shuttlesworth came before the local federal district court, and in October 1961, Judge Harlan H. Grooms ordered that Birmingham's parks and other public facilities integrate by January 1962. In reaction, the commissioners announced they would close all sixty-eight city parks, thirty-eight playgrounds, six swimming pools, and even the city's four golf courses.

Although some supported the commissioners' actions, backlash against the closing of the city's facilities built steadily. Editorials in both the *Birmingham News* and the *Post-Herald* protested the actions. According to Paul Friedman Sr., the YMBC was the first to take a public stand that the city could not oppose a court order and must integrate parks and schools. YMBC members persuaded others, including the Jaycees (Junior Chamber of Commerce) to join their stand. The vote among the Jaycees was unanimous. Community leaders including Rabbi Milton Grafman, Bishop George Murray, Father Allen, Tom Moxley, and Vernon Patrick appeared on local television to "prevail on the city to keep our parks and schools open."[150]

Bob Hart of the Jaycees expressed his concern about the impact the parks closings would have on the economy, as well as the precedent that would be set. He warned that schools were next in the integration picture. "We've got to take a stand whether three people [commissioners] have the right to say whether your child or mine gets an education."[151] Other groups who opposed the closings included the Birmingham Chamber of Commerce (after bitter infighting and a "study"), the Birmingham Committee of 100, the Downtown Improvement Association, the YMBC, and various church groups. "Dozens of letters opposing the closure and asking commissioners to reconsider their decision poured into city hall. Some were from organizations. . . . Most came from concerned individuals. A few correspondents tried, however incongruously, to strike some middle ground; the Highland Golfers Association suggested a unique solution, writing that while they were in agreement with 'most of the ideas expressed, . . . we strongly feel the exception of the golf courses should be made since there is no personal contact involved.'"[152] Mayor Art Hanes supported this strategy.[153]

To their credit, the Park and Recreation Board members—James Downey, Mrs. J. H. Berry, Dan Gaylord, and former mayor Jimmy Morgan—although appointed by the commissioners, refused to close the parks, saying doing so would hurt the community's children. David Vann recalled, "Former Mayor Jimmy Morgan . . . didn't get on the park board to close the parks. He got on the park board to build a zoo."[154]

According to Edward Harris, Vann and Clarke Stallworth thanked each of the Park Board members who voted against closing the parks. Stallworth was a *Post-Herald* political reporter (and future editor for the *News*), who covered the YMBC meetings as well as KKK activities. He had also documented the relationship between Black Belt interests and Birmingham's Big Mules. "He worked quietly getting stories in the papers, stories that needed to be told about the accomplishments of black folk . . . He was, in the sixties, essentially the program chairman of the Young Men's Business Club, getting speakers whose talks would then be covered in the paper." Harris quoted Stallworth as saying, "Newspapers can't make people change their minds, but what is covered will decide what is talked about. It can set up an agenda."[155]

But the commissioners responded by cutting the city's parks budget to $50,000, the minimum required by state law. When the city facilities were closed, Mrs. J. H. Berry resigned from the board in protest.[156]

Segregationists threatened those who supported open parks. "One woman stated ominously that Klan members had taken their robes out of the closet.

Now they carried the robes in their cars at all times, ready for action on a moment's notice."[157] But other voices refused to be silenced. In September, the *Post-Herald* quoted William P. Engel of Engel Realty Company as saying that the "massive resistance [to desegregation] harmed the community."

Connor threatened to sell off the public property before allowing integration. Abe Berkowitz responded in a letter to the editor on November 7, 1961: "I prefer to keep the park and sell Commissioner Connor." A month later, he added, "It is the Supreme Court which guarantees Mr. Connor's right to express his 'pity and contempt' for it, and mine to express my pity and contempt for him."[158]

The Jewish Community Center gave a dinner honoring Engel for his leadership. At that dinner, Engel challenged Birmingham's citizens: "My conscience and my love of Birmingham will not permit me to ignore our present plight. Either we go forward or we go back, and if we go back, we go back into the depths. . . . Are we going to follow our course already established as a progressive city, or are we going to become a city of infamy known for violence?"

When Connor read Engel's statement in the following day's paper, he called him, asking if the quote was accurate.

"Bull," Engel replied, "that wasn't the half of it."

A *Birmingham News* editorial observed that Engel " has always been blunt and willing to say and even do the unpopular. It is fact, as the *News* sees it, because too few have done so, that our troubles now are multiplied."[159]

Connor's critics included his own pastor at Woodlawn Methodist Church. The Reverend John Rutland, an outspoken liberal, lectured Connor about his treatment and language toward Blacks. Despite "the burning of a cross on his front lawn . . . and pressure from his own bishop, [Rutland] did not mute his voice for racial justice."[160]

Another critic was businessman Jim Head. In November, he asked local businessmen to sign an innocuous letter to maintain law and order. "This was an indirect, but clear rebuke to local police and politicians, who had looked the other way while Klansmen and their sympathizers beat Freedom Riders, assaulted 'uppity' Negroes, and tried to prevent school desegregation." Eighty-nine businessmen signed the letter. From their perspective, massive resistance was a dark stain on the reputation of the city and its prospects for economic growth. A representative of the Southern Regional Council, the parent organization of the Alabama HRC, commented that he had never seen "such a general mobilization of community leadership on the moderate side of a segregation issue."[161]

But the commissioners plowed forward to shut down the city's recreational facilities. Connor had "No trespassing" signs posted. Golfers tried to sneak onto the links to play. On the last day of 1961, city workers filled the holes on public golf courses with cement.

Inscribed on the paneled wall above the City Chamber doors, bold words proclaimed, "Cities Are What Men Make Them." From the raised dais inside those doors, the three commissioners looked down at four spokesmen presenting a petition on January 9, 1962, calling for a cooling-off period and reconsideration of the closing of the parks: "James A. Head, director of the Chamber of Commerce's Committee of 100; Dr. Henry Stanford, president of Birmingham-Southern College; the Reverend David C. Wright, rector of the prestigious St. Mary's on the Highlands Episcopal Church; and Barney A. Monaghan, president of Vulcan Materials Company." The commissioners rejected the petition outright. Then "Bull Connor and Mayor Hanes treated the delegation to an hour-long 'bombastic and abusive' discourse on segregation."[162] Mayor Hanes asked how many of the businessmen lived inside the city and then—though more than half of the 1,200 people signing the petition lived inside the city limits—scolded them as hypocrites, noting that the men presenting the petition all lived in the suburbs cocooned from integration.

This treatment alienated the influential members of Birmingham's elite and played right into Sid Smyer's hands. The commissioners' stubborn insistence gave an impetus and rationale for Smyer's efforts to oust Connor and his cohorts. According to Sol Kimerling, it created the readiness for change necessary in the public's mind. The Bar committee Smyer had asked to look at the issue of changing the city's governmental structure had reported months before (in October 1961) with a finding recommending the mayor-council configuration as allowed by Alabama law, but adroitly avoided the issue of personalities, merely stating that "defects in the current government were purely structural."[163] With this study in his back pocket, and riding the wave of outrage over the closed parks and amenities, Smyer began planning the next steps toward implementing a change in the form of government.

11

A Failed Assassination

During the crisis over the shutting down of the city's parks and facilities, Police Chief Jamie Moore talked Bull Connor into inviting Chief Laurie Pritchett of the Albany, Georgia, police department for a visit to Birmingham. Moore hoped Connor would listen to how Pritchett had handled Martin Luther King Jr.-led demonstrations the year before, avoiding the violent confrontation he feared was coming to Birmingham.

Pritchett had known that King was committed to nonviolence, and the Albany chief spent time in the library studying Gandhi's philosophy and tactics. He understood that if King could not provoke a confrontation, he would gain no moral ground in Albany. Pritchett kept the behavior of his police department low-key, avoiding violence in arrests, just as the protesters did, and negating overcrowding complaints by arranging for jails in nearby counties to take overflow prisoners. He also kept his officers from making arrests for violations of segregation laws to avoid possible appeals and federal precedents if any were overturned.

Pritchett's "success" had not gone unnoticed in Birmingham. Lankford had accompanied Moore and Tom Cook (who had been promoted to lieutenant) to Albany to study King's method firsthand and to learn from Pritchett's response. For Lankford, the trip had been an education in more than tactics. It provided a stunning personal revelation.

He recalled the hot summer day in July 1962 when he and Moore sat in rocking chairs, eating peach ice cream cones—Moore's favorite—on the rickety, wooden front porch of the New Albany Hotel, just across from city hall. Martin Luther King, however, was sitting in Albany's jail. The protests by students and local activists continued without him. With King in jail, arrests and demonstrations had increased. Lankford would later report that the White community watched but didn't interfere, leaving that up to law enforcement. "Moore said whatever prejudices or resentment the whites may have had, they were kept under control."[164]

Pritchett stopped by the hotel while Lankford, Moore, and Cook relaxed on the porch. Pritchett was a "hulking man, six feet one inch and 220 pounds in 1961, ballooning to 265 pounds by the end of 1962 during Albany's civil rights crisis. He often clenched a cigar with his teeth; but any resemblance to the stereotypical Southern lawman ended there. He was as smart and bright as the gold badge (Albany Police #1) he wore on his stiffly starched white shirts."[165]

Pritchett advised the Birmingham trio to rest up, as it was going to be a long night. "And if you're going to the doings, better get a seat early. One church won't hold the crowd that'll show up tonight," he added, referring to the nightly meeting at the nearby Shiloh Baptist Church, which followed the same pattern as the mass meetings in Birmingham.

Lankford attended, settling down to listen and report the plans. For the media, he reported the time for the planned demonstrations in reporter's shorthand as "CPT," Colored People's Time, which meant the events would actually be later. Demonstrations were deliberately started late to make sure the maximum amount of people and police were there.

The rallies were familiar turf for Lankford, but late that evening back in the hotel room he shared with Cook, he heard something that did surprise him. Cook sat on his bed at one end of the room sipping a whiskey. Never a drinker, Lankford sat with his soda at a small table on the other side.

Cook was the quietest, most private individual Lankford had ever known. He was a loner, a man of sharp intellect and keen loyalty, though Lankford suspected he was more loyal to Connor's public safety commissioner office than to the man himself. In Lankford's opinion, Cook was too much of a deep thinker to be swayed by Connor's rhetoric and bluster. He had no evidence that Cook himself was a Klansman, only that he cultivated the KKK relationships in order to report to Connor.

Lankford and Cook had spent a good bit of time together, and Lankford had never heard him utter a word of personal disrespect for the Reverend Fred Shuttlesworth. Fearless, Shuttlesworth always stood first in the line of marchers, earning him the respect of many law enforcement officers. Yet something weighed on Cook's mind that evening in the shadows of their hotel room. He spoke softly from his bed where he nursed the whiskey, talking about an incident that had occurred years ago, when Lankford was still a student at the university. At that time, Shuttlesworth was making headlines leading marches and sit-ins at the Birmingham bus station and making life miserable for Connor, as well as infuriating the Klan.

Cook told the story weighing on him in a quiet, dispassionate voice that belied the words' jolt. At first, Lankford was not sure he heard correctly: Connor had ordered Cook to have Shuttlesworth killed. Lankford was silent, listening not as newsman but as friend and confidant. Sensing Cook needed to get it off his chest—or perhaps was bragging, Lankford was never sure—he asked no questions. Cook relayed how he had carried out Connor's instruction by rounding up his most trusted "snitch," a Black informant. Cook made the informant an offer "he had better not refuse." The man was to shoot Shuttlesworth with a shotgun at close range outside a church that had a double set of steps leading up to the main entrance where Shuttlesworth was to preach.

As per the pattern of meetings, the congregation finished eating in the basement and moved upstairs for the prayer meeting, prepared to listen to Shuttlesworth preach against "Bull" and the plight of the Black community. The informant, armed with a shotgun, took his position as planned under a small porch. Cook parked down the street, watching.

Just as the service was ending, a city police cruiser, unaware of the setup, was making its rounds and slowly approached. Frightened, the informant fled his hiding place, running down the alley behind the church.

The incident was many years old, but Lankford told Sheriff Mel Bailey what Cook had revealed, only to discover that Bailey already had knowledge of the alleged failed plot. In recalling the incident years later, Lankford said he "probably discussed it at some point with Townsend," but neither he nor Cook ever mentioned it again.[166]

CHIEF PRITCHETT HAD KING and Ralph Abernathy released from the Albany jail after only three days, notifying them that an "anonymous black man" had paid their bail. They would have preferred to stay in jail as a symbolic gesture. Abernathy later joked, "I've been thrown out of lots of places in my day, but never before have I been thrown out of jail."[167]

It was not until August, after his third arrest, that King agreed to leave Albany and announced a frustrated halt to demonstrations. Now he had turned his attention to Birmingham where Moore hoped Connor would listen to Pritchett and emulate his tactics and avoid a violent confrontation.

When Pritchett was ushered in, Connor was sitting in his large office chair talking on the phone with his back to the door. Pritchett, expecting a large man from the size of his "great big" chair and deep voice, was surprised when Connor turned around. Connor told him he'd been talking to the city's recreation department. "That the Blacks wanted to play golf on the municipal courses, and that he [Connor] was going to let them, but he was going to put cement in the holes. They would never get a golf ball in any of the holes."[168]

Pritchett came away from the meeting with the conviction that Connor had paid no attention to his recommendations. Yet Connor subsequently sent Lieutenant House as a liaison to Klan leaders to tell them to stay out of dealings with King and the demonstrations.[169] This move may have been why Klan members reportedly began to collaborate with previously shunned Ed Fields and J. B. Stoner of the NSRP.

12

Secret Meetings

While controversy raged in Birmingham about closing its parks, a secret meeting was going on in the Donnelly House, an elegant plantation-style house on Highland Avenue that usually hosted social events. In the basement, the city's top attorneys, White and Black, met with an agenda. Led by Abe Berkowitz, the group's goal was to open the door for Black membership in the Birmingham Bar Association.

Another Jewish attorney, Alan Heldman Sr., supported the effort to admit Black members. Like Karl Friedman, Heldman Sr. had gone out of his way to sit with Black attorneys in court when they found themselves sitting alone. Years later, Heldman's son became an attorney and after presenting a case in federal court was called into the judge's chambers. The judge was U. W. Clemon, Alabama's first Black federal judge. Clemon said, "I just wanted to tell you that when I first came to Birmingham and started practicing law, there were two lawyers in this community who treated me graciously. One of them is Bill Acker, my colleague down the hall now a fellow judge"—and, incidentally, a right-wing Republican—"and the other was your daddy."[170]

Heldman Sr. refused to join the Birmingham Bar, making his point by returning the annual membership form with a note added informing the organization that he would join when the Black lawyers could join.

Those in attendance at the Donnelly House planned a more organized effort. They gave Charlie Cleveland the job of obtaining a nomination form, a simple task stymied by a suspicious Bar administration that told him there were no forms available. It would take several years before the all-White bar would admit the first Black attorney.[171]

Meanwhile, Sid Smyer, encouraged by Jim Head, started secret meetings of his own with Black leaders to discuss ways through the minefield of negotiations. Those meetings often included David Vann.[172] In Karl Friedman's opinion, while Smyer's motivation was the local economy, Head's was humanitarian.[173]

Alabama Council on Human Relations director Jim Jimerson quietly acted as a go-between. Walking the line between the two groups, while keeping the trust and respect of each, was not a simple task. It was a role he played for three years with little recognition.

The fact that both the Black and White leaders were themselves divided in their positions enhanced the difficulty. Paul Rilling of the Southern Regional Council reported, "One of the most depressing factors of the Birmingham situation is the apathy and divisiveness of the Negro community. The [J. L.] Ware [Baptists] group, the Shuttlesworth group, the [A. G.] Gaston circle are working at cross-purposes and constantly at loggerheads." Likewise, he observed that "the white leadership seeking to reduce tensions fell into two camps: those who urged moderate action but refused to meet with Black leaders under any circumstances, and a second group of businessmen willing to consult with black leaders." Head and Sid Smyer fell into the latter category.[174]

Other meetings had long been taking place in First Congregational Christian Church at 1024 Center Street North, a small Black church just across the street from attorney Arthur Shores's house in the heart of an area that had seen so many bombings it was nicknamed "Dynamite Hill." The founders of the church in 1882 had been associated with Talladega College, a private Black liberal arts college about an hour east, founded by emancipated slaves at the end of the Civil War. Several prominent Black leaders, including educator Odessa Woolfolk and attorneys Arthur Shores and J. Mason Davis, belonged to the First Congregational Christian Church.

Since at least 1958, the church had served as one of the meeting places for the interracial Birmingham Council on Human Relations. The BCHR attempted other venues, but a reason to eject the group would arise, or members would come out of a meeting to find their tires slashed. But they found sanctuary at First Congregational.[175] Attorney Shores would often sit quietly in the back of BCHR meetings and listen.[176] Members tried to keep the meetings quiet to avoid bringing attention to themselves or identifying their fellows, which could put them in danger. Not only did their agenda mark them for supremacists' vitriol, but Blacks and Whites sat together, making such meetings illegal under the Jim Crow laws.

Tom Lankford had no idea that Bull Connor had targeted the BCHR when after a long day he headed to his car in the *News'* parking lot. Before he made it to his vehicle, Lieutenant Tom Cook—Connor's man—pulled up beside him, rolled down the window on his unmarked black Ford, and asked him to show up with his camera at the detective bureau at 6:45 p.m.

Giving up on going home for the night, Lankford reported to city hall where he learned that Cook wanted him to help expose an illegal, racially mixed meeting at the First Congregational Christian Church.

On the way, Lankford called his friend Wendell Harris, a WAPI-TV news anchor, and asked him to help. Lankford called on him partly because Harris's news director was a close personal friend of Townsend, but more importantly, Harris was an ace reporter, and Lankford predicted he would not want to be left out of a story. Even so, Harris was nervous. His job did not normally entail breaking into buildings, but the church doors would be shut to protect the BCHR participants, who feared the Klan would learn their identities.

What Cook wanted (on Connor's behalf) was for Lankford to get inside the church and take photos of the meeting while the plainclothes police remained outside. It was a warm day. Cook and a couple of detectives stood with Harris and Lankford outside their car near the church, talking. Lankford's camera hung from its shoulder strap the way he liked to carry it for fast action.

Lankford's plan was for Harris, who was recognizable from television news, to go in the front door and create a distraction, while Lankford rushed in the other door and grabbed his photos then made a getaway with the film. The police would remain outside; they had no excuse to enter the church. It didn't bother Lankford that Cook was using him to do so. He felt such a meeting should have been open to news reporters in the first place. For him, it was not an issue of right and wrong; it was a news story he had to break.

Ramming his shoulder against the door, Lankford burst through and ran to the pulpit where an open-mouthed speaker stood. Lankford's flash illuminated an equally stunned audience. Before Lankford could take more photos, the speaker leaned forward and threw out his hand, blocking the lens. The upset crowd surged around Lankford, wanting to confiscate his camera. He refused. Harris was nowhere in sight.

Lankford recognized the man who grasped his arm and pulled him aside as attorney Chuck Morgan. In a low voice, Morgan said, "Tom, we're brothers from The Machine. Let me have the film."

Lankford was shocked, having no memory of Morgan as a member of the secret organization at the University of Alabama. But Morgan had been in Tuscaloosa a few years before Lankford.

"The Machine don't count here, Chuck," Lankford managed to say, torn between Lieutenant's Cook's expectations, his job, and giving Morgan the film out of loyalty to their college connections. "We'll let Townsend decide," he finally said.

Morgan agreed to the terms. He asked the unhappy BCHR members to wait outside and stepped away to call *News* VP/General Manager Victor Hanson. He returned to say, "Tom, Victor said for you to bring the film straight to the *News*."

Outside, Cook and his "boys" had departed, although Harris had waited for him.

Lankford drove to the *News* and delivered up the film. He was not terribly surprised to learn that it was returned to Morgan without being developed. Although some claim it an Alabama myth, Lankford believed connections between members of The Machine made it the most powerful secret force in the state.

13

The Spark that Lit the Birmingham Movement Fire

City officials reluctantly reopened the parks under U.S. District Judge Hobart Grooms's court order in January 1962. By the middle of the month, three Black churches were bombed—St. Luke's AME Zion, Triumph Church and Kingdom of God in Christ Temple No. 7, and New Bethel Baptist.

About the same time, Black students from Miles College formed an Anti-Injustice Committee (AIC) to address inequality with economic pressure. Miles was a Black college sponsored by the Christian Methodist Episcopal (CME) church and located in Fairfield, a small town on Birmingham's western edge. Led by a thirty-one-year-old student government association president Frank Dukes, and supported by President Dr. Lucius H. Pitts Sr., the AIC students discussed how to change the treatment of Blacks as customers and employees in stores in downtown Birmingham. Ironically, some of the most outspoken local civil rights supporters were members of the Jewish community, yet Jewish-owned businesses were the AIC's target, because Blacks shopped at those stores, and that was where the Black community could make an impact.

Some early Jewish immigrants found a niche as peddlers. A few who were successful grew their trade into stores, then into department stores, predominantly in the heart of Birmingham's downtown. Miners and steel workers, Black and White, lived in company towns, like Fairfield, near the mines and mills. They could buy food and small items on credit at company stores, and the company would deduct the charges from weekly pay envelopes. But company stores were not always trusted. Many working families came downtown on Saturdays to shop at the Jewish-owned stores, which treated them fairly and also offered credit.[177]

Dukes noted that before the AIC launched any direct actions, the Miles College business department did studies based on Chamber of Commerce information to figure out the impact Black shoppers had on the local retail economy. It turned out to be $4 million per week, about 25 percent of sales. Meanwhile, the department stores operated on a 12 percent profit margin. Higher-end stores—Porter Clothing, Kessler's, and Burger-Phillips—sold to middle-upper class Blacks, although the stores didn't allow Black customers to try on the clothes before buying or to return merchandise afterward.

As a young man, Dukes had resented everything about Jim Crow. His mother wanted him to leave Alabama because she predicted his defiance would get him in trouble.[178] "I did get into fights with white boys growing up," he said. "I didn't like them wanting me to step off the sidewalk and let them pass. I never got arrested for that, because by the time the police got there, I was gone."

In 1949, he left for the U.S. Army, to his mother's relief, and swore he would never come back to Alabama. After serving his military term and working in a Detroit factory, he reenlisted in 1954 and served in Korea. Returning to Detroit, he resumed his former job in the Chrysler factory. But, reeling from the recession of the late 1950s, Chrysler laid him off for nine months, so he came back to Birmingham to bide time. It was 1959. "I was good at pool and dice and I played to support myself. One day I was playing pool, and a friend suggested I go to Miles College. 'You can go on the G.I. bill.' I said I didn't have the money to register. He said, 'Mrs. Allen [at Miles] will let you enroll for forty dollars and pay the rest when your checks start coming.'"

Another friend loaned him the forty dollars. Dukes enrolled the next day, a move that changed history. When the call came to return to Detroit, he decided to stay in school. By 1961 his fellow students elected him president of the student government association, and he was point man in the planning to address the treatment of Black citizens.

Despite his youthful tendency to confrontation, Dukes understood the White community's reluctance to change. Addressing fellow students, Dukes said, "There are many among us who would like to express our views but . . . fear economic reprisals, and that same thing holds true for members of the white race. They would like to stand up and be counted, but the same retaliations would be directed upon them."[179]

DUKES RECALLED THAT DR. Lucius Pitts was "a genius at making friends." He had made a point of meeting top Black businessmen, and through them he met top White businessmen. Pitts suggested that Dukes's group, before initiating a boycott, meet with the White power structure to discuss several goals: drop the prohibition against hiring Blacks in sales positions; take down "Colored" and "White" signs; allow Black shoppers to use department store dressing rooms; make returns on clothing; and address other inequalities perpetrated by Jim Crow laws.

Jim Jimerson of the Alabama Council on Human Relations worked as a liaison between the groups. Emil Hess, the Jewish owner of the Parisian clothing store, introduced Dr. Pitts to Episcopal Bishop George M. Murray at the Cathedral Church of the Advent. Murray worked it out to bring the parties together at the church. It was a risk. "If Bull Connor had known that Whites and Blacks were meeting, he would have put all of us in jail," recalled Dr. Jonathan McPherson, advisor to the Miles College senior class.[180]

The first such secret meeting included White business and community leaders Roper Dial, Paul Johnston, Rabbi Milton Grafman, Jim Head, Sid Smyer, and Hess. Dukes recalled that the Pizitz, Newberry, Burger-Phillips, and Kessler's stores did not send representatives.

"The Whites didn't feel safe [meeting with me]," Dukes said, "because I had been described as a hothead." He added wryly, "though not as much as Shuttlesworth," with whom the businessmen also would not meet, considering him "too rough." Dukes recalled ironic progress: "They [possibly Smyer] called us 'niggers' the first three meetings. Then we became 'colored boys.'"

In response to the Anti-Injustice Committee's requests, the businessmen explained that they knew Birmingham was lagging behind Atlanta and changes were needed, but they wanted to wait. Although the plan to change the city's form of government was not yet public, the wheels were in motion. The AIC was unwilling to wait. "We'd been waiting four hundred years," Dukes said. "Emil Hess was kicked out of the meetings because he said we were right. He agreed with us that Blacks were being discriminated against, and they should have jobs according to their abilities. He wanted to desegregate and hire Blacks. The other committee members thought he was going too fast and put him off the committee."

But there may have been other fears. Dukes said the White representatives "confessed they couldn't talk to Bull Connor because they were afraid of him, like all of the Black people and most of the White folks."[181]

The biracial group met weekly for about a month, and finally the businessmen met with Connor. Reporting back, they said they could not get Connor to budge, and, as predicted, he threatened to put them all in jail if they took actions toward desegregation.

THE ANTI-INJUSTICE COMMITTEE DETERMINED to move ahead with the boycott, which they called a "selective buying campaign" because boycotts were illegal in Alabama. "There are only two men who have power in this city," Dr. Pitts told Frank Dukes—"Bull Connor and Fred Shuttlesworth." Shuttlesworth flew in for his organization's Monday night mass meetings. Dukes appealed to Shuttlesworth and his organization, the ACMHR, asking for support for the boycott, which was promised.

Dukes produced a public statement titled, "This We Believe," calling for educational and employment opportunities for Blacks. During the selective buying campaign, hundreds of students and other citizens signed Dukes's statement, including a few brave Whites. Dukes, along with fellow student U. W. Clemon and Dr. McPherson, presented the signed statement to the city commissioners. Connor responded with racial slurs.

As the campaign heated up, Black minister Herbert Oliver asked Jimerson to help plan an interracial human relations workshop at Miles College. Black and White speakers from across the South attended.

The boycott was successful, cutting downtown business significantly, especially during the Easter season. But in April Connor retaliated. In a below-the-belt blow, he proposed that the city cut off food appropriations to the county's needy families. The other two commissioners joined in voting for the draconian measure.

In May, at the Southern Christian Leadership Conference meeting in Chattanooga, Shuttlesworth renewed pressure on Martin Luther King Jr. to come to Birmingham. Shuttlesworth used the boycott effort and what Miles College had done, as well as the work of his own organization, to persuade King that Birmingham was ready to stand up with direct action. King announced that SCLC would have its annual September meeting in Birmingham.

In the swelter of Birmingham's summer, the commissioners who were running for reelection—Connor and Waggoner—met with the Chamber of Commerce, believing these White businessmen to be totally behind the commissioners' opposition to desegregation. To their shock, the Chamber members tried to convince them to change their stance. The commissioners walked out in a huff.[182]

By June, the city lost one of its progressive leaders. Birmingham-Southern President Dr. Henry Stanford resigned in frustration after numerous difficulties with his conservative board, alumni, and community. The KKK had even burned a cross in his yard. The actions of a Black maintenance man illustrated the measure of Stanford's personal reputation and relationship in the Black community. For several nights after the cross burning, the maintenance man, armed with a shotgun, took up a protective post "at serious risk to his own life" in the president's front yard.[183]

Stanford became president of the University of Miami about the time the Birmingham boycott concluded, but the student movement had helped the Black community experience the power of unity and its economic influence, a precedent for the coming demonstrations. And the White business community had become "more favorable to negotiations."[184] Civil rights activist Joe Dickson called the boycott, "the single most important event which led to the coming of Martin Luther King to Birmingham."[185]

IN RETROSPECT, SEVERAL LEADERS of the 1962 boycott have stated that the Miles movement had "invaluable and secret support from white citizenry." Dr. Willie Clyde Jones: "There were a lot of white folks who supported us." Jeff Drew: "It amazes me how quickly we forget. . . . We could not have done it without them [White people]. They knew it was the right thing, and they wanted to participate."[186]

Such was not the case in the broader White population of Alabama. Gubernatorial candidate George Wallace had been campaigning on his new segregationist platform. He promised to stand in schoolhouse doors if necessary to prevent integration. Understanding clearly what the segregationist voters of Alabama wanted to hear, he hired Asa Carter, Klan leader and White Citizens' Council member, to write his speeches to "stir up the rednecks." Carter was a radical's radical. It was his KKK chapter members who had attacked Nat "King" Cole on a Birmingham stage in 1956, kidnapped and castrated Judge

Edward Aaron in 1957 in one of the most brutal acts in Birmingham's history, and attacked Freedom Riders in Anniston in 1961.

Although the *Birmingham News* had supported Wallace in 1958 when he ran for governor as a racial moderate, the newspaper "vigorously opposed him when his politics turned to race-baiting in the 1962 campaign." Wallace claimed the paper's Jewish New York owner, S. I. Newhouse, had ordered the paper to oppose him. The *News* ran a front-page response: "Wallace Is a Liar."[187]

Wallace beat Ryan DeGraffenried in the Democratic primary runoff of June 1962. As Alabama was basically a one-party state at the time, winning a Democratic primary was tantamount to election anyway, but the Republicans didn't even field a candidate in the general election that November. Wallace's inauguration as governor in January 1963 would whip the state into a fury that profoundly affected the direction of local and national politics and policy and shook the world.

14

Prelaunch & Clash

Tom Lankford spent most of August 1962 working with law enforcement, tracking the horrific kidnapping/murder of a White eleven-year-old boy. The incident sent Connor on a rampage against "perverts." He ordered them rounded up from their "hangouts" across the city and jailed. Meanwhile, the kidnapper/murderer was arrested out of state and Lankford drove Blount County Sheriff J. C. Carr and state investigator Harry Sims to Baltimore to pick up the defendant, also White. Lankford stopped at pay phones along the way back to call in the story when the man confessed. With the arrest, Connor quickly turned his attention back to racial issues.[188]

The weeks before Dr. Martin Luther King's scheduled appearance at the SCLC's September conference in Birmingham "sizzled with tension," according to Jim Jimerson. The year had seen Black students at Miles College rise up in the selective buying campaign. The integration of the University of Mississippi and the University of Alabama loomed. The multiple bombings of Black churches reported earlier in the year and the unrelated bombing of an under-construction apartment building for Blacks drove home the message that groups were willing to use violence to attain their ends.[189] The city was still spinning from the 1961 Mother's Day attack and feared further incursions of Freedom Riders and "trouble from outside agitators."

Shuttlesworth planned demonstrations to coincide with the SCLC conference, but moderate Black leaders "feared violent confrontations that could ignite the city's volatile racial antagonism. White city leaders prepared for armed clashes. The Klan mobilized its forces to oppose the expected demonstrations." Paul Rilling with the Southern Regional Council observed, "'the mood in the city is ugly, the reactions of Bull Connor uncertain, and some elements in the Negro community no longer seem wedded to nonviolence.'"[190]

In this atmosphere, Sid Smyer considered how to move forward on two fronts: obtaining the required signatures and momentum to change the city's governmental structure and stopping Martin Luther King from coming to Birmingham—or at least stopping demonstrations, which Smyer feared would negatively affect the referendum. The Birmingham Bar committee's study had presented a favorable report for a new mayor-council form of government. Now Smyer needed a group to spearhead a campaign and sell the idea to the public. The Chamber demurred, saying they were not the appropriate organization, so Smyer asked the YMBC to pick up the cause.

It was a wise choice. Attorneys Abe Berkowitz and Erskine Smith began the campaign by giving speeches to civic groups and anyone who would have them. To call for a referendum on the issue, Alabama's state law required documented signatures from 7,500 registered voters, a daunting challenge.[191] On a morning in mid-August 1962, attorney and YMBC member David Vann pondered how to get those signatures.

During his drive to work, Vann was listening to Dave Campbell, a well-known radio personality whose call-in show, "The People Speak," was "one of the few places that blacks and whites talked and listened to each other. The moderator [Campbell] was scrupulously fair. He asked gentle and challenging questions, and he let people have their say."[192]

In that morning's radio broadcast, Campbell remarked on the discussions regarding the change in government. "'Well,'" he said, 'we ought to get up a petition and have an election on it, or we ought to get behind the government we got. It's not good for a city to be split.'"

Vann's immediate reaction was, "'He [Campbell] can sit up on the mountain and pontificate easily, but [to] get a petition [is not as easy].' Glen Iris Civic Club on the Southside had tried to get a petition, and Mr. Connor had sent plain clothes detectives around to pick up petitions as fast as they were signed." But by the time Vann arrived at his law office, it hit him he might be able to use the upcoming special election to his advantage.

The election was to fill seats after the decennial reapportionment of state legislators and was being held as a result of *Reynolds v. Sims,* the one man, one vote lawsuit originally filed by YMBC members. Although the U.S. Supreme Court had not yet heard the case, a lower court had issued an order giving ten additional house seats to the Birmingham area, and the state legislature had called for the special election. The Democratic primary was scheduled for August 29, ten days hence.

Vann realized that if he could set up a petition booth across the street from every polling place, he might gather enough petition signatures in a single day. "We could use voting lists that are published in the newspaper. We could check people off, make sure the signatures were valid, and we could send somebody around to pick up petitions once an hour so. If Connor tried to get some of them, we'd [still] have most of them, because we would have a security system of our own."

Vann phoned Berkowitz and said, "Abe, you really want to change the city government? I have figured out how to do it."

Berkowitz arranged an emergency meeting of the executive Chamber of Commerce in Smyer's office. At Vann's insistence, Don Stafford, representing organized labor, was included. Vann knew Stafford from their mutual work on John Kennedy's campaign. The businessmen balked at trying to pull together something so complex on such short notice, but Stafford said, "I've been sitting here thinking, yeah, why hadn't we thought of this before? Let's go."

AFTER MORE DISCUSSION, THE businessmen agreed but wanted ten to twelve leading citizens to head the public relations part of the operation. Vann drew up a list of twenty-five possibilities, but none would sign the petition, afraid of damaging their business relationships with the city. Smyer said, "If you can't get twenty-five silk-stocking people, let's get five hundred anybodies."

The group mimeographed a page that said, "I hereby agree to be a member of the Birmingham Citizens for Progress to sponsor a petition to give the people of Birmingham the right to decide for themselves what form of government is best for their city." Realizing a hunt for that many signatures could never be kept from the press, Vann asked for permission to go to the newspapers and ask them to keep it out of print until the committee was together. He wanted to keep a low profile, knowing the fact that he had clerked for Justice Hugo Black during the *Brown* decision could be used to taint the committee's efforts. The *Birmingham News* and the *Post-Herald* agreed.

The cat was out of the bag, however, by August 20, and Connor responded by crying it was "outsiders trying to run the city's business."[193] Despite Vann's fears, phone calls poured in with offers to help and be part of the effort.

Many of those who stepped forward were modest businessmen like Elbert A. Hobson, who owned a roofing and construction company and belonged to the East End Optimist Club. He and doubtless many others received threatening phone calls during the campaign.[194] Nonetheless, the group met at the Bankhead Hotel three days later with well over five hundred names and formed "Citizens for Progress," chaired by William Jenkins, a retired painter and member of the AFL-CIO. Vann and the committee agreed it would not hurt to have the name of "William Jenkins" listed as chairman, as it coincidentally was the same name as a local judge.[195]

For days prior to the election, messages in large print at the bottom of page one of the *Birmingham News* urged people to the polls. "It's your privilege and your responsibility," "Make your ballet count," and "Fill House seats with the best men—Don't fail to vote."

Volunteers created packets with instructions and petition forms before the election. The plotters decided not to put up petition booths near the Black voting places, avoiding the possibility of their antagonists painting the effort as a segregation issue.

MEANWHILE, KING WAS SCHEDULED to appear in Birmingham for the upcoming SCLC meeting, and planning for street demonstrations was underway. Fearing the Black activity would have a negative effect on the upcoming referendum effort, the Chamber was finally ready to take action, perhaps swayed by Townsend and Smyer's arguments that the city was strangling itself of opportunities, or by arguments on moral grounds for desegregation put forward by Berkowitz, Jim Head, and Emil Hess. Whatever combination of factors were at work, the Chamber formed an *ad hoc* group of eighty-nine men to work on solving the "race problems."

The special Chamber committee emerged on August 27, 1962, two days before the referendum, and became known as the Senior Citizens Committee (younger businessmen also participated). The committee was to address five issues or crises, only one of which was racial, but on that topic its charge was to "make the necessary communications with the Negro leaders of Birmingham, establish the necessary communications and maintain such communications."[196]

Prominent Jewish department store owner Isadore Pizitz requested that he and other Jewish store owners not be officially included in the membership list, fearing retaliation by white supremacist groups should their names be uncovered as part of the Senior Citizens Committee. The few Black leaders who participated included businessmen A. G. Gaston and John Drew, attorney Arthur Shores, and Miles College President Dr. Lucius Pitts. The membership of the Senior Citizens Committee was kept secret for many years.

On election morning, half of the people who had volunteered to take the packets did not show up, having absconded with them. "We had to get volunteers to make up new packets," Vann recalled. "We hired Kelly Girls. By midafternoon, we had about two-thirds of the places covered."[197]

Attorney Charles Cleveland was one of the YMBC members staffing a booth located across the street from a polling place in the Glen Iris neighborhood. Vann had given Cleveland a list of voters registered at Glen Iris so people could print and sign their names exactly as they appeared on the voting list, a requirement of the probate judge.[198]

VANN'S BRILLIANT IDEA PRODUCED eleven thousand signatures, several thousand more than required. Approximately a third of voters had signed the petitions. Erskine Smith guarded the petitions with a shotgun in his law office as they came in, and they were locked in the First National Bank vault overnight.[199] On September 6, a photo appeared in the *News* of Vann, realtor J. H. Berry, and the chairman of Birmingham Citizens for Progress, William A. Jenkins, turning in the signatures petitioning for a referendum.[200] Jefferson County Probate Judge J. Paul Meeks certified the petition, but Mayor Art Hanes decided not to call for the election, to "leave it to the courts."[201]

Opponents attacked the petition, claiming that a fee of ten cents per name was due. Vann said he would deposit the money. "I literally raised that money walking from Second Avenue to the courthouse. People stopped me, gave me $20 bills, $10 bills and by the time I got to the courthouse, I had $750, which is what I needed."

Meeks, a former state legislator and one of the sponsors of the Mayor/Council Act that allowed cities to decide on their form of government, said the money wasn't necessary, but Vann insisted he hold it. Meeks called for the referendum vote on November 6, 1962, and afterward called Vann to come get his money.[202]

With the requirements to hold a referendum met, Citizens for Progress intensified its efforts to prepare for the actual election where people would vote on the form they wanted for their city government. Four days after turning in the petitions, a *News* staff writer interviewed Vann in a front-page article, giving him an opportunity to explain the forms of government being proposed.[203]

Working on another front, Vann called Jim Jimerson and asked him, as president of the Alabama Council on Human Relations, to try to get King to change his mind about coming to Birmingham or at least to postpone or delay demonstrations that might put the referendum voting in jeopardy. Jimerson agreed and flew to Atlanta, without an appointment, in late August 1962.

He arrived at King's headquarters and sat for several hours, waiting to see King or anyone who would talk with him. Disappointed, he returned to the airport where he spotted SCLC executive director Wyatt Tee Walker. Jimerson cornered Walker, explaining what was taking place in Birmingham and how critical the timing was to get a vote on restructuring the city's government. Removing the commissioners would create a path forward for desegregation. He asked that the SCLC change its plans and not come to Birmingham or if they came, to call off plans for demonstrations. His pleas with Walker met a stone wall. "It's up to the folks in Birmingham," Walker told him, meaning Fred Shuttlesworth. This encounter and exchange, however, alerted King's organization to the events and efforts in Birmingham and the stakes involved.[204]

Meanwhile, ACHC chair Jimerson and Miles president Pitts were moderating the Senior Citizens Committee's subcommittee meetings on race relations. Frustrated at their lack of progress and afraid King's appearance and demonstrations by Shuttlesworth's followers would negate their attempts to rid the city of Connor, Smyer met with Jimerson and Pitts, but determined that these men "had little influence over movement activists or the black masses." He called for a direct meeting with Shuttlesworth.[205]

At A. G. Gaston's personal urging, Shuttlesworth agreed to meet a representative group from the Chamber's Senior Citizens Committee and the downtown businesses at Carpenter House adjacent to the beautiful sandstone Church of the Advent. In that meeting on September 16, 1962, a suspicious Shuttlesworth focused his bitterness on Isadore Pizitz. Rabbi Grafman, though not present at the meeting, later expressed his disappointment and surprise, given not only the Pizitz store's large Black clientele, but the historic generosity of Pizitz's father, Louis Pizitz, with the Black and White community.

Considered one of the city's foremost humanitarians, Louis Pizitz emigrated from Poland where he had trained to be a rabbi. He became a pack peddler, working up to own a small dry goods store in Georgia and moving to Birmingham in 1898. The Louis Pizitz Dry Goods Company grew rapidly to employ about 750 people. When the mines shut down in 1908, and thousands faced starvation, he bought mines to allow the miners to work and sold the coal at cost. Five years later, cotton prices dropped to eleven cents a pound. Pizitz bought it from farmers at fifteen cents and stored it. During the Depression years, he opened his store on Thanksgiving to feed anyone who was hungry. With Birmingham's beloved Brother James Alexander Bryan, a Presbyterian minister and founder of a mission, Pizitz delivered truckloads of food to prisoners for Christmas, again bought coal mines to put miners to work, and when banks closed and teachers could not cash their checks, said, "Bring your checks to me." Without knowing if the state would ever make the teachers' checks good, he cashed them.

Louis Pizitz's philanthropy knew no color line. He was not only a director of the Tuggle Institute, Fund Chairman for Tuskegee Institute, and founder of and co-chairman for the campaign to build a hospital for Negroes in the Black community of Ensley, but he was also instrumental in establishing the first local swimming pool for Negroes and gave a substantial donation to start the first YMCA for Negroes.[206]

Nevertheless, Shuttlesworth "beamed [his] main points at [Isadore] Pizitz." He threatened that he, King, and SCLC vice president Ralph Abernathy would be happy to be arrested in Pizitz's store and "dragged out by Bull Connor's efficient police."

When Shuttlesworth challenged the White store owners to make a good faith effort at concessions, Roper Dial, owner of the Sears store, offered the first one. According to Shuttlesworth, Dial said, "Well . . . tell you the truth, that door to my toilet, I can just probably have my janitor paint [over the 'White Only' sign]." Dial left the room and returned, saying his janitor was painting the sign now. Most of the other merchants followed suit.[207]

As Smyer, Vann, and the Senior Citizens Committee feared, King arrived in Birmingham for the annual SCLC convention, September 25–28, 1962. Influenced, however, by the downtown businessmen's efforts to remove signs and promise of changes, Shuttlesworth had halted the planned demonstrations a week before the SCLC meeting.

When the convention was over, Connor put intense pressure on the businesses that had removed the signs, reminding them that the segregation ordinances were still the law. He threatened fines and fees, to withdraw their business licenses, to arrest Pizitz and anyone else, and to "hold them up to public ridicule and ruin their businesses."[208]

Richard Pizitz recalled that "Bull Connor walked into his father's store and said, 'I think you may have some issues here [with this building]. I need to send the fire inspector over and shut this place down.' People thought my father [Isadore Pizitz] was a friend of Connor's. That was not true. My father hated Bull Connor, but he had to keep a dialogue going."[209]

Reluctantly, the businesses put the signs back up, triggering the SCLC's decision to make Birmingham the site for a massive nonviolent campaign the following spring. The memory of and frustration with Connor's actions would also make business owners reluctant to commit to reforms in the coming days of conflict, setting the stage for a showdown.

15

Fireman's Hall, Hat on the Table

October 17, 1962, dawned mild and rainless. After roll call and the customary coffee with a handful of detectives in the city hall basement cafeteria, Lankford took the elevator to the press room. The stairs were easily navigable for the young reporter, but riding the elevators gave him a chance to chat with the older Black women operators. From the perches of their wooden seats, they opened and closed the elevator doors with levers and punched in the floor requests, privy to the diverse threads of conversations deposited between floors. Their donations of gossip or cheerful comments on the weather started the day as much as the basement cup of coffee.

On the fourth floor, "Railroad" waited outside the press room door, twisting his hands. "Man, where you been?" the slender Black man asked as he followed Lankford inside. "I been waiting here for the longest."

Furnishings in the shared media room were stark—a table, a few chairs, and a telephone. Adjoining that room, two smaller offices housed the satellite stations for the *Post-Herald* and the *News*. Covering the crime beat required relationships with law enforcement and politicians but also with those who inhabited the dark corners of the city. Though a neat dresser in his late twenties, Railroad was a junkie, and not a particular one. He used any drug he could get his hands on.

Trying to explain the forces that drove him, he had once told Lankford, "If I just received a paycheck, and my baby was sick, and my wife sent me to the pharmacy for medicine, I would spend the money on my habit. You can't help yourself. You don't have a soul no more, no way to tell the difference between right and wrong. What might have been there before inside a person is gone, burned out, and it ain't coming back."

Lankford could tell from Railroad's shaking that he needed a fix now . . . badly. Unaware the addict standing before him was about to give him explosive information, Lankford picked up the phone and dictated the previous night's crime report to the *News'* state desk, news that included a major fire in a downtown building.

Railroad listened, shifting from one foot to the other. When Lankford hung up, Railroad said, "They asked me to burn that building."

"What building?"

"The one you just called that story in on."

"Did you?"

"No."

"Who burned it, then?" Lankford tested, not too ready to trust a man obviously desperate and fishing for money.

"Mr. Jones, the owner," Railroad replied.

Knowing the owner's name gave credibility to Railroad's information, plus he regularly provided good information to Sergeant Carl Limbaugh, head of the Safe Burglary and Narcotics Detail. But Railroad might do or say anything to get his fix.

"Well," Lankford said, "Did you burn the building *for* him?"

"No, I gave the job to my friend, Hosepipe."

Lankford considered. Intuition urged him to take the chance on Railroad's veracity, and Lankford was a man who acted on his instincts. "How much do you want for the information?"

"Twenty-five dollars."

That was a large sum for a reporter in 1962, but by luck Lankford had the money. He handed folded bills to Railroad, and together they walked the half-block from city hall to Fire Department No. 1 and up the stairs to Fire Marshal Aaron Rosenthal's office.

While Railroad gave a statement to the fire marshal, Lankford wandered back to Captain Bill Berry's desk to share the information about the arson.

"Thanks, Tom," Berry said.

Lankford knew the property owner as a decent man and was aware he had gotten into financial trouble holding onto a downtown property too long. Businesses were fleeing the city to the new shopping centers, plunging downtown property values. He must have set his own building afire to collect the insurance.

"I feel sorry for the guy," Lankford said.

Berry looked up sharply. "Tom, he's an arsonist. It was a big blaze. Firemen could have been killed. Save your sympathy."

Lankford decided a change of subject was in order. "How about you and the wife coming over tonight?"

"Can't," Berry replied. "We've got that meeting with Bull at the Fireman's Union Hall."

Goosebumps pricked the back of Lankford's neck. What he heard in Berry's casual pronouncement of an unannounced meeting between Connor and the firemen was the possibility of a big story. The special election to determine whether a new form of government would replace the commissioner triumvirate loomed only a few weeks away. If the vote passed, Connor's job would disappear. At best, he'd have to run for mayor or city council member. With a strong united front to do away with their jobs, the commissioners were all desperate. What would they offer the firemen for their vote? Would the "differential"—the controversial pay difference between firemen and policemen—be thrown into the pot? Lankford couldn't hide his excitement, but Berry was blasé.

"Why is Bull meeting with the firemen?" Lankford asked.

"Don't know. The chief just said to go."

Lankford made sure he arrived at the Fireman's Hall early. For five dollars, the janitor was glad to let him in. It was an old building. Rows of metal folding chairs had been set out to accommodate about 150 persons. The speaker's table was on the north side of the building and behind it was the type of old-fashioned window that cranked outward to let in fresh air.

He had come prepared. Lankford spent Sundays in the *News'* deserted newsroom hunting for leads for investigative or features stories. He browsed through the Reuters and AP worldwide wires and stacks of newspapers from around the country, including the thick Sunday papers. With his position on the crime beat, he developed a particular interest in criminal investigations, and he read everything, including ads on the latest in police hardware.

It was in one of these Sunday paper inserts that he found an ad for a Sears and Roebuck recorder housed in a wooden case for just under $100. "There was no place on the expense account for this sort of stuff," Lankford recalled. "Only mileage and expenses for meals to develop sources, but I realized off the bat there were times you needed proof when you were quoting folks on controversial issues." On the hunch it could become useful, he ordered the equipment and stopped by an electronics shop to purchase a few miniature microphones, a roll of wire, friction tape, and a soldering iron. When the recorder arrived, he practiced with it several times, getting ready to tape an interview or any secret meeting that might occur.

Lankford had learned the value of eavesdropping early. But this was his first real attempt at recording a conversation. From his camera bag, he fished out a tiny condenser microphone, taped it under the podium and strung the wire to the window, intending to listen outside below the window. But with the sudden realization that someone could spot him there, he changed his plan. Fire Station No. 1 was too close to city hall. He was sure to be noticed if the meeting lasted longer than a few minutes. Pulling the wire back inside, he ran it instead about fifty feet to a side door, then down the hall to the men's toilet. It took about an hour to conceal the wiring under the molding and carpet.

When the meeting started at 7 p.m., he was inside one of the building's toilet stalls with the stall door locked. The reception was not broadcast quality, but clear enough to make out what the speaker was saying. Connor was in rare form, reminding Lankford of his pre-political days when his loud, clear voice and colorful descriptions, his ability to "shoot the bull," about the city's baseball team had given him fame as the "Voice of the Birmingham Barons."

The men of the firemen's union, angry over the pay differential, weren't clapping much.

"You know me," Bull roared, as if still announcing one of his ball games. "You know I support you firefighters. We've got to stick together against these carpet-bagger Jews from New York who come down here with their newspapers and TV stations trying to tell us how to run our business!"

That Connor was courting the firemen didn't surprise Lankford. Firemen—more than any other group of municipal employees—got out the vote.

"Vote to keep me," Connor declared, "and no matter what you read in the paper, or hear on TV and radio, I promise to give you a 7 percent pay raise." Mayor Hanes joined in, promising an "8 to 10 percent" raise and to eliminate the pay differential.[210]

Lankford knew he had hit pay dirt, but there might be more, so he remained in his cramped position with the cheap portable recorder resting on his knees. Then everything unraveled.

A cracking noise over his earpiece alerted him. Someone was pulling up the wire that ran around the wall from the auditorium across the hall. Bursting out of the toilet stall, he stopped dead, startled to see Sergeant John Preddy, Connor's executive assistant, holding the other end of his wire.

"Tom," Preddy said, "Bull is your friend. He trusts you and will be very disappointed to know this."

"Sergeant, this is for *Townsend*," Lankford retorted, "and if you get in the way, I'll report what's happened here, and you'll have to answer to him."

Lankford could see that Sergeant Preddy was struck with indecision. He was a Mason and an active member of the Zamora Shrine where he associated with Birmingham's businessmen, including Townsend. Torn between his loyalty to his boss and knowing full well the power of Townsend and the *Birmingham News*, he backed down.

"Okay," he said with reluctance, handing Lankford the wire, "but I don't know anything about this."

When Lankford ran up the long sidewalk leading to his mentor's Southside home and rang the bell, Townsend answered the door in his bathrobe, though he hadn't retired for the night. Townsend often discussed strategy about the Citizens for Progress campaign into the wee hours.

This was nothing new. Lankford was a frequent visitor to Townsend's home and was present for many after-hours discussions about Birmingham's need for change and progress on topics from the need for highways, business diversity, and changing the status quo for the city's Black community, although Townsend believed, liked many, that it needed to happen gradually. His home was a revolving door for city leaders, who sat with him into the night or stood in the kitchen, often with the refrigerator door open while he puttered with tiny bowls of spicy relishes, taking experimental bites and seasoning until he got it right, all the while talking about what needed to be done to make Birmingham better.

The city leaders who passed through his door included Alabama Power Company head Thomas Martin; former mayor and current president of the county commission, William Cooper Green; and men destined to be Birmingham mayors—Albert Boutwell, George Siebels, and David Vann. The University of Alabama football hero and future Hall of Famer, Fred Sington Sr., was a frequent guest. Sington owned a well-known sporting goods store and had his hand in almost every civic venture, to the point he was nicknamed, "Mr. Birmingham." His wife, Nancy, was close to Julia Townsend and both were well schooled in everything Birmingham. They often joined in the conversations, plans, and dreams.

But this night, Townsend was alone. Without comment, he listened to the taped segment about the promised 7 percent raise, and then picked up the phone and dialed Vann.

"David," Townsend said, gripping the phone tightly, "We've got what we've been looking for. Be in my office at seven in the morning."

The *News* transcribed Lankford's recording and put a verbatim copy in the paper. Edward Harris recalled the radio ads Citizens for Progress produced:

What really happened at the secret meeting with the firefighters?

Listen as your honest firefighter asks your city commissioners, "Where is the money coming from to pay the pay raises?"

Then you would hear the actual voice of Mayor Art Hanes saying:

[What] do you care where the money is coming from? We are here to talk about raises, not taxes.

Then there would be a closing line in another voice:

Let's end this kind of corruption in city hall—vote Mayor-Council.

The six ads were the talk of the town. The radio stations got requests for the ads and some stations played them in response.[211]

City hall pressured the media. When Vann had tried to buy television ads, both stations refused, saying a change in the city government was "not of sufficient public importance."[212] Despite their decision, a week before the election, Channel 6 called to say they had sold Connor a half hour show, and the law required them to offer Citizens for Progress the same amount of airtime. The program cost $800, which CFP did not have. Vann and Erskine Smith borrowed $1,000 personally for the production and advertising expenses.

Soon after the incident at the Fireman's Hall, Townsend ordered Lankford to join him for breakfast and endorsed the concept of working with law enforcement using eavesdropping and wiretapping equipment to keep him informed on what was happening behind the curtains of the Magic City.

BIRMINGHAM, ALONG WITH THE world, held its breath for almost two weeks in October 1962 through the Cuban nuclear missile crisis standoff with the

Soviet Union. Afterward, the city turned back to its own affairs and the item highest on its agenda—taking its destiny into its own hands with the opportunity to change the city's form of government.

At the annual meeting of the Jewish Fairmont Club, Abe Berkowitz asked for the floor. He spoke passionately about changing the governmental structure. "'We'll never get any place, as long as we have this kind of city. . . . Blacks will always be outside the circle. So, we're gonna have to stand up for black people, just as if we're standing up for Jewish people. I, and members of my law firm, are going to start a fund raising. We can't do anything without money.'

"He put his own hat on the table and put money in it, saying that was all he had, but 'don't leave here until you take a part in this new beginning for the Jewish community. Please, everyone here tonight, put something in the hat. Go home without any change.'"

In fact, Karl Friedman remembered, "We did go home broke. That night we raised $600, not a significant amount, but a commitment."[213]

As Lankford remembers: "The good folks were mad about the bribe offered to firemen. And they wanted a change. Townsend and the *News* wanted a change. Women were tired of not being able to shop at Pizitz, Loveman's, or the five and dime stores without treading over demonstrators sitting in the streets, on the floors, and everywhere else. All were weary of the constant bad press and the city not having a robust future for their kids. They wanted the new businesses, overpasses, and freeways that Atlanta had. It was not a black versus white thing, Bull versus King, or anything like that. It was a change for a better Birmingham."[214]

While progressive voices and the *News* pushed for change, others pushed in the opposite direction. In October 1962, weeks before the election, the NSRP's *Thunderbolt* published:

> There can be no doubt that the vast majority of the White citizens of Birmingham favor our present strong form of government. Our three city commissioners are all strong segregationists. If they were liberal race-mixers, there would be no attempt to change our form of government to the weak and influenced Mayor-Council system.[215]

David Vann was betting the other way. He had studied the election returns of the May primary when for the first time "the black [voting] boxes and the Southside boxes and the over-the-mountain boxes had all voted against George Wallace. Wallace was unable to carry Jefferson County." Vann was banking on "putting those forces together—the liberal Democrats, the Republicans and the Black vote"—to win.[216] Quietly, he worked with Black leadership that included political leaders W. C. Patton and Emory O. Jackson and attorneys Arthur Shores, Orzell Billingsley, Oscar W. Adams Jr., and J. Mason Davis.[217] Simultaneously, a group from YMBC spoke at every opportunity, explaining how the mayor/council government would work and pointing out that the three commissioners had no checks and balances. "The same people who pass the taxes spend the money."[218] He was also counting on the exposure of the firemen's bribe to work in their favor.

But the fight was on. Connor claimed Vann had been "brainwashed in the office of U.S. Supreme Court Hugo Black." He accused Vann of attending meetings of the Greater Birmingham Council on Human Relations. "If you want your town integrated," he said, "vote for the change." The *News* ran that story in October on page 26.[219]

On November 2, a large ad paid for by Connor's campaign appeared in the *News* on page 31, asking David Vann three questions: 1. As Justice Hugo Black's law clerk, did you help prepare the briefs for the Supreme Court's infamous 1954 decision integrating schools? 2. Do you favor integration of our schools, swimming pools, and restaurants? 3. Have you ever attended and participated in any integrated meetings?[220]

ELECTION DAY ARRIVED IN November 1962. Voters had to consider all three forms of government—commissioner, mayor-council, and city manager. Vann feared that if there was a runoff, the usual "Black hand" politics would come into play and they would lose.

Townsend, Vann, and the members of the Senior Citizens Committee watched the poll results coming in mixed anxiety and hope. Stakes were high—the future of the city—and those who had worked so hard for this new, progressive change held their breath when the final returns for the special election came in. The turnout was slim and the count was close, but the people endorsed the change to a mayor-council government.

Vann called it "one of the most dramatic demonstrations of democracy that any of us will ever witness." But he added that the job of bringing progress to Birmingham had just begun. "We will have won no victory unless we now bring into our city government the type of devoted citizens who have a grasp of the vision of our city's great potential."[221]

Lankford received a $500 bonus the next day from a widely grinning Townsend. Connor of course did not share the enthusiasm. Though he had said he would not run for mayor under any circumstance, he promptly changed his mind. The progressives who had worked to get him out of office had no time to draw a breath before taking on this new challenge—keeping him out of the mayor's office while deciding who to support for the nine new city council seats. Regardless of whom the people elected to the offices, the city was stuck with the three city commissioners until April 15, 1963, when the new government would take its seat in city hall.

Soon after the election, state Democrat Party chairman Judge Roy Mayhall spoke to the YMBC. "'If integration comes to Alabama—by court order or whatever—I favor enforcing the law.' Alabamians should accept this and move on, rather than 'kicking a tree because you've run your car into it.' He later wrote a guest article in a local newspaper revealing the 'voluminous' responses to his published remarks, the majority of which were supportive." He also received negative responses, such as one that accused him of being "afraid to stand up for the white race . . . just plain NAACP scared."[222]

More rabid segregations made their point with a bomb at Shuttlesworth's Bethel Baptist Church where children were rehearsing a nativity play. The explosion ripped up the front of the church. Fortunately, no one was hurt.

Ruth Barefield-Pendleton and Deenie Drew went to check on Shuttlesworth. To their surprise, they saw their White friend Eileen Walbert coming out of the door, having arrived at Shuttlesworth's residence to express her concern before them. Barefield-Pendleton teased Walbert, a beautiful, willowy woman who had been a model in New York before moving to Birmingham, that she had "out-blacked" her.[223]

PART
Two

❧

16

Year of Infamy

"The year 1963 was schizophrenic," Houston Brown recalled. "One minute you were feeling good about race relations and the next something happened that set us back."[224]

George Wallace began his term and the infamous year with fiery words he later said he regretted, words that set the stage for confrontation, courage, and death. At his inaugural speech, he proclaimed, "In the name of the greatest people who ever trod this earth, I draw the line in the dust and toss the gauntlet before the feet of tyranny, and I say segregation today, segregation tomorrow, segregation forever!" It was no coincidence that Klansman Asa Carter wrote Wallace's speech or that the Klan motto was "The Klan today, tomorrow, and forever."

In Birmingham, Alvin Rosenbaum, a Jewish student at Indian Springs School, wrote a letter to the *News* calling Wallace's speech "the most shocking display of bigotry and short-sightedness he had ever seen." Rosenbaum received more than a hundred pieces of anti-Semitic hate mail and death threats.[225] Eleven White clergymen reacted to Wallace's speech with a more measured response, "An Appeal for Law and Order and Common Sense." The ministers represented Baptist, Methodist, Roman Catholic, Episcopal, Jewish, Presbyterian, and Greek Orthodox churches. They gave their hand-delivered statement of January 16, 1963, to the newspapers [See Appendix A]. The statement said that:

| Hatred and violence have no sanction in our religious and political traditions. | There may be disagreement concerning laws and social change without advocating defiance, anarchy and subversion. | Laws may be tested in courts or changed by legislatures, but not ignored by whims of individuals. | Constitutions may be amended, or judges impeached by proper action, but our American way of life depends upon obedience to the decisions of courts of competent jurisdiction

in the meantime. | No person's freedom is safe unless every person's freedom is equally protected. | Freedom of speech must at all costs be preserved and exercised without fear of recrimination or harassment. | Every human being is created in the image of God and is entitled to respect as a fellow human being with all basic rights, privileges, and responsibilities which belong to humanity. |

The ministers were not in a vacuum among their peers. A poll by *Pulpit Digest* revealed that of those questioned a majority of White Southern ministers favored the *Brown* decision, including 53 percent in Alabama, but "the gap between pulpit and pew was disquieting."[226]

The backlash from the ministers' public statement was quick and painful. "Each of the men received an outpouring of vicious letters, harassing midnight phone calls, and, as [Bishop] Carpenter later wrote, 'other expressions of hatred' from radical segregationists . . . and from inside their congregations, admonishments that their 'job was to tend to the spiritual needs of their congregation, not to lead a social revolution.'"[227] As Robert Powell, a White Baptist pastor who grew up in the South recalled, "Religion . . . for most white people in the South . . . was individual between us and God. We did not have much social awareness."[228]

ONE OF WALLACE'S FIRST acts as governor was to fire Alabama Public Safety Director Floyd Mann—the lawman who had jumped into the assault on Freedom Riders in Montgomery and fought off attacking Klansmen. Wallace replaced Mann with Al Lingo, a former career highway patrolman who had served as a pilot for Wallace during the 1962 political campaign.[229] According to Lankford, Alabama law enforcement professionals disdained Lingo and kept their distance as much as possible. Lingo gave himself the title of colonel and renamed the highway patrol to "state troopers." In the hands of Lingo and Wallace, the troopers became a strategic weapon to enforce segregation.

Wallace also modeled two state agencies after the subcommittee of the U.S. Senate Committee on Foreign Relations on which the later disgraced Joe McCarthy famously red-baited witnesses during hearings. The subsequent Alabama Commission to Preserve the Peace and Alabama Sovereignty Commission added to Wallace's arsenal of intimidation that could be used against any, Black or White, who might dare question segregation in the state. The purpose was to go after "all known integrationists and subversives. [Wallace] armed [the agencies] with subpoena power, the authority to issue contempt citations, and [he brought to bear] the investigative power of Lingo's Department of Public Safety." "Photographs, phone tappings [*sic*] and investigative reports were used to harass and embarrass citizens."[230] Through the State Department of Public Safety, dossiers were collected on more than three hundred subjects and "photographic negatives of more than seven hundred persons, as well as identification data and other materials."[231]

Staff from these organizations traveled to probate offices across the state to instruct voter registrars on how to keep Blacks from registering by requiring impossible tests, tests not administered to Whites. Besides the cumulative poll tax, which required back taxes for all the years a person was a resident, the 1946 Boswell Amendment added to Blacks' obstacles to voting; this was a constitutional amendment that required a person attempting to register to vote to "understand and explain" any section of the U.S. Constitution to the satisfaction of a county registrar.

Edward and Sandra Harris were scrutinized and harassed by the Commission to Preserve the Peace. They took part in a Unitarian church program where White and Black couples visited each other's homes. On one such occasion, a young Black couple arrived at the Harrises' home. All were conversing when David Vann called to warn that one of the neighbors had complained to Vann that Harris had "niggers in his house." A few minutes later, Harris observed a man with a professional camera "creeping around in the trees and grass of the vacant lot across from the house." The photographer was obviously waiting to get a shot of Harris and his Black guests. As the Harrises walked out onto their screened porch, the photographer moved into the street for a better angle.

Enraged, Sandra Harris rushed toward the man, yelling, "Stop taking pictures of my house and guests!" The photographer bolted, running up the alley behind a neighbor's house, but Harris had already alerted his neighbor, Joe Wilson. Wilson met the photographer with a shotgun and demanded to know who employed him. The response was "the Commission." Harris recalled that "Joe walked the man down the alley and back to his car and told him not to be coming around here anymore."[232]

SCLC LIEUTENANT ANDREW YOUNG began preparing for the Birmingham demonstrations (dubbed "Project C" for Confrontation), by reaching out to the only White person he knew in Birmingham. Young had met Peggy Horne Rupp during their days with the United Christian Youth Movement. Now, Rupp was with the Alabama Episcopal Diocese, traveling across the state to work with youth groups in Black congregations. The Episcopal churches were open to Blacks, though the races used denominational buildings at different times. If a Black came to the church during a White service, Rupp recalled, "They would be welcomed but seated at the back. That was just how it was."[233]

Young described Rupp as "charming" and having "the vitality one must have to work with young people." He asked if she would help set up meetings with members of the White establishment in Birmingham. Agreeing to help, she asked Episcopal Bishop George Murray to meet with Young, which he did.[234]

Murray offered the Birmingham headquarters of the Alabama Episcopal Diocese as a location for negotiations. The diocese's Carpenter House already had a history of interracial meetings, having been the location for the negotiations around the previous year's student boycotts. Though the site was considered a "safe place," Blacks who attended the meetings took care to enter one at a time to avoid attention from the authorities.[235]

17

Scratch Ankle, the New Sheriff, and Spies & Lies

Melvin "Mel" Bailey was the new sheriff in town. At six-foot-five and 240 pounds, the square-jawed, curly-headed lawman was an imposing figure. Bailey began as a bicycle patrolman in the Birmingham police department, worked his way up to auto-theft detective—where he and Lankford first met and formed a close relationship—and then followed in the footsteps of his father, who had served as a sheriff in Louisiana. Bailey ran for sheriff of Jefferson County in 1962 and took office in January 1963. At that time, the sheriff's department was obscure, with about seventy personnel who mostly didn't wear uniforms, drive marked cars, or answer many complaints, according to Jim Woodward, who eventually succeeded Bailey. The deputies "primarily served court papers, directed traffic at funerals, and suffered embarrassment at the actions of corrupt fellow deputies."[236]

Bailey was one of a select few law enforcement officers in the state to have graduated from the FBI National Academy. With publicity help from the "braying and guitar twanging" Country Boy Eddie [Burns], a radio personality, Bailey campaigned on a promise to professionalize the department. He wanted the best equipment he could get and the services of those able to use it and teach his deputies. Vincent Townsend had backed Bailey's campaign and promise.

One lazy Sunday morning, Lankford found an intriguing ad in one of the hundreds of exchange newspaper Sunday magazines received by the *News*. He told Sheriff Bailey about his find. With authorization, Lankford called the advertised number to order the sheriff's department's first surveillance equipment. It was to be the start of a long friendship between Lankford and electronics expert, R. B. Clifton, president of ACE Electronics in Miami,

Florida. Because Bailey had just taken office and didn't yet know who was trustworthy in his own department, he gave the nod to ship the equipment to Lankford's home address.

Lankford kept the equipment at his home or in his car. As the collection expanded, he moved it all to the basement of police detective Marcus Jones's home where the two spent many hours modifying it, preparing devices for installation, listening to tapes, and erasing tapes for reuse. The sheriff had no budget for such purchases. Townsend paid for the equipment, raising money from the business community and later from Rabbi Grafman.

One of Bailey's first actions as sheriff was to call on Lankford and his skills to root out corrupt deputies, including one who was a Klansman. When the sheriff had the information he needed, he summarily, but quietly, dismissed the offenders or let them voluntarily resign.

One day, Townsend told Lankford that Bailey needed him for an operation that would tie him up for a while. "I'll cover for you with the city desk," Townsend said.

Lankford went, aware this was another opportunity for his direct supervisors at the *News* to grumble at his "side assignments." He met Sheriff Bailey at a most unlikely location—a "skid-row room" in a stretch of dilapidated restaurants, boarding houses, and pawnshops between Fifth and Sixth avenues on Twenty-sixth Street North, across from the railway terminal station. The area was home to the down-and-out and a shady criminal element and was known to locals as "Scratch Ankle." The principal attraction of the grimy boarding section on the second floor of Jeb's Seafood was that it overlooked The Corral, a cafe notorious for its unsavory clientele. Lankford had already installed a tiny transmitter inside a pay telephone located inside the cafe.

Bailey introduced Lankford to the stern-faced David Orange from the Bessemer Division of the sheriff's department. A former Birmingham police officer, Orange rose rapidly under Bailey, eventually becoming a major and still later a two-term president of the Jefferson County Commission. He and Lankford became lifelong friends.. To Lankford at the time, Orange seemed more like "a serious-acting federal agent than the normal sort of sheriff's deputy." Orange would later refer to Lankford as "a character without match."[237]

Bailey, Orange, and Lankford joined Lieutenant Maurice House and

Sergeant Carl Limbaugh with the Birmingham Police Department in a small room on the second floor of Jeb's Seafood. Bailey addressed them all: "What we've got here is a bunch of thieves aided by some of our fine lawyers, who are running an illegal operation right out of the Tennessee State Prison into Birmingham. And I want some people put in jail over it."

After many long hours of listening, the officers and Lankford obtained information on the next expected transport of stolen goods from Tennessee. They trained a telephoto lens on the location. Indeed, a tractor-trailer full of stolen suits, fur coats, and other luxury goods arrived, and the team shot photos of the attorneys who showed up to pick out whatever took their fancy and then left, as if they had just gone shopping at a department store. Lankford recognized one of the lawyers as a part-time city judge. The taping captured him arranging for burglary tools for the city's most notorious safecracker and bail-bond favors for the thieves.

Because no court order had been obtained, the phone-bug evidence was not legally admissible, and the sheriff couldn't arrest that attorney. The photos, however, were another matter, and other arrests were subsequently made. Bailey "had himself a secret unit up and running that would serve him well and often during the next eight years." He put Orange in charge of the sheriff's department Intelligence Unit, sending him and the two deputies who had worked on the Tennessee tractor-trailer case to Florida to train under R. B. Clifton, the man Lankford had found through an ad and who became the department's chief supplier of surveillance equipment. Bailey accompanied the men to Florida. The *News* paid for Lankford to go with them and train with them on equipment designed to bug telephone, room, and car conversations and on a vehicle-tracking device.[238]

At the time, no state or federal laws forbade wiretapping, although a federal law prohibited the disclosure of information gained through wiretapping.[239] The Supreme Court had ruled that law enforcement could not use evidence obtained by committing a trespass, and in a subsequent case, the court determined the Fourth Amendment right against unreasonable search and seizure did not apply to telephone lines outside a person's property. In response to these decisions, Attorney General Robert Jackson ordered a halt to FBI wiretapping without warrants.[240] This left the FBI to lean on partnership with local law enforcement, which could still tap phone lines without a warrant, as long as they did not trespass onto the individual's property to do so. This would be the state of wiretapping until federal legislation in 1968 clearly defined what was legal and illegal.

By EARLY 1963, IT was well known that Martin Luther King Jr. was coming to town with the SCLC to push for racial equity demands with street demonstrations. The Klan was a stirred hornets' nest. Birmingham was in the throes of change in its government, and Connor was fighting for his political life. The potential for violence hung over the city.

Reflecting years later, Orange said, "At the time, we thought that the public good outweighed the illegal [or warrantless] aspect of the [wiretapping] action. We felt that to have advance intelligence to cope with the very unusual conditions [civil rights unrest], the best was by use of wiretaps. The same rationale had been applied in regard to criminal activity."[241]

For both the police chief and the sheriff, the key to maintaining order and peace was not severe suppression, but information. With good intelligence, they could anticipate conflict and make sure they had the police presence necessary to control volatile situations.

Lankford echoed Orange's perspective: "As the operations were with full knowledge of the FBI and state troopers, as well as city and county law enforcement agencies, there was no effort to obtain legal permission from a court. All those involved felt the illegal [or warrantless] aspect of gathering advance intelligence at this critical juncture in history was overshadowed by the public good."

Neither Sheriff Bailey nor Chief Moore agreed with Connor's methods or ideals. Both supported the idea of moving toward racial equity, but they believed it should come through changes in the law they were sworn to uphold. "We were just people dealing with long-established, complex customs," Lankford later said. "There were disagreements, of course, but those I associated with, including many in law enforcement, felt blacks needed more rights. How that was going to be brought about was the question."[242]

Moore and Bailey were long-term friends who respected each other. As those who knew them attested, they acknowledged racial inequities, but their first duty was to the law they had sworn to uphold and to keep the peace. Unlike Connor, neither had any desire to work with the Klan. Bailey later recalled, "I had many identified Klansmen call me and say, Sheriff, you just give us the word, we'll take this thing and handle it if you want. You won't ever know what happened. Well, that incensed my . . . personal integrity they thought they could call and get that kind of sanction."[243]

At one point, in anticipation of the coming protests, Bailey met with the local Black ministers. "You got a great responsibility, and I'm depending on you to help keep order in this city. There wouldn't be enough police in all the South, there wouldn't be enough troops if this thing triggers to a point of . . . war, you might say."[244]

Bailey warned his deputies, "Whatever our feelings may be, we have no right to them in this situation. Our sole job is to keep peace in the streets."[245]

Law enforcement's concerns were aggravated by the 1962 riot on the campus of Ole Miss—the University of Mississippi—over the enrollment of Black student James Meredith. Lankford never forgot what he saw there or even where he was the day he was assigned to that story.

It was late September 1962, just before the city's referendum on government structure. Lankford had responded to a homicide call—the stabbing of a truck driver asleep in his cab at the Farmer's Market. At the scene, a call from the *News*' city editor came in over his CB radio/scanner: "Townsend wants you at Ole Miss to cover Meredith."

Intelligence sources in Birmingham had reported that local Kluxers were headed to Mississippi, joining their brethren across the South to stop what they saw as a terrible threat—a Black man enrolling in a White college. The situation was ripe for violence, and Moore feared a similar eruption was possible in Birmingham. Moore wanted his own people on the scene in Mississippi to see the situation firsthand and learn from it, so he sent Lieutenant House and Sergeant Limbaugh. Townsend sent Lankford.

Since the officers would be out of their jurisdiction and only observers, they rode with Lankford. In Oxford, they checked into a motel just off campus. Later, Major Bill Jones and Lieutenant Harry Sims arrived from the Alabama State Highway Patrol. Norman Dean from the *News* and George Metz, a Mississippi-based *News* staffer, joined Lankford. Even in the motel, the air crackled with tension and anticipation. Nearby, the AP had a field photo developing lab with machines to transmit their photos and reports.

Listening to his CB radio/scanner, Lankford knew when the plane bearing

Meredith was landing and when authorities planned to enroll him. Metz clued him into the behind-the-scenes deal between Governor Ross Barnett and the Kennedy administration. Despite all Barnett's public protestations, the federalized head of the National Guard was to put his hand on his pistol butt, and the governor would stand aside, allowing Meredith to cross the police lines, foreshadowing future events at the University of Alabama. With sunset on Sunday, September 30, four hundred armed and helmeted U.S. marshals brought Meredith onto the campus.

Hundreds of protesters had gathered. Lankford sat in a car with the officers, watching. As darkness fell, madness erupted. It began with a smashed camera. A mob surrounded Dallas television reporter George Yoder, who was sitting with his wife in his station wagon. One man reached in and grabbed his camera, throwing it toward the marshals stationed there, then reached into the car toward Yoder's wife, yelling, "Nigger-loving Yankee bitch!"

State patrolmen moved the Yoders to safety, but the crowd threw missiles at the marshals, beginning with eggs and degenerating to bricks and firebombs. One hit a marshal on the arm, burning him. A piece of pipe dented another's helmet. Lankford wrote, "It was obvious to us that this was no pep rally, no demonstration that would break up soon. The shrieks were getting louder, more intense. Students and persons in the crowd were armed. There were rocks, Molotov cocktails, bottles, bricks and weapons."[246]

In response, the marshals fired tear gas, covering the campus in a haze, and retreated to the Lyceum Building. Klansmen climbed into trees and fired real bullets at the marshals.

Lankford watched the surreal scene as Birmingham Klansmen unloaded a drum of gasoline to make homemade Molotov cocktail bottle bombs. Marshals returned fire with tear gas and shotguns loaded with rock salt. Students joined in, rags tied around their noses for protection from the gas, scooping up the smoking canisters and hurling them back at the marshals.

Lankford unbelievingly watched a national TV crew, unsatisfied with its footage, rehearse a group of students before shouting "Now!" and rolling cameras to catch the "spontaneous" action. But the rioting was real.

As Lankford drove across campus, a mob moved toward them, overturning a manned TV rig just in front of his car. Lankford's passengers—House, Limbaugh, Jones, and Sims—jumped out of the car, pistols drawn, to confront the rioters. Before the situation deteriorated further, a shotgun blast of rock salt by a marshal inside the Lyceum wounded one of the students.

"Here, give him to us," Lankford shouted to the mob. Hesitating a moment in confusion, two of the students dragged their wounded companion over and dumped him in the car. Lankford drove the young man to a local hospital and then returned to the surreal scene where the desperate marshals, besieged by bricks, bottles, and gunfire, were running out of tear gas.

At last, the Army marched in to join the marshals and federalized National Guard and restored order.

THE NEXT DAY, THE campus looked like a war zone—burned cars flipped over, some still smoldering, black smoke and remnants of tear gas in the air. Federal troops camped on the school grounds and just outside of town.

Reporters were barred from the campus, but history was unfurling, and Lankford was not about to let the news opportunity slip through his fingers. Soldiers were stopping and searching every car that came onto campus, so Lankford crawled several hundred yards down a ditch, sneaking past the marshals to get on campus and make his reports. For several days, Meredith went to class, often through harassing crowds, and always under escort by the marshals. Photo opportunities were limited. Getting a shot of him actually in class had eluded reporters and photographers.

On Friday, Lankford, dressed as a student, along with AP reporter Jim Boudier and Norman Dean, fell in behind Meredith's entourage, following him and the marshals up the stairs to class. Marshals yanked Boudier out of line and Dean's camera was confiscated, but Lankford's cover held and he slipped unnoticed into the classroom and took a seat.

When the teacher started class, Lankford slipped the camera from its hiding place and jumped up, snapping frames as he made his escape. Outside the classroom, he made a quick final shot before dashing down the stairs. Pursued by the marshals, he called on the speed that had earned him positions on his high school and college track teams.

Outdistancing the marshals, he made it back to the AP darkroom. Within minutes, the first photo of Meredith in class was transmitted worldwide with Lankford's credit line (for which he later received recognition and a $25 check from the AP).[247]

Townsend and the *Birmingham News* used the Ole Miss riot and failed efforts of segregationists as an example of why more Alabamians should accept the inevitability of desegregation. But the *News* editorial stirred opposing views from White readers who felt "the federal government had not only violated Mississippi, it had stained her honor [and] humbled her before the world."[248]

The National States Rights Party, headquartered since 1960 in Birmingham, took a similar stand, but with a different rationale. Under the same logo that Hitler's SS Elite Guards had worn, the NSRP's racist news-sheet, *The Thunderbolt*, declared, "God Bless Mississippi Students' Courage and Valor. Few events to save the South from 'mongrelization' have been more encouraging."[249]

Chief Moore had taken in the lesson learned from the reactions and the firsthand reports of what happened at Ole Miss—not to mention memories of Autherine Lucy's 1956 attempt to desegregate the University of Alabama and even the 1943 Detroit race riot that was quelled by six thousand federal troops. Violence was brewing—a cocktail mix of seething Klan and neo-Nazis and a frustrated Black community. As Moore later told an interviewer, "Counter-intelligence was our salvation in order to keep these people apart."

The emotional dynamite of racism had been lit in Mississippi and exploded, and experienced lawmen feared the same could happen in Birmingham. Hence, four law enforcement "Intelligence Units" were operating in Birmingham in 1963. Three were in the Birmingham Police Department: Lieutenant Tom Cook's unit, which worked civil rights and extremist groups and reported to Police Commissioner Bull Connor; Sergeant Marcus Jones, who worked civil rights and extremist groups and reported to Birmingham Chief Jamie Moore and; Lieutenant Maurice House's Intelligence Unit, which worked criminal cases and some civil rights/extremist group assignments, either with Sergeant Jones or independently, and reported to Moore. Separately, Lieutenant David Orange's Intelligence Unit reported to Sheriff Mel Bailey.

For the most part, the chief's units (House and Jones) and sheriff's units worked together, sharing information to help guide law enforcement and the city's "peacemakers," with some information also going to Rabbi Grafman and Townsend. The latter two in turn informed the Ministerial Council, the Jewish Committee, and the business community, including, one must assume, key decision-makers like Sid Smyer, although Lankford said that Townsend did not reveal his own sources except to Rabbi Grafman, whom he trusted explicitly.[250]

Lankford adroitly skirted internal commissioner/police/sheriff's department politics, working his way into positions of trust with all of them by keeping confidences, working whatever hours and in whatever conditions required, and responding when a law enforcement officer called on him to take a photograph or write a story. Although he came to regard many of the lawmen as close personal friends, for him, his role was ultimately about getting whatever Townsend needed. And Lankford was well aware the buck did not stop with his boss. "Townsend was not acting alone in his decisions to eavesdrop on Birmingham. Norm Newhouse, formerly with the CIA,[251] who ran the *Times-Picayune* in New Orleans gave his approval." Newhouse was close to his brother, S. I. Newhouse, owner of the *Birmingham News* and probably shared information with him. [252]

Meanwhile, the SCLC wasn't the only group making preparations for King's 1963 arrival in Birmingham. An assignment asked of the intelligence units found Lankford late one night standing in the street at Sixth Avenue and Twenty-first Street North with Sheriff Mel Bailey, Lieutenant Maurice House, Sergeant Carl Limbaugh, and several other detectives, at the behest of the local FBI. They were looking down the dark opening of a manhole into which Sergeant James Earl Smith had lowered himself.

Since 1956, FBI Director J. Edgar Hoover had focused COINTELPRO—counterintelligence program—on suspected communist activists, basing his authority on the Communist Control Act of 1954. Declaring the U.S. Communist Party an agency of a hostile foreign power, the law stripped the party of "the rights, privileges, and immunities attendant upon legal bodies created under the jurisdiction of the laws of the United States." Hoover ordered his FBI agents to infiltrate and destabilize the party. Because close King associate Bayard Rustin was a known party member, King was an object of Hoover's attention.

There was no evidence that King was affiliated with the communist party (to the contrary, he spoke privately against its ideology). However, the U.S. and the U.S.S.R. were engaged in Cold War espionage. In that context, the concern of the Kennedy administration and FBI was perhaps understandable, although the fear of communist influence became a Hoover obsession.

Despite that concern, Attorney General Robert Kennedy and his Justice

Department were trying to control Hoover's spying. From Lankford's and local special agents' perspectives, the Birmingham FBI's attempts to gather information were made increasingly difficult because Kennedy was "imposing regulations on the special agents and refusing to allow them even [to seek the] necessary court orders for such an operation." To get around the restrictions, agents often got local law officers to set up the wiretaps and recordings unofficially, thus the feds were not directly violating orders but simply "accepting" information.

David Orange later wrote a book, *From Segregation to Civil Rights*, in which he said sheriff's department wiretaps were known to the FBI. "We usually had two agents who received our wiretap information and recorded it in the FBI files. At times we had special agents actually sit and listen as the information came from the wiretaps to our receiver, usually located in a parked car." He said federal and local officers exchanged information and notes. When Jones, House, or Orange met with agents, Lankford hung back and was briefed later. When the local intelligence units initiated their own wiretaps, information on phone box layout came from Don Donahue, a retired FBI agent, who got it from another retired agent who worked for the phone company. Local law enforcement intelligence units later developed their own relationships with phone company security employees. [253]

The cluster of law enforcement officers peering that day into a Southern Bell manhole waited for Smith to emerge. He was as close to an expert in tracing color-coded telephone wires as the units had. The space below the street housed a labyrinth of wires, into which the FBI had run a half dozen radio-balanced telephone lines that reduce external noise. The lines ran from phones of civil rights activists and extremists, including members of the KKK and the NSRP. The lines converged at one small aluminum telephone box. Although the feds had run the lines, they didn't have permission from Washington to listen to or record the conversations. So, they gave House the location of the box and its wire pair information and asked him to have his intelligence unit record the conversations and keep the FBI apprised.

Smith, however, shouted from the depths that the junction box was not present. House was skeptical, saying "the Bureau doesn't make stupid mistakes." After more searching, the missing junction box was located on the wall of the basement of a nearby housing project building.

The wiretappers verified that the phone lines of interest were in the box and ran wires from selected pairs to a radio receiver, voice switch, and recorder. When they finished, the listening equipment was strung out on one long worktable in the basement. The tapes ran twenty-four hours, and Jones or members of the Unit would return a few times each day to swap out tapes and recover the valuable information.

Weeks later, an FBI agent rushed into the basement listening post warning of a foul-up. Sergeant Jones had left a transmitter on the frequency of a Birmingham TV station, and an old couple living upstairs reported to the FBI that over their television set they heard a conversation between a reverend in Birmingham and Dr. Martin Luther King in New York.

LANKFORD AND MARCUS JONES teamed up on racial politics situations, including White Citizens' Council meetings that were often held at the Jefferson County Courthouse. They also followed Klan figures, particularly Mary Lou Holt, an attractive woman who had been married to two Klan leaders and who showed up at meetings attended by some of the most violent local Klansmen—"Dynamite Bob" Chambliss, Robert "Bobby" Frank Cherry, and Thomas Blanton. Klan wives were normally subservient but Mary Lou seemed to be an exception; Lankford and Jones passed along what they learned about her itinerary to the FBI and local law enforcement.

On another occasion, Lankford inched precariously along a narrow eighth-floor ledge to climb through a window to get into position to drill a hole and slip a wire into a room of the Ramsay-McCormack Building in Ensley in west Birmingham. Connor would be holding a secret meeting there with merchants. Lankford's expense report for the drill he used was questioned by a *News* editor, and Townsend let it be known that from then on Lankford would report directly to him and that expenses should be approved without question. That didn't endear Lankford to the editors, but he didn't care much about office politics.

The Ramsay-McCormick adventure was a bust; Connor's comments at the meeting added nothing for intelligence or a story for the *News*. Meanwhile, Lankford's secret missions with law enforcement appeared over when FBI Special Agent William Hall reported to the *News* management that Lankford was unlawfully aiding law enforcement in bugging operations that needed to be stopped.

Townsend alerted Lankford that a meeting was to be set up with him, Agent Hall, Townsend, *News* publisher Clarence Hanson, and *News* attorney James "Jim" Barton. Lankford was ordered to sign a statement, drafted by Barton, where the *News* disavowed wiretaps and illegal surveillance. It also stated that if Lankford had ever been engaged in such activity, it was to cease and never be repeated.

Lankford obediently signed the document. Afterward, riding down the elevator to the newsroom with Townsend, Hanson, and Barton, he asked, "What do I do now?"

With a snort, Townsend replied, "Continue as usual."

On the many operations Lankford worked with the FBI after that, no one objected again to his involvement.[254]

18

Sin in the City

Lankford admired and respected the Reverend Fred Shuttlesworth and other members of the movement, including the Reverend Edward Gardner, and was friendly with the SCLC's Martin Luther King Jr., Ralph Abernathy, and Hosea Williams. Lankford's intrusions into the personal lives of a couple of other local pastors, however, left a bad taste in his mouth, as he heard them use their positions as church leaders to leverage women into their beds.

It was no secret that FBI Director J. Edgar Hoover had a deep personal dislike of King. President Kennedy's hesitancy to embrace King was due not only to the fact that a key King aide had suspected communist ties, but also to the "FBI's notorious surveillance of King, which produced evidence of womanizing." Kennedy possibly did not want to throw stones in that direction because of his own affairs. Berl L. Bernard, staff director of the U.S. Commission on Civil Rights from 1958 to 1963, noted in an oral history at the Kennedy Library that "the FBI's file on King's sex life was dauntingly thick. I do think the president was aware of it, and I know [darn] well some people in the administration were aware of it."[255]

Abernathy, King's ally throughout the campaigns, stated that King was always a gentleman but acknowledged in his 1989 autobiography, *And the Walls Came Tumbling Down,* his close friend's extramarital affairs and "weakness for women." Other biographers, including Taylor Branch and Pulitzer prize-winning biographer David Garrow, noted that King's sexual activities were an "open secret" among civil rights activists. King's time in Birmingham was no exception, and Lankford's first exposure to it was through King's brother, the Reverend A. D. King, who lived in Birmingham and was the pastor of First Baptist Church in Ensley.

Prior to the SCLC's official campaign, King periodically came to the Magic City to visit his brother and preach. He was often a guest at John and Deenie Drew's home, and their son Jeff knew him as "Uncle Martin."

One spring night, Lankford, at the request of Lieutenant House, strapped on his climbers and belt and shimmied up the telephone pole at the first junction box from A. D. King's house, his mind occupied with the barking dogs leaping and snarling below him. House, Limbaugh, and J. B. Jones moved the black, unmarked city car down the alley, hoping that would calm the dogs. It didn't.

Lankford dialed King's phone to make the connection. When King answered, Lankford apologized, saying he had the wrong number. Then it was a simple matter of "running" the metal tool between the pairs of small screw-like posts. A click over his handset confirmed he had the right pairs, and he attached the two leads from the tiny transmitter to them, sliding the antenna over a prong on the side of the transmitter, taping the device inside the plastic junction box to keep it dry, and running the antenna along the telephone line with plastic friction tape. It took only moments.

Lankford jammed his steel spikes into the creosoted-pole and started down. Just above the dogs, he took a piece of leftover steak from his gadget bag and threw it far up the alley. While the dogs scampered after the meat, he jumped down and ran to the waiting car.

THAT NIGHT THEY LISTENED for a while from the police car then retreated to the listening post on a hilltop Lankford had chosen earlier, a deserted street a mile away in a straight line from the transmitter. Several detectives from House's Intelligence Unit sat outside the van in the warm air on lawn chairs. House considered the information from A. D. King's residence so valuable, he assigned extra men to operate two shifts to monitor the tapes. Normally, Lankford and Marcus Jones would change tapes several times a day, listening to them in the basement of Jones's house, making notes and then erasing them on a magnetic bulk tape eraser for reuse. But Jones was not involved in this assignment.

Most of the phone activity took place at night, but the stakeout became a hangout where Lankford and detectives gathered to discuss the days' events and listen to the revealing and sometimes humorous conversations. Nearby, rose a water tower. Smokestacks of U.S. Steel's coke plants belched out noxious fumes that dusted the tops of cars with black fallout.

The detectives listened to telephone conversations from A. D. King's house. The operation continued for several weeks. One day, A. D. King was speaking to a woman in his congregation about his recent accident, telling her about the plaster leg cast that rose to his hip. Lankford never saw him in a cast or noticed any injury, but he recalled A. D. King asking a woman to come "visit" him while his wife was out shopping. When she demurred, asking if that wasn't a sin, he assured her as long as nobody found out and therefore weren't hurt, it wasn't a sin, but God's will.[256]

Days later, after Dr. King's arrival, amidst conversations of marches, meetings, and court proceedings, the Unit overheard a phone call from A. D. King making a date for himself and his brother with Black "call girls" working out of the post office downtown across the street from Birmingham's federal building on Fifth Avenue North.

"Okay, boys," House barked. "We're going to bust them. We wait at the church, follow them to the rendezvous, then make the arrests."

Heads snapped up in surprise, and Lankford exchanged looks with the detectives—Carl Limbaugh, J. W. Jones, and J. B. Jones. Could the city be willing to take such a risk? Who would believe them if they made that arrest?

"We'll record it and take photographs," House explained. "We don't know where they're meeting, so we'll follow, try to hear what's going on inside. But we know there's going to be sex, so we go in at the right time."

"Tom," he said, addressing Lankford. "They will probably be naked, but if not," he quipped, "yank their pants down and take the best pictures you can. [Otherwise,] it's their word against ours."

"What about the girls?" Lankford protested, "I'm not gonna take their clothes off."

Smiling for the first time, House said, "Don't worry. Their clothes will already be off. We can be sure of that." Then he added, "Boys, we're on our own. The Bureau and state don't want to go with us."

Despite their surprise at this new twist in the operation, the call for action brushed away the frustration of weeks of waiting, surviving on donuts and stale coffee. And the hypocrisy of the "men of God" had rankled.

While Martin Luther King spoke at the church, the Unit waited outside. J. B. Jones started the engine of his unmarked car as people exited the church. When A. D. King pulled out, they allowed two more cars to get between them and then followed. The convoy headed north and then west past Legion Field.

It was Friday night and a football game had just concluded. Cars streamed into the streets, separating them from their quarry.

Breaking the radio silence, House snatched the mike and barked, "All cars in the vicinity of Legion Field, 10–78. We need backup fast."

In minutes, police cars responded, recognizing the voice of the veteran House and knowing the call was important. But it was too late; there were too many cars on the road, and A. D. King's vehicle was lost among them. The operation was abandoned.

In later years, Lankford decided the failure was the luckiest break the Unit was ever to have. He realized the national media would have given Birmingham a hard time if they had arrested Martin Luther King on a "morals" charge, considering it a fabrication . . . and if they had, how would it have affected history?

19

A Vote for Birmingham's Future

Stakes were high for the upcoming election to determine who would be the new mayor and sit on the city council. Progressive Whites and the traditional Black leaders—those invested in changes via court actions, rather than direct action—feared that street demonstrations would play into Connor's hand, allowing him a campaign platform and a backlash vote. Dr. King would leave town, but those who called Birmingham home could never regain the lost opportunity. At the business community's urging, Miles College President Lucius Pitts and businessman A. G. Gaston conferred with President Kennedy, who agreed that it was important to convince King to postpone demonstrations until after the election/runoff. Shuttlesworth, normally against any delay, realized this was Birmingham's chance to rid itself of Bull Connor, and he finally agreed.[257]

For the SCLC, having Connor out of the picture would have been a handicap. They counted on Connor to create a confrontation that would garner national attention, hoping to push President Kennedy into supporting a comprehensive civil rights bill in congress. The SCLC could not afford another Albany, but this was Shuttlesworth's town and his people who would be marching, so the delay was agreed to. But regardless of the vote outcome, the new administration would not take office until April 15.

A little-remembered possible factor in the SCLC decision was that the *New York Times* and *New York Post* writers were on strike. The *Birmingham News* had a reputation for downplaying the early demonstrations, no doubt a combination of the fact that they seemed "minor" news at the time and that Townsend was trying to safeguard his city's image. Whatever the reason, the paper's coverage of demonstrations had been limited. That would soon change.

The SCLC agreed to delay its campaign until after the March 5th election. The most critical new governmental position was mayor, and the most likely mayoral candidate to challenge Connor was Albert Boutwell. Boutwell was a segregationist, but by this time (and compared to Connor) he was considered a racial moderate who recognized the necessity of yielding to court orders and proceeding with change in an orderly and peaceful manner. Boutwell and Abe Berkowitz had been roommates at the University of Alabama. It is speculation whether the outspoken, passionate Berkowitz had influenced Boutwell as Jim Head had influenced Sid Smyer.

David Vann was one of those who asked Boutwell to run. "He was an outgoing lieutenant governor," Vann recalled, "a member of my church, and a very good man. He was just part of the culture that we had, and he had sponsored an amendment to the constitution to have freedom of choice on schools. But he agreed we had to change."

On March 4, the *New York Post* resumed publication, but the *New York Times* remained on strike. Birmingham businessman John A. Williamson told the Chamber of Commerce, "The image of Birmingham and the state of Alabama is that of a state of reaction, rebellion and riots—of bigotry, bias and backwardness." That distorted image "is an image of the people who speak for us." Chamber members who went on record supporting Williamson's message calling for new leadership included Rabbi Milton Grafman of Temple Emanu-El; Episcopal Bishop C. C. J. Carpenter; John C. Evins, president of the Downtown Improvement Association; Lamar Jackson, pastor of Southside Baptist Church; S. D. Jackson, president of American Cast Iron Pipe Company (ACIPCO); Carl C. Brown, president of the Birmingham Real Estate Board; Albert L. Mills, past president of the Real Estate Board; and Ferd Weil of the Downtown Action Committee.[258]

On March 5, voters braved thundershowers. That night the election results under the new Mayor-Council Act came in, requiring a runoff between Boutwell and Connor.

Smear sheets printed "suggestively in red"—to emphasize a link between Boutwell, the Black vote, and communism—appeared throughout the city. Boutwell accused Connor of stooping "to a new low in his panic," and Connor accused Boutwell of putting out the fliers himself to have "something to cry about." Boutwell clung to his segregationist background, reminding voters that when he had been in the legislature, he had written "the laws which today successfully maintain our traditional segregation in Birmingham public schools."[259] He was referring to the Alabama Placement Act that allowed local school boards to decide on a case-by-case basis who could attend particular schools. He insisted, however, that Birmingham was "not going to be a city of unrestrained and unhampered mockery of the law"; that qualified him as more moderate than Connor.[260]

Two days before the runoff, both daily newspapers and the Black *Birmingham World* endorsed Boutwell.[261] Townsend and other progressives worked behind the scenes on behalf of Boutwell. Like Boutwell himself, his proponents walked a fine line, not wanting to alienate the White vote or cause a backlash, focusing on better government.

On election night, April 2, 1963, Lankford was at Boutwell's campaign headquarters when the vote came in. An amazing 75 percent of registered voters cast ballots, perhaps the largest turnout for a city election to that time. Connor and Boutwell each had a half of the White vote; the eight thousand Black votes tipped the scales in Boutwell's favor.

The *Atlanta Constitution* reported, "The citizens of Birmingham, Alabama, fooled their critics recently. It turned out not to be Bull Connor's town after all. A tide of political change is running in that city. . . . The turning has come in Birmingham's direction and its leadership will be felt throughout Alabama."[262]

Nine White moderates who had campaigned to open the city parks when the commissioners shut them down rather than desegregate them were chosen for the council: Dr. John Bryan, Don Hawkins, George G. Seibels Jr., M. E. Wiggins, Alan Drennen Jr., Nina Miglionico, John Golden, Dr. E. C. Overton, and Tom Woods.

A new day seemed to be dawning for the beleaguered city, but the tribulations that would set the world's eyes on Birmingham were just beginning.

AFTER THE ANNOUNCEMENT OF the winners on election evening, Boutwell strolled to city hall to visit his new office. He and a group of compatriots, including Lankford, stopped at a nearby church to offer thanks and pray for guidance. While the new mayor was at the altar praying, Lankford watched his executive assistant, Billy Hamilton, scribbling Boutwell's acceptance speech on a notepad. Boutwell would pledge to accept the future's challenge "in full knowledge of its difficulties. We accept it with full confidence in the good sense and good faith of the people, of all classes, races and creeds we represent as heads of government. We shall find the solution to old problems and new achievements."

The day of the election, SCLC leaders set up a command post in Room 30 of the A. G. Gaston Motel. King, who had been fundraising in New York, would move in the next day. The motel was close to the action at the 16th Street Baptist Church, Kelly Ingram Park, the downtown retail businesses, and city hall. Gaston, a successful Black businessman, had constructed the hotel because no upscale facility for Blacks existed before it. Interestingly, Blacks and Whites frequented the lounge and restaurant in flagrant disregard for local Jim Crow laws, but the facility was not harassed or shut down.

President Kennedy personally asked King to wait the two weeks until the actual installment of the new mayor-council government. Had King agreed, history may have unfolded differently. But he refused. The *New York Times* strike had been resolved, and having Connor still in office was the SCLC's best bet for a confrontation that would draw national attention and support for a civil rights bill. There was no stomach for waiting for incremental, theoretical local changes. The goal was much broader.

20

The Perfect Storm

On April 3, 1963, the day after Connor's defeat, the front page of the *News* carried a rare color photo of a golden sun rising over the city skyline, with Vulcan atop Red Mountain, and a headline proclaiming, "New Day Dawns for Birmingham." The *Boston Globe* wrongly noted that the April 2 election "was a revolution in itself more significant than any change likely to develop from the demonstrations."[263]

The day also marked the beginning of Project C. Dozens of protesters—many of them students from Miles College led by Frank Dukes—targeted downtown lunch counters at Woolworth's, Loveman's, Pizitz, and Kress department stores, where it was illegal for Blacks and Whites to sit together at lunch counters. Blacks also boycotted the stores, trying to put economic pressure on the downtown businesses as the Miles students had done the previous year.

The White community was "shocked" that demonstrations began the day after a historic election that promised significant change. "White moderates felt betrayed by 'outside agitators' intervening in local political concerns. David Vann said: 'This is the most cruel and vicious thing that has ever happened to Birmingham.'"[264]

Later that day, Martin Luther King Jr. and Ralph Abernathy arrived in Birmingham. It was a historic moment. Shuttlesworth had been trying to get King to bring the SCLC's desegregation campaign to the city for years. Most sources speculate that King chose Birmingham because the SCLC needed a victory after the Albany failure to capture the nation's attention. Activist Frank Dukes added his perspective:

> In the later part of 1962 or early 1963, King had come to Birmingham to speak to a Baptist Ministers conference. I was also addressing them about the [student] boycott. King, his father, and Ralph Abernathy were there and heard my speech to the ministers. King later got in touch with me and told me,

"When you think black people are ready to demonstrate, go to jail, and die if necessary, get back in touch with me." And that's how we got King to come to Birmingham. It was the student boycott. He would not have come were it not for the student boycott.[265]

What actually brought King to Birmingham was several factors—Fred Shuttlesworth's foundational work with his grass roots organization and his constant urging for King to come; the prospect of creating a more dramatic confrontation with Bull Connor that could give the movement a national platform; the building pressure on the downtown retail businesses; and the demonstration by the Black community of its willingness to sacrifice and even go to jail in supporting the student boycott. "If we can crack Birmingham, we can crack the South," King said. While King's public stance was that Birmingham was the most racist city in the South, Andrew Young admitted to Jim Jimerson that Birmingham had been chosen in part because the city's climate had improved to the point they felt demonstrations could be held without anyone being killed."[266]

That night Dr. King, his brother, the Reverend A. D. King, who lived in Birmingham, and his SCLC lieutenants retired to Room 30 at the Gaston Motel and caught sight of Birmingham police lieutenant House ducking into a room that adjoined the hotel suite. The contingent appeared to assume that House's presence was for their protection and were (or acted) surprised and pleased. King invited House to open the locked door separating their rooms, noting that this was not the sort of attention he normally received from policemen serving under Police Commissioner Bull Connor. He asked House if aides could outline for his benefit the route of a proposed nonviolent march the next day.[267]

Lankford interpreted King's reaction to a recognition of the strategic value of planning, even with White law enforcement officials, a lesson perhaps learned from the violence that had greeted the Freedom Riders. House took notes while listening but warned King that his superiors could order the demonstrators arrested, as they would be marching without a permit. Thirty minutes later, the lieutenant again locked the adjoining door, and his detectives inside put on earphones to monitor conversations in Suite 30 over listening devices planted only minutes before King's arrival.

Their recorder whirred silently to capture any conversation, no matter how low, in King's room. Another recorder was hooked to a voice switch, and then to a receiver that would intercept King's telephone calls. The eavesdroppers were not in a hurry. The powerful room transmitter had a thirty-day battery supply, and the matchbox-sized telephone transmitter would transmit indefinitely from the phone's power supply. Within hours, agents would be listening to the conversations and air shipping their reports to the FBI forensic lab in Quantico, Virginia. Lankford was told Director J. Edgar Hoover reviewed these reports with personal interest.[268]

Mayor-elect Boutwell expected to take up residency in city hall on April 15; he decried the civil rights activists as "outsiders." Both daily newspapers downplayed coverage of the demonstrations. A *Birmingham News* editorial called on citizens to ignore the protests:

These outsiders created "strife and discord" in the city's streets, and, the paper claimed, they only desired headlines and publicity. Prophetically, the *News* predicted the demonstrators would receive media coverage in full measure if they provoked the city. But at the time, their "sideshow" was "playing to an empty house." Editor Emory O. Jackson of the Black *Birmingham World* branded direct-action campaigns "wasteful and worthless."[269]

On April 5, the *News* quoted Governor George Wallace complaining he had difficulty finding the stories about the protests. Shuttlesworth, in what had to be a rare agreement with Wallace, said, "We have ceased to be page seven news. We are front page business around here." That story and one about that day's arrests from Lane-Liggett and Tutwiler drug stores appeared on page two.[270]

Shuttlesworth then led a march from 16th Street Baptist Church to city hall, for which police arrested forty-five protesters, including Shuttlesworth. The police remained "calm and businesslike," possibly because Connor was seeking an injunction against the protestors that he assumed would end the matter.[271]

Another possibility was that Captain George Wall was put in charge of the protests. Wall was tall, a veteran of the Army Air Force and nineteen years in the police department. "He kept a level head when it was not popular to be emotionally under control." Sergeant David Orange recalled that Wall had set an extraordinary example, sitting down "to eat a meal with the blacks from 'the other side' and try[ing] to reach some agreement to keep things calm. In those days it was unheard of for a white man to eat at the same table with black folks."[272]

THE FIRST MEETING WITH Dr. King that Karl Friedman recalled attending was held at the conference room of A. G. Gaston Insurance Company.[273] When King spoke, he reflected on his "failure" in Albany, saying he had learned from it. He concluded that it had been a mistake to protest segregation in general, and that a more focused approach might yield better results. He announced the intention of the SCLC to target businesses in Birmingham and his position against "gradualism." Emil Hess, owner of Parisian, spoke for the White businessmen, saying the protests were making things worse and suggesting a cooling-off period. He volunteered to lead the merchants and present a plan within that week.

King did not wait for a plan from the businessmen. Not long after his arrival, however, he made it known to Jim Jimerson, president of the Alabama Council on Human Relations, that he wished to meet with the local White clergy and members of the Ministerial Council, including Episcopal Bishop George Murray, Ed Ramage of First Presbyterian, and Earl Stallings of First Baptist. Dr. King, his brother A. D., Andrew Young, J. L. Ware, and Shuttlesworth joined them. The White ministers expressed their belief in moving race relations forward, but they worried demonstrations were unhelpful and would stir violent reactions on both sides. For them, racial understanding came from small, steady steps. This philosophy irked and disappointed King.

Although Grafman, rabbi of the Reform Temple Emanu-El, was perhaps the most outspoken of the ministerial group, he had not attended that meeting. According to Karl Friedman. Rabbi Mesch of the Conservative Temple Beth-El was "a powerful speaker for minorities," but essentially within his own congregation, while Grafman was "up front and spoke loudly and constantly."[274] Grafman's stance was held long before 1963. In 1956, the University of Mississippi invited him to speak for their religious emphasis week. A fellow speaker, an Ohio Episcopalian rector, announced he was donating his winnings from a TV show to the NAACP. In response, the university withdrew its invitation to the rector. In solidarity, Grafman declined to attend the university's program. Grafman received so many harassing and threatening phone calls in response, he purchased a whistle and blew it over the phone to discourage the callers.[275] When Grafman attempted to buy property in suburban Mountain Brook two years later, the seller refused to sell to him because he was Jewish.[276]

"Some of the Jewish people, Friedman recalled, were upset [at first] that Grafman was in the middle of controversy swirling around the demonstrations, worried he might alienate the white community." The rabbi carried the additional burden of concern for extremist backlash against the Jewish people and kept an alert eye out for any trouble in that direction through his contacts, which included Sergeant Marcus Jones and Vincent Townsend.

Although not recorded in other historical accounts, according to Friedman, Grafman met at some point with King to discuss strategies and see if they could come to terms. Grafman never mentioned this, perhaps because he suffered from the backlash in being linked to a plea for a gradual solution. Grafman hoped to convince King to hold off on the protests and marches and to sway him that the best course was to make progress gradually to prepare society for the changes. Episcopal

After a lot of "pondering and evaluating," Grafman decided to recommend a plan "to have one Negro hired in one month and then two the next month and so forth, until all of the reservations of the white people would disappear. He went head-to-head with Martin Luther King."[277]

Paraphrasing somewhat, King said, "Rabbi, we are through with gradualism—we have lived with that long enough and it's not productive. The time for change is now, today, and not tomorrow; so you might as well change your direction if you want to accomplish anything." King also told the rabbi he [Grafman] was promoting resistance rather than progress. The rabbi told him that the entire Jewish community was behind the Grafman plan, and many on the Ministers Council [The Greater Birmingham Ministerial Association], to which King replied, "Gradualism is dead," and he left.[278]

Both the Shuttlesworth-King alliance and those who embraced "gradualism" recognized that segregation had to be changed. The *impasse* was that one perspective believed—given the long, entrenched culture—change needed to be forced through nonviolent pressure and happen now. The other believed—given the long, entrenched culture—moving in increments would result in meaningful, lasting racial progress.

Those who believed in gradual change were hit from both sides. Even from his camp of immediate change, Edward Harris noted, "Good people, like Bishop C. C. J. Carpenter, who had been instrumental in bringing together blacks and whites using his prestige and office very constructively was captive of his white constituency."[279]

REGARDLESS, THE DEMONSTRATIONS CONTINUED. On Palm Sunday, April 7, police, this time with Connor present, intervened again, briefly bringing in K-9 dogs as King, Abernathy and the Reverend John Thomas Porter of the Sixth Avenue Baptist Church led another march. Thousands of spectators lined the street.

During that Palm Sunday march—Porter, Nelson H. Smith, and A. D. King—dropped to a knee in prayer. That night, another minister prayed when the Klan sent their own message about the demonstrations.

Charles Billups, an associate pastor at New Pilgrim Baptist Church and a key member of Shuttlesworth's ACMHR, worked at Hayes Aircraft. After ending his shift around 1 a.m., he and two of his co-workers were kidnapped, blindfolded, taken into the woods, tied to a tree and beaten. The kidnappers branded "Klan" onto his stomach. After Billups prayed aloud for his kidnappers, they finally released their captives.

While Billups was held captive and tortured in the woods, three men met in secret to begin negotiations. The rendezvous took place in the home of the Reverend Joseph Ellwanger, the White Lutheran pastor of a Black church on the south end of downtown. Although Ellwanger was not present, he left his house open for the visitors. Arriving at midnight, the three men—Jim Jimerson, Andrew Young, and David Vann—parked a block away and walked to the house to avoid arousing suspicion. "In this secret meeting, Young and Vann agreed that each of them would find five or six people to represent both the black and white communities for informal discussions . . . [to] provide communications channels in preparation for full negotiations." [280]

21

A Bad Good Friday

Two days after the initial secret meeting of Vann, Jimerson, and Young, another meeting took place. Jimerson again helped set it up, between A. D. King, Fred Shuttlesworth, Young, Nelson Smith, Bishop George Murray, Sid Smyer, and other businessmen, including YMBC member Chuck Morgan. They met in the library/conference room of the Church of the Advent on April 9, 1963, the same day the YMBC issued a statement urging a halt to the sit-ins and appealing to Black leaders to use their influence to stop demonstrations so the newly elected government could proceed "toward the solution of the city's problems in a responsible manner."[281]

During the meeting Shuttlesworth was chilled, and Morgan, who "liked air conditioning," gave him his coat. "I remember the fellow sitting across the table," Morgan recalled. "The look on his face! He looked across the table and he says, and I quote, 'Tell me, what is it that you niggers want?' End quote. I just said, 'Well, one thing—probably they don't want to be called niggers.'"[282]

Shuttlesworth's presence at the Episcopal Church of the Advent meeting gave a new dynamic. Although the discussions thus far had been, like the preceding boycott, focused on downtown businesses, Shuttlesworth did not feel the need to follow King's lead and confine his demands to the businesses. He demanded the desegregation of schools. The downtown businessmen could not change school policy; Connor and his fellow commissioners were still in power. Even the businessmen's involvement in the discussion was contrary to the city and state position of no negotiation over segregation.

On April 10, eight activists integrated the Birmingham Public Library. The police did not intervene, possibly no complaint was made, or because the activists were with Deenie Drew, who was so light-skinned she often passed for White. Farther downtown, however, police arrested a couple of dozen picketers. The boycott pressure on the stores intensified to the point that Black protestors stood outside the doors of the retail stores to dissuade

Black shoppers, even snatching purchases from people's arms. What made the boycotts more effective, Richard Pizitz recalled, was that Whites, afraid of the disturbances, wouldn't come downtown.

Meanwhile, State Circuit Court Judge William A. Jenkins Jr. issued an order that was to have history-making repercussions. Jenkins based his decision on affidavits of police captains G. V. Evans and George Wall and testimony from Tom Lankford that he witnessed SCLC leaders encouraging others to march downtown. Lankford identified those leaders in court. Jenkins's subsequent injunction against King, Shuttlesworth, Abernathy and 133 other civil rights leaders prohibited involvement with "mass street parades or mass processions or like demonstrations without a permit" and any other "acts calculated to cause breaches of the peace." This gave Connor the legal authority to arrest violators.

The morning of April 11, the injunction against marching was served on the movement leaders at the Gaston Motel. The march was scheduled for the next day. King knew if he defied the court order he would be jailed. Several SCLC leaders argued that King in jail would be devastating; they needed him to raise money. Several hundred people were still in jail from previous demonstrations, and available bail money was not enough.

King did not show up at the negotiations meeting with the Senior Citizens Committee that day as he had promised. Instead, he prayed and anguished over the decision. In the end, he concluded he had to march, and he made the decision to lead it, announcing, "The path is clear to me. I've got to march. . . . We cannot in good conscience obey such an injunction which is an unjust, undemocratic and unconstitutional misuse of the legal process."

The next morning, which dawned as a pleasant spring day despite a forecast of rain, was April 12, Good Friday. In the sea of Black marchers was a sole White face, Miles College professor Robert Brank Fulton. Fulton, a graduate of Yale and Union Theological Seminary, had attended the mass meeting the previous night and announced he would march.

Connor ordered the arrest of the marchers, including Fulton, Abernathy, and King. Birmingham police captain Jack A. Warren effected King's arrest. The charge was marching without a permit, ironically an ordinance passed in 1930 to "protect Negroes from Ku Klux Klan marchers."

King was held incommunicado for twenty-four hours. President Kennedy returned Coretta Scott King's worried phone call. When Dr. King later called her from the jail, she was able to tell him she had spoken to the president. King, realizing he had gotten President Kennedy's attention, said, "This gives it a new dimension" and instructed her to get in touch with SCLC executive director Wyatt Tee Walker, who had not marched and was thus not in jail and could coordinate Project C.

That same day, April 12, saw the publication of a second letter from the group of ministers who had formalized a response to Wallace's inaugural speech in January. This new letter [See Appendix A] was in response to the demonstrations and stated that "responsible citizens" were working for a "new constructive and realistic approach to racial problems." Believing that court decisions and the change in the city's governmental structure were moving in the right direction, they urged patience and agreed with the local "Negro leadership" that the best solution was to continue negotiations with them, rather than with outsiders and demonstrations.

Considering that the White ministers faced opposition on both sides of the issue from their congregations, this letter was a bold step. Grafman said that his congregation stood solidly behind him, but internal pressures would eventually force out two of the ministers from their churches. The problem, one White minister observed, was "'how to lead without being appropriated by one or the other extreme, which immediately destroys the effectiveness of your leadership.'"[283]

Civil rights leaders interpreted the ministers' use of the phrase "law and order" as code for maintaining segregation. The White ministers were not the only voices disagreeing with the strategy of King and the SCLC. Along with many in and outside the Black community, the *Birmingham World* agreed with a cessation of demonstrations.[284] Others urged King to delay demonstrations, fearing they would lead to violence. Those included U.S. Attorney General Robert Kennedy and the Reverend Billy Graham, neither of whom was branded a racist for their statements, though the White ministers would be.

On Easter Sunday, two days after the publication of the minister's second letter, another public statement was issued, this one by a racially mixed group of nine Birmingham citizens. It affirmed the "constitutional right of every American citizen to demonstrate peaceably for what he believes to be his just rights . . . the rightness of the aims of all who seek equal employment opportunities and equal access to all public facilities regardless of color or creed."

The statement concluded with a call to elected officials and "other persons of influence" to open communications with "responsible Negro leaders" and urged "all citizens to speak and act for justice honestly and without fear in their various spheres of activity." The signers were Paul E. Cosby, Joseph W. Ellwanger, Robert Brank Fulton, Harold D. Long, Louis L. Mitchell, Ervin R. Oermann, J. E. Robinson, G. L. Terrell and H. C. Terrell.[285] Unlike the ministerial letters, this statement went largely unnoticed in the media, perhaps due to the more compelling news of Easter Sunday arrests and activists' integration of White churches.

Birmingham police arrested about twenty-eight marchers though King was already in jail. The *News* reported, "There was some scuffling, during which several Negroes threw rocks at the police."[286] While protesters marched, other Black activists attempted to attend White churches. Several churches turned them away, but at least two White pastors refused to do so.

At Earl Stallings's First Baptist Church, when Andrew Young and two college-age Black women arrived at the crowded sanctuary, they were seated, along with two women who came later. Nearly "seventy white worshippers immediately left in protest. Stallings—a signee of both ministerial letters—later commented that these segregationists 'did not characterize the way most of us felt about welcoming them [Blacks] to our worship.'"

After the 1954 *Brown* decision, the church had adopted an open-door policy for any Black visitors, but until that morning it had never been tested. Reporters and movement leaders gathered outside the church, expecting confrontation, but "as the visitors exited the sanctuary, Stallings greeted Young and his group on the steps of the church with a heartfelt smile and a warm handshake." Stallings received support from many inside and outside of the congregation but was also vehemently condemned. Two other Baptist ministers stood by him and supported his stance, Dotson Nelson at Mountain Brook and Darold Morgan at Hunter Street. Eventually, however, Stallings left the church because of the internal strife.[287]

At downtown's First Presbyterian Church, the Easter Sunday visits sparked an internal revolution. The church was the pastorate for Dr. Edward Ramage, also a signer of both earlier ministerial letters. Within the Presbyterian church, the Session, an elected board of elders, governed all aspects of church life other than the delivery of the services. Ramage, trying to move the church toward acceptance of integration, had been in disagreement with the Session. Receiving advance warning about a planned integration attempt on Easter Sunday, some elders had the doors shut and locked as soon as the White parishioners were seated.

Furious, Ramage strode to the front doors and threw them open with a bang. Then he marched up to the pulpit and said, "I don't care if it tears the church asunder. I am a minister of the gospel of the church of Christ, and these doors will stay open."

Some members left, but the majority kept their seats. When the singing began, two young Black women entered the church. Ramage's daughter, Katherine, watching from the balcony, recalled they were "finely dressed, walking arm-in-arm, bravely, like two Joan of Arcs, heads held high and proud, their shoulders square."[288] One was Dorothy Vails, an instructor at Miles College who had been a student leader in protests at Talladega College. No seats were available in the back rows. Motioned to the front by Ramage, they made their way down the aisle. The singing trailed off. The Black women took seats in a front pew.

One church member slapped his hymnal closed, strode across the aisle and handed it to the women, showing them the page for the music. More people left. As a young man, Ramage had experienced destitution, hunger, and homelessness. Perhaps his past was on his mind when he prepared to offer communion. Pointedly, he said, "We welcome those who God welcomes." That ad-libbed line became a permanent addition to the church's liturgy.

Vails later told a newspaper reporter that after the service she and the woman with her were "welcomed 'most cordially' by church members. 'They had a lovely service, which we enjoyed very much.'"[289]

But the controversy broke apart the church. More than three hundred persons—a minority of the membership—withdrew. Ramage received death threats, and his family suffered harassing phones calls, slashed tires, and broken windows. The Ramage children were beleaguered at school. Although, like Stallings, Ramage ultimately left the church, the congregants who had remained stood firm behind the values and cultural core he laid down.

Although the number of churches that had allowed Blacks to walk through their doors on Easter Sunday 1963 was limited, there were some changes. First Methodist member Peggy West recalled that her church stationed men at the doors to "prevent trouble," but added, "Now, if they came to worship, that would have been different, and not long after that we had a black couple from Miles College join as members."[290]

Other churches kept their doors closed to integration.

While Blacks pushed boundaries at White churches, Martin Luther King read the ministers' plea from his solitary jail cell. The letter he read was their second (published on April 12) asking for the demonstrations to stop to give more time for negotiations and the new government. King's reply, scribbled in the margins of the newspaper and on scraps of paper brought by a jail trusty, was smuggled out by King's attorneys over many days. The finished letter, edited by Wyatt Tee Walker, wasn't published until May. It became the "Letter from Birmingham Jail," a seminal and enduring document of the civil rights movement.

King and the SCLC used his letter and the drama of the situation to capture media attention and sway the president and the nation. Though it was addressed to the White ministers who had signed their April 12th letter (see Appendix), none ever directly received a copy from King.[291]

Published in June, King's eloquent defense of the "just refusal to obey an unjust law" and his attack on "gradualism" was a bombshell. Black attorney Demetrius Newton said he believed it "pricked the hearts of the White ministers."[292] It also had devastating, if unintentional, ramifications on the ministers to whom it was addressed.

In 1957 in Atlanta, a similar letter signed by a group of eighty ministers called for citizens to obey the law, support freedom of speech, keep the public school open, and communicate with each other in a spirit of humility and equality, though the document was careful not to support the "amalgamation of the races."[293] This letter resulted in the lauding of Atlanta as a place of racial moderation, a city "too busy to hate." Birmingham's ministers, however, received a far different reaction.

According to Professor Jonathan Bass in his book, *Blessed Are the Peacemakers*: "Already called communists and 'nigger lovers,' now King and some of the civil rights activists denounced them [the ministers]; arrogantly uninformed white northerners wrote each of them harsh letters of reproach. The most hostile condemnation, however, came not from King or northern liberals, but from Southern white racists. Each clergyman experienced petty harassment and received scores of hate letters, midnight phone calls, and death threats. A few of the ministers endured bare-knuckled segregationist reprisals, such as cross burnings, vandalism, and assault."[294]

According to historian Taylor Branch, "King was aware they [the ministers] were the same 'liberal clergymen' who 'had risked their reputations' in responding to Wallace in January."[295] In that letter the ministerial group had challenged Wallace by calling for obedience to laws and courts, protection of freedoms, respect, and "the basic rights privileges and responsibilities which belong to humanity."

Bishop Nolan B. Harmon, one of the signees, lashed out at a major Methodist board for printing King's letter without any attempt to contact the religious leadership or coming to Birmingham "to find out what exactly happened." King's letter, he said, "comes out frankly for the breaking of any law a privately appointed lawbreaker may not call 'good.'"[296]

Although many of the traditional Black leaders also disagreed with the marches, many others would accept no support short of the White clergy marching in the streets, and they castigated the ministers cited as the object of King's letter. Shuttlesworth even declared that Rabbi Grafman was "a bigot." Bishop Carpenter received mail branding him the "Apartheid Bishop."[297]

In response to those extreme accusations, David Vann noted, "What the [White] clergy was saying was often unpopular with its parishioners. Dr. King couldn't understand what they were saying. But no one was more hurt [than Grafman] by King's letter. Rabbi Grafman is anything but a bigot. He was a critically important leader who had a great moral commitment to end segregation . . . [during the days] of the Bull Connor show."[298]

Episcopal Bishop George Murray recalled Rabbi Grafman explain that in defending the rights of Blacks, he was also "'defending the rights of Jews. If people are allowed to move against one group, we're all in danger.'"

Rabbi Mark Elovitz said, "Rabbi Grafman was 'anything but a bigot . . . [but rather was] enlightened, social-minded, and interested in the well-being of all peoples. People who say that he's a bigot are ignorant, uninformed. Saying that he's a bigot is a vicious canard."

'I was glad that Dr. King attained his objectives,' Bishop Murray reflected. 'They were my objectives too. But I would still object to the tactics used.' [Murray] knew how many Klanners were around and every night he 'checked the shrubbery' outside his house. Like Grafman, Murray received phone threats from callers he suspected were Klansmen. Eventually, he took his name off the mailbox and moved his children's beds from their rooms to the center of the house in an effort to protect them from a potential bomb.[299]

Despite the movement leadership's criticism for the ministers' position of "gradualism" and for not marching with them, "campaign leader John Porter . . . refused to condemn the white ministers for not taking a more active role. 'You have to be careful when you boast about what I did and what you did not do,' Porter emphasized. 'Even getting involved as much as they did placed the eight white clergy on shaky ground.' Porter said he saw 'tremendous suffering' in the white pulpits of Birmingham. 'Any attempt to address the [racial] issue from a moderate point of view and you were penalized gravely.'. . . Belligerent segregationists carefully scrutinized the actions and rhetoric of the white clergy. 'The intensity was just unbelievable.'"[300]

22

Two Mayors, a King, and a Crisis

While Police Commissioner Bull Connor asserted he wouldn't waste manpower protecting Martin Luther King Jr., Sheriff Mel Bailey allocated resources and personnel to the Birmingham Police Department during the demonstrations, coordinating with Chief Jamie Moore to supply officers where needed. Both men believed their duty was to keep order and, as Bailey later explained, "This is how . . . law enforcement must work. . . . The innocent passerby . . . they're just as entitled to protection as those who have the . . . so-called bit in their teeth, running with it. . . . We had a multisided [*sic*] duty to perform."[301]

Although the progressives had won the vote for a change in government, and Connor had lost the mayoral runoff, the three sitting commissioners refused to leave their offices while a Connor-initiated lawsuit challenged the vote and the transfer of office set for April 15, 1963. When that date came and went with the former commissioners still in city hall, it led to the quip that Birmingham was the only city with "two mayors, a King, and a parade every day."

Pleas by White leaders such as Abe Berkowitz to the commissioners to step down were fruitless.[302] Meanwhile, for White negotiators such as Sid Smyer and David Vann, further discussion with the SCLC seemed pointless until who was running city hall was established. Negotiations thus also waited for resolution of the lawsuit, with devastating consequences.

Unfortunately—or perhaps fortunately, depending on historical perspective—the police and fire departments still answered to Connor. After the election, Tom Lankford, anticipating that Connor would be ousted from office, wrote that "Birmingham Police Chief Jamie Moore, who hasn't had a chance to be a real chief in his seven years in office, will play a big role under the new mayor-council form of government." Connor's intransigence, however, kept Moore in the background and that probably significantly affected history.[303]

The combination of King's presence and the fact that Birmingham had two vying governments and no effective leadership produced what businessman Richard Pizitz called "a perfect storm."

On Wednesday, April 17, Shuttlesworth sent Moore and Mayor Art Hanes a telegram requesting police protection for a register-to-vote march to the county courthouse. Moore responded by going in person to the voter registration clinic in the basement of the 16th Street Baptist Church. "I don't have anything against your registering to vote," he said. "You know that. But if you march out of here as a parade, you will be in violation of a city ordinance, and we will take necessary action to keep you from violating the law."

Sixteen who then marched from the church were arrested.

A week later, on April 23, three White students from Birmingham-Southern—Martha "Marti" Turnipseed, Barbara McCord, and Sam Shirah—attended First Baptist Church to hear King speak, and Turnipseed pledged to join the sit-in the following day. She walked two miles from Birmingham-Southern's campus to join seven Black women at a sit-in at Woolworth's store downtown. Police arrested the Black women, but Connor had Turnipseed taken back to her college. When she refused to promise she would not break segregation laws in the future, the administration expelled her. (A year later, the college allowed her to return and graduate.)[304]

"Why was Marti so alone?" wrote another former Birmingham-Southern student years later. "Why did I and approximately one thousand other students fail to join the righteous social revolution that swept Birmingham and America in May of 1963?" Journalist and author Howell Raines lamented his youthful decision not to defy the college's threat of expulsion: "I was among scores, indeed, hundreds of students who thought George Wallace was a buffoon and the violent attacks on Dr. Martin Luther King Jr. and his demonstrators were both unchristian and unconstitutional." Alvin Rosenbaum, the high school student whose letter to the editor castigated Wallace's inaugural speech, learned about the demonstrations at Gene Crutcher's liberal bookstore on Southside and showed up at Shuttlesworth's mass meetings. After Rosenbaum's second visit, Shuttlesworth told him he was going to get himself killed and to stop coming.[305]

Seventeen-year-old Ingrid Kraus, a senior at Shades Mountain High School and the daughter of Frederick and Anny Kraus, wanted to join the downtown marchers. Her parents walked the talk in their commitment to equality, attending and hosting integrated discussions, but Anny Kraus forbade her daughter to join the marchers. Ingrid found an outlet for her ideals by initiating an integrated discussion group with Black friends she had met through her contacts at summer camps in Vermont.[306]

OVER THE NEXT FEW days, there were a few demonstrations and additional sit-ins at lunch counters, but Project C in Birmingham faced a crisis. King and many protestors were in jail. The *News* had printed the names of those arrested, and the Black community felt the pressure. The cost for participation was high. Employers fired participants from jobs that put food on the table for many families.

Not every White employer fired his workers. In Tennant McWilliams's home, Mary Martin was a part-time domestic worker. She was also a foot soldier in the protest marches. McWilliams told an interviewer, "Every time Bull Connor's people put her in jail, my parents or several of their friends, who also employed Mary, would go bail her out."[307]

With dwindling participation, demonstrations ebbed. The marchers' efforts had not triggered a reaction from Connor that would land on the front pages of local newspapers, much less attract the national attention the movement needed. A plan brewed to change all that.

Most historians credit the idea of putting children in the forefront of Project C to James Bevel and Ike Reynolds, but during those tense weeks Lankford and Marcus Jones spent countless hours surveilling the SCLC leaders. Based on intelligence gathered via bugs, wiretaps, and follow-up interviews, Lankford claimed the idea of using the children actually came from Hosea Williams, an SCLC staffer who was WWII veteran and Purple Heart recipient who had served under General George Patton. Wyatt Tee Walker jumped on the idea. In the Black Baptist church tradition, a child who accepted the Christian faith could join the church, and that tradition of youth stepping up to responsibility may have played into the decision to let them march and "testify for justice."

While the formal local negotiations awaited an outcome of who reigned at city hall, and the SCLC leadership was kicking around the idea of a children's march, meetings with the downtown businessmen continued. Karl Friedman recalled that most meetings began on an optimistic note, but tensions often surfaced. Some meetings were informational, but others focused on formulating ideas to address the issues. At one open session in the conference room of Gaston Insurance, "a lot of hollering and screaming and a modest degree of cursing" took place. There were also a couple of meetings at the Gaston Motel where some "nose-to-nose" negotiations took place when vigorous debate degenerated into personal arguments. Friedman recalled:

> That happened frequently, but it was very rare that anyone challenged Dr. King. Since every meeting had a different mixture, there were often declarations about those who were not present. Everyone always agreed that the status quo had to change, but how to do it was debatable. Frequently, the discussions were between King and Shuttlesworth. In conferences where there were white people, there was very little anger. I don't ever remember a white person cursing Dr. King, and hardly ever Reverend Shuttlesworth, who upon some occasions picked up and left and went his own way. No meeting ever ended without at least one point agreed.[308]

The regular mass meetings of Shuttlesworth's AHRC also continued. One of Lankford's duties as a reporter was attending them. Black churches were the focal point across the South to gather volunteers for sit-ins, lay-downs, marches, and other demonstrations. The evening meetings would typically entail an early fried chicken dinner in the basement, then prayer and gospel singing upstairs in the main sanctuary—preambles to the rallying speeches.

Lankford had attended dozens of such meetings, more often than not at the 16th Street Baptist Church across from Kelly Ingram Park. Lieutenant Cook's two plainclothes policemen would sit on the front row and record the meeting on microphones hidden under their coats, broadcasting the signal to an unmarked car just outside, which fooled no one, where Cook sat and listened. Lankford would watch in amusement from his own front-row seat on the opposite side as the "undercover" officers succumbed to the music, heads swaying or miscreant feet tapping to the compelling rhythm. Everyone knew they were police officers and sometimes subjected them to hoots and jeers. Shuttlesworth had tried earlier to bar cops from the mass meetings, but the courts ruled those was a public assemblies and the police had as much right as anyone to be present.

At some point, Cook realized that Lankford, as a reporter, was more welcome than his police officers and asked him to wear the microphone. He did on several occasions, dressed in the only suit he owned, a vested Cricketeer, and his only pair of dress boots. Skipping the chicken meal, he would secure a seat as close as he could get to the pulpit. The information obtained helped the police plan for the next day's demonstrations.

The quality of the transmissions was often compromised. When wearing the hidden device and sitting with the congregation, even close to the front, Lankford's microphone might pick up someone blowing his nose, sneezing, or just loud breathing. At this point, Lankford had attended over thirty mass meetings in a row. One night he had the bright idea—an idea he later classified as one of the stupidest in his career—that detectives receiving and taping the signal could get better reception if he located the transmitter closer to the speaker.

During the actual service, prior to Dr. King's stepping to the pulpit, Lankford boldly walked up to the front of the church in plain sight of Dr. Ralph Abernathy, whom he knew well. Figuring it was common knowledge that mass meetings were being taped and that it would make little difference where the actual bug was placed, he taped a transmitter to the microphone cable.

When it was Abernathy's time to talk, the minister walked to the pulpit, unloosed the bug and talked into it as if it were a microphone. "O.K., 'Bull' Connor," he said. "We know you are spying on our meetings, but it won't do you no good. We are tired of being beat over the head, Bull, tired of being kicked around and abused by the white man."

The excited audience came to its feet as Abernathy's chant rose: "We are tired of our black women working in the white woman's kitchen, Bull. We are tired of not having a say at city hall. We want freedom, Bull, and we intend to get it! And you can't stand in our way!"

"Amen," the audience shouted back.

A crimson-faced Lankford jumped up and hurried to the podium to retrieve the transmitter. With a smile, Abernathy handed it to him.

23

Children, Dogs & Hoses, Meetings

King had agreed to letting Birmingham schoolchildren meet at the 16th Street Baptist Church, but after his release from jail on April 20, 1963, he listened uneasily to the idea about using children in the demonstrations. Many in the Black community shared his concern, and there was a backlash from parents. But popular radio talk show hosts Shelley "The Playboy" Stewart and "Tall Paul" White got involved. They invited to lunch about thirty influential students—star athletes, cheerleaders, beauty queens—they had grown to know at "platter parties" where they had entertained as disc jockeys. At the luncheon, they urged the students to start a "whisper campaign" at their schools and to listen for coded messages the deejays would give out on the radio.[309]

While King met with angry Black leaders and parents in Room 30 at the Gaston Motel, unable to decide what to do, some teachers in the Black schools looked the other way while the children climbed out windows and over chained gates to listen to Bevel at the 16th Street Baptist Church. Andrew Young credited Bevel's charisma and understanding of black youth to motivating and organizing the children and training them for nonviolent protest. When the noon deadline for the march passed with no King appearing, Bevel, Williams, and Walker moved forward with the plan, and the Black youth in Birmingham responded.

On Thursday, May 2, 1963, freedom songs filled the air as clusters of youth emerged from the church and down its steps. Laughing, clapping, singing, and holding picket signs, groups headed to different targets, south toward downtown and east toward city hall. Using a walkie-talkie to communicate with group leaders, Walker coordinated the strategy. Waiting police arrested the youths, first putting them in squad cars and then calling for vans.

An agitated and unsure Connor watched. As Glenn Eskew writes in *But for Birmingham*, "For weeks he had kept his cool, 'nonviolently' arresting demonstrators, keeping the vigilantes at bay. As police surveillance reports informed him, the movement had 'run out of niggers.' But with the deploying of the schoolchildren, Connor began to crack. Captain Jack Warren recalled, "'You could see Bull moving, looking, concerned, fidgety. He was just desperate. What the hell do I do?'"[310]

When there were no more police vans, sheriff's department vehicles and school buses were used to transport the children. Within a few hours, a thousand Black youths were in jail. Connor called out the fire department to block the intersection at Fourth Avenue and Seventeenth Street, the heart of the Black business district, known as "Little Harlem." Fire hoses were unfurled that day, but not turned on. The dogs stayed in the patrol cars.[311]

At that night's mass meeting, jubilant people filled the Sixth Avenue Baptist Church, celebrating the successes of the day. King said, "I have been inspired and moved today. I have never seen anything like it."

The youth involvement shocked and dismayed the White community. Mayor Boutwell denounced "people who are not residents of the city and who will not have to live with fearful consequences . . . [of] using innocent children as their tools." Attorney General Robert Kennedy warned, "School children participating in street demonstrations is a dangerous business. An injured, maimed or dead child is a price that none of us can afford to pay." From Harlem, New York, activist Malcolm X declared that children should not be exposed to possible violence and said, "Real men don't put their children on the firing line."

King announced, "We are ready to negotiate, but we intend to negotiate from strength. If the white power structure of this city will meet some of our minimum demands, then we will consider calling off the demonstrations, but we want promises, plus action."[312]

Tom Lankford respected Hosea Williams, whom he considered an honorable and truthful man. He asked Williams if, as a minister, didn't he think depriving the kids of time in class was hurtful to their future. Hosea replied, "Tom, one day of marching in the streets for their God-given human rights will benefit these youngsters more than any schooling."

The following day, May 3, was "D-Day" for the movement. Vincent Townsend made an urgent call to Burke Marshall, an assistant attorney general in the fledgling Civil Rights Division of the Justice Department, alerting him to the situation in Birmingham. Besides Townsend, Marshall's connections in Birmingham included his Yale classmate Douglas Arant, with whom Sid Smyer had initially discussed the idea of changing the city's form of government. Marshall had also established contacts with Chuck Morgan and Abe Berkowitz and read reports from Jimerson.

Following the call with Townsend, Marshall met with Robert Kennedy, and then tried to reach King at the Gaston Motel.[313] Meanwhile, two thousand children in Birmingham were listening to King's warning: "If you take part in the marches today, you are going to jail, but for a good cause." The impatient children, buoyed by the previous day's success, were ready to march.

Connor had firefighters at the scene and roadblocks around the area and called police dogs to the park. In 1960 he had instigated a K-9 corps for the police department. Sergeant Marvin McBride directed the program, based on his training with police dogs in Baltimore, Maryland. The dogs' primary duty was patrol but, ironically, police had used them against the White mob at the bus station two years prior to protect the Freedom Riders inside. Chief Moore opposed their use in the demonstrations,[314] but Connor—still presiding as commissioner while his lawsuit crawled through the court system—overruled Moore.

Once again students spilled down the steps of the 16th Street Baptist Church in waves, headed in different directions to confound efforts to stop them. Many crossed the street into Kelly Ingram Park and toward the police roadblock. Some of the Black community's well-to-do women, including the Den Mothers from the Miles College student boycott days, picked up students from schools.[315] They drove "their Cadillacs and Buicks behind the 16th Street Baptist Church and took demonstrators around the barricades to sit in locations downtown."[316]

Earlier that day, Connor had instructed Captain Jack Warren, who headed the patrol division, to keep the marchers from crossing a certain point. Warren recalled the confusion: "At the beginning, the orders were they can't come past this point, but nobody [in the department] had ever gotten down to the crucial point of having to make a decision. That is to say [if they do threaten that boundary] to use the dogs, the hoses, shoot, or whatever. You can understand the reluctance of all these policemen. Nobody wanted to do the damn thing first. . . . There must have been three thousand, four thousand [children] out there. I mean, it was just solid."[317]

Although the jails were full and police arrested more, still more children came. Arrested youth were placed in animal pens at the State Fairgrounds (also known as Fair Park). Connor decided to end the demonstrations and ordered the fire hoses turned on. At first it was a light spray.[318] Lankford recalled, "The atmosphere in Kelly Ingram Park was not a fearful one that day. I'm sure the high-pressure water stung, but the youthful demonstrators were mostly laughing and dancing around, with occasional brief screams as the water struck them."

In the beginning the children did dance in the spray, but when some refused to move, the pressure was turned up to a level that a fireman later said would "skin the bark off a tree." Black spectators uninvolved in the demonstrations changed from a cheering crowd to an angry mob, showering police and fire officers with rocks, bricks, and bottles.[319]

According to the *News*, Connor brought in the leashed dogs for crowd control after the bricks and bottles began to fly. "Several yelling Negro youths pulled off shirts and waved them at the oncoming dogs." A dog was hit with a brick. At one point, a youth grabbed an officer's gun and ran with it, dropping it after he was chased. Police arrested a white man who tried to run his car into the protestors.[320] The crowd moved back, but then refused to give any more ground, and the dogs were brought closer. Although others may have been treated elsewhere, what has been documented is that two youths were treated for dog bites at University Hospital.[321]

Lankford was one of the many journalists at the scene:

> As for those awful pictures of the dogs biting the shirts of protestors: I was up close with the photographers . . . and the event was staged. SCLC organizers shoved black kids in front of the dogs, photographers just behind. The SCLC guys reached around them, waving mostly shirts, which they had taken off, and making taunting noises. . . . I had watched the City's first K-9 dogs in training, and they are trained to lunge at movements, guns, etc. Don't know if any [media] shots captured the waving. I was so close I could have reached out and touched the guys.[322]

One of the most famous pictures representing that day was of fifteen-year-old Walter Gadsden, who came to the park as a spectator. Officer Dick

Middleton arrested him for "parading without a permit" when he moved around the police line into the street. A photo of the encounter, snapped by Bill Hudson with the Associated Press came to symbolize the extremes to which Birmingham had gone in oppressing the civil rights of their people. It was front page news nationally, but none of the pictures involving K-9s appeared on the second-page stories of the local papers.

Lankford was close by. According to him, "at one point, a young black man was threatening Officer Middleton and his dog with a piece of terra cotta pipe, and Middleton, not knowing if the object was a weapon, let his dog lunge at the suspect, again keeping his dog on leash. The man was knocked against my parked car, damaging a rear-mounted antenna."[323]

Assuming Lankford is referring to Gadsden, photos do not show anything in Gadsden's hands at the time they were taken, but Gadsden, "who had a big dog at home, had not only thrust his knee into the dog's chest but had grasped Officer Middleton's wrist with his left hand."[324] Middleton had a reputation among his peers as being even-handed and fair in his dealings with Black and Whites. Veteran Birmingham police officer Louis Snow recalled, "Dick [Middleton] told me that the whole mob was trying aggravate his dog."[325]

Author Bill Nunnelly wrote that "Injuries resulting from the use of police dogs and fire hoses were minimal." Over the period of SCLC-led confrontations with demonstrators, from April 5 to May 9, "eighteen policeman and firemen, two newsmen, and five blacks suffered injury requiring medical attention . . . by University Hospital, where those injured were taken for treatment. The majority of policemen, firemen, and newsmen suffered bruises and lacerations from being hit by thrown objects; two blacks were treated for dog bites, one for facial injuries, one for a knee injury and another [Fred L. Shuttlesworth] for chest pains after being hit by water streams."[326]

The nuances of what actually happened were swallowed by the national media's portrayal and, perhaps rightly, faded in historic relevance in light of the reasons for the demonstrations, the underlying inequities and abuses suffered by the Black community over the centuries. The photos taken may have been framed for dramatic impact, the dogs deliberately agitated, the police assaulted by onlookers, children (as young as four) put at risk, but the fact that snarling police dogs and powerful water blasts were used against children shocked the nation. The photos and reports scalded the city with a deep and lasting brand. The eyes of the country opened and focused on Birmingham.

DAVID VANN SAT IN on some of Mayor-in-waiting Boutwell's meetings with the Black leaders who had worked on his campaign and heard his commitments to them. Vann understood that some of the Black leaders who had "worked their fingers to the bone to change the city government, to elect a new government . . . felt they had chips on the table, and that King was going to come in here and pick up their chips and claim credit for them."[327]

But Connor's aggressive reaction to the children's marches changed everything. Even A. G. Gaston, who had not approved of King, his methods, or the use of children in demonstrations, said, "I'll swap my salary for their [SCLC] expense account any day . . . but lawyer Vann, they've just turned fire hoses on those black girls, right there in the middle of the street now. I can't talk to you no more."[328]

According to Karl Friedman, the children's marches also upset the downtown merchants who had agreed to work on hiring Blacks in their stores. It took time to find someone who would do a good job and hire them, but King wanted it done immediately. "He didn't like the speed at which we were doing it."[329]

The combo of dogs, hoses, and children in a Birmingham park was an irresistible lure for the media. From across the country, they flooded the city, hungry for information and stories. Chuck Morgan made himself available as a source of information, using his reputation as a defender for unpopular people and causes. Morgan's wife, Camille, recalled that "white people wouldn't talk to the outside media, so they would talk to Chuck. People from the *New York Times, Los Angeles Times, World Press,* the *Wall Street Journal,* and *Time Magazine* would come to dinner at our house. Jack Nelson [a Pulitzer Prize-winning reporter and former Washington bureau chief for the *Los Angeles Times*] said Chuck was best source of information during the Birmingham civil rights struggle. He never led them astray."

She added that it was sometimes frightening. "We had to install lights in front of the house because people were constantly driving by. A Jewish man named Arnold Shiland drove Chuck around and protected him, because Chuck was afraid he would get pulled over." Shiland, who had a wholesale food business, was a friend who often helped Morgan with various tasks.[330]

"Chuck and I grew up together," Shiland recalled. He drove Morgan many nights to nearby suburb Homewood to converse with the media who gathered there to rehash the day's events or to discuss what possible options the government might have to intervene. "Chuck was a very smart man," Shiland said, "and very involved in politics. He could have been governor had all this [racial] stuff not happened, but for the times, he was a thorn."[331]

THAT FRIDAY NIGHT OF May 3, Sid Smyer called a secret meeting in a back room of his offices at Birmingham Realty Company. It was the first biracial meeting of the businessmen since the halted meetings in the Episcopal Diocese's Carpenter House. Vann had agreed to represent the merchants, providing they gave him "enough to work with." Abe Berkowitz, Townsend, and Smyer joined Mayor Boutwell's representative, W. C. "Billy" Hamilton. Deliberately excluded were the city commissioners and the Big Mules. The smaller group wanted to work out the problem, not protect the status quo.[332]

At the hastily called meeting, the businessmen discussed that 1) they did not have the authority to speak for the city government; 2) they did not know how the Alabama Supreme Court would rule on the municipal governance issue and when or if the newly elected officials would take office; and 3) even if Boutwell was seated as mayor, he would not control the school board, which had threatened to expel the marching students. Thus, changes had to come in the private sector.

At the Friday night mass meeting, King—perhaps sensing the impending possibility of a real victory nationally and willing to compromise to get one—backed away from earlier demands for the desegregation of parks and schools and municipal reforms and focused on hiring Negroes and removing the "Colored" and "White" signs from stores.

THE FOLLOWING MORNING, SATURDAY, May 4, segregationists hung Martin Luther King Jr. in effigy outside St. Paul's Cathedral, the same Catholic church where forty-two years earlier, a Klansman had murdered Father James Edwin Coyle for marrying the Klansman's daughter to a Puerto Rican. Undeterred by the threat, the demonstrations continued.

Administrators at the White Phillips High School downtown chained its doors from the inside lest marchers might burst in. Large high-capacity fire hoses at the park's edge blocked the route to the business district. Connor shut down the exits from the 16th Street Baptist Church, effectively stopping the demonstrations.

Violence then erupted among the unorganized Black bystanders who had gathered. They began by taunting the police. By mid-afternoon up to three thousand persons had flooded into Kelly Ingram Park. "Angry black men mockingly danced about the elms and waved their arms, daring the defenders of white supremacy to sic the dogs and shoot the water. Connor's troops obliged as the hoses opened at full force." For an hour, police tried to disperse the crowd, but protestors on the rooftops hurled rocks and brick shards on them and the dogs. Movement leaders, afraid the violence would negatively impact what they were trying to accomplish, worked with city officials.[333]

Burke Marshall, with Attorney General Kennedy's blessing, arrived from Washington to help with the negotiations. He stayed in contact with a young attorney in the Justice Department's Tax Division, Louis Oberdorfer, who had deep roots in Birmingham and was no newcomer to civil rights conflicts— Robert Kennedy had dispatched him to the scene of the attack on Freedom Riders in Montgomery in 1961. Oberdorfer's father had been a respected Birmingham attorney. "My dad," he said, "was president of the Birmingham Bar in 1928. His election as a Jewish lawyer, at the time and since, was viewed as a manifestation of the determination of the bar and the [Birmingham] community to free itself of the influence of the Klan."[334]

As soon as his plane landed in Birmingham, Marshall met with Sheriff Mel Bailey, who told him law enforcement was containing the situation. "For how long we don't know. There's a possibility it could get out of hand."[335]

Police officers and deputies, issued helmets to protect them from thrown objects, were riding four to a car. Others took up stations on the rooftops to prevent rioters from raining rocks and bricks down onto their fellows and to spot rock throwing in the crowds.[336]

Townsend asked Marshall to explain to King that the city government couldn't take action until the courts settled the election dispute. Marshall had that conversation with King. Afterward, he realized that King's phone was tapped and Townsend knew everything he had said. That ended up being "a great asset" because it established "good faith with the whites" that he was carrying their message.[337] Marshall shuttled between the merchants and the SCLC, trying to work through negotiations by representing each party himself. Shuttlesworth, believing the meetings should be face-to-face, was not happy with Marshall's presence or strategy, but he bowed to King's decision to cooperate with the Kennedy administration.

Pressure mounted on law enforcement. Alan T. Drennen Jr., one of the new city council members, recalled, "Police were under a good deal of stress; anything could have set off a very serious racial problem throughout the city." Although he was "shaking in his skin," unsure what would happen, Drennen and a friend met with Shuttlesworth to ask him to get the children off the street. The visit had no effect, but later he received a night phone call: "Hey, Nigger-lover, we will get you."[338]

For Moore and Bailey, having children involved ratcheted up the already serious tension. We saw "using juveniles as a problem," Bailey recalled:

> Number one, endangering their lives, [but] more than that, drawing them out of public school where they ought to be. . . . [Boys and girls] were in the [State Fairgrounds] yard like cattle and being herded into buses, and moved to family court, and then remanded and bused back here to a county jail to get them in shelter, get them in safe and secure places. . . . At one time I had here in this building [county jail] on the seventh and eighth floor, over twelve hundred male juveniles, black, on top of our regular complement of probably near a thousand. . . . We managed all of that over a period of about seven weeks without one added person. . . . There was no such thing as off days, everybody working seven days. Sleeping, cat napping, and just holding fire.

Bailey told the *News* that the children were being well fed and taken care of, that some were homesick and cried, but most were "having a picnic." He invited anyone to come inspect the jail or the holding facilities.[339]

Bailey and Moore met every morning to evaluate the situation to make certain police were present at hot spots. Both men received intelligence nightly from their respective "eyes and ears"—Marcus Jones and David Orange. The situation fluctuated daily, a "perfect set up for someone to do something terrible."[340]

The arrested children crammed the jails, the exercise yards, the 4-H dormitories, and the animal pens at the State Fairgrounds. Sheriff's Department detective Dan Jordan recalled being assigned to "guard the kids as the Birmingham police arrested them." He didn't like the assignment on principle. He didn't care for Connor or his methods but acknowledged that the Birmingham officers were following Connor's orders:

> I couldn't help but feel for the kids. . . . As the bus pulled away from the curb, I stood in the aisle and worried about them. They had no idea where we might decide to take them. Were they frightened? The bus ride with the children changed me. . . . The assignment taught me that all children, regardless of color, are worth loving. . . . I began to realize that . . . my badge did not really stand for justice for all.[341]

While Jordan was concerned for the children, Jeff Drew remembered how excited and fired up the youth were, writing in his memoir:

> We were like "a school of fish" ready and proud to swim in whatever direction King pointed us. It was a badge of honor to be part of the marches, and the youth "begged their parents to let them march." The night before the mass meetings and marches, King had empty shoeboxes put outside the churches. Youths would put any knives or anything that police could construe as a weapon in the boxes. Such was the solidarity and communal purpose that when they later claimed their belongings out of the shoeboxes, there was never an argument or missing item taken by anyone other than its owner.[342]

According to a film by the Birmingham Bar Association, it was more difficult to keep up the children's spirits in the holding pens when it rained. Charles Avery was one of the children imprisoned there. He later recalled that he had never seen rain like that, even in Vietnam's monsoons while he served in the military. "Thunder and lightning. Lightning hit the fence. We thought even God don't want us. We just felt as though we had lost it all."[343]

24

Miracle Sunday and a City on its Knees

On Sunday, May 5, 1963, Charles Billups—still recovering from his kidnapping and beating by Klansmen—led 1,500 marchers, clothed in their Sunday best, down Sixth Avenue South toward the city jail. Firemen and police confronted the march near the jail. Police Captain Glen V. Evans stepped forward and asked the group to return to its starting point at New Pilgrim Church. In response, Billups and the marchers dropped to their knees. Connor had cleared journalists and White spectators from the scene. Accounts vary but reportedly, as the marchers prayed aloud, Billups stood and called out, "Turn on your water; turn loose your dogs. We will stand here until we die."

Evans would later claim he never heard Connor's shouted orders to turn on the hoses or sic the dogs onto the crowd, but the marchers had, and when the fire and police officers refused to obey Connor, it was as if the Red Sea had parted before Moses, allowing them to pass. Directed into a nearby "Negro" park (now Memorial Park), the marchers held a prayer meeting until dusk.

Another miracle occurred that Sunday. While marchers prayed elsewhere, four White Birmingham churches—St. Paul's Catholic, First Presbyterian, Sixth Avenue Presbyterian, and Grace Episcopal—welcomed Black worshipers.

Also that day, YMBC members David Vann and Erskine Smith met with Burke Marshall and Sid Smyer and a cadre of merchants, who understandably were reluctant to make any concessions while Connor was still claiming to hold office, lest Connor make good his threats to shut down their businesses and arrest them for violating municipal segregation laws. The downtown merchants felt they bore the full weight of the demonstrations, and that other Birmingham businesses needed to step up or at least stand behind them. They finally agreed to consider the negotiations if they had the backing of the Chamber's Senior Citizens Committee.[344]

Getting that backing would be a daunting hurdle. For the eighty-nine members of the Committee, it would mean putting themselves, their families, and their businesses at risk of a backlash. Marshall called Attorney General Robert Kennedy and asked for assistance persuading the Committee to meet and discuss the impasse. Both the attorney general and the president joined other senior government officials over a two-day period making personal calls to the committee members.

DR. KING, MEANWHILE, WAS preaching at Ebenezer Baptist in Atlanta on Sunday, the 5th. He returned to Birmingham on Monday, the 6th, for a fruitless meeting with Burke Marshall where Marshall tried to convince him to call off the marches, conveying Robert Kennedy's concern about the building potential for violence. But hundreds more children still took to the streets that day. By late Monday night, Smyer and the Senior Citizens Committee representatives, fearing the building impetus, proposed a compromise—if the marches stopped, the downtown businesses would desegregate department stores and lunch counters. Perhaps finally feeling in power, the Project C leaders declined, calling the offering "too little too late." Other issues were important to them, particularly to Shuttlesworth and his followers: desegregation of schools, the hiring of Black police officers, and most critically, the people still in jail. None of those were issues the business community could fix.

Monday night's mass meeting, spurred by renewed excitement, was attended by so many people that it spilled over to two other churches, reversing waning participation from the previous weeks. Joseph Ellwanger, the pastor at the Black St. Paul's Lutheran Church, was often the only White face at the meetings, other than the detectives and Lankford.

A new strategy sent the city center to its knees on Tuesday, May 7. Students left the 16th Street Baptist Church and marched around Kelly Ingram Park. Hundreds more emerged through the church doors, taking off in different directions. Spectators joined them, overrunning traffic barricades and firemen. Thousands congregated on Twentieth Street, the heart of downtown, winding in and out of stores, some singing or kneeling in prayer on the sidewalk. Historian Glenn Eskew wrote, "Powerless to act, policemen stood by helplessly as civil order collapsed in the heart of the city."[345]

While masses crowded downtown streets, representatives of U.S. Steel Corporation and the United Steelworkers looked down from the windows of the Steiner Building onto the commotion. Howard Strevel and Reuben

Farr represented the Steelworkers. C. Thomas Spivey represented the powerful U.S. Steel Corporation, owned by northern interests. Black and White workers in the same positions at U.S. Steel received equal pay, but Blacks were not promoted to the top jobs. The union men in the Steiner Building that day were completing an agreement to "end the racial division of labor at the city's huge steel factory."[346]

"The clashes [on the streets below their window] caused Farr to hesitate. He suggested that they 'back off' for a bit because there would be 'hell to pay'" as a result of their agreement. Strevel, his fellow union representative, replied, 'If we back off now, we are through.'" They pushed forward.

Since *Brown,* race had been cast as a civil liberties issue—"the right to equal schooling, to vote, to serve on juries in the South—not an economic one."[347] But the union reps knew that a level playing field for jobs was critical, and they turned back to the table. As union lawyer Buddy Cooper recalled, "while there was this great conflict with the merchants, we were trying hard to get our job done where it really counted."[348]

On the street negotiations, the calls from the Kennedys had accomplished what had seemed impossible—gathering the entire Senior Citizens Committee in two days. That Tuesday afternoon, Burke Marshall and the Committee assembled in a wood-paneled conference room at the Chamber of Commerce. Eskew wrote that White "presidents of banks, industries, major businesses and utilities, editors of newspapers, and partners in prestigious law firms—grimly greeted each other with reserved familiarity. . . . Leaning over to Vann, Marshall said: 'I don't think I'll ever see a city sit down with itself like I'm seeing today.'"[349] In a later interview, Marshall told journalist Anthony Lewis, "There were fire engines going by all the time outside, sirens screaming. Reports would come in from the police chief and the sheriff that they didn't think they could handle the situation for more than a few hours. It was very tense."[350]

Vincent Townsend was, of course, at these meetings, though he preferred to wield his influence behind the scenes. Another quiet but influential progressive influence was Alabama Power Company President Thomas Martin, a national leader in the electric industry.

After former mayor Cooper Green called the meeting to order, former governor Frank M. Dixon, a World War I veteran and Dixiecrat, declared they "should immediately, right then and there, call the governor and get martial law declared and send in the troops and suppress the whole business."[351] Smyer quickly suggested compromise was a better answer. Encouraged by Smyer and Marshall, the committee discussed the issues. Smyer recalled, "Person after person just got up and said, 'Gentlemen, we've got to get this thing straight. . . . ' It was a dollar-and-cents thing. 'If we're going to have a good business in Birmingham, we better change our way of living.'"[352]

The committee, with only two or three dissents, voted to support negotiations.[353] Attorney Vann would represent the downtown merchants, Smyer and a few select others would speak for the Senior Citizens Committee, and a representative of new Mayor Boutwell's office would represent the city government with hope that the courts would soon resolve the issue of conflicting governments.

While the committee met, Alabama Public Safety Director Al Lingo had increased state troopers on Birmingham's streets from 250 to 600, arming them with "submachine guns, sawed-off shotguns, carbines, and tear gas." Brigadier General Henry V. Graham appeared in the city to assess the need for the Alabama National Guard. President Kennedy put the Second Infantry Division at Fort Benning, Georgia, on alert. He also contacted the former public safety director and veteran of the 1961 Montgomery Freedom Riders attack, Floyd Mann, asking for his help.[354]

Law enforcement was on edge, fearing the forces that were building—the Klan and Nazi elements and the Blacks whose frustrations might erupt beyond the peaceful boundaries set down by their leaders, especially if police were not present to keep them apart. Lankford, Marcus Jones, and Lieutenant House kept long hours listening on their devices and gathering intelligence to keep Chief Moore, Sheriff Bailey, and the FBI informed.

LATE THAT AFTERNOON, MORE children marched out of 16th Street Baptist Church despite warnings that armed state troopers were in place and that the children would be walking into danger. Black bystanders hurled rocks at officers and firemen. Bull Connor put a lightly armored urban assault vehicle on the streets. Firemen blasted water from their hoses, while angry bystanders taunted, "Bring on the dogs!"[355]

Bailey's deputies joined Birmingham police, as did officers from surrounding municipalities and a "posse of irregulars" led by Sheriff Jim Clark of Dallas

County. The combined law enforcement beat back the rioting mob.

Through the chaos, the Reverend A. D. King walked with Birmingham Police Captain George Wall down 16th Street, asking protesters to go home. "You're not helping our cause," he told them.

Eventually, the crowd drew back.

Shuttlesworth emerged from the 16th Street Baptist Church and heard someone shout, "Let's put some water on the reverend!" The powerful spray knocked him off his feet and into a brick wall, and he was hospitalized at Holy Family Community Hospital.

When Connor arrived on the scene, the ambulance had just left and he remarked, "I waited a week to see Shuttlesworth get hit with a hose. I'm sorry I missed it . . . I wish they'd carried him away in a hearse."

As firemen pumped water out of the church basement, Captain Glenn V. Evans wondered, "What does it all accomplish? What do we hope to do here by doing these kinds of things?"[356]

Smyer requested an emergency meeting with the two claiming to be mayor—Boutwell and Hanes—and Moore, Bailey, Lingo, Connor, and their staff officers. The meeting took place in Moore's office. While the streets boiled outside, the "mayors" accused each other of usurping the other's authority:

"'Get the hell out of here, you're not mayor.'"

"'You aren't either.'"

Bailey intervened. Not only was the sheriff physically imposing, he had the legal authority to commandeer law enforcement functions. Standing between Boutwell and Hanes, he said, "'Gentlemen, I want to tell you something. And it's regrettable I have to say this to two men of such esteem. As sheriff, I'm gonna have to come over here and take over this matter of policing this city. We have a crisis on our hands.' . . . Both of them apologized and immediately left the room."[357]

Bailey informed Smyer that the situation "could erupt in a holocaust should a spark be struck."[358] This was precisely what the moderates and "gradualists" on both sides had always feared would happen.

Birmingham News PUBLISHER CLARENCE Hanson sent a telegram to the White House: "Mr. President, if these were white marches, demonstrations, open defiance of uniformed law officers, we believe your administration would have taken vigorous action to discourage them. Our aim is the restoration of domestic tranquility, cessation of open disruption, and provision of a basis for calm negotiation toward concrete results which will answer legitimate complaints of Birmingham Negroes."[359]

But President Kennedy did not want to bring in troops or federalize the National Guard. He had put his influence behind the negotiations and had Burke Marshall on the scene to lend whatever sway the federal government had in the volatile situation. That evening, the negotiators met secretly downtown in the office of Black insurance businessman John Drew. Drew's relationship with Martin Luther King Jr. dated to their undergraduate years at Morehouse College.[360]

Those present at the volatile May 6 night meeting included Smyer, Vann, Boutwell's executive secretary Billy Hamilton, Roper Dial of Sears, Roebuck, and Andrew Young. Shuttlesworth was still hospitalized. Young proposed a settlement. For three hours, details were discussed regarding desegregation and hiring, but the businessmen balked on dropping charges against demonstrators and removing segregation ordinances—those required government authority. A smaller group, which included Burke Marshall, Smyer, Vann, Young, Wyatt Tee Walker, and Chuck Morgan continued the discussions late into the night at the Drews' home on Dynamite Hill.[361]

According to Young, "Debate centered on two issues: first, how to word the biracial agreement so as not to embarrass the white negotiators, to give them an opportunity to save face while convincing the Black community that it had achieved something; and second, how to deal with the thousands of arrested school children if the city refused to drop the charges." Walker ranted and raved. Young played the role of calm facilitator, although he was no neutral party. At one point, according to Young, "Vann broke down and cried. The whole city was hanging on these negotiations."[362]

The informal gathering broke up at three in the morning with the "white businessmen in general accepting the watered-down demands of the movement."[363] There was still no answer to the problem of the jailed demonstrators, and the negotiators faced the uncertain task of getting agreement from their respective groups.

25

The Invasion of the Rabbis

While the negotiators debated into the night and early morning, Karl Friedman was awakened by a call from a friend and client who was in New York on a buying trip: "You got a problem coming. Some young rabbis, members from the Jewish Theological Seminary and the Rabbinical Assembly, are coming to Birmingham to witness for the black people. They're on the plane now. We have pictures of them on the plane."[364]

Jewish tradition called for rabbis, before coming into a community, to check with its elders to find out what was going on. Friedman knew that intense negotiations were ongoing. Surprised by the violation of protocol and fearful that the delicate situation in Birmingham could be upended, Friedman called several people in leadership positions to alert them.

The rabbis from New York equated what they perceived as silence on segregation from the Birmingham Jewish community with the atrocities of the Nazi Holocaust. They came to Birmingham as a "testimony on behalf of human rights and dignity." Birmingham Jewish leaders understood this, but the downtown Jewish merchants were in the middle of the controversy. The negotiators walked a precarious line and feared that the rabbis' presence and message would thrust the Jewish community into a position that could affect the negotiators' ability to bring everyone to the table.[365]

In addition, the local community saw these rabbis—the "nineteen messiahs," as they came to be called—as outsiders who risked nothing by coming to Birmingham but could put the local Jewish residents at grave risk.

The fears were not unjustified. The Jewish community was on high alert. In reaction to demonstrations, the Klan had just held a large rally on the city's outskirts. A "stepped-up campaign to distribute anti-Jewish and anti-Negro hate literature" had nerves on edge. Synagogues and the Jewish Community Center had hired off-duty law enforcement to keep watch.[366]

A group of local Jewish leaders that included Rabbi Milton Grafman,

Friedman, Dorah Sterne, Abe Berkowitz, and William P. Engel hastily convened to meet the New Yorkers at the airport on May 8, 1963. They hoped to greet the rabbis and explain the local concerns and the extremely volatile local situation. Their goal was to talk the rabbis into returning home or at least not participating in civil disobedience.

It was raining when the plane arrived at 2:15 a.m. on the city's single runway. The local contingent had no problem recognizing the rabbis, but a welcoming committee of Black activists had already encircled them.

When the Jewish group could at last get through, Berkowitz acted as spokesman. He asked that the rabbis speak to someone from the local Jewish community before they took part in any demonstrations. According to Friedman, the visiting rabbis' leader was Richard Rubenstein. "He was outspoken, angry, unpleasant, and disrespectful." Grafman—who knew the rabbis would be aware of an advertised six-month vacancy at Birmingham's conservative Temple Beth El—responded to Rubenstein's tirade by asking, "If you are so interested in changing things in Birmingham, why don't you become a rabbi here?"

According to Friedman, the New York rabbis:

> . . . split up. Half of them came with us, back to my office, and we started talking about the problems. We said, "Look, we're not deterring you from coming to witness anything. We want you to know what you are walking into."
>
> Well, the ones who went with us asked good questions, said what they thought, and we differed with some and agreed with some. And mostly what we agreed about was the timing was wrong.
>
> The others scattered around town, and they headquartered themselves at the A. G. Gaston Motel. . . . They decided to march with Martin Luther King and some of his Alabama emissaries, up to city hall, right up Twentieth Street. They all got arrested and put in jail. That [was] part of the plan, to get put in jail. . . and we bailed them out.[367]

The afternoon of the rabbis' arrival, two other complications threatened the negotiations. The first was the high bond set by the judge for King and the others who had been arrested on Good Friday. But A. G. Gaston, recognizing that the moment was too crucial for King to be out of the picture, posted the exorbitant bond. The second issue was local leader Fred Shuttlesworth.

That afternoon, police officers and blue-helmeted state troopers, primed for a confrontation, clustered at every intersection around the Kelly Ingram Park, waiting for marchers to exit the 16th Street Baptist Church. A crowd of sullen, restless onlookers also waited in the boiling heat. King, under pressure from the White House, and hoping for the approval of the negotiated agreement, called a moratorium on the marches.

Shuttlesworth was still in the hospital from being hosed down the steps at the church when he heard that King had called a moratorium. Livid that such an agreement had been made without his input, he left the hospital to confront King in the Drews' living room. When King refused to back down, Shuttlesworth announced the moratorium was over and headed out to lead another march.

Joseph Young, one of the Justice Department's team, stood between Shuttlesworth and the door while deputy assistant attorney general John Doar frantically got Robert Kennedy on the phone. Turning to Shuttlesworth, Doar offered him the phone receiver. "The attorney general would like to speak with you, Reverend Shuttlesworth."[368] Grudgingly, Shuttlesworth took the phone, and Kennedy convinced him that all the progress made would be jeopardized should the marches continue at this point. King's assurance that demonstrations could resume should an agreement not be in place by 11 a.m. the following day mollified Shuttlesworth.[369]

That evening the nineteen rabbis from New York visited services at the New Pilgrim Baptist Church. They marched down the aisle in full regalia, enthusiastically greeted and welcomed by the Black congregants. Several spoke, "including Richard Rubenstein, who compared Bull Connor's actions to police repression in East Berlin. The rabbis taught the congregation a song in Hebrew: 'Behold how good and how pleasant it is for brethren to dwell together in unity' . . . The mass meeting adjourned as the activists exited the church singing 'black and white together, we shall overcome, someday.'" Though the rabbis' visit was disturbing to the local Jewish community, it was a psychological boost to the members of the civil rights movement.

Media connections of the Jewish Committee members kept coverage of the visit out of the newspapers. Most likely, Grafman called into play his close relationship with Vincent Townsend.

The rabbis left on Thursday.

An agitated Grafman said later, "I would . . . be much more impressed if the men who have all the answers to this tragic problem which confronts the entire nation, not only the South, were to take pulpits in Alabama, Mississippi, and other areas of genuine tension instead of sublimating and expiating their failure to tackle problems in their own communities by indulging in homiletical [*sic*] heroics at a safe distance."[370]

UNRELATED TO THE VISITING rabbis, anti-Semitism was an issue of serious concern to the local Jewish community. Aside from Bull Connor's remarks about out-of-state "Jewish-owned newspapers," neither Lankford nor Friedman ever heard him express anti-Semitic comments. In fact, Friedman recalled two productive meetings with Connor in connection with a publication that was feeding the flames during the turmoil of demonstrations.

The Thunderbolt tabloid of the National States' Rights Party was described by Friedman as "a hate-sheet distributed throughout the community that clearly attacked Jewish people, black people, and Catholics. In those days the [major] newspapers had racks on the street where you could purchase the paper for a nickel. Next to it was a little stand with the [free] *Thunderbolt*."[371]

Its articles used religion and anti-communism to encourage violence should the races intermingle, with passages like these:

> Segregation is not a Southern prejudice; it is an Anglo-Saxon principal (*sic*). The Bible states, "everything after its own kind" and segregation is in keeping with this command.
>
> SEGREGATION OR MONGRELIZATION? THE CHOICE IS YOURS. Completely destroy segregation and mongrelization will follow as night follows day.
>
> Most important of all is the fact that GOD IS A SEGREGATIONIST.[372]

Friedman gathered information on the NSRP, and in spring of 1963 he and two others approached Connor. "'I want to tell you what's happening to your city,' Friedman told him. 'There is a group here publishing a newspaper, *Thunderbolt*. They don't have a license from the city of Birmingham to do that, and they're operating Sundays too.'"

"Connor replied, 'Well, I'll see what I can do about it.'"

It is difficult to know what motivated Connor. His reaction after the attempted synagogue bombing was outrage. With obvious serious intent, he had the police attempt to make a criminal case on the primary suspect.[373] He considered the NSRP "outsiders."

The following Sunday, a great number of police officers appeared at the two-story residence that housed the printing of the *Thunderbolt*. They "tore down the front doors, pulled out the equipment used for printing, all the supplies and everything, and threw it on the sidewalk, and that was the end of *Thunderbolt* [in Birmingham]." The paper, however, continued to be published in Georgia, and the NSRP headquarters remained in Birmingham until 1965.[374]

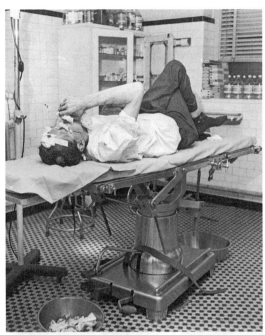

LEFT: Tom Lankford photo of Freedom Rider Jim Peck in Carraway Hospital ER, after KKK beating at Birmingham Trailways station, 1961.

BELOW: Robert Adams or Ed Jones photo of Fred Shuttlesworth (center) with Freedom Riders who survived the same incident. (Both photos courtesy of Alabama Department Archives and History/ Alabama Media Group/ Birmingham News)

RIGHT: Tom Lankford's photo scoop of James Meredith (top) in first class at University of Mississippi, 1962 (Courtesy of Alabama Department Archives and History/Alabama Media Group/ Birmingham News.)

Onlookers agitating police dogs at Kelly Ingram Park (16th Street Baptist Church in background), 1963. (Courtesy of Alabama Department Archives and History/Alabama Media Group/unknown photographer, Birmingham News.)

OPPOSITE PAGE, BOTTOM: Tom Lankford at front right, talking to news desk on portable radio and holding a fireman's hat, during demonstrations in downtown Birmingham, 1963. (Courtesy of family of Bill Berry.)

ABOVE: Norman Dean photo of Tom Lankford near Bull Connor's "urban tank" with rioter-set fires in background, after bombing of Gaston Motel,1963.

LEFT: Racist state trooper head Al Lingo at edge of Kelly Ingram Park, 1963.

(Both photos courtesy of Alabama Department of Archives and History/ Alabama Media Group/ Birmingham News.)

Above: Detective Marcus Jones, left, and Arthur Shores examining aftermath of bombing of Shores's home on "Dynamite Hill" in west Birmingham, 1963. (© 1960s/ Birmingham News. All rights reserved. Reprinted with permission.)

Opposite page, top: Tom Lankford, middle, and other Alabama reporters taking cover at riot following bombing of Shores's home. (© 1960s/Birmingham News. All rights reserved. Reprinted with permission.)

Opposite page, bottom: Tom Lankford photo at Bloody Sunday march in Selma, March 7, 1965. SNCC leader and future congressman John Lewis, with backback, is at the center of the photo just ahead of club-wielding Alabama state troopers. (Courtesy of Alabama Department Archives and History/ Alabama Media Group/Birmingham News.)

RIGHT: After cows were poisoned on a farm owned by Black Muslims, this warning note taped to a rock was thrown through the window of the home of White supporters Janet and Gene Griffin, 1970. (Courtesy of Janet Griffin.)

BELOW: Some of the surveillance equipment used by Tom Lankford and law officers during the 1960s. (Courtesy of Tom Lankford).

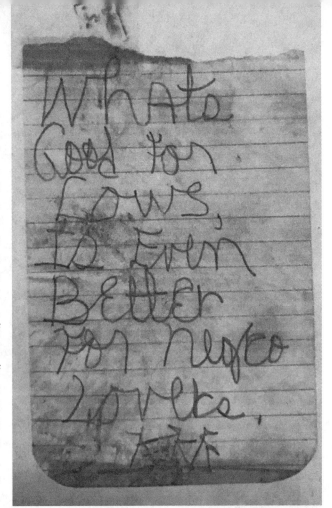

FBI Special Agent Bill Fleming, left, and BPD detective-sergeant and later FBI Intelligence Analyst Ben Herren, bombing investigators, on the steps of the 16th Street Baptist Church. (Courtesy of Teresa K. Thorne)

Longtime friends and law partners Karl Friedman, left, and J. Mason Davis were among those who charted a new path for Birmingham during the turbulent civil rights period of the 1960s. (Courtesy of J. Russel Photography)

26

'It Takes a Village'–Behind the Curtain

Meanwhile, more than a thousand children were in custody, many sitting in the rain where they were held in the open stockyards at the state fairground. Bonds were set at $500 per person for a first offense and $750 for a second. When the SCLC ran out of money for bonds, individual members of the Black and Jewish communities, members and connections of Friendship and Action, and the Birmingham Council on Human Relations contributed.

Other help came from an unusual source. Many White youths came to Fourth Avenue North near the Gaston Motel and the office of radio personality Shelley Stewart. The youths gave their pocket money to any movement leaders they saw.[375]

Karl Friedman's brother-in-law, Dr. Arnold Royal, tried to administer medical aid to the children through the fence. Friedman recalled, "The kids were standing at the fence crying, or parents couldn't find their child, and it was terrible. . . . There was a furious uprising [at the children's plight] by the whole community. I'm sure that there were many people who called or contacted or sought to remedy the situation," but Connor made it known he was going to hold the children until a court tried them.

Friedman and Eugene Zeidman discussed how to approach Connor. The two Jewish attorneys met with the general manager of USF&G, a nationally famous bonding company that normally did corporate bond work. The company agreed to issue bonds for the children if Zeidman and Friedman would guarantee them at about fifteen dollars each should a child not appear in court. Friedman said the total exposure was "more than Gene and I had in net worth together," but they committed to pay the charge and determined to go to the community and raise the money if necessary.

They told Connor the bonds were being issued and that the way the children were being held was "damning his wonderful reputation." Connor responded to this backhanded flattery. After exacting a promise that the Jews would not support any "unauthorized marching," he agreed to release children into the custody of their parents in lieu of bonds, as long as the parents accepted the responsibility to see they showed up in court.[376]

When the weary negotiators awoke on May 8, they learned that Judge Talbot Ellis, with concurrence from the police and sheriff, was releasing children on signature bonds, unless they were "previously known to the Juvenile Court."

Although the processing had begun for release of the children, hundreds of adults and children remained in jail, a key sticking point in the negotiations. Movement leaders insisted on their release, but the businessmen were not able or willing to make bail for the adults, and Connor refused to drop the charges. To make matters worse, the city had raised the cost to appeal the charges to $160,000 to $200,000.[377] It seemed an insurmountable barrier. But the White House refused to accept defeat and searched for a solution.

Sometime close to midnight, a ringing telephone woke Birmingham attorney Jerome "Buddy" Cooper. It was a surprising call from the general counsel for the steelworkers' union.

Born in Brookwood, Alabama, a small mining town near Tuscaloosa, Cooper was exposed early to the community and culture of miners, but when he was six, his family moved to Birmingham. After graduating law school at Harvard, he became the first clerk for Supreme Court Justice Hugo Black, an Alabama native and former Birmingham attorney. Black's life had arced from brief early membership in the Klan to being a New Dealer U.S. senator to becoming one of the Supreme Court's strongest supporters of civil rights. When Cooper became Black's clerk, the *Harvard Crimson* headlined "Harvard Jew Appointed By Hugo Black To Be Law Clerk."[378]

After service in the Navy, Cooper returned to Birmingham to practice as a labor attorney, where he could apply the principles that guided his life. He wanted to "even out the scales of justice."[379] Cooper litigated groundbreaking union labor cases, giving Blacks the opportunity to be promoted into jobs previously reserved for Whites.

Bomb threats and harassing, denigrating phone calls shadowed Cooper's work. They became so vulgar and nasty that Cooper told his daughters never to answer the phone. "Those phone calls are really bothering me," Cooper mentioned to a phone company union employee, who traced the source of the calls. Six union men knocked on that door and let the harasser know that "if Mr. Cooper received any more such calls, the caller would not see the light of day."[380]

When Cooper heard from the United Steelworkers' general counsel in the middle of the night in 1963, he recognized the caller. David E. Feller was a well-known figure in the fight for equality. He had helped prepare a friend-of-the-court brief in *Brown*, among other civil rights cases. But what Feller asked him to do stunned Cooper.

Feller said that President Kennedy and Robert Kennedy wanted the Steelworkers (USW), the AFL-CIO, and the United Auto Workers (UAW) to put up the bond money for the Birmingham demonstrators. Cooper recalled the conversation:

> I said, "Davy, I don't know whether we legally can do this. This is trust money that the unions own."
>
> "Well, maybe not, but the president wants this done."
>
> "Well, then we'll do it."
>
> I had to clear it with Mr. [Reuben] Farr, the [district] director, and Howard Strevel. I called them in the middle of the night, got them up, gave them this outline, and said, "We've got to do it. The president wants us. He thinks the interest of the country requires it, and I think it does. Of course, all three of us know that when word gets out, we'll be looking for a job."
>
> They said, "We know that, but if the president says that this is what is required, then this is what we'll do."
>
> I said, "I'll pass the word."
>
> I called Davy [back] and told him that it would be done.[381]

Andrew Young later pointed out that the union's trust money was never at risk because it was expected that the courts would strike down the issue on appeal. The act was, however, an extraordinary personal risk for those that made it happen.

CONTRARY TO KING'S PROMISE to Shuttlesworth to resume the protests if an agreement was not in place by 11 a.m. on Thursday, May 9, King canceled the scheduled press conference, giving the negotiations more time. Presumably he had been told the unions were working on getting bond money and that Nelson D. Rockefeller might help too. Having the bond money would take some pressure off the negotiations. Three times that day, King postponed the press conference. Shuttlesworth seethed as King made statements that appeared to back away from many of the Project C demands.

By noon, the UAW, working through Buddy Cooper, had agreed to supply $160,000 for bonds.[382] SCLC attorney Clarence Jones flew to New York where Rockefeller at Chase Manhattan Bank handed him $100,000 in cash from a huge vault protected by "a big circular door with a driver's-wheel-like handle."[383]

Late that night, the parties reached a final settlement, the "Accord of Conscience," and work began on the crafting of the statement by attorney Chuck Morgan, activist Vincent Harding, and two others, probably Arthur Shores and Andrew Young. None of the White businessmen wanted to speak, so the Black leaders would.[384]

Feeling their authority usurped, the commissioners and Boutwell lashed out publicly. The political pressure was intense, and Sid Smyer received at least one death threat. He protected the other White negotiators by refusing to give up their names, further infuriating Hanes, who called them "quisling, gutless traitors" and—apparently without a blink at the irony—accused them of "selling the white folks down the river."

The media event to announce the negotiation settlement took place in the courtyard of the Gaston Motel. Shuttlesworth, flanked at the table by King and Abernathy, read the statement: "The city of Birmingham has reached an accord with its conscience. The acceptance of responsibility by local white and Negro leadership offers an example of a free people uniting to meet and solve their problems."[385]

The compromise "Four Points for Progress" included "desegregation of lunch counters, rest rooms, fitting rooms and drinking fountains in large downtown department stores and variety stores within the next ninety days; the promotion and hiring of Negroes on a nondiscriminatory basis in stores and appointment of a private fair employment committee; the release of jailed Negro demonstrators on bond or on their personal recognizance; and the establishment of a biracial committee within two weeks."

Shuttlesworth collapsed after reading the statement and was taken back to the hospital. King promised to remain in Birmingham for two weeks and said, "We must now move from protest to reconciliation."[386]

Smyer commented that the White businessmen were "proud to have been in a position to be of service to our city, though we share the bitterness which every citizen must feel about these demonstrations and their timing." He claimed that the agreements made were not "inconsistent with plans which already were in the making before these disturbances." For two years, Smyer had been working on creating an environment for change. Though the names of the other Senior Citizens Committee members and negotiators were eventually determined and published, Smyer had refused to give them up, allowing himself to be the target for angry city commissioners and possible retribution by radical Klansmen.

Whether the new government or progressive voices would have brought about that change without Project C will never be known. By Wednesday, May 13, all but five of the 1,500 arrested children had been released.[387] Ten days after the Accord, the Supreme Court threw out the convictions of lunch counter sit-in demonstrators and "declared it unconstitutional for a state to require segregation and use its powers to enforce it."[388]

But the conflict was far from over, and Klansmen would soon express their rage.

27

Bombings and Riots

Despite the agreement, or because of it, tension continued to brew the day after the historic accord, but Al Lingo called a May 11, 1963, meeting of his state troopers staff to announce he was "ordering the troopers back to their home stations unless someone knew of a strong reason for them to remain in Birmingham." State investigator Ben Allen spoke up.

Allen was a segregationist, but he was also a professional law enforcement officer. He had been Governor James E. Folsom's point man in an effort to stop the Klan in 1949 and had later hunted down the Klansmen responsible for kidnapping and castrating Judge Edward Aaron in Birmingham. He was the most knowledgeable KKK investigator in the region, and he relayed to Lingo and his staff information from an informer who had "never given him wrong information" that the Gaston Motel, where King was staying, would be bombed at a "given hour."

"I will take care of [Robert] Shelton," Lingo bragged, brushing off Allen's warning.

Asked later what inference Allen drew from Lingo's remark, he replied, "Draw your own conclusions."[389]

An informant also called the Gaston Motel and warned the switchboard operator of a bombing attempt. The operator said he notified the police department, Sheriff Bailey, and the FBI. The county and city told him they were aware of the Klan rally and that "the motel was under surveillance and not to worry about it."[390] Wyatt Tee Walker also told local police that men had been seen "casing the hotel" and asked for the police to keep an eye on the building and other possible targets.[391]

That night, more than 2,500 people rallied with the Klan on a field in Bessemer. UKA (United Klans of America) leader Robert Shelton led the rally. Two burning twenty-foot-tall crosses illuminated the scattering of American and Confederate flags. Standing on the bed of a truck, Shelton targeted the merchants and civil rights leaders for retribution.

Klan bombers hit two sites that night. The first was the home of Dr. King's brother, A. D. Rumor spread that a uniformed police officer had thrown out dynamite. A crowd gathered, expressing their anger by puncturing the tires of the responding police cars and fire trucks. Some threw rocks at them. A. D. King tried unsuccessfully to calm the crowd.

According to witnesses, around midnight that same night, four White men, their faces "smeared," tossed a bomb from a car as it passed the Gaston Motel on Fifth Avenue North. The bomb's target was assumed to be Room 30, where King had been staying. Four people were injured in the explosion. Unbeknownst to the bombers, King had left the day before to preach at his own church in Atlanta the next morning.

Some police officers apparently knew about the bombing plan. Sheldon Schaffer, the White economist who had presented a scathing report on Black life to Sid Smyer, had gone to a movie downtown that evening with his wife, Harriet, and then they went late-night grocery shopping at the Liberty Supermarket. While his wife waited in the checkout line, Schaffer stepped to the side and stood beside an "elderly white, white-haired Birmingham policeman." A loud explosion to the east startled everyone except the police officer. Schaffer asked, "What was that?" The officer replied, "That's the nigger motel getting blown up."[392] The Schaffers drove from the grocery store to a vantage point a block from the scene to witness utter chaos. Harriet convinced her husband to leave.[393]

As THE DUST FROM the bomb settled, people flocked to the scene. Arriving patrol cars were met with bricks and bottles and shouts of "Kill 'em!"

The presence of White police officers incensed the crowd. Inspector W. J. Haley called for help from the sixty-two-man Black Civil Defense force, planning to let them stand between the police and the crowd. According to James Lay, the captain of the force, in trying to implement this plan to move the police force back and out of sight, Haley was hurt.[394]

State troopers had not withdrawn far after the earlier meeting and had quickly returned to Birmingham's streets. The sight of the troopers further incensed the mob, which ransacked the area, smashing windows of the mostly

Black and Italian businesses. Historian Glenn Eskew wrote: "Innocent travelers caught in the area attracted rocks thrown from the crowd and suffered most of the white injuries. A police officer received stab wounds. Captain Lay saved the life of a white cabbie, W. A. Bowman, who inadvertently drove into the riot and was knifed by black men. They torched his taxi after turning it over."[395]

Sheriff's detective Dan Jordan was called out to the riot. As he neared the Gaston Motel, he saw "burning and smoke curling up in the air." A half brick crashed into his passenger door, then another into the left front door, the windshield, and all the doors "like machine gun fire." His windshield smashed, he could not see and had to pull over on Fifth Avenue as soon as the rocks quit hitting his car.

Thousands of angry Blacks lined the street. He later learned the mob had looted a liquor store and many had been drinking the spoils. The rock throwers were attacking anyone who didn't have the overhead light on in their car. The existence of such a prearranged code, along with a supply of half-bricks at hand, made Jordan conclude the riot was planned beforehand. It was also obvious to him that "these violent people weren't the usual nonviolent marchers from the black churches of Birmingham."[396]

When Sheriff Bailey arrived on the scene, he saw the overturned, burning taxicab. As he approached the Gaston Motel, "hundreds of black people [were trapped] in the courtyard of the motel. They had boiled out of the rooms of the motel, out of the lobby and from around the neighborhood, and they had been herded into this fenced area [inside the hotel courtyard]" where a bomb had just exploded. Al Lingo and his troopers were not allowing the panicking people to leave.

Disk jockey Shelley Stewart approached Bailey and told him, "Sheriff, can't we get these people out of here? They're about to stampede and somebody's going to get hurt, probably smothered and killed."

Bailey had trouble getting the state troopers to understand they weren't solving the crisis; they were creating it. "Let these people go," he insisted.

It was not his first conflict with the state troopers or Lingo, Bailey recalled. "There was truly a difference between what had to be done and what the state Department of Public Safety was trying to do as a force coming from the governor's . . . philosophy of 'segregation now and segregation forever.' Likewise with Bull Connor . . . but these men [troopers] were sworn officers, and I was banking on that oath . . . deep in their mettle, to carry out their responsibilities."[397]

And they did. The crowd was released from the motel courtyard.

But it was too late to stop the violence that erupted elsewhere. An enraged mob set fire to several Italian-owned grocery stores. The flames spread to the Black neighborhood. Mobs prevented fire trucks from reaching the flames. While Blacks looted stores, three White men were seen throwing bricks through the windows of Parisian, owned by Emil Hess. As related by David Vann, "every piece of glass in Parisian's stores was broken that night. Emil Hess . . . called every glass company in the county. By the time the sun came up, every window was intact. There was no broken glass."[398]

Bull Connor appeared shortly after 1 a.m., driving around Kelly Ingram Park in his light-armored vehicle, siren wailing. Behind him marched hundreds of troopers, instructed by Wallace to shoot in self-defense. "Wielding carbines as clubs, the steel-helmeted troopers stormed into the mob, beating rioters with impunity. Some officers ran up on front porches and into tenement houses, attacking innocent occupants. They were as incendiary as the dynamite."[399]

Moore asked Lingo and his associate Dallas County Sheriff Jim Clark to leave. Lingo replied that the governor had sent him, and he wasn't leaving. "'We don't need any guns down here,' Moore told him. 'You all might get somebody killed.'

"'You're damn right it'll kill somebody,' Lingo said, slapping his automatic shotgun."[400]

Thousands flooded the streets. From inside the armored urban assault vehicle, an unheeded voice on a megaphone exhorted people to go home. When police brought out three K-9 dogs, the crowd pelted them with gravel; one was stabbed.

Amid all this, reporters including Lankford responded to the various scenes of "rock throwing and firemen being driven back from the fires that were set." Outside the Gaston Motel, he joined a long line of people trying to use the phone and was able to dictate the story. "Some reporters, the *News* said later, "who attempted to use telephones on the street in the riot area were trapped, overrun."[401] Because of the tall buildings near the area, Lankford wasn't able to reach Al Stanton at the newspaper's city desk with his CB radio. Finally he connected with a CB user in Cullman, about fifty miles north of Birmingham;

the man used his landline to relay Lankford's story to the *News'* city desk.

Wyatt Tee Walker, the energetic pastor who was King's chief of staff, came to the scene and was hit over the head with a trooper's gunstock. Before he could lunge at the trooper, the Mississippi United Press International reporter Bob Gordon tackled him, knowing what would happen if Walker struck the White trooper. Despite the incident, Walker called for peace, walking the streets with a megaphone, waving his free arm, calling out, "Please do not throw any bricks anymore. Ladies and gentlemen, will you cooperate by going to your homes?"

In response, a brick arced from the crowd toward him.

A. D. King left his damaged home to come to the motel. Witnessing the bedlam, he attempted to contact President Kennedy, but succeeded only in reaching the FBI. "You've got to do something," he pleaded, "the whole town has gone berserk . . . the Negroes are up in arms."

King drew several hundred persons into a nearby parking lot, leading them in songs and preaching that violence was "the tactic of the white man." They should "forgive them for they know not what they do."

It was a night of horror and heroes on all sides.

THE FOLLOWING DAWN BROUGHT what Lankford described as an "eerie quiet" to a war zone with armed officers watching almost deserted street corners. It was Mother's Day, two years from the day that a White mob attacked Freedom Riders at the Trailways bus station. Lankford had been at the scene most of that night, as had Townsend. Both were back in the newsroom, Townsend directing the writing and publishing of the first extra edition of the *Birmingham News* since World War II. As the newsroom buzzed, someone called out, "Lankford's gotta go to Montgomery to pick up the AP news writing award!" Townsend snapped, "Tell them he's busy winning next year's awards."

"Tom, I know it was a chaotic night," Townsend said as he rewrote the lead on Lankford's piece, "but this time next year, Birmingham will be designated an All-America City and peace will prevail." In his capacity as head of Operation New Birmingham, Townsend had already spearheaded hiring a New York public relations firm to work on the coveted designation.

It seemed a bold statement at the same moment that Mayor Boutwell was calling for President Kennedy to resist sending federal troops into the city and declaring martial law. With "Operation Oak Tree," the president had moved Army troops to standby status at the closer Fort McClellan in Anniston and had an order prepared to federalize the National Guard if needed.

Boutwell thanked the general community for not panicking. He also thanked the police, noting "their vigilance and efficiency, in spite of the physical toll upon endurance, in forty days of so-called 'nonviolence' deserves national tribute, which they are unlikely to get."[402]

President Kennedy told King, "If the Negroes begin to respond and shoot at Whites, we lose." But all those who had worked hard for the accord—President Kennedy, Attorney General Kennedy and their staff, the chamber's Senior Citizens Committee, the downtown businesses, the SCLC and local Black leaders—wanted to keep painstakingly built bridges from breaking.

Kennedy sent Burke Marshall back to the beleaguered city. Dr. King also returned. Smyer met with both. All, perhaps optimistically, agreed that the negotiated agreements were still in effect, and that their problems could be handled locally.

Although Connor and Wallace vowed to keep violence at bay, Shuttlesworth saw the presence of the state troopers as a "brutal provocation" and said, "The governor is trying to sabotage the agreement. He wants to provoke incidents by Negroes. We'll guarantee against violence from Negroes if the troopers leave. We want the city to return to normalcy."[403]

King toured the Black pool halls and juke joints, passing around a hat to collect weapons. "There may be more blood to flow on the streets of Birmingham before we get our freedom," King warned, "but let it be our blood instead of our white brother."[404]

The atmosphere was still brittle. Despite Shuttlesworth's request, Lingo's troopers remained, standing guard on the streets and working with Connor to put up police barricades around the 16th Street Baptist Church to prevent attendance at services or meetings that might inflame the tensions.

Robert Kennedy, still trying to decide whether to deploy federal troops, called Bailey.

"Sheriff," he said, "this is Attorney General Kennedy, Bobby Kennedy. I'm advised by reliable people that you are a trusted person. They trust you. I've got to ask you a question."

"Yes, sir."

"Are you going to be able to hold it?. . . Twelve thousand troops are at Fort McClellan, [and] here's this monkey on my back again. You know, when do you want martial law? Can you handle it?"

Bailey replied, "If you get Dr. Martin Luther King out of Birmingham."

"Is that right?"

"Yes, sir, we can handle it if you can do that."

Bailey later recalled, "[King] left that night to Memphis. You see, we had another problem. We had intelligence that he [King] was a marked man. It was to either happen in Birmingham or Selma. I didn't want it to happen here."[405]

28

Bugging and Long Hot Summer

Although the bombings of the Gaston Motel and A. D. King's home were never solved, it appeared obvious to most that the Klan was responsible. Gary Thomas Rowe, the FBI informant who had saved Lankford during the assault at the Trailways station two years earlier was supposed to check in with his FBI handler after the Klan rally the night of May 11, 1963, but he had gone missing for several hours. Suspicion also fell on a well-known Klansman bomber, Bill Holt. Though Lankford and Marcus Jones had spent many hours following Mary Lou and Bill Holt, that night they were occupied elsewhere.

Meanwhile, the Black school children who had left school grounds to march for their freedom faced expulsion the week before graduation. The school board's edict would cost many seniors their high school diplomas. NAACP lawyers hastily sued in U.S. District Court, but the judge sided with the school superintendent. Ten women from the Birmingham Council on Human Relations, including Florence Siegel, Anny Kraus, and members of the Unitarian Church met with Superintendent of Education Theo Wright to protest the suspensions, also without success. It took the U.S. Fifth Circuit Court of Appeals to reverse the District Court's decision and send the children back to class.

The following day, May 21, the Alabama Supreme Court ruled against Bull Connor's lawsuit that had delayed the change in government. Mayor Albert Boutwell and the new city council took office, dismissing Connor and the commissioners. Connor declared it the worst day of his life. A career politician, there is little doubt that Connor would have jumped back into the next race and worked to hinder desegregation and stymie any progress the city had made. Well aware of this and unwilling to see all the work to remove Connor from office come to naught, Townsend called Lankford into his office. "We have to get Connor out of the city," he said.

Marcus Jones, who worked nights, was just finishing breakfast when Lankford arrived at his house. He was eager to hear what Townsend wanted.

"He wants Bull out of Birmingham," Lankford told him.

"Okay," Jones said. "Let me finish my coffee, and we'll get started."[406]

Since Connor was no longer at city hall, they needed to tap his home phone. Connor lived within a mile of Jones's residence in Crestwood. It was a simple matter to drive past Connor's house and follow the overhead telephone line. Lankford had no worries about tracing it. He and Jones had developed a close relationship with security at Southern Bell and one call would provide the location of the junction box and the number of the "pair" of wires leading back to Connor's home telephone. If needed, they had access to a Southern Bell lineman's truck with the logo stamped on the green door. In addition, the telephone company had supplied Lankford with a lineman's gear—a belt and gadget bag, a telephone handset, sharpened steel climbers, and all the wire and accessories needed. They taught him to climb with the new gear and how to "run" a box to find the correct pair within thirty seconds of opening the double door on the junction box. Jones and Lankford used the "set-out" car to record Connor's phone calls.

For weeks after the election there was nothing much to report, except one conversation Connor had with Fred Taylor, an old friend and city editor of the *Birmingham News*. Taylor encouraged him to seek the open seat in the upcoming Alabama Public Service Commission (PSC) election.

"You can haul off the money in a pickup truck," Taylor told Connor. "The PSC regulates everything in the state—electricity, telephone rates, even the type of fire extinguishers for public buildings and trucks."

Connor was interested.

When Jones and Lankford told Townsend, he recognized the opportunity. He said, "I hate to wish him off on the people of the entire state, but he must leave Birmingham." Townsend strode to the door that connected with the managing editor, John Bloomer.

"Get Bull in here, John," Townsend snapped, "the *Birmingham News* wants to talk to him about running for the PSC."

Lankford later reflected, "Townsend would have supported Bull for president of the United States if it took that to protect the image of his city."

The *News* supported Connor's bid, and he was elected to the PSC. He voted with regularity to raise utility rates, holding the job until a few months before his death seven years later.

UNAWARE OF TOWNSEND'S MACHINATIONS, newly installed Mayor Boutwell quietly arranged for the first official biracial meeting with city hall figures. Rabbi Grafman attended as a representative of the religious community. Boutwell did not announce the meeting, wanting to keep it secret, but Lankford learned of it from Billy Hamilton, the new mayor's administrative assistant. The day before the meeting, Lankford waited until darkness and used his police lock picks to open the outer door of the mayor's conference room.

After a quick scan of the room, he decided one of the framed portraits of past Birmingham mayors afforded the best location, close enough for clarity and with enough hidden area for a transmitter antenna.

From his gadget bag, he affixed the bug to the back of a large portrait of former mayor Jimmy Morgan with friction tape, coiling the antenna and pointing the end upward toward the press room, where he would be receiving and recording the conversation. He planned to give the information to Townsend—to keep ahead of events.

Retreating to the pressroom, he set up the receiver and tape recorder to check out the sound quality. To his satisfaction, he heard a continuous, loud hiss, indicating an ideal connection. He locked the receiver and recorder in his desk. The whole operation had taken five minutes.

Back home, he called Lieutenant House and filled him in on the details, including where he had placed the bug. Then he couldn't sleep. Something felt wrong. Having learned to listen to that inner voice of warning, he got out of bed, dressed, and headed back to city hall.

Hastily, he took down the installation and searched for another place. There were few options. To conceal the device in the ceiling or walls would take too long. There was only one place where no one would look, and it was the worst location in the room for a bug. Windows of the conference room looked out over Woodrow Wilson Park, and a valance held the window blinds in place. The groove in the valance was a perfect place to conceal the small device and stretching the antenna lengthwise would send a strong signal. Extraneous outside noises, however, would make the proceedings inside harder to decipher. Lankford saw no other choice and put the bug in the window valance.

The next day, just hours before the meeting was to start, he again checked his equipment, listening for the signal from the room below. He could hear furniture being moved around and other strange sounds. Racing down to the room, he found Margaret Lasakow, Temple Emanu-El's education director, under the conference room table, making slits in the chairs' upholstery looking for a transmitter. He later learned she had already checked behind the mayor's portrait, where House had told her the bug was located. Lankford could only imagine that House had felt guilty about taping Rabbi Grafman. Or perhaps he decided it was in the city's best interest to keep the meeting secret and tipped off Lasakow.

Regardless of his reasons, he had left Lankford exposed to Margaret's distress. Seeing him, she almost burst into tears, asking how he and Townsend could betray the rabbi's friendship, especially since Grafman had raised money for the very equipment Lankford had used.

Stung by her pain and House's perfidy, Lankford assured her that it was nonsense. But as much as he valued her friendship, his first loyalty was to Townsend. He retreated back upstairs to the pressroom, closed his door, and got ready for the meeting. The attendees were local and said nothing noteworthy. When Marcus Jones later became privy to the tape, Lankford told him what happened. This was one time Jones did not pass the information on to Lasakow and Grafman. It became an event that "didn't happen."[407]

MEANWHILE, ALTHOUGH BATTLES HAD been won in Birmingham, the fight for equality and school desegregation was far from over. By June 1963, after some punting, the U.S. Fifth Circuit Court issued a ruling on *Armstrong v. Birmingham Board of Education*, a lawsuit filed by Black Birmingham barber James Armstrong Sr. six years earlier to allow his children to attend a White school. The court found for Armstrong on all the substantial points but decided it was too late to require the school board to desegregate an entire grade by the start of school, so it required the Birmingham Board of Education to submit a plan, using the law in place to choose which students would integrate which schools.[408] On June 2, Vernon Patrick, a leader in YMBC, said that organization was "nearly unanimous" in agreement that schools must desegregate. "Public schools and equal opportunities," he said, "are fundamental to the American way of life."[409]

While school officials scrambled to satisfy the court's requirement, the eyes of the country shifted from Birmingham to Tuscaloosa, where tensions were mounting over the impending desegregation of the University of Alabama. The university requested a delay, citing the unrest in Birmingham. Grooms denied the request, saying to do so would be tantamount to declaring that law and order had broken down.

U.S. District Court Judge Harlan H. Grooms had denied the university's request for delay by citing the unrest in Birmingham, saying that would be tantamount to declaring that law and order had broken down. Perhaps with a bit of irony he brought to the attention of university representatives that Governor Wallace—who had already declared he would stand in the door of the university to prevent desegregation—had promised to maintain law and order.

Wallace brought National Guard troops to the campus in preparation. President Kennedy, who could have snatched control out of Wallace's hands by federalizing those troops, decided to allow Wallace his show as the best strategy to keep violence at bay. But he sent Deputy Attorney General Louis Oberdorfer to Birmingham to meet for several days in secret sessions with Alabama state officials to plan out the confrontation and facilitate the registration of two Black students. So detailed was the scenario they worked out that chalk marks on the sidewalk would indicate where each player was to stand.[410]

Lankford was present in Tuscaloosa days before, taking photographs and reporting on the whirlwind of happenings, including the presence of the National Guard and the arrest of some Birmingham area Klansmen stopped en route to Tuscaloosa with a car full of weapons. Lankford also interviewed the UA student government association president, Don Stewart, on students' efforts to prepare for a peaceful desegregation of the campus.

On June 11, Lankford observed for the *News* the drama that ensued under a scorching sun when Wallace "stood in the schoolhouse door" at Foster Auditorium. Birmingham actors had roles to play in that performance. Real estate executive and National Guard Brigadier General Henry Graham stepped forward and told Wallace it was his "sad duty" to order the governor to step aside.[411]

Wallace, playing his part, stepped aside.

The Black enrollees, Vivian Malone and James A. Hood, had already registered. They waited in a car until the end of the theatrics, which Alabama

Attorney General Richmond Flowers later called "the greatest production since *Cleopatra*." Malone, Hood, and onlooking White students, many of whom had actively worked to ensure a peaceful desegregation, then entered Foster Auditorium, ate in the cafeteria, and continued with their day in classes.[412]

President Kennedy spoke that night on national television. The time was ripe to take a stand and draft a civil rights bill. "The events in Birmingham so increased the cries for equality that no city or state or legislative body can prudently choose to ignore them," he said. More than seven hundred demonstrations had roiled the country since Birmingham's marches in May. But the turning point in the decision to draft a civil rights bill came when Burke Marshall returned to Washington after the negotiations in Birmingham. "Everyone concluded," Marshall later told a *New York Times* reporter, "that the president had to act and . . . not only face this himself, but somehow bring the country to face the problem and resolve it." [413]

Kennedy used the desegregation of the university and cited the actions in Birmingham to ask "Congress to enact legislation giving all Americans the right to be served in facilities which are open to the public." Segregation was simply wrong, and it should be clear in "hearts and minds" that the fundamental reason for enacting such legislation was "because it was right."

Not everyone's heart and mind was open to that moral point. The following night, Medgar Evers, an NAACP field secretary, was shot and killed in his driveway in Mississippi by a white supremacist. That news rippled across the country, reinforcing the need for action.

President Kennedy was not the only White person to speak out against Wallace's grandstanding at the University of Alabama. So did Birmingham's Methodist Bishop Nolan B. Harmon, a signer of both ministerial letters calling for law and order and racial understanding. "In June 1963, Harmon stood before the Annual Conference in Birmingham and read a public protest. Neither segregationist governors nor civil rights activists had the right to defy the law, the bishop underscored. Harmon regretted that Wallace had attempted to 'defy the sovereignty of the United States' and deny fundamental human rights."[414]

Kennedy took a further step, convening 244 lawyers from across the country for a June meeting in the East Room of the White House. Kennedy and

Vice President Lyndon B. Johnson, despite his previous voting record against civil rights legislation, joined Attorney General Robert Kennedy to urge the lawyers to "use their training and influence to move the struggle for the protection of civil rights from the streets to the courts." One of those attendees was Birmingham labor rights attorney Buddy Cooper. Another was a Unitarian, Paul Johnston. Later named the Lawyers' Committee for Civil Rights Under Law, the prestigious group became a powerful force in educating the bar on civil rights and providing pro bono assistance to victims of discrimination.

Before Project C, President Kennedy had said he did not think the nation was ready for a civil rights bill. But during the negotiations in Birmingham, Attorney General Kennedy made private assurances that the administration would pursue a comprehensive bill.[415] By June 20, the Omnibus Civil Rights bill was introduced to the House of Representatives.

Two days later, President Kennedy invited civil rights leaders to the White House. In a conversation with municipal representatives from Birmingham, the president said, "We had no legislative proposals before the Congress until the events in Birmingham last April and May happened to light off a whole fire around the country."[416] He quipped, "I don't think you should all be totally harsh on Bull Connor. After all, he has done more for civil rights than almost anybody else." Shuttlesworth reported that the president added, "But for Birmingham, we would not be here today."

29

Change in the Magic City

For Blacks in Birmingham, the world changed in some ways in 1963, but in some ways it did not. The Project C success did not suddenly produce money in Black pockets.

New Mayor Albert Boutwell, despite his promise to act with honor, drug his feet on creating the promised biracial committee. A month after the negotiated agreements, the city still had not reopened parks and public recreational facilities on a desegregated basis or rescinded the segregation ordinance. The *Birmingham News* blasted the city, claiming "nothing was being done to take action on the Negro-White agreements." Relations with the police department were tense in the aftermath of the marches and riots, and three Black men were shot, two fatally, between the end of June and August.[417]

But change did come. On July 23, the first city council in Birmingham's history rescinded all of the city's segregation ordinances at once. According to David Vann, Birmingham was "the only city in America that ever did that."[418]

The new government and progressive leaders took steps to ensure desegregation was not just applied to downtown businesses but implemented throughout the city.

The NSRP's Edward Fields would have dearly loved to know the days and locations that desegregation of lunch counters would take place. Connor had shut down the NSRP's production of *The Thunderbolt* at the urging of Karl Friedman and the Jewish community, but the racist organization now dispersed another hate sheet. The mimeographed *Birmingham Daily Bulletin* pointed fingers at individuals, including their names and addresses, who capitulated to desegregation. Fields wrote in the *Bulletin* that information about the schedule for "lunch counter mixing" was the "most tightly guarded secreted in Birmingham."[419]

Local movement activist Calvin Woods called Vann daily to discuss what building would be desegregated that day. Vann then notified Chief Jamie

Moore, who would assign plainclothes detectives to the store for protection. Vann recalled that after the third day, a representative of Eastwood Mall called and asked to be included, saying "We're going to have to face this. We would rather do it with police protection." Vann told interviewer Horace Huntley, "So, we sent the integration team out to Eastwood Mall. . . . Five Points West called and asked would we come and integrate them too. So, we sent teams to Eastwood Mall, Downtown, and Five Points West."[420]

At one site, members of the NSRP protested. Police arrested four, including Fields, who waved a Confederate flag in a police captain's face.

YMBC member Charlie Cleveland recalled that the Blacks who tested the lunch counters "found themselves segregated all over again," i.e., sitting alone. No White person would sit with them.[421] To remedy this, "white members of the Birmingham chapter of the Alabama Council on Human Relations waited at the counters to sit near the blacks when they came in."[422] Peggy Fuller organized Unitarian women to participate, including Cleveland's wife, Ruby, and Marjorie Linn.[423] Jackie Mazzara, also a Unitarian, took both of her children to Woolworth's and sat with a Black customer at the lunch counter to "show that it made absolutely no difference to us."[424]

Edward Harris recalled how the SCLC's James Bevel "took a bunch of white folk and taught us how to . . . be nonviolent, how to lay [sic] down and cover your head if you were being attacked." Harris, who'd organized the student discussion group in the library of Birmingham-Southern, had joined the Unitarian Church in Birmingham. He and his wife were part of a team that desegregated more than forty restaurants, hotels, and other venues. Ideally, a team consisted of two White couples and one Black couple. Harris and his wife with their baby would go in and sit at the counter with the Black couple. "If everybody got up, we didn't move. Then we would encourage the waitress . . . that it was okay; they [the Blacks sitting at the counter or table] are only people. The other [White] couple would then come in and they would be observers if there was violence or something happened. . . . There was a policeman on the scene, and he was observing too."[425]

Virginia Sparks (later Volker), a White graduate student in anatomy at the School of Medicine, joined a summer biracial college fellowship group that met at Thirgood Memorial C.M.E. Church, a downtown Black church. "The students would talk with one another, no small thing at that time, and go out in small groups to test desegregation at the lunch counters. Most of the time, we encountered no problems, but sometimes when we sat at the counter, the business would put a 'Closed' sign in the window."

Sparks often got a ride home from Tommie Wren, a Black SCLC field worker who owned a large car. Jack Greenberg, a White Jewish attorney from out of state, rode with them. The white supremacist NSRP knew him well as "Jew Jack."

Greenberg was the director-counsel of the NAACP Legal Defense Fund. Thurgood Marshall (later to be the first Black U.S. Supreme Court justice) had pegged Greenberg as his LDF successor to work on Jim Crow laws. Greenberg had been the youngest member of Marshall's legal team that brought *Brown v. Board of Education* before the Supreme Court. He had also participated in the litigation of *Meredith v. Fair* in 1961, the case that allowed James Meredith to integrate the University of Mississippi. Martin Luther King Jr. had called on Greenberg to oversee SCLC's demonstration cases, which is why he was in Birmingham in 1963, riding with Wren to give Virginia Sparks a ride home.[426]

Wren pulled up across the street from her house, and Sparks had just exited the car when blue lights from a patrol car behind them startled them all. After searching Wren, one officer said, "Boy, don't you know these white folks are going to get you in trouble?" He turned to Greenberg, "You smell like a nigger." To Sparks he said, "What are you doing here? Does your Daddy know you are here? Do you want to have a nigger baby?"

Sparks's back stiffened. "My father is a minister and would care about how these people are being treated."

Anger flushed the officer's face red and his hand went to his gun.

"My father taught me to speak my mind," Sparks later recalled, "but I changed my tune when I realized I could be killed!"

The next day, Greenberg called to check on her, afraid information about the encounter had leaked and she might have received flak from the School of Medicine. One of her professors did call her into his office.

"Virginia, we have to go slow on these issues," he cautioned.

"Well, if not now, when?" she replied, unknowingly echoing the question of an ancient Jewish sage.

"They've just got to be ready," he replied. "They've got to be educated."

"Professor, the Whites are the ones who have to get ready."[427]

"GETTING READY" FOR DESEGREGATION was not an easy task for the School of Medicine. The Birmingham school was still part of the University of Alabama, so director Joseph F. Volker answered to UA president Frank Rose in Tuscaloosa. Both supported desegregation, but Volker's role as administrator of a state-supported school required him to tread carefully to keep from losing funding. In June, he called on Charles Zukoski, the Unitarian member whose long-time civil rights stand had gotten him dismissed from First National Bank the previous year. Volker asked Zukoski to use his contacts to help identify a Black student for admission to one of the academic programs.[428]

Progress inched forward in other ways.

Edward Harris not only participated in testing the desegregation of lunch counters but also served as youth leader at the Unitarian Church. In that capacity, in the summer of 1963, he started the first interracial summer youth camp at the Sandridge Country Club for Negroes in the Oxmoor community of Birmingham. Black radio personality "Tall Paul" Dudley White leased the facility. Disc jockey Shelley Stewart recalled that the country club was a "hangout" for Black and White youth, a "safe" place where the love of music fostered many interracial friendships.[429]

Love of music—and good barbeque—also brought the races together at "Gip's Place" a backyard juke joint in Bessemer. Beloved owner Henry "Gip" Gipson, a former railroad man and gravedigger, would quip, "No blacks, no whites, just the blues." Like A. G. Gaston's far more upscale restaurant in Birmingham, which escaped scrutiny by law enforcement and city officials, Gip's Place had operated freely from 1952 on, despite violations of Jim Crow laws.[430]

Another cultural racial breakthrough occurred via youth with the arts. Laura Toffel Knox, a daughter of Jewish Polish immigrants, made her own statement against segregation. With Marilyn Sheffield,[431] she founded the Birmingham Creative Dance Group (later Southern Dance Works), a racially integrated company that defied Jim Crow laws and garnered national attention. Knox's 2011 obituary quoted her having said, "I read things about the Holocaust, how when the Jews were segregated, they brought together an orchestra at a concentration camp. It made me wonder about my connection with black children in Birmingham." Knox's daughter recalled her mother would go into Black communities and pick up the kids for rehearsals. In 1963, Knox presented the first integrated dance program at the Unitarian Church.[432]

THAT SUMMER, DOWNTOWN RETAIL merchants discussed how to enact their promises to hire Blacks in management and on sales floors. Karl Friedman helped design a program to hire Black employees in the department stores. It was important to the merchants to have a plan that would be uniform in each department store "to explain to and pacify the White executives and employees."

Led by Emil Hess, the group developed a plan for stores to simultaneously carry out four steps at intervals. First was the removal of "White" and "Colored" signs from water fountains. About two weeks later, the same would occur at restrooms. Restaurants would follow as the third step. Parisian, Pizitz, Loveman's, and Newberry's department stores all complied, removing the "Whites Only" signs and serving Blacks in their restaurants. Sears, however, was a national chain; its Birmingham store shut down its restaurant and reopened with only vending machines.[433] The final step called for Black employees on the sales floor and in administration. All the retailers knew the date to enact each step.

During this period, stores received threatening phone calls and bomb threats. When Richard Pizitz made his way one day to his family's store at Second Avenue North and Nineteenth Street, he saw Blacks demonstrating along the Second Avenue side and Whites demonstrating along Nineteenth Street. Police stood at the corner between the groups. Inside the store, he found his father and quipped, "I think we've achieved the perfect balance."

Convinced of the importance for the city that the entire community got involved rather than only a few downtown retailers, Pizitz approached the biggest bank in town, First National Bank, and Alabama Gas Company, asking them to hire or promote Blacks as tellers. Both refused. The bank told him, "The problems of the retailers are not our problems." Pizitz also visited the *Birmingham News* to ask they stop segregating the Sunday society page that featured White betrothals and weddings on the front pages and Black ones on back pages. A *News* employee (not Townsend) refused, saying the city wasn't "ready for that yet."[434] Edward Harris would later seek a job with the *News* and managing editor Leroy Simms, chomping on a cigar would tell him, "I would rather hire a nigger than a nigger lover."[435]

Rabbi Grafman proposed that the merchants announce the final and most controversial step, the hiring of Black staff on the sales floor of the downtown retail stores. Doing so was risky on two levels. First, there was a fear that Whites would refuse to have Blacks wait on them. Second, White employees might feel a Black person had taken a White person's job.

Without the support of other institutions, and under pressure from Blacks and Whites, progressives and segregationists, the downtown retailers moved forward. Most of the department stores strove to fulfill their end of the understanding, but finding the right people, especially on the sales floor, was a challenge. It required, in Friedman's words, finding a "competent and cooperative black person who was willing to take the risk." Hess, who led the group, asked for the help of each department store owner in finding suitable people.

The stores made good on their promises. Pizitz put three of the store's Black employees on the sales team, including Molly Davis, an elevator operator, and Doris Hicks from housekeeping. Threats and protests continued for a while, but Pizitz reported that after a few months, "The whites accepted the changes."

Friedman reflected that although Grafman had led the concept of gradual change, "he reversed his direction, saying 'You know, doing the job quickly is better than not doing it at all.' That took courage."

Some efforts by White business owners to hire Black employees resulted in unintended collateral damage. Friedman recalls that two of his clients' businesses received a visit by civil rights leader Abraham Woods during the boycotts and marches.

> Reverend Woods came to their stores and told them they had to hire black people, or he was going to boycott their stores. Both acquiesced and hired young black boys. They stole from them, shorted the cash register, gave away goods. So, Pete [Cohen] fired those employees, and Reverend Woods came back and threatened them again, telling them that if they did not rehire them, he was ready to march. So, they hired them once again, and then they proceeded to dissolve their businesses and go out of business. Just around the corner, Sidney Ziff had a similar experience. These were Jewish merchants who were not wealthy, nor were they ready to retire, but it was necessary.[436]

Although he had appointed none of the approximately twenty Black members to the important steering committee, Boutwell honored the unsigned "Accord of Conscience," and appointed 153 citizens, Black and White, to the Community Affairs Committee (CAC), giving it a broad reach into many areas of concern. When the full body met for the first time, segregationists crammed the hall outside the city council chambers where the group was to meet. "These leaders of Birmingham walked through the lines of the Klan demonstrators," Vann said, "and held their meeting; they refused to be intimidated, and I believe that was one of those very critical times again as we went forward in that summer."

Boutwell addressed the CAC: "'Here tonight,' he said, 'a dream begins to unfold' which could be the beginning of Birmingham's 'finest hour . . . a solemn . . . hopeful and historic occasion.' Frank Newton, of Southern Bell, the first president of CAC added, 'The time has come when we must take a position and stand on it . . . united.'"[437]

Union attorney Buddy Cooper was a founding member of CAC (and the JCCEO), a commitment he kept for many years. Richard Pizitz, son of Isadore Pizitz, also attended the CAC Monday breakfasts. "For many," he said, "it was the first time blacks and whites sat down to eat together and talk." The Black preachers and police, who had confronted each other on the streets, now had the opportunity to salve the wounds and begin positive changes. At the breakfast meetings, people breathed a new "air of community and conversation."[438]

Sheriff Bailey, who supported the goals of CAC, designated Major David Orange to attend the meetings and report back to him. Early meetings moved from city hall to the ballroom of the Parliament House Hotel. The mood of the meetings, Orange recalled, was always hopeful, though he remembered nothing of "real significance" coming from them.[439]

Community leaders grew frustrated with Boutwell's lack of response to CAC recommendations, prompting Vann to break with Boutwell and charge him with failure even to call most of the subcommittees together. Grafman also grew frustrated with Boutwell's refusal to invite Blacks to apply to the police department.[440]

PROGRESSIVES MAY HAVE BEEN frustrated at the slow progress in race relations, but others were determined to stop it altogether. On August 21, Lankford wrote, "A carefully placed bundle of dynamite blew another notch into Birmingham's notorious 'dynamite hill' . . . damaging the home of Negro Attorney Arthur D. Shores at 1021 Center Street." The blast heard for miles brought out about a thousand angry protesters. "Rocks, bricks and half bricks struck most of the policemen, but only two required treatment at a hospital, Sergeant T. L. Jones and Patrolman H. J. Deal. A door window and headlight on a sheriff's car were broken and tires on four police cars were slashed." It took one hundred riot-trained, armed officers to control the crowd without further injuries. Six men were arrested. The city offered a reward of $50,000 to find those responsible for Shores's house and other recent bombings.[441]

In a rare revelation, U.S. Attorney Macon Weaver announced his conclusion that the attack on police officers at Shores's home was the result of the previous accusation of an "unidentified Negro person to FBI agents and an unnamed New York congressman" that two police officers had bombed the house of A. D. King earlier (May 11), a rumor that was "'well known in the Negro community." The FBI had determined the accusations against the officers were false, but prior to Weaver's statement the FBI's investigation and determination had been unknown to the community.[442]

The following month, two hundred thousand Americans gathered in Washington, D.C., on August 28 to rally for the March on Washington for Jobs and Freedom, an event historian Glenn Eskew said was "simply a celebration of the victory in Birmingham."[443] The march was conceived in the A. G. Gaston Motel in Birmingham. Birmingham's Peggy Fuller and the Reverend Alfred Walters Hobart were among those marchers. On the Washington mall, King gave a dramatic and memorable speech from the steps of the Lincoln Memorial, knowing the battle was not yet won—"I have a dream that my four little children will one day live in a nation where they will not be judged by the color of their skin, but by the content of their character."

30

Countdown to Calamity

While the city braced for desegregation of high schools in the fall of 1963, the first Black student admitted to a regular academic program at the School of Medicine quietly enrolled. Without a word of protest from anyone, Luther Lawler, a Black high school teacher, began the master's program in education.

But the high schools were a different matter. With the final resolution by the courts of Birmingham's school desegregation case, the new city officials and law enforcement prepared to take whatever steps necessary to ensure a lawful transition and protect the Black students who would not walk unchallenged through the formerly White school doors.

Public opinion raged back and forth, and the papers printed letters reflecting the gamut. The newspapers' editorials supported a peaceful desegregation of the schools, and several articles carried a message asking for peaceful compliance with desegregation orders. At a meeting of Methodist women in August, First Methodist's the Reverend Denson N. Franklin said, "We must keep our schools open and we must avoid violence." Newly elected city councilwoman Nina Miglionico said, "The law is here, and it must be faced in Birmingham."[444]

One headline in early September read "Amidst Crisis—Ministers of All Denominations Call for Order." Dr. Lamar Jackson of Southside Baptist Church asked that "the people of the city and county, young and old alike will conduct themselves with the dignity that makes for civil tranquility and with the decorum which responsible officials have requested."[445] The Birmingham Jaycees passed a resolution 27–9 "commending and supporting the Birmingham Board of Education and the Birmingham Police Department in their efforts to maintain our public school system in an atmosphere of law and order through peaceful compliance with court-ordered desegregation."[446]

Alton Parker, a prominent Birmingham attorney who had been oblivious about racial issues as a youth, recalled his parents' position about segregation. "I don't think they had any problem with desegregation, but they thought it was dangerous."[447]

A group of White parents, fearing violence for their children, filed a petition with the U.S. Fifth Circuit Court of Appeals asking for a stay against the *Armstrong v. Board of Education* injunction. Some cast dire warnings, pointing to the problems encountered by schools in Washington, D.C., which had started integration a little more than a week after the 1954 *Brown* decision. At the same time the Birmingham school board received another petition urging it to keep public schools open for all Birmingham children, Black and White; Unitarians had secured eleven thousand signatures.[448]

Perhaps the best endorsement for the fact that local leaders were trying to move forward— even though it was a course they might not have chosen without the pressure of court decisions and social unrest—came from the radical NRSP. In a rally against integration, Edward Fields, J. B. Stoner, and Jerry Q. Dutton "lambasted NBC and CBS television networks, the *Birmingham News*, the Kennedys, Mayor Albert Boutwell, Sheriff Melvin Bailey, [and] members of the Birmingham City Council [for] assisting in integrating Birmingham."[449]

As feared, not everyone accepted a peaceful desegregation. On Sunday, September 1, the NSRP set up near Graymont Elementary and Ramsay High School. Fields "planned to lead flying columns of white supremacist volunteers through police lines and onto the school grounds where they would proceed to destroy the schools rather than allow them to be desegregated."[450]

Governor Wallace tried to pressure Boutwell and the school board into delaying desegregation, but both the city council and the school authorities told him they could handle the situation themselves, although they decided to allow only two Black students (Dwight and Floyd Armstrong) to register at Graymont Elementary the next day and to proceed with Ramsay and West End schools the following day. But Wallace continued his defiance. He had used state troopers to shut down Tuskegee High School. Now he pulled away some of those officers, sending them to reinforce the troopers in the Magic City.

Knowing the KKK and NSRP were ready to disrupt integration and provide the violence he needed for troopers to step in, Wallace kept about six hundred officers on standby in the area hotels. Burke Marshall flew back to the city and reported to Robert Kennedy in Washington. The Justice Department,

aware Wallace was baiting the feds and wanting interference, issued a statement: "Governor Wallace knows the schools will be opened and the Negro
students will attend them in accord with the orders of the courts. We hope it
will be accomplished swiftly by the people of Alabama and their officials."[451]

ON WEDNESDAY MORNING, SEPTEMBER 4, schools opened in Birmingham, and
the Armstrong boys registered at Graymont Elementary. A hundred or more
protestors organized by the NSRP's Fields were on the scene. Tom Lankford
was also present and wrote, "A rush on Graymont School by a handful of
shouting whites set off street skirmishes between police and demonstrators. . . .
'Get the niggers out of that school,' the group shouted. Police blocked the
demonstrators at steps to the main entrance."[452]

Reinforcements and a sudden heavy rain caused Fields to back away in
frustration and call for a move to Ramsay High School. Perhaps the NSRP
had been expecting cooperation from the police, but Bull Connor no longer
controlled law enforcement in Birmingham. At Ramsay, four NSRP members
were arrested after taunting and assaulting the police, who again "held their
ground to the horror of the NSRP contingent."[453] The segregationists accused
the police of being "Nigger lovers" and yelled "Keep America White!"[454] A
newspaper photographer snapped a photo at Ramsay of a policeman carrying off a White demonstrator who had in his grip a large Confederate flag.[455]

Joe Rhodes was one of the Birmingham officers assigned to guard the Black
students. His daughter, Kelly Rhodes, later recalled that "Dad was a police
officer when West End was integrated . . . It was a big deal. He was there to
protect those children. That was most important to him."[456]

All that day, Lankford ran from trouble spot to trouble spot, keeping the
city desk at the *News* informed by CB radio and calling in from pay phones.
That afternoon, Boutwell praised the actions and restraint of the police. Police
had made six arrests, and one officer was injured.

That night, the Klan bombed Arthur Shores's home on Dynamite Hill
for the second time in two weeks. Shores, his wife, Theodora, and seventeen-
year-old daughter Barbara were home, but not seriously injured.

Houston Brown, a Black student at Talladega College, was visiting his
parents across the street from the Shores residence when the bomb exploded,
and he ran out of the house to see five Birmingham police cars already parked

along the streets. One had backed into his driveway and an officer in riot gear, shotgun in his lap, sat on the passenger side, his door open and his feet on the ground.

Although police were still patrolling that area, as well as the schools—some perceived the bombing of the Shores house as an effort to pull police away from guarding the schools. For Brown, however, the officer could not have been in that position if he hadn't been expecting the bombing. If true, it indicated there were still Birmingham police officers in league with the Klan, a belief bolstered by the false but persistent rumor that police had bombed Shores's home earlier.

The shotgun-cradling officer told Brown to get back to his house, but Brown replied that the policeman would have to shoot him in the back to stop him as he ran to help Shores get through the smoke and debris to his wife, who had been asleep in a back room of the house.[457] The officer did not attempt to stop Brown.

Despite having worked all day, Lankford rode with Sergeant Marcus Jones that night and responded with him to the scene. With fellow journalist Joe Campbell, Lankford wrote, "The thunder of the bomb scarcely had died before Negro residents of the area boiled into the streets. They met the first officers who arrived with a rain of bricks, bottles and rocks. Frequent shots crackled through the ranks of officers, many of whom had battled White demonstrators outside schools that faced desegregation Wednesday." Police fired shots over the heads of the protestors, however, John Coley was shot "when he burst from a house shooting a gun." The following day, however, the *News* reported that an "investigation revealed he did not have a gun." The coroner ruled Coley was killed by "stray pellets from a shotgun."[458]

IN THE END, THE injured included eleven Blacks, four officers, and six Whites, including men and women who had just been passing by. The incident, along with additional pressure from Wallace, resulted in the school board postponing further integration. By Friday, September 6, the Fifth Circuit Court of Appeals heard and denied a request by White parents for an injunction to stop integration of the schools.

The original eight White Birmingham ministers issued another public statement calling the bombing of Shores's house a "dastardly act." Many others spoke up. Despite protests from newspapers all over the state, Wallace was not deterred. Saturday night he appeared in Birmingham to speak at a meeting of five hundred United Americans for Conservative Government. Former Birmingham Mayor Art Hanes introduced him. Bull Connor and Edward Fields joined Wallace on the stage where Wallace assured the crowd he was "willing to take any risk" and was ready "to go the last mile" to prevent school desegregation.

On Sunday night, September 8, the governor appeared on TV to declare, "We cannot win this fight if we resort to violence. If you stand with me in this fight, you will observe law and order and avoid violence." Segregation extremists apparently heard another message: That night they firebombed another home, this time that of Black businessman A. G. Gaston. Mr. and Mrs. Gaston had just returned the night before from a state dinner with President Kennedy in Washington. Gaston was reading in his living room and his wife was in the bedroom when a firebomb landed in the yard and another crashed through the window, setting the venetian blinds and a lamp on fire. The Gastons were not injured.

Schools were to open the following day. But Wallace ordered that "no student shall be permitted to integrate the public schools" in three Alabama cities—Tuskegee, Birmingham, and Mobile.

That Monday morning in Birmingham, carloads of state troopers ringed Graymont School where the Armstrong brothers, accompanied by Shuttlesworth and attorneys Ernest Jackson and Oscar Adams walked with them from their home to the school. A girl commented to her friend that "the school looked like a jail" with the hundred officers ringing it. Lankford watched as State Public Safety Director Al Lingo carried out Wallace's edict and blocked the boys' entry. White students leaned out the windows, watching. When one of the adult escorts tried to speak, Lingo said, "You will leave immediately."[459] It was the same scenario enacted earlier at Ramsay and West End high schools.

Governor Wallace and President Kennedy meanwhile battled with words over school segregation, while Judge Frank M. Johnson Jr. called the state's other federal district judges—Lynne, Allgood, and Grooms in the Northern District, and Thomas in the Southern District. All five judges issued a temporary restraining order (*United States v. Wallace*) against the governor and his troopers from "implementing or giving force or effect to [Wallace's] executive order of September 9, 1963." The order enjoined Wallace from "physically preventing or interfering with students, teachers, or other persons" or from "interfering with or obstructing" the three boards of education.

Federal marshals served Al Lingo with the restraining order, and Lingo warned Wallace, who was holed up in the capitol, surrounding himself with troopers who refused to allow marshals inside, thus preventing them from directly serving him with the court order.

On Tuesday, September 10, while Wallace still dodged the federal order, National Guard troops sent by him arrived at the schools, prepared to keep Black students from entering. President Kennedy played the trump card, federalizing the Guard and ordering the soldiers to return to their respective armories. That left local police in control in their own cities.

Richard Walker quietly desegregated Ramsay High School. One can only imagine the courage it took to be the sole Black in a White high school or the courage of James Eber when he "broke the ban of silence" and dared to sit with Walker in the school lunchroom, an act which earned Eber a beating after school, and for which he was "ostracized and hated."[460]

Peggy and John Fuller's daughter Carolyn had a similar experience when she "committed the sin of speaking to the one black student" desegregating Ramsay, and many [of her fellow students] stopped speaking to her. In her words, "the only people I considered real friends came from that [Unitarian] Church. I'm not sure I would have survived emotionally if it had not been for the church." One day a friend warned that someone waited for her to leave the school grounds and planned to hurt her. Her activist mother received a terrifying phone call and a threat that her daughter would return home in pieces.[461] She and her brother slept under the dining room table "for some measure of safety from the threatened bombings."[462]

Her father said in reflection, "the difference [was] the black kids that were integrating the schools, they would leave school and be heroes, but the white kids that were supporting them were ostracized and had no support system." Carolyn's younger brother experienced harassment at McElwain School. Other kids danced around him, calling him a "nigger lover." Another time, they strung him upside down from his feet from a tree, and in yet another incident, an older boy held a knife to his throat.[463]

On the poorer side of town, where Connor found his base, the Armstrong boys found 60 percent of the students at Graymont Elementary School absent, but there were no incidents. At West End High School, however, Patricia Marcus and Josephine Powell sat quietly, enduring scorn and mockery by White students in their classroom. A thousand protesting students, along with teachers and NSRP members or sympathizers marched around the campus. It took busloads of police in riot gear to break up the crowd. In the chaos, nine arrests were made, including that of a man who struck Detective Marcus Jones with a brick.[464]

Police inspector Bill Haley went to the NSRP headquarters to note tag numbers to match with vehicles involved in the day's disorder at the schools. Students who should have been in school were hanging around the headquarters; one had an effigy of Martin Luther King. Knowing that would incite emotions, Haley tried to convince him to give it up. NSRP members interfered, attacking Haley, who managed to call for help.[465]

After the drama at West End, Lankford was driving *News* photographer Ed Jones down the Bessemer Highway at his usual "full tilt." When they heard Haley radio for help over the police scanner, "full tilt" got faster. Haley gave his location as the NSRP office. Lankford was well familiar with the brown sandstone house with a Confederate flag and the signs that said, "Keep America White, National States Rights Party" and "Niggers, Jews, Dogs, and FBI Agents Not Allowed."[466] He and Jones were the first responders to arrive, skidding to a stop next to Haley's car. One of the NSRP members had Haley pinned down on the front seat of his car, beating him.

Lankford "yanked the Nazi off Haley." A bloody but angry Haley scrambled out of the car and held the offender while Lankford returned the favor. Other NSRP members poured out of their headquarters. Jones snapped pictures. Lankford stood his ground. One photo caught his fists connecting with two assailants simultaneously, while a bloody Haley held one, a photo that made Lankford appear to be the aggressor. Lankford recalled that when motorcycle police arrived in response to the call for help, "There was some real serious stuff that took place in the back seat of the inspector's car."

Lankford responded to a summons to Moore's office. While he was there, an "official [at the courthouse] called Moore for advice, explaining that Edward Fields, head of the NSRP, was seeking a warrant on Lankford. Moore said,

'No warrant.'" When asked if the *News* wanted to press charges, Townsend simply said he was "satisfied with the way it had been handled."[467]

ALTHOUGH MANY STUDENTS STAYED home that week, some continued to protest and their numbers grew by Thursday, September 12, to an "angry, roving mob" of more than a hundred cars. With headlights on, drivers honked horns and passengers waved Confederate flags, as the Klan had done over the years in random displays throughout the metro area. Placards and bumper stickers read, "'Keep your children out of integrated schools'; 'Kan the Kennedy Klan'; 'We've been betrayed'; 'We want private schools'; 'Close mixed schools'; 'We want a white school'; and 'Obey little, resist much.'" In the back of one pickup truck were two caskets. A Black "person" was dragged in effigy from the trailer hitch.[468]

Police tailed the parade as it traveled to various schools. Protestors massed at Phillips High School, where Shuttlesworth was beaten in 1957 while trying to register his children. At Woodlawn High, student leaders tried to turn the group away, and a fight broke out that police had to break up. Football players stationed at the doorway kept the protesters out of the building.[469]

Woodlawn's teachers were pressured "to refuse to teach and hold out against integration." Mrs. Ann (Moon) Gray and her husband M. P. Gray were members of the Unitarian Church and supporters of integration. Despite her principal's instructions, Ann Gray stood up at a teacher's meeting and stated she "would be happy to have the first Negro children to be integrated in the school in her classes." Despite the ostracism and harassment, she encouraged others to "do what is right."[470] She faced threatening phone calls and the "sneers of bigots" by herself. "I am a teacher," she said, "a professional teacher, and the color of students will make no difference to me."[471] Her husband, the principal of Graymont School, also welcomed its first Black students.[472]

The student efforts to encourage a total school boycott were unsuccessful, and police arrested the NSRP's Fields and Stoner. But the next day, Friday, September 13, about five hundred students gathered outside city hall with representatives of other supremacist organizations, Birmingham Regional Association for Information and Needs (BRAIN) and the United Americans. The White students chanted, "Eight, six, four, two, Albert Boutwell is a Jew!" A group burst into the mayor's office, "put out cigarette butts in his carpet and climbed atop his desk to wave the battle flag."[473]

Amid the turmoil and anger surrounding school integration, an action squad of the Eastview Klan met under the Cahaba River bridge just south of Birmingham to foil FBI bugging of their conversations. These "Cahaba Bridge Boys" or "Cahaba Boys" were likely responsible for many previous bombings. They were right to be concerned about bugs. They didn't trust the FBI's primary informant, Gary Thomas Rowe, despite the fact that Rowe had a history of violence. Determined to send a warning that could not be ignored, the Cahaba Boys did their planning under the bridge and worked on a bomb, probably at Klansman Troy Ingram's house. Final preparations occurred under the cover of night in a sign shop only a few blocks from 16th Street Baptist Church.

31

The Unthinkable

In the thick darkness around 1 a.m. Sunday, September 15, 1963, a 1957 two-toned white-over-blue Chevrolet with a whip antenna pulled slowly in front of the 16th Street Baptist Church. Taking advantage of a diversionary fake "bomb threat" call to a nearby hotel, the car crept around the corner and headed to the back alley where it stopped. Inside the car were four Klansmen: Robert "Dynamite Bob" Chambliss, Thomas Blanton, Robert "Bobby" Frank Cherry, and Herman Cash, members of the Cahaba Boys' action squad.

Unbeknownst to them, two women disguised in wigs and hats sat watching in the shadows a block away. The women were Flora "Tee" Chambliss, Dynamite Bob's wife, and her sister, Mary Frances Cunningham. These extraordinary women who lived in the shadow of the Klan had done their best to alert law enforcement. They had leaked information through a trusted county deputy. Today they risked their lives to be witnesses and saw Thomas Blanton's Chevrolet park and Bobby Cherry exit the car carrying a black bag, watching as he took it around to the east side of the church. The bomb was left on the church's northeast side, under a stairway and outside the ladies' lounge. Understandably reluctant to come forward, Cunningham nonetheless eventually went to the FBI (along with her niece, Elizabeth Cobbs).

Years later, Cunningham denied that she had sat outside the church that night or even that she had ever reported it to the FBI. However, the state investigator who spent the most time with Cunningham, Bob Eddy, believed the women were there that night and that she recanted out of fear of the Klan and to protect her sister. The details of their account too closely matched that of another witness, Gertrude Glenn, a Black woman who worked in a hospital laundry in Detroit. She was in Birmingham that night and staying with a friend in a house behind the church. She pulled the car she was driving right behind the Chevrolet just as a man was exiting the car. Its dome light came on and from the back seat "Dynamite Bob" Chambliss turned, looking right into her headlights. She later identified him.

The men drove away, and the women hastened home. At about 2:30 a.m., Cunningham called a county deputy who had been the recipient of her frequent reports of information about Klan activity and plans. Tragically, the deputy told her to meet him the following morning and then hung up on her. She did meet him the next morning to warn him, and he later told investigators that he headed to the church, but he was too late.

MID-MORNING SUNDAY, FIVE BLACK girls primped and chatted in the ladies' lounge at 16th Street, getting ready for the church service that followed Sunday school. It was a special occasion, Youth Day, when the children would usher. They wore their best white dresses. The girls were Cynthia Wesley, Addie Mae Collins, Sara Collins, Carole Robertson, and Denise McNair. All were fourteen except Denise McNair, eleven, and Sara Collins, ten.

Investigators in the following years theorized the bomb's timing device (probably a water-drip trigger) clogged and failed to go off as planned during the night. Prosecutors would claim in court that the explosion went off just as planned. In any case, at 10:22 a.m., the bag of dynamite blew through thick layers of brick, stone, and mortar, cascading debris onto the girls in the lounge and killing four instantly. Sara Collins, badly wounded and blinded in one eye, survived. The last she'd seen of her sister, Addie Mae was tying Denise McNair's sash.

From under the debris, Sara called out in the darkness for her. There was no answer.

Lankford was one of many who rushed to the scene. He wrote, "A church became a tomb as ten sticks of dynamite dug a grave for four children. Gunshots echoed in the streets while police hunted a killer-bomber."[474]

A young Alton Parker was leaving the nearby Methodist church, crossing the street a couple of blocks away, when the bomb exploded and a plume of brown dust billowed from the front of the church. It seemed to him that sirens wailed only seconds later, leaving him with a lifelong impression that emergency responders were expecting the blast.

Police, however, were already in the area because of the tense atmosphere related to the school integration, the recent bombings of Arthur Shores's home, and the May bombings of the nearby Gaston Motel and A. D. King's house. In fact, Officer Charlie Dunnam, who had just been hired only a week before, was working Car 13 with his training officer, E. L. Lewis that morning. Dunnam was driving past Phillips High School, only a few blocks away, when he and Lewis heard the explosion and drove toward the sound. Dunnam was "shocked and saddened" by what they found.[475]

People reported hearing the explosion as far away as the city airport, about six miles. A large crowd formed as the churchgoers, dazed and some wounded, found their way outside. Chaos erupted. Angry Blacks pelted responding police with rocks and debris. One officer yelled, "We didn't do it. We are here to protect you!"

According to the *Washington Post*, "Thousands of hysterical Negroes poured into the area around the church this morning, and police fought for two hours, firing rifles into the air to control them." The church's Reverend John Cross took up a bullhorn and pleaded, "The police are doing everything they can. Please go home. . . . The Lord is our shepherd," he sobbed. "We shall not want."[476]

The children's charred and mangled bodies were taken to Hillman Hospital where their parents had to identify their daughters based on the remnants of the clothes they were wearing. Cynthia Wesley had to be identified by her shoes and the ring on her finger.

Sheriff's detective Dan Jordan recalled, "Blacks were throwing rocks that morning at innocent Whites who happened to drive through a Black neighborhood. . . . Unknown retaliators set fire to a large downtown building and a vacant house."[477]

Two additional homicides followed. In the aftermath of the chaos, sixteen-year-old Johnny Robinson was one of a group of Black youths throwing rocks at White teens in a car draped with a Confederate flag. When a patrol car pulled up (according to the police report), he also threw rocks at the officers. He fled. Officer Jack Parker shot him in the back. Parker was president of the local chapter of the Fraternal Order of Police and had recently signed an ad in the newspaper "arguing against integration of the department."[478] Local and federal grand juries reviewed the Robinson shooting and did not indict Parker.[479]

The other homicide victim was Virgil Ware, a thirteen-year-old Black youth who was riding on the handlebars of his brother's bicycle near Pratt City northwest of Birmingham. The boys had not participated in any of the violence but were simply headed home when two sixteen-year-old White youths rode by on a red motorcycle and shot Ware with a .22 pistol. The boys were Eagle Scouts and students at Phillips High School. That day they had attended a Klan rally and purchased a Confederate flag for their motorcycle.

When Detective Paul Couch of the Mountain Brook police department heard about Ware's murder, he took it upon himself to get in his car off-duty and, on a hunch, drive around the Fultondale area looking for the suspects, though it was miles from his jurisdiction. His hunch paid off. "I found myself driving behind what looked like the two shooters riding double on a red motorbike. I thought I saw a pistol bulging in the pocket of the boy riding on the rear . . . and I wrote down the motorbike license number, M-5403."[480]

Because of Couch's initiative, the case would be solved in two days. Usually clearing a case would be a cause of satisfaction, but Jordan was saddened and discouraged that the "racism of grownups in Birmingham had spread into the lives of two young Eagle Scouts." The White youths, Michael Lee Farley and Larry Joe Sims, were convicted of manslaughter and given probation.

Fires set in Black businesses burned sporadically throughout the night of the church bombing, accompanied by periodic gunfire. Wallace sent three hundred state troopers back into Birmingham to augment law enforcement, and they broke up any gatherings. At Birmingham armories, five hundred National Guardsmen stood by.

THE CITY SEEMED TO go into shock from the church bombing and the deaths of the young girls. The Magic City's curtain had ripped apart.

Chief Moore called the church bombing "the most awful, senseless, uncalled-for act of violence I can remember occurring in the city in my thirty-six years as a policeman."[481]

"'It is a tragic event,' Mayor Boutwell said, with tears in his eyes. 'I never could conceive that anyone existed with such universal malice. It is inconceivable to me. It is just sickening.'"[482]

Councilman Alan Drennen was working late alone at city hall when he heard sirens wailing. Leaving the office, he stepped into the elevator and asked the operator what was happening. At the news, he got into his car and drove to the Hillman Hospital where the children's bodies had been taken. He sat in his car in the parking lot and wept.[483]

At the Unitarian Church, the Reverend Alfred Walters Hobart received the news while he was in the pulpit. He stopped his sermon, telling the congregation that "nothing could be said in the face of such a murderous act—only action would suffice." Afterward, numbed congregants "remained to talk about how they might best respond to the tragedy." Two of the girls killed had been participants in a summer program at the church to prepare youth for the upcoming school integrations.[484]

When the Unitarian congregation learned of the fifty-eight people hospitalized after the bombing, a member who was a nurse offered her help at the hospital and several others gave blood. Gene Crutcher, the owner of a Southside bookstore, spent the afternoon contacting other Whites and urging them to give blood. "Many responded."[485] Ed Harris and Peggy Fuller representing the Unitarian Church, along with Lutheran Reverend Ellwanger, went to the hospital and afterward called on the Collins and Robertson families, offering assistance. Harris wrote that "in visiting the black neighborhoods, reported to be seething with hatred and dangerous to all white people," they were received in the spirit for which they came, "to express our sorrow at their loss."[486]

ALTHOUGH THE FBI HAD refused to intervene in the many previous bombings, Attorney General Robert Kennedy ordered the Bureau to investigate the 16th Street Baptist Church bombing. Dozens of agents and support staff poured in from around the country. By the next day, the *News* reported, "A growing task force of angry officers, including FBI bomb experts, today sifted through slim clues in the ruthless blasting of a Negro church that murdered four young worshippers."

U.S. District Court Judge Clarence A. Allgood voiced his anger in a public statement to a special federal grand jury before it retired to secret deliberations. "We have witnessed what amounts to mockery of our laws—a mockery by those who would cut the very roots of our American system of justice." He called the bombing a "hideous example of those who are completely in disregard of law, order, justice and plain common decency. I can think of no greater heresy or blackening sin against humanity." Then he did something that could not have been part of the bombers' plans—he ordered the federal grand jury to indict anyone who obstructed the federal court order to allow the five Black children scheduled to attend White schools.[487]

J. B. Stoner, the virulent anti-Semitic and racist Georgia attorney who had been the primary suspect of the 1958 bombing of Temple Beth-El, was on the list of top suspects for the church bombing. Not long before, law enforcement had received word that Stoner planned to meet with Klan members in the north Jefferson County woods. Lankford accompanied Sheriff Bailey, Major David Orange, and a couple of other deputies. Carefully working their way through the trees to observe the gathered "Kluxers," they got close enough to observe Stoner demonstrating in great detail how to make a timing device for a dynamite bomb.

An internal FBI memorandum from the Birmingham office to headquarters mentioned that Stoner was arrested in October 1963 for reckless driving. Stoner complained that the FBI was following him and that agents were "contacting neighbors, landlords and employers." The memo stated that the FBI wasn't following him, but he was "under local police surveillance."[488]

In fact, the FBI had planted listening devices inside the NSRP headquarters and Stoner's car. Marcus Jones and Lankford also had a more primitive eavesdropping device installed on a telephone pole inside a junction box in an alley behind the headquarters. Just yards away, they sat inside Jones's unmarked police car using a neighbor's empty garage for cover. Jones and Lankford had spent months periodically listening, especially when the FBI notified them that Stoner was coming to town, but everyone, including the feds, was frustrated with the lack of helpful information their efforts had produced.

After the church bombing, in a move described by Lankford as a "typical FBI tactic to get things moving in those days," the local agents decided to stir things up. At their request and under the direction of Lieutenant House, Jones and Lankford accepted a highly secret mission. Around midnight, they drove to the NSRP headquarters at 1865 Bessemer Road, where Lankford had tangled with the men who'd attacked Birmingham police inspector Haley. Lankford had no qualms about what federal and local officials asked him to do. "I always had an adversarial relationship with . . . the Nazis."

House and an FBI special agent watched from a patrol car in the Church of God parking lot across the street as Jones swung his unmarked police car across the middle lane and lined up alongside Stoner's empty convertible.

Lankford, who had been down on the back floorboard, rose up, "stuck a double barrel 12-gauge shotgun out the window and let go both barrels at point blank range at the car's cloth top."

As the FBI had hoped, the ensuing stir produced a flurry of phone calls from within NSRP headquarters. None resulted in any new leads.[489]

ALTHOUGH SOME CONSPIRACISTS SPECULATED that civil rights activists had placed the bomb at 16th Street as a way of gaining sympathy, most blamed those who had a history of setting off explosions—the Klan, the NSRP, and other extremist groups. The tragedy rippled across the country and even across the ocean. But it most intensely affected Birmingham. Despite the many bombings that had taken place in the city over the years, these were the first deaths.

The tragedies touched people across the spectrum of views on segregation.

Virginia Sparks Volker recalled that people who knew of her involvement in civil rights but had never spoken to her before came up to her and apologized for their racist views, as if they needed confession to lift their grief and guilt. They said things like, "I'm so sorry, this should not have happened. This is taking it too far."[490]

Young Earl Tilford, who would later become an Alabama writer and historian, watched his stalwart segregationist father, a Presbyterian minister, break down in tears when he heard about the children's deaths. "'If this is what 'defending our Southern way of life' means . . . then it's not worth defending.'"[491]

The deaths of the girls hit attorney Chuck Morgan hard. The day after the church bombing, he attended YMBC's Monday luncheon at the Redmont Hotel and gave a bitter and impassioned speech:

> Every person in this community who has in any way contributed during the past several years to the popularity of hatred is at least as guilty, or more so, than the demented fool who threw that bomb. Four little girls were killed in Birmingham yesterday. A mad, remorseful worried community asks, "Who did it? Who threw that bomb? Was it a Negro or a white?" The answer should be, "We all did it." Every last one of us is condemned for that crime and the bombing before it and a decade ago. We all did it.

But not everyone felt the blow. Morgan's wife, Camille, recalled that when she played bridge the Friday after the church bombing, "not one person mentioned that the church had been bombed. They just never acknowledged it." She felt that large segments of the White community were unaffected by the entire period of marches and bombings.

After Morgan's speech to the YMBC made the media, the family had to install a second phone line and number because of threatening phone calls. Morgan's son, Charles III, later recalled a family story about the intervention of a union man when the calls got really nasty, that Morgan was in his law office when a burly guy he had never seen came in and asked him to take a ride with him. When Morgan got into the passenger seat, the union man introduced the man in the back seat as Robert "Dynamite Bob" Chambliss.

The union man said over his shoulder, "Mr. Chambliss, tell Mr. Morgan who you are with."

"The Klan," Chambliss said.

"Now tell him what I told you I would do if those calls continue."

"You said you would break my neck."

"Do you believe I would do that?"

"Yes, sir, I do."[492]

The calls stopped for a while, but then picked up again. The Morgans endured all this because, as Camille affirmed, "Chuck loved Birmingham." But the breaking point came when the second phone line rang late at night with the warning, "'When you turn on the ignition to your car, a bomb will go off.' One of last things the caller said—and what made us finally make the decision to leave—was they knew the route our son took and the alley he walked through to the nearby Crestline School." Although Morgan had just signed a lease for a new office, the family packed up and left "the city he loved—the city that had broken his heart."[493]

On September 18, a funeral was held for three of the church bombing victims. King returned to Birmingham to give the eulogy. Thousands gathered. Of them, about eight hundred city pastors, priests, and rabbis—Black and White—met downtown and marched to the church, the largest interracial clerical gathering in the city's history. John Porter, a Black minister who led the impromptu march, recalled, "I felt great joy in seeing the togetherness of leaders of the religious community, but great sadness that it took this event to bring us together."[494]

On September 19, Rabbi Grafman, who had attended the funeral, was so distressed he tore up his notes for his sermon the day before one of the holy days in Jewish tradition, Rosh Hashanah, the Jewish New Year. Sick at heart and horrified at the bombing, for the first time in his career, he did not have prepared remarks. He simply spoke from his heart:

> For days about twenty of us have been meeting—colored and white—. . . since this terrible thing happened. . . . I said to them that if Birmingham has anything to repent of, to atone for, let it be the white community of Birmingham that makes the atonement. . . . You can't repay these people for the loss of their children, but whatever we can do to help them, hospital expenses, . . . let us do it! Let the white people of Birmingham do it! . . .
>
> I want to know how many Jews sitting in this room have written a letter to the editor of the *Birmingham Post-Herald* or the *News*. What's the matter, haven't you got the guts to do it? You afraid you might have harassing calls? I've had them since 1955 [and recently] because I referred to the Governor two months ago as bellicose and signed a statement to the effect that everyone, including him, has to obey laws until they are changed and court decisions until they are reversed. My life was actually threatened, though no one knew about it, and for . . . two and one half months my home [has been] under surveillance. . . .
>
> This isn't the way I like to talk on Rosh Hashanah. I told you, I have never done this before. These are terrible times. And it's time to stand up and be counted. It is time to do things. It is time to pay the price whether it is in personal safety and security or whether it is in money. The question is—are you ready to pay the price, because if you are not, God help this city. . . .
>
> Let us bow our heads in silence. In memory of Denise McNair, Carole Robertson, Addie Mae Collins, Cynthia Wesley, [John] Robinson, Virgil Ware. Wantonly killed, insanely slain, brutally murdered, whose deaths we mourn, whose families we would comfort and the shame of whose murders we would, and we must have our city atone.[495]

At the Unitarian Church, the Reverend Hobart delivered a memorial sermon titled "Requiem for Six Children" for the four girls and two boys killed on September 15. Marjorie Linn, a local poet, wrote the *Birmingham News.* "How can responsible, clear-thinking White people possibly believe that there is any excusing such acts?"[496]

After the editorial, Linn received an invitation to the next Birmingham Council on Human Relations meeting and took her close friend Gertrude Goldstein. Goldstein had little personal experience with Blacks, but she listened to the details of the bombing and stories about mistreatment of Blacks, stories that opened her eyes. "You couldn't get it on radio and television." She attempted to share the reality of what happened to Birmingham Blacks with her friends. "There were no discussions in front of me," Goldstein recalled, "because they knew that I had gotten involved. . . . I wanted to talk about it, and everybody would just shut up about it. They were just really steering clear."[497]

Historian Wayne Flynt called the bombing of the 16th Street Baptist Church "our moment of epiphany when . . . someone held up a mirror and we had to look at ourselves and think that is really who we are, and we can't deny it anymore. That is who we are."[498]

On September 22, Jim Jimerson of the Alabama Council on Human Relations attended the funeral services of Ware and Robinson. Unlike the funerals for the girls killed in the church, Jimerson was the only White person to attend. He and his family later visited the Wares' home. Virgil's father had lost his job as a coal miner and worked as a yardman when he could. His mother worked as a maid when she could. The visit affected Jimerson's young son, Randall, who later wrote, "We talked with her and let the family know there were people concerned with the loss of their son. Mrs. Ware thanked us over and over for coming to visit. The Ware family literally didn't have enough food to eat, and they had never heard of the food stamp program. You had to pay two dollars to get enrolled in the program, and it was a long time since they had seen two dollars."

The Jimersons gave the family the two dollars and offered to help find financial support. As they drove home past the deserted road where the two teenagers shot Virgil Ware off his brother's bicycle, the Jimerson children stared out the car window in silence.[499]

After the bombing, the school demonstrations and motorcades died down, and White students settled down to the inevitability of having a token few

Black students in their schools. Those students reported that there were some efforts of friendship and several incidents of harassment, but no violence.

A year later, the FBI office in Birmingham recommended to director J. Edgar Hoover that the Justice Department review evidence in the bombing case. They stated that there was in Birmingham a "climate of public opinion favoring prosecution." Hoover declined their request.[500] It remains debatable whether Hoover blocked prosecution of the church bombing or recognized that the case was not winnable without court-admissible evidence. Although local police and the FBI knew (through informants, primarily "Tee" Chambliss, who told her sister Mary Frances Cunningham, who relayed the information to a deputy who reported it to the FBI) the identities of the bombers, at the time the key witnesses—White and Black—fearing for their lives, refused to testify.[501]

The Birmingham Klan appeared to go underground after the church bombing. Few wanted to be associated publicly with the group or to be subjected to the intense federal investigation that followed, even though the FBI did not make a case until years later. As journalist Donald Brown reflected, "The church bombing itself put a clamp on the outcries that had gone on all summer from the Klan and the National States' Rights Party. [But] the inability of national, state and local law enforcement to come to grips with those who put the bombs at the church, the inability to do that hung very heavy over us for a long time."[502]

PART

Three

32

Bullets and Beatles

It took three months after the abolishment of Birmingham's Jim Crow laws for a resolution from University Hospital's new medical facility council and a memo from Black employees to prompt President Joseph Volker to desegregate the dental and medical schools. "Black employees began using the faculty—the cafeteria, the bathrooms, the water fountains—just as Whites did."[503]

In October 1963, the Reverend Fred Shuttlesworth, backed by Martin Luther King Jr., threatened more demonstrations, once again holding non-violence workshops with the city's youth. This time one issue was the demand for a meeting between the city council and SCLC leaders. The city refused, partly because both Shuttlesworth and King were considered "outsiders" (Shuttlesworth had taken a pastorate in Cincinnati in 1961).

A. G. Gaston and attorney Arthur Shores confirmed that they still "have faith in Birmingham and believe that a majority of the people of Birmingham deplore and are ashamed of the recent climate of hate, bombings and violence which exist in our community, and we feel that our local problems can better be solved by local leaders of our community, white and colored, if there is continued open communication between members of the group[s]."[504]

A second issue was the city's failure to hire Black police officers. Exacerbating the fact that few Blacks applied was the requirement that the Civil Service Board had to test and approved all city hires. In December, two Blacks passed the civil service exams. According to the *Birmingham News*, Cecil Hayden refused to fill out a police application form. Jonathan McPherson, a chemistry instructor at Miles College, was also certified, but failed to show up for his interview, and his application was thrown out. According to the article, McPherson said he never received notification of an interview, however he later recalled having an interview with Connor where Connor asked him if he would arrest a White person.[505] The *News* also reported that a school would soon offer instructions on passing exams, and that Black leaders had begun a drive to encourage people to take the civil service exams and apply for police positions.[506] It remains an open question whether Black applicants were not qualified or simply designated so, but King and Shuttlesworth called off the threat of demonstrations over the issue, admitting some unpreparedness in "getting Negroes to apply for police jobs."[507]

The *News* and *Post-Herald* supported the call for hiring Black police. "We have put this matter off for years, and we are paying the penalty for inaction. It is past time we faced up to reality." Petitions supporting the hiring of Black officers appeared in the newspapers as ads, one from ninety city residents and one from forty-four prominent business leaders. The YMBC and Birmingham Trade Council were among the White voices raised in support of hiring Black officers.[508]

Yet another reason for the foot-dragging was a bow to the newly formed Community Affairs Committee on Group Relations, which was discussing the issue. That committee of ten Blacks and fourteen Whites, chaired by Episcopal Bishop C. C. J. Carpenter, recommended to Mayor Boutwell and the city council that "the mayor make a public statement immediately that the city will employ Negro police when they have qualified under civil service regulations and are certified."[509]

BY NOVEMBER, THE DOOR had cracked wide enough for James T. Montgomery, a Black cardiologist, to step through and become the first Black physician to practice at University Hospital, a position previously reserved for physicians who belonged to the private and all-White Jefferson County Medical Society. The effort to open that door began five years earlier when President Volker discussed it with a few liberal physicians, including Dr. Abraham "Abe" Russakoff, a Jewish physician who had come to Birmingham in 1946.[510]

A few years after beginning practice in Birmingham, Russakoff accepted an invitation to teach interns on the segregated wards of University Hospital. He refused to follow the custom of calling Black patients by their first names. The chief threatened that he must "conform to the local mores, 'or else.'" Russakoff chose the "or else," returning only after a change in administration allowed him to treat all patients with respect.

The only board-certified chest physician in Alabama until the late 1960s, Russakoff was considered one of the "fathers" of pulmonary medicine. He spent fifteen years studying the effects on the lungs of people living near steel mills, accumulating data that led in 1970 to Alabama's first air pollution law.[511]

Known for his compassion with patients, Russakoff also disobeyed Jim Crow laws in his private practice, keeping his waiting rooms integrated, which did not "win him friends" in the White community. Soon after opening his office, he hired a Black woman as a custodian. "It became apparent she had much more potential. . . . We taught her how to take an electrocardiogram, to take and process chest x-rays, and other technical patient-connected procedures." He lost patients, but she continued to work with him for more than thirty years.[512]

Russakoff's initial efforts to convince the Jefferson County Medical Society to admit a Black physician were unsuccessful. "Volker, Zukoski, Russakoff, [Mathew] McNulty, and Walter Frommeyer initiated a full-court press on the Medical Society's discriminatory practices; telephone calls, 'serious conversation' over lunches, letters, and McNulty's pleading remarks before the society." James Montgomery finally acquired the letters of endorsement needed from current members in October 1963. In a unanimous vote of the membership committee, the medical society accepted him as a member. A few weeks later, he applied for and received "an appointment to the active staff of the University Hospital and an appointment as clinical assistant professor of medicine."[513]

As the "Pink One" and the School of Medicine's top administrator, Volker had to tread cautiously. He found ways around his constraints. When emergency room physicians related that they were treating Blacks with lacerations and wounds from Birmingham police officers, Volker phoned Bull Connor and threatened to go to the press "unless Connor intervened, which apparently he did for a while."[514]

Volker's desire to move the School of Medicine forward was fueled in part by the realization that negative national attention added to the already difficult task of recruiting top-notch faculty. State legislators, some expressing concern about the "medical center liberals in Birmingham," didn't help. One state representative proposed a bill that would require a "loyalty pledge" to Alabama's racial laws on the back of state paychecks, in effect requiring employees to sign the pledge to endorse their checks. Volker spoke to Governor Wallace about the issue, and Wallace backed him. The bill died before ever being introduced.[515]

Dr. Leon "Chink" Weinstein, whose Jewish grandparents emigrated from Russia, was another professional who rejected Jim Crow laws in his private office. His daughter, Lynn Raviv, recalled, "Growing up in Ensley, [my father's] family lived in a multicultural area, neighbors to an African-American family with whom they shared an outhouse." As a dentist, he cared for African American patients at a time when few White doctors and dentists served Black patients unless at night and on Sundays.

Weinstein and his wife Phyllis invited groups of dentists to their home for "dinner and a parlor type meeting to prepare the groundwork for a smooth integration of the Birmingham Dental District Society." As president, Weinstein would oversee that integration in 1964 and 1965.[516] Phyllis Weinstein was known for her passion in promoting Holocaust education and for her "commitment to building bridges and communication between various communities in Birmingham," including later working with the Birmingham Civil Rights Institute. [517]

Meanwhile, in November 1963, segregationists aimed a low blow at Lutheran minister Joseph Ellwanger, a White minister with a Black congregation. Besides taking two Black teen girls to a White church in Tuscaloosa, he had attended mass meetings and stood in picket lines in front of downtown businesses. Unnamed "officials" called Ellwanger to city hall to disclose an accusation against him. While Ellwanger waited to find out what was going on, a police officer led in a nervous Black man, a jail trusty. The officer said, "This prisoner reported that last week, when he was cleaning the men's room on the first floor of city hall, you made a pass at him, tried to have sex with him, and he had to push you away and run to get away from you." The officer threatened to charge Ellwanger with attempted sexual assault. A few weeks later, Ellwanger received a call from someone who claimed to be in the district attorney's office and could drop the charges if he left town. Indignant at the absurd allegation, Ellwanger refused, and the matter dropped.[518]

WITH THE REST OF the world, Birmingham watched in shock as President John F. Kennedy was assassinated November 22, 1963, in Dallas, Texas. In many Black Birmingham homes, a photo of Kennedy hung on the wall alongside those of Martin Luther King Jr. and Jesus. No doubt there was celebration in the homes of extremists. Some children remember students and even teachers clapping at the news. Others remember it as a somber, tearful moment. Although some saw Kennedy as a Northern federalist meddler, he was their president, and his death rocked the nation and the South.

1964 began with the Beatles' first appearance on the Ed Sullivan Show. Spring brought waves of unrest across the country. Racist vigilantes beat Black groups in Florida, and White Mississippi geared up to challenge the interracial voter registration activism of what would be called the Mississippi Freedom Summer.

Throughout the turbulence of the era, "a group of young white lawyers, bankers, businessmen, and scientists met quietly. "In the companies they worked for, they were trying to be change agents. They were hiring the first blacks in non-traditional jobs. . . . They tried to find candidates to run for office. Most were never going to go to a demonstration or write a letter to the paper, but they worked to make their city better. Saturdays, Clarke Stallworth, the newspaperman, held class in the home of Jack Hurley and told these men, preoccupied with business affairs, what was really going on in their city."[519]

In the quiet suburb of Mountain Brook, just south of Birmingham, Julian L. McPhillips Sr. took on the pastorate of St. Luke's Episcopal Church, preaching "bold sermons on civil rights-related topics." McPhillips and his wife Eleanor Dixon McPhillips had moved from Montgomery where "he organized the city's first biracial clergy group, led services at . . . a black parish [and] with assistance from Birmingham's Bishop Murray, helped found a facility for black children with mental disabilities and served on its board of directors." [520]

Eleanor McPhillips joined the women in the community who took on segregation, a list that included Peggy Fuller, a Unitarian and the wife of well-known architect and YMBC member John Fuller. Peggy was an outspoken leader supporting integration, writing a "stream" of letters to the local newspapers. Her pastor, Alfred Hobart, "recounted that Peggy waged a continuing battle with 'the prejudiced, the hate-mongers, the Klan and members of the White Citizens' Council during the bad days in Birmingham.'"

Another outspoken woman was Cecil Roberts. Born in England, Roberts had a successful career in New York as a fashion designer but followed her husband to Birmingham where she engaged in a myriad of activities, from igniting the area's cultural opportunities to supporting projects for the sick, poor, and Planned Parenthood. Involved in more than thirty civic projects and boards, she quipped, "All I need to get sold on a project—and I don't care if it's for Catholics, Jews, or Negroes—is to pull my full weight."[521] Roberts is credited for the first integration of the Alabama Symphony when she took Dr. John and Ethel Nixon as her guests. "She also brought Ralph Bunche to the Mountain Brook Country Club for dinner," Councilman John Katapodis reflected, "to the objection of other patrons who did not care that he was a diplomat that had won the Nobel Peace Prize . . . he was still black and better suited, in their minds, to waiting on tables there."[522]

Several Black and White women had met each other over the years at the integrated Council on Human Relations meetings. Dr. Lucius Pitts invited a group of those women to Miles College. They asked him, "What can we do [about race relations]?" Dr. Pitts said, "You can sit down and have a cup of coffee or tea, and you will find out that you have more in common than you think."[523] Later in 1961, the women began to gather in each other's homes to discuss issues and get to know one another. "They met first in the Black women's homes because it was too dangerous to meet at the White homes."[524] Besides socializing in secret, the women discussed issues of "integration, racial equality, women's rights, and resisting peer pressure to conform to the South's racial exclusion."[525]

Virginia Jimerson recorded in her diary on November 16, 1961: "Went to Jackie Mazzara's group. Had interesting discussion on race. Eileen Walbert has very compassionate feelings. Ann Thorpe . . . felt that not enough of us speak out—not willing to be unpopular. Helen Knox finds it difficult to talk with people on opposite side [segregationists]—it upsets her. . . ."[526]

By 1964, Peggy Fuller had formed the group of women into a more formal interracial organization called Friendship and Action or Friends in Action. The group hoped that "getting to know one another on a personal level . . . could dispel myths and misconceptions that often smolder beneath the surface of polite society."[527]

The Friends' early White members included Anny Kraus, whose husband Frederick had been recruited by the medical school; Eileen Walbert; Sidney Fiquette; Sandra Harris, wife of activist Edward Harris; Carolyn McCoy; Peggy Fuller; Helen Baer, and Bette Lee Hanson, whose husband Roger was president of the Birmingham Council on Human Relations. Under her maiden name, Bette had a radio talk show on WAPI where she invited Black guests such as Lucius Pitts.[528]

Friendship and Action was not just about socializing and talking across racial lines. Two of the White Friends, Walbert and Kraus, teamed up with Black attorney Oscar Adams's wife, Willa, to investigate inequities at Black schools. After seeing the conditions in Miles College's science labs, Kraus persuaded professors at UAB to donate equipment.[529]

The summer after the church bombing, the New York-based African Cultural Society granted Friendship and Action $5,000. That money developed an integrated play school for approximately sixty children, invited weekly speakers to the Unitarian Church, sent an integrated group of eight children to a camp in New York State, and started a tutoring class to prepare Black children for attending integrated schools. Member Kay Hall taught students at Miles how to take tests effectively. The Friends sponsored an integrated public forum on "Problems of American Democracy," held at the Unitarian Church.[530] In the years to come, several of these women would take on even more activist roles, stepping up publicly to share their perspectives and to initiate difficult discussions in the community.

THE YEAR AFTER THE children's marches, hate still hovered over the city. On the morning of March 18, 1964, Sol Kimerling opened mail at his home that put an icy chill in his heart—it was as if Nazi Germany had stepped over his threshold into his home. The letter was from Alex Rittenbaum, president of the Birmingham Jewish Community Council. It contained a warning about anti-Semitic literature being passed around Birmingham and enclosed, as an example, a 1938 copy of a German newspaper, the *Estiirmer*. In it was an article referencing the "Jewish Murder Plan," along with a large cartoon of a Jewish man holding a bowl to catch blood from the throats of Aryan youths for a Passover ritual.[531]

On the other side of the spectrum, the U.S. Congress on July 2, 1964, passed the landmark civil rights bill that Martin Luther King and many others had worked toward. President Kennedy had pushed for the bill after the 1963 events in Birmingham, though he did not live to see it become law. President Lyndon B. Johnson shepherded the bill through congressional committees. Believing the voting rights section would hold up the entire bill, he removed that section, but the Civil Rights Act of 1964 made it illegal to discriminate because of race, color, religion, sex, or national origin. The act outlawed racial segregation in facilities serving the general public, as well as strengthened voter protections and allowed the Justice Department to initiate school desegregation and other civil rights suits. On July 13, a three-judge federal court panel, while declining to order statewide desegregation, enjoined George Wallace and the State Board of Education from interfering in court-ordered desegregation "anywhere in Alabama"—a sweeping ruling that affected Birmingham's future as well as the state's.

More local legal battles lay ahead as Southern segregationists swore resistance. In Birmingham, Ollie's Barbeque on Greensprings Highway still refused to serve Blacks, leading to a landmark Supreme Court case (*Katzenbach v. McClung*) upholding the 1964 Act; Alabama's Hugo Black was one of the concurring justices.

The climate was changing. The Reverend C. Herbert Oliver, who had headed the Inter-Citizens Committee in Birmingham and for years had documented sworn complaints of police brutality, stopped preparing the reports because "he could not find cases for the past several months."[532] On June 5, 1964, for the first time since the bombing of the 16th Street Baptist Church, congregants had returned to their rebuilt building, a sign of healing and hope. The church held an interracial service in August to rededicate the church. That same month, Miles College opened its first interracial day camp.

YET BIRMINGHAM AND ALABAMA and the South continued to struggle with race. In the Freedom Summer of 1964, hundreds of youth flocked to Mississippi to help register Black voters. In June, Mississippi Klan members abducted and murdered one Black and two White civil rights workers—James Chaney from Meridian, Mississippi, and two young Jewish men, Andrew Goodman and Michael Schwerner from New York City. Their bodies were found buried in an earthen dam.

In Birmingham, many were still reeling emotionally from the 16th Street church bombing. Edward Harris rented the Unitarian Church for a memorial service for the children killed. The newspaper didn't print his press release, so he paid for an ad, listing the names of the six youths who were killed that day, including the two boys, Virgil Ware and John Robinson.

"At that time," Harris recalled, "I was not a minister, and I didn't really know what I was doing. It all fell into place, because very shortly somebody came forward and said, 'I play the piano,' and then from Carole Robertson's school, the choir director called and said, 'Can I bring some of our children to sing?' Dr. Oliver said he would do the prayer, and then Mrs. Ware called me and said could she come. I said, 'Absolutely, please do.' She said, 'It's the first time that anybody has acknowledged that my boy was killed then too.'"[533] Lawrence E. McGinty, a native Alabamian who was now the Unitarian minister, gave the welcome to the mixed attendees. When a bomb threat was received, the attendees refused to leave and instead continued on with the memorial service.

Fall was also the time for the State Fair, which was held on the fairgrounds in west Birmingham. The Klan planned to set up an exhibit at the fair as they had for years, staffing the booth with robed Klansmen who passed out pamphlets and little Confederate flags. Rabbi Grafman asked that the National Conference of Christians and Jews appeal to the Fair Authority to bar the exhibit. The request was granted, after which the Klan threatened the rabbi and his congregation with a million-dollar libel lawsuit.[534]

Harris, along with three or four Black activists and a half a dozen White friends, integrated that fair. Joan Sidney (Malloy) Fiquette, a White Birmingham schoolteacher who worked with autistic students, was one of the friends who accompanied him. As a high school student she had written letters-to-the editor supporting desegregation, and she had taken part in an early effort by the Alabama Council on Human Relations to desegregate Birmingham's public elevators. "She and a black teen-age boy went downtown one day and rode up together in the 'White Only' elevator of the Brown Marx Building. Blacks had to take the freight elevators in that building."

The integrated group walked together through the fairgrounds, tailed by law enforcement. Six thugs, probably frustrated Klan members, attacked Harris, knocking him to the ground and kicking him repeatedly. The police stepped in. The attackers and Harris's group scattered, except Fiquette, who stayed with him. Police arrested Harris for inciting a riot, taking him and Fiquette to jail. A few days later, the city school where Fiquette worked fired her for "drinking beer in a public place with a man other than her husband."[535]

33

The Color of Money and Trouble Down the Road

In 1964, Karl Friedman and a few other businessmen boldly decided to do something they had talked about and planned for a long time—to create an integrated bank, owned and operated by Blacks and Whites and serving both segments of the community. The three White and seven Black businessmen knew the State of Alabama would not welcome a bank with Black owners, so they went for a federal bank. The Kennedys were pushing to get minorities into professional positions, but not a single national bank had been brought to Alabama.

With extensive contacts in the Black community, Friedman determined he could help make this dream come true. As the attorney for the Birmingham group, Friedman studied the requirements to get a federal bank charter. One of his partners had connections in the U.S. Senate that would possibly be of help. Each of the ten put up about $10,000 as seed money. They would need approval by the Office of the Comptroller of the Currency, an independent bureau within the U.S. Treasury Department that chartered, regulated, and supervised all national banks. Friedman began a long, tedious series of communications with the assistant comptroller in Memphis, Tennessee.

Friedman responded to every demand of the assistant comptroller. At last, they reached a critical point where the coalition needed to find a location. A building at Fourth Avenue and Nineteenth Street North seemed perfect—in the heart of the White retail business area yet only two blocks west of the Black business sector. The former clothing store was now empty and owned by a corporation. One-third of the ownership interest belonged to a well-known businessman Friedman referred to as "an industrialist." The Aland family owned the other two-thirds. Leon Aland, a client of Friedman's, was happy to have a prospective occupant for his vacant building, and they drew up and entered into a lease. But the other partial owner "blew his top" when Aland told him about the deal. The next day he appeared at the store with his attorney and told Aland:

"You know, you could have some terrible problems if you let them occupy your property there. White people won't trade in your stores if you do that."

Aland replied, "Let me see if I understand. You don't want me to have a lease, because a black person is involved."

The attorney said, "That's right, Mr. Aland. We ain't having no niggers on Nineteenth Street."

Mr. Aland said, "Please leave my office before I throw you out."

Leon Aland called Friedman that afternoon and told him what happened. "I'll be damned if they're gonna run my business for me. We'll have a showdown."

"Mr. Aland, that might be a mistake," Friedman cautioned him. "You know, you don't own that [business] by yourself. You've got three brothers and a sister that own it along with you. You ought to consult them before you have that showdown."

Aland said, "They'll do whatever I tell them."

"Well, at least get their blessing." Friedman said.

He [Aland] called me the next day and said, "They're scared to death."

So, I said, "You need to get out of the lease, tear up your copy, and I'll tear up mine, and we'll go elsewhere."

He was very grateful, but he really was disappointed in himself.[536]

Friedman pursued another opportunity that had just opened up. The Steiner Bank had operated in the Steiner Building at First Avenue and Twenty-first Street north. The bank had moved, leaving the building vacant. The location was excellent, and the physical layout was better than Aland's property. Friedman explained to the owner, Bernard Steiner, what racial issues might arise. Friedman said, "We created a lease, signed it, and waited for the explosion." Steiner also had a "visitor," who confronted him about signing a lease with the interracial group. Steiner replied. "Oh, I made a mistake. I am so sorry, but I have already given them a lease and I can't withdraw."

Friedman sent in the lease, the last requirement the assistant comptroller had put before him, only to receive a list of new issues. It was obvious they were being stonewalled. Frustrated and angry, most of the ten partners gathered, while others listened in on a loudspeaker. The mood was dour.

Arthur Shores spoke up. The distinguished Black attorney, whose home had twice been bombed by extremists, had been among those representing Martin Luther King during the Montgomery bus boycott. He garnered respectful attention. "I want to make one more try at it," he said.

Throughout the crisis days of 1963, the Kennedys frequently consulted Shores, and he had a phone number to the switchboard in Robert Kennedy's office. Shores called that number and spoke with the attorney general. "'I know that your family is trying to get [more] minority businesses. We tried to form a federal bank down here, but we've been closed out by a bunch of bigots." After a moment, Shores said, ". . . I'd like for you to talk to my lawyer.'"

Friedman took the phone, recalling, "That was the first time I had a hello with the Attorney General of the United States." Kennedy asked if Friedman was confident he had complied with everything asked, and Friedman said, "They're running out of things to complain about," and he related the story in detail. Kennedy asked a few questions and then asked where he could get in touch with Friedman.

The first call that arrived the next morning was from the assistant comptroller, who was suddenly eager to have another meeting about the bank. He assured Friedman there were no further issues. Three days later, Friedman had the certificate, and the consortium was in the banking business. "There was rage and anger, and pride and happiness all over town. We had an integrated bank, the American National Bank of Birmingham, the first such in over one hundred years."

A. G. Gaston bought a $10,000 certificate of deposit, though his primary banking remained with First National Bank of Birmingham. The partners convinced their friends and business acquaintances to deposit their payroll tax withholdings in the new bank, which helped but was too little and too late. "Almost no one in the black community patronized us." Friedman recalled. "They didn't have any confidence in a black bank to succeed. So, it was a pyrrhic victory. We put it on the market and sold it, and we came out pretty good, financially, but it was sad." The American National Bank of Birmingham closed in 1964 and became the National Bank of Commerce.

The day the bank sold, Friedman walked out of the building with one of the Black members of the consortium, Dr. James T. Montgomery, Fred Shuttlesworth's doctor, the head of the department of medicine at a hospital in nearby Bessemer, and Friedman's good friend and client.

"'Doc, I know how you feel,' Friedman told him. 'Jewish people have lived with this for thousands of years, but we think we are making progress.'"

"'Karl, I appreciate that,' Montgomery replied, 'but when you and I walked out on this street, what everybody noticed is that I am Black, and you are White . . . and *nothing* is changing.'"

That comment made a deep impression on Friedman. For his part in the venture, Friedman received "a multitude of nasty telephone calls at my home, embarrassing my daughters, and telephone calls to our office asking for Arthur Shores, several little nags like that. On the good side, it established my legitimacy with the Black community. I already had several Black clients, and more came."

Friedman was in Israel the week of July 4, 1964, when he learned that someone had scorched the words "Nigger lover" with hairspray onto the grass of his front yard. The eight-foot tall words stretched from one end of the hundred-foot yard to the other. His brother-in-law repaired the yard, but when Friedman returned from his trip, he was walking through the living room and saw "a little flash [in the window] like the sun shining in a certain way." It turned out to be a bullet hole. "Nobody knew anything about it, and nobody ever wrote me, or commented about it. So, all I know, in the middle of civil rights, someone saw fit to shoot a bullet through that window."

Despite that, no one in the mostly Jewish residential area in Mountain Brook where he lived ever complained to him or, to his knowledge, to anyone else about any of his activities, about the dozen or so cars parked at his house, or about the police car that the Mountain Brook police department sent to watch over them. Although his children took the "nasty telephone calls" in stride, his upset wife asked whether it was right for him to create a situation of risk for the family. Friedman himself was uneasy, but he carried on in the spirit of his mother, who had opened the doors of his mind and their home when he was a child. The interracial meetings in his home—with Black clients or other civil rights activists—continued.[537]

As BIRMINGHAM'S TRIALS AND tragedies of 1963 receded, new ones were coming into focus ninety miles south in Selma, the seat of Dallas County and the largest city in the west Alabama Black Belt. The SCLC had staff members working with the Dallas County Voters League by 1963, and by the next year so did SNCC. While Project C's focus had been on general discrimination in retail and employment, the target of the Selma Campaign was voting rights: In 1960 Census data, Dallas County was 58 percent African American, but only some 150 of the 15,000 voting-age Blacks were registered.

Two years of demonstrations, mass meetings, and marches to the courthouse had limited success, but the effort spread to adjacent counties. On February 18, 1965, Army veteran and church deacon Jimmie Lee Jackson was shot by state trooper James Bonard Fowler during a voting rights demonstration in Marion, Alabama, thirty miles west of Selma. Jackson died eight days later, prompting an outcry by civil rights workers to carry his body to the State Capitol and symbolically lay it at the feet of Governor George Wallace, whose fiery rhetoric was blamed for instigating the assault by local and state police officers on the Marion demonstration. Jackson's body was not taken to Montgomery, but the call to do so led the next month to the Selma to Montgomery March.

Meanwhile, two White Birmingham women, disturbed by the events in the Black Belt, made a trip to Selma to "see for themselves" what was happening. What one of the women, Mary Gonzalez of the Birmingham Council on Human Relations, saw burdened her. Dallas County Sheriff Jim Clark was terrifying the Black community and suppressing Black voter registration.

The BCHR subsequently invited the SCLC's Hosea Williams, one of the activists in Selma, to meet with them. The Reverend Williams spoke to the group at the First Congregational Christian Church on Center Street (Dynamite Hill) about the oppression of Blacks under the harsh hand of Sheriff Clark. He gave more details about the shooting of Jackson in Marion.

Eileen Walbert asked, "What can we do to help?" Williams replied, "I'll tell you one thing you can do to help. You can take some warm, white bodies down there and show yourselves and that you care."[538] The subsequent decision to get involved was not unanimous among BCHR members, but several took the challenge to heart. To give them organizational status, attorney Abe Berkowitz, who had attended the meeting, drew up the incorporation of Concerned White Citizens of Alabama.[539]

CWCA then asked SNCC to send some trainers to help plan what the inexperienced Whites from Birmingham could do in Selma. Helen Baer, a member of Temple Emanu-El, spoke up to say she was "tired of having black people do all the work"—lead and demonstrate for voting rights—and "I don't care if anyone else goes to Selma. I'm going if I have to go alone." Gonzalez joined her. Their determination moved others.[540]

Led by the Reverend Joseph Ellwanger of St. Paul's Lutheran Church, the group made phone calls and sent delegations to other Whites throughout Alabama to rally in Selma with a march to the courthouse. Eileen Walbert recalled that brief newspaper coverage brought in warm letters and contributions from across the country. With only ten days' notice, seventy-two people—forty-six from Birmingham—answered the call.[541]

Peggy Rupp, Marjorie Linn, the Walberts, and representatives from the Jewish community—the Siegels, Krauses, Goldsteins, and Baers—were among Birminghamians who stepped forward. When the group arrived in Selma, they were welcomed at the Reformed Presbyterian Church by the SCLC's James Bevel and Father Maurice Ouellet, who like Ellwanger served a Black congregation.[542] Helen Baer recalled that there were "quite a few Blacks there. They were so happy and so astonished. They were just not used to having Whites come on their side."[543]

Local Unitarian pastor James Rongstad, however, asked the group why they had come to Selma. "We didn't come to Birmingham to tell you what to do," Rongstad said. It was an ironic echo of the response of Birmingham Jews in 1963 to the New York rabbis. In both cases, the outsiders took a risk, but they also could return home, leaving the locals to pay the price for their stand. However, the rabbis returned to the safety of the North, but the White Alabama marchers would return to the same environment that threatened the Selma Unitarians. Frederick Kraus, speaking unknowingly to a *New York Times* reporter, said, "'We have remained silent for a long time, trying to give moral support to Negroes. I personally felt it was time to show that a group of demonstrators can have a face other than that of the Negro."[544]

From Broad Street, the group marched two by two with signs reading "Silence Is No Longer Golden" and "Decent Alabamians Detest Police Brutality." SNCC workers made sure the White marchers followed the law by keeping a certain distance apart and not blocking sidewalks. The marchers were prepared to be arrested, but that was not their purpose. At Alabama Street, "There on our right," Ellwanger recalled, "were about one hundred white men . . . with baseball bats or pipes and using foul language to let us know what they thought of us. To our left, on the far side of the intersection, in the street and on the grassy area around the federal building, were about four hundred blacks giving us words of encouragement."[545]

Peggy Rupp, who had worked with Black youth across the state through the Episcopal parish in Birmingham, said, "We had training to ignore all the taunts and shouting. We were just there to let people know that there were white people in Alabama who believed blacks should have equal rights." Helen Baer recalled that jeering bystanders tried to trip them. "We just had to keep our faces straight ahead." Her husband, Maurice "Max" Baer, remembered that she had carefully dressed befitting her Vestavia Garden Club. "Mary Gonzalez was [also] focused on maintaining order and dignity as they approached the courthouse steps."[546]

Amelia Boynton, longtime stalwart activist in the Dallas County Voters League, said, "I can never do justice to the great feeling of amazement and encouragement I felt when, perhaps for the first time in American history, white citizens of a Southern state banded together to come to Selma and show their indignation about the injustices against African Americans. . . . They had everything to lose, while we . . . had nothing to lose and everything to gain."[547]

Through the jeering segregationists, Ellwanger led his group to the courthouse steps where he read their proclamation protesting the treatment of arrested Negroes in keeping them from voting and gathering in lawful assembly.[548] When he finished, seventy-two voices lifted in "America the Beautiful." The segregationists tried to drown them out with "Dixie." But from across the street, the hundreds of Black witnesses joined in with their strong voices to finish "America the Beautiful"[549] and then to sing "We Shall Overcome."[550]

"You could feel the danger in the air, the hatred . . . from the whites," Helen Baer remembered. As Ellwanger led the group from the courthouse steps, a law enforcement officer approached. It was CWCA's good fortune that Sheriff Jim Clark was out of town, leaving Selma Public Safety Director Wilson Baker in charge. Baker had often de-escalated situations, perhaps playing a role in relation to the brutal Sheriff Clark as Police Chief Jamie Moore had to Bull Connor in Birmingham.

Baker quietly advised Ellwanger to take a different route back to the Presbyterian Church. Along the way, White men knocked down a photographer, but others pulled the assailants off, and there were no further incidents.

Advised to leave quickly, the White marchers got in their cars, "rolled up the windows, locked the doors and drove away." They made it home safely, despite a frightening encounter with two carloads of Klansmen who followed them part of the way.

34

Selma Repercussions in Birmingham

On March 7, 1965, some six hundred Blacks set out from Brown Chapel AME Church to march to the State Capitol, fifty-five miles away. Two abreast, the column marched through downtown Selma and across the Edmund Pettus Bridge over the Alabama River. At the foot of the bridge on the Montgomery side, the marchers were beaten and teargassed by state troopers and Sheriff Clark's horseback "posse." The day would become known as "Bloody Sunday."

Afterwards, Dr. Martin Luther King Jr. and the SCLC put out a call to community leaders and clergy of all faiths across the country to join in a march of protest and solidarity for those who had borne the onslaught on the Selma bridge. On March 9, Birmingham's Joseph Ellwanger and Eileen Walbert and her son David joined hundreds of Black and White clergy and citizens in Selma, perhaps a total of 2,500 persons.[551] At least two dozen marchers came from Birmingham and, of those, at least fifteen had marched a few days earlier with the CWCA. Meanwhile, U.S. District Judge Frank M. Johnson Jr. of Montgomery had issued a restraining order against continuing the march until he could hold hearings to sort out constitutional issues and protection for the demonstrators. Not wanting to defy Johnson's order, King led the large crowd to the Selma side of the bridge and held a service, then turned the march around and went back to the church.

That night, Klansmen severely clubbed White Unitarian minister James Reeb of Boston as he was leaving a Selma restaurant. He was taken to Birmingham for emergency surgery and died. A week later President Lyndon Johnson held a televised news conference to deplore Bloody Sunday, support the marchers, and announce an impending voting rights bill, ending his address with "And we shall overcome." That and Reeb's death galvanized even more people to come to Selma to show their unity and support.

The Birmingham Unitarian Church issued a public statement expressing sadness and aligning with the marchers. "We share the moral sentiments which have stimulated these outbursts of protest." Gertrude Goldstein, Marjorie Linn, and an unknown third woman from Birmingham's Friendship and Action and BCHR traveled alone to Montgomery in hope of meeting with Governor Wallace and persuading him to allow the Selma to Montgomery march and protect the marchers. They were told the governor was too busy to see them.[552]

With much angst, the Birmingham Unitarian congregation debated whether to go to Selma, but the response from Unitarians across the country was overwhelming so the local church members decided to stay in Birmingham to act as a way station. They transported hundreds of people from the airport, housed them, arranged for buses to Selma, and provided food.[553]

Rowena Macnab rode with her father, John Macnab, an active member of YMBC, to the Unitarian Church to pick up and host overnight three out-of-towners en route to Selma, a White couple and a Black man. "I knew that this was clandestine, and you could get hurt," she recalled. "I was pretty scared most of the time, because I had been coached by my parents that I couldn't talk about it. Just before turning the car into their neighborhood, her father said, "Okay, it's time to get down." Rowena was mystified, but the Black man knew exactly what he meant and hunkered down out of sight. They proceeded down the street with their headlights off and pulled around to the back of her house. When she woke the next morning, their guests were gone. Others who hosted travelers received threatening calls. Joseph and Virginia Volker were among those who sat up all night with a host family that had received a bomb threat.[554]

While Wallace played brinksmanship with both Judge Johnson and President Johnson, Birmingham's White Ministerial Council hosted a memorial service at the Church of the Advent for the slain Reeb. About half of the four hundred persons attending were Black.[555]

On March 19, twelve days after Reeb's murder, Judge Johnson, after receiving assurance from President Johnson that the demonstrators would be protected, ordered that the Selma to Montgomery march could proceed. On March 21, Dr. King led thousands back over the Edmund Pettus Bridge headed for Montgomery. That same day, U.S. Army soldiers Robert M. Presley and Marvin M. Bryan of the 142nd Ordnance Detachment at Fort McClellan rushed to Birmingham where police had discovered bombs.

White supremacists had showed their displeasure with five bombs in "green, hat-sized boxes" with "up to fifty sticks of dynamite, clocks, batteries and wires. . . . Each one capable of wholesale slaughter." One bomb was near the Reverend A. D. King's former home and the others were "not far from the 16th Street Baptist church," one at a Black Catholic church and one at a Black high school. The two demolition experts arrived and "disarmed each bomb, when several of the devices were within minutes or even seconds of explosion." They risked their lives, not knowing that the batteries in the timing devices had failed to hold a charge.[556]

Learning their lesson from the failed batteries, White supremacists planted more bombs. One was placed in front of City Councilwoman Nina Miglionico's home. "Miss Nina" was a Birmingham-born first-generation Italian American, one of the first women attorneys in the city and a fierce defender of women's rights and civil rights. When Wallace had pressured Birmingham to close the schools in 1963, Miglionico worked to keep them open.[557] Like Abe Russakoff's medical office, her law firm, Gordon, Miglionico and Cleveland, had never had separate waiting rooms for "Colored" and "White."[558] Miglionico was one of the first city council members seated after the change in Birmingham's governance. That council voted to eliminate the city's Jim Crow laws. Objecting to the sign over the city council chamber doors, "Cities Are What Men Make Them," she had the "M" turned upside down and the "n" removed so the sign read, as it does to this day, "Cities Are What We Make Them." Shortly before the bomb showed up on Miglionico's porch, "Tee" Chambliss, the wife of church bombing suspect Robert Chambliss, called Miglionico and whispered over the phone, "I can't talk, but you be careful because they are going to kill you." Miglionico's elderly father found the box with sixty sticks of dynamite on their porch, heard a clock ticking, and reached in, yanking out the clock and throwing it into the yard.[559]

A few blocks away, a similar bomb in a green box was found in shrubbery on the grounds of Mayor Boutwell's home. Birmingham Police Captain J. H. Wooley, risking his life, disarmed it. The mayor had angered white supremacists when he joined other mayors to meet with President Johnson. Police checked other targets, including the Unitarian Church, but they were too late to stop a bomb from going off at the home of a Black man unaffiliated with the movement. Fortunately, no one was seriously injured.[560]

Sheriff Mel Bailey attended a meeting to address the lack of controls on possession of dynamite. Years earlier, when Chambliss was interviewed by law enforcement about possessing dynamite, he claimed he needed it to blow up stumps on Klan property. Sheriff Bailey now remarked wryly, "If everyone blew up stumps who said they were going to, we wouldn't have a tree left in Jefferson County."[561]

Law enforcement never identified the green-box bomber(s), although similar boxes were found in wooded hillside around the suburb of Irondale. FBI reports pointed to Chambliss and his Cahaba River Boys as the most likely suspects.

WHITE BIRMINGHAMIANS INVOLVED IN the several marches in Selma were subjected to harassing and threatening phone calls. They raised money to pay for guards around Ellwanger's church and residence. Marjorie Linn's car was a total loss after it was pushed over an embankment, and she lost her job at the *Shades Valley Sun*, a suburban newspaper.

Burton "Burt" Zell, a Unitarian, was a successful furniture manufacturer's representative who lived with his wife and children in Mountain Brook. Zell disagreed with segregation and took part in the Selma marches. His customers received anonymous warnings if they bought furniture from Zell, they would discover broken windows at their own businesses. Overnight, Zell lost his customers. Depressed, he started drinking, lost his home, and lost custody of his children. "Eventually he got on his feet again."[562]

After the Selma marches, the Birmingham Council on Human Relations held a short march protesting police brutality. "This time," Eileen Walbert recalled, "the police were driving beside us, protecting us."[563]

DESEGREGATION WAS NOT INTEGRATION. Only a few selected Birmingham schools had been desegregated in the fall of 1963 by a few selected Black students. Now the city needed to open all its schools. In May 1965, Shuttlesworth's organization, along with the CWCA, NAACP, and the Alabama Council on Human Relations formed a committee to accelerate and support school desegregation. Throughout the rest of the year, they worked to address "fear and apprehension," getting out information and working with Black families to integrate the schools.

Eileen Walbert walked alone through the Black community of Rosedale in the suburb of Homewood, knocking on doors and encouraging the residents to integrate the White schools. She found thirteen willing children and parents and drove many to school in an old black car that friends referred to as the "civil rights car."

The sight of a White woman driving Black children angered school officials, city businesses, and strangers, but Walbert was undaunted. She regularly picked them up after school, along with other children in the community, and brought them to her home where they swam and played in her backyard pool. Her mentoring made a difference for many, and she stayed in touch with them over the years. Verbal abuse, a cross burned on her family's lawn, and threatening phone calls from Klan members did not stop her. "I was learning how to be brave," Walbert said. "A bully, if you let them know you're not scared, they'll back off."[564]

An article in the civil rights-oriented *Southern Courier* newspaper reported that in the prior year Birmingham had "seven Negro students in all-white schools. This year [1965] fifty-four Negroes integrated Birmingham schools. . . . This is still tokenism, but at the same time, there is significant progress in comparison to previous years."[565]

Not all Birmingham Jews supported integration. Rabbi Grafman asked Gertrude Goldstein, a member of BCHR, to host a young Black Jewish convert from Boston who was preparing to attend school in Tuskegee. Goldstein and her husband agreed, and the young man attended services with them at the synagogue. Afterward, a woman at the Hillcrest Country Club confided, "You know they would really like you all to resign from this club." The Goldsteins did.[566]

As racial violence rippled across the state in the August heat, the National States' Rights Party—plagued by the FBI, internal theft of its membership lists, and criticism from other conservative groups—closed its Birmingham office. In an editorial for the *Southern Courier*, freelance writer Joseph Wilson wrote, "The main reason that the NSRP abandoned Birmingham to the hells of integration was economic. Party income was dwindling. The reason? The National States' Rights Party is a nay-saying organization and even Birmingham now knows better than to say 'never.'"[567]

That same month, a pen in Washington, D.C. brought sweeping consequences on a broader stage. President Johnson signed the promised 1965

Voting Rights Act, which prohibited the literacy tests still in force and provided the basis for eliminating poll taxes in state and local elections in Alabama and other states.[568]

Wayne Flynt, a twenty-four-year-old new professor at Birmingham's Samford University, worked to put the momentous legal changes into local action. He persuaded the Young Democrats to take on a voting registration drive in Rosedale, the same small Black community where Eileen Walbert had recruited youth to integrate the schools. Flynt and his fellow Young Democrats also walked door to door, but their aim was to help people register under the Voting Rights Act. Few residents in Rosedale owned cars, so the volunteers offered rides. "We were not well received at the registrar's office in Homewood. If looks could kill, I would have been killed one hundred times, because every time I walked in, [it was] with an African-American, most of them elderly who had never voted in their lives, never been registered to vote."[569]

A second undertaking by the Young Democrats involved a tutoring program at Rosedale High School. Flynt was appalled to discover the school had no microscope, no language courses, no physics, chemistry, or advanced mathematics courses. Student and teacher volunteers split into two groups. Some worked with the many youths who were not reading at their grade level or couldn't read at all. Others focused on students who needed help preparing for college. Most of the youths' parents were blue-collar workers at steel mills and plants around Birmingham.

In the fall of 1966, Flynt worked with a young woman named Elizabeth Sloane—"painfully shy and quiet, but really bright." By spring of her sophomore year, Flynt asked where she planned to attend college. It had not dawned on him someone of her intelligence would not go to college. She told him she was not. "'Why?" he demanded.

"I don't know how to go to college. How do you get in college?. . . I couldn't pass college."

"Of course, [you could]. You are as smart as a whip, Elizabeth. You can do whatever you want to do."

He suggested she apply to Samford University. When she balked at not having the money, he encouraged her and walked her through the application process for financial assistance and scholarships. Two years later, she was the first Black woman admitted to Samford (three Black basketball players had been recruited a few months prior). White parents did not want their children to room with Sloane, so at first she had a room to herself. But students and tutors supported her. Flynt recalled that Samford never had many Black students in that era. There were, he noted, "philosophical segregationists," but "in terms of social relationships, it is amazing how warm [they were], warm in the sense that [although] they didn't know how to treat an African American . . . the minute any of the students were integrated into a group, like, for instance, the three basketball players, they were just part of the basketball team and the object was to win basketball games."

Flynt proudly noted that following Sloane's success at Samford, she went on to become a manager of Alabama A&M University's WJAB-FM radio, earned a masters there in urban and regional planning, and became the school's director of telecommunications and distance learning.[570]

A few years later (1969–1970), Samford Dean Gilbert L. Guffin presented a proposal to the executive committee of the Birmingham Ministerial Association to commit to a public stand on the principle of "The Open Door of the Church to All People." The committee was hesitant to act and wanted to postpone a decision. Denson Franklin called on Rabbi Grafman for an opinion. According to Franklin, Grafman said, "'This is a matter for the Christian Church to face.'" But after a moment of silence, Grafman gave a sweep of his hand to the assembled men and said, "'How many of you have read that series of little books called the New Testament? I have. How many of you ever walked [in Israel] in the footsteps of Jesus Christ? I have. When you read those books and when you walk in his path, you will have your answer.'"

The executive committee and later the Ministerial Association passed the resolution unanimously.[571]

35

Selma Post-Op

By July 1965, many perceived that race relations had improved significantly. Recent Miles College graduate U. W. Clemon reported to the *Southern Courier* that Birmingham seemed to be on a course toward racial harmony and progress. "There is a feeling of optimism on the part of a great number of citizens, white and Negro." He cited that public utilities were hiring Blacks, many attended downtown movies and concerts regularly without incident, and reports of police brutality were "not nearly so rampant" as they had been. He admitted that it was difficult to hire "Negro policemen [because] the better qualified Negroes simply do not seek these jobs."[572] Despite Clemon's optimism, others were unhappy with and suspicious that none of the Blacks taking the police applicants' civil service test were able to pass it or the associated background checks. Mayor Boutwell appointed a biracial committee to study the tests.

Also, despite setbacks, the Klan was alive, as Birmingham attorney Matt Murphy loudly declared. Murphy had made a name for himself defending Collie Leroy Wilkins, one of three Klansmen charged with murdering White civil rights worker Viola Gregg Liuzzo during the Selma to Montgomery march.

For other individuals, Black or White, there was little perception of improving race relations. Edward Harris received a too-familiar phone call during an integrated social gathering at his home. The call put him on a new path.

"Are you Harris, the nigger lover?"

"Yeah, I am. You got the right guy."

"Well, we're going to come over to your house and kill you, your wife and children."

"Well, why don't you just come on. We are here waiting on you."

I went back into the dining room and said, "You know what, Sandra? I think we have just been called to the ministry."[573]

According to Tom Lankford, Governor George C. Wallace was unhappy with state trooper director Al Lingo's disobedience in the Selma marches. Lingo officially resigned in October 1965, but some insist that Wallace forced him out. Lingo then ran against Mel Bailey for sheriff of Jefferson County. Lingo saw Bailey's "moderate position" toward civil rights as "a tool to be used against him in a race for sheriff."[574]

Lankford had no love of Lingo. Among other things, he distinctly recalled Lingo ordering state troopers to attack the marchers in Selma on Bloody Sunday. Lingo and history would place the blame for that violence on George Wallace. Lingo claimed afterward that Seymour Trammell (Wallace's financial director) told him to stop the march "by whatever means necessary."[575] Wallace did announce that he had told the troopers to halt the march, but what the governor said in private, like the staged "stand in the schoolhouse door," was often different than his public stand. Lankford had on occasion been privy to Wallace's behind-the-scenes remarks. On the day before Bloody Sunday, he had spoken with the governor by phone.

"'Tom,'" Wallace said, 'I've told Al [Lingo] to let those people march tomorrow to Montgomery. I told him I want them out of Selma with no more trouble.'

"'Yes sir, governor,'" Lankford said. Then, knowing Lingo and his hatred of the marchers, he added, 'Think he'll do it?'

"'He damn well better,' Wallace said."

Wallace's words came to mind the following day as Lankford stood next to Al Lingo on the west side of the Edmund Pettus Bridge and saw the head of the state troopers fidgeting "as if he had ants in his pants." Lankford felt fortunate to be covering the biggest national story of the day, but watching Lingo, he knew trouble was coming. And it did. Blood flowed that day at Lingo's order.

When Lankford learned Lingo planned to attend a Black caucus meeting at the 16th Street Baptist Church in Birmingham to seek the Black vote for his run at the office of sheriff, Lankford planned a little surprise for him. Lankford held in high esteem (even while recording his conversations) the Reverend Edward Gardner, president of Birmingham's Alabama Christian Movement for Human Rights (Shuttlesworth's group), and asked for his assistance. "Lingo knows it is a lie that Wallace ordered the assault on blacks on the Selma bridge, and I know you don't have any use for him," Lankford said. "After you introduce him and he speaks, there'll be a collection, right?"

"Right," Gardner agreed. "That's the way we do. You know that."

Lankford requested that Garner ask Lingo to get in line as the minister and congregants marched down to the collection plate, "as a show of respect to the folks whose votes he [Lingo] is after."

Gardner agreed to do it.

Lankford slipped into the church prior to the ceremony and hid. As predicted, Lingo blamed Wallace for ordering the assault on Blacks on the Selma bridge. "I argued for two days to let those people march . . . but I was ruled down by my superior . . . I'm tired of being a scapegoat for that Selma incident."[576]

In an ironic counterpoint to the photo Lankford had taken of mayoral candidate Tom King years before, he jumped out and snapped a photo of Al Lingo standing in the collection line at a Black church. Lingo snarled at him but was helpless to do more. The next edition of the *Birmingham News* carried Lankford's byline on a front-page story with the headline, "Lingo Blames Wallace for Selma Bridge," and the photo of Lingo dropping money into the collection plate at the church where a Klan bomb had killed the four girls two years before.[577]

Asked about the story, Lingo said: "It might cost me 50,000 white votes, but it'll get me 100,000 black votes in return." It did not. Bailey was reelected by a landslide.[578]

ATTORNEY GENERAL ROBERT KENNEDY had offered a job to Chuck Morgan when he left Birmingham after the church bombing, but he chose the ACLU Southeastern office in Atlanta. He and Orzell Billingsley filed a federal lawsuit to desegregate Alabama's prison system. "Throughout the South, prisons were bad. Prisons for blacks were terrible," journalist Wayne Greenhaw wrote. In 1966, Sheriff Mel Bailey appeared as a witness in that suit before Judge Frank M. Johnson. The State of Alabama defense called Bailey as its witness for the current system, but when Judge Johnson leaned down and asked, "'Is there any instance in your experience where it is necessary to classify solely because of race in order to maintain and operate your prison properly?' Bailey answered, 'I would have to say no.'"[579] The court found that segregation of the prisons in Alabama was unconstitutional, a finding upheld by the Supreme Court two years later.

Around this time, Edward Harris, wishing to build a case for a civilian review board over the Birmingham police department, studied forty-four local police shootings from 1949 to 1963. He was surprised that of the 450 police officers then on the force, "three men shot most of these forty-five people. There are only six police officers out of the whole police force that were present at all of these killings."[580]

He and Peggy Fuller took his findings to new city council members Nina Miglionico and John Bryan, both of whom Harris had noted quietly attended the 16th Street Baptist Church bombing victims' funerals. The council members thanked him for the information but advised that it was not "proof," and warned him not to talk about it, asking him to let them handle the situation. He left "in deep grief."

About a year later, however, Harris saw David Vann at an awards dinner. Vann whispered, "'They are all gone.' Harris asked, 'Who? What?' Vann replied, 'The policemen you were worried about. They are all gone. Off the force or brought in for administrative duty. They aren't on the street carrying guns anymore.'"[581]

THE CITY AND COUNTY secret intelligence units continued their work after 1963, utilizing their equipment and skills to investigate crimes, including a corruption investigation of Public Service Commissioners. The wiretappers also monitored Black Muslims and the Students for a Democratic Society (SDS), and continued to investigate the Klan, which included bugging the home of notoriously vicious Troy Ingram.[582] Ingram took part in the Trailways bus station attack on Freedom Riders in 1961. He had traveled around Mississippi to fire up protests against James Meredith's admission to Ole Miss. He was the "exalted cyclops" of the "Cahaba Boys," the violent offshoot of the Eastview 13 Klan in Woodlawn, a small community east of downtown Birmingham. That Klan chapter's members included Robert "Dynamite Bob" Chambliss, Thomas Blanton, Bobby Frank Cherry, and Herman Cash. Although their main meeting place was under the Cahaba River bridge, members also met in Ingram's garage, where Ingram made bombs, drawing on knowledge of dynamite from his days as a miner and mine owner.

Ten days after the 16th Street church bombing, a nasty double bombing occurred that would be linked to Ingram. The day's headline, co-written by Lankford, read, "Plans to Kill Negroes and Police misfires as 'bait' bomb fails to lure crowd into shrapnel trap." The first bomb exploded in a Black neighborhood on Center Street in Titusville at about 1:30 a.m. It was not an area known for racial trouble, so there were no police stationed there, but police quickly responded.

The FBI's bomb team, which was in Birmingham investigating the church bombing, also raced to the scene. About fifteen minutes after the first explosion, there was a second blast, this one from a metal container "filled with large nails and scrap metal" that riddled a half-dozen homes, damaged an automobile, and toppled a telephone pole. It was the first shrapnel-type device of the forty-eight bombs that had exploded in Birmingham since World War II. The second bomb was about fifteen feet from the first. At the scene, Lieutenant House said the apparent purpose of the first explosion was to "draw residents of the sleeping community outside their homes where flying shrapnel could cut them down."[583]

Pieces of the recovered shrapnel were similar to items from Troy Ingram's garage, but there had never been enough evidence for an arrest. Investigators also suspected Ingram was one of two White men seen running on foot from the 16th Street Baptist Church just before that deadly bomb went off. Investigators postulated those men might have been checking on the bomb, which was supposed to have gone off hours earlier.

Lankford was present when Sheriff's Department Sergeant James Earl Smith, under Lieutenant David Orange's orders, installed a bug on a telephone line that connected to Ingram's garage, not far from the infamous Cahaba River bridge. The phone bug "yielded a lot of insight as to what made the Kluxers tick, their goings and comings, suspicions, doubts, etc., but nothing that resulted in an arrest." Something heard, however, prompted Sheriff Bailey himself to want to listen in one night, and he asked Lankford to accompany him, Orange, and Smith. The listening post was on the side of a lonely road near the telephone pole that hosted the bug and transmitter. The deputies would intercept the calls on a receiver hooked to a recorder in their car. No buildings or shrubbery concealed the unmarked county car, clearly visible in the moonlight.

Lankford, Smith, Orange, and Bailey were in place, waiting for a call over Ingram's bugged phone, when a car slowly drove by. Smith recognized the occupants as Klansmen. Ingram, who was driving, hit his brakes, turned around in a wide spot in the road, and headed back to investigate. Bailey ordered the officers' car to move out fast, so as not to jeopardize the surveillance. Ingram chased for a while but lost them.

Troy Ingram was never prosecuted. He died of a heart attack while driving a volunteer fire truck in 1973.

WHEN PRESIDENT JOHNSON'S 1964 Economic Opportunity Act (EOA) became law, it provided funding to address poverty in local communities. Birmingham and Jefferson County desperately needed the assistance, but the federal government required data. One man fit the bill to provide it—Sheldon Schaffer, a freethinking Jew and an economist with Southern Research Institute whose research had helped change Sid Smyer's outlook on how racism affected Birmingham economically. Schaffer directed research projects to define the type and location of the county's poverty.[584] This work provided the basis to solicit federal funds and the authorization to create the Jefferson County Committee for Economic Opportunity (JCCEO). The agency's goal was to provide neighborhoods with equal access to social welfare programs.[585]

Erskine Smith, one of the young White lawyers in YMBC, had led the change in government effort. He also led in bringing the opportunities of the EOA to the community and became the first board chairman of the JCEEO. Under political pressure from Governor Wallace, Smith was forced to resign early, but he gave his "knowledge and support" to Schaffer, who took the reins of the organization as president and chairman of the board.

Schaffer did not just sit in the "ivory tower" of the boardroom. "Sheldon took his job very seriously. He spent many of his evenings giving talks in little churches in the poor black areas. We received some threatening phone calls, and I worried some," recalled his wife, Harriet.[586]

Although hampered at the state level by Wallace's efforts to control the JCCEO board of directors, by December 1965 the new organization had put into place a Head Start for preschool children and a Neighborhood Youth Corps program for teens. The JCCEO also became "the first effective quasi-public interracial group in the community, a feat of no small consequence."[587]

Houston Brown, who worked on designing the questionnaires and maps and collecting data, gave this accomplishment a more personal perspective: "Everybody was learning how to get along with each other. You had to say, 'I'm sorry' a lot." Brown worked closely with Schaffer and Harold Wershow, a Jewish social worker and sociology professor at UAB who had taken part in the Selma March. He recalled that Schaffer and Wershow were open and that in discussions "we would explore and [gain] a sense of pride and respect for one another." Brown felt that JCCEO was a bold attempt to help level the playing field for Blacks in the city of Birmingham and was key in breaking down segregation.[588]

Though progress that had been unimaginable under Jim Crow was made, for Birmingham and many parts of Alabama, it was slow, particularly in education. In an ironic consequence of desegregation, White flight from urban areas exacerbated problems of inner-city communities, as did Black flight, which stripped neighborhoods of their professional and middle class people. Several Black-owned businesses folded as Black customers' choices broadened to include formerly off-limits White-owned businesses.

36

Chases & Cracked Ceilings

In a random fit of racist pique, Klansman Thomas Blanton once tried to run over a Black man crossing the street. On another occasion, he surreptitiously put a toxin on raw meat at a store owned by a Jewish grocer who served Black clientele. Blanton was one of the primary suspects in the 16th Street Baptist Church bombing.

Two years after the bombing, an FBI agent showed a Klansman from a small town north of Birmingham the photos of the four girls' remains. Mitch Burns, an ex-Marine in WWII, was a segregationist and a Klansman out of family tradition. But when he saw the photos of the young girls' torn bodies, he was moved and agreed to help build a case on Blanton. Throughout 1965, Burns and Blanton "honky-tonked" in Burns's car around the sleazier parts of Birmingham on Friday nights with a hidden microphone in the dash and a reel-to-reel tape recorder running in the trunk. Blanton was a dangerous man. If Blanton had looked in the trunk of Burns's car or otherwise suspected him, he would not have hesitated to kill him.[589]

Lankford and Marcus Jones, acting on their own, had bugged Blanton's home phone earlier in 1965. On one occasion, they sat in Jones's car, listening to the Blanton's conversation with Robert Chambliss. "Somebody's gonna burn for this," Blanton said, his shrill voice crackling with fear. "We gotta meet!"

Although Lankford and Jones didn't know what specifically Blanton was referring to, they realized that Blanton would hook up with Chambliss, who might get in Blanton's car and talk about the bombing. They couldn't let such an opportunity pass by.

Lankford and Jones were parked near Blanton's home. Knowing he had only moments before Blanton would leave the house, he raced to Blanton's driveway and tossed a transmitter under his car's front seat. Normally, Lankford would have used a sticky substance that would have fixed the transmitter to the floorboard, but he didn't have any with him. With no time to improvise, he slammed the door and ran to the car's rear bumper, where he hid an expensive magnetized signal device that would allow them to follow the vehicle.

Lankford just made it back to Jones's Ford Falcon when Blanton burst out of the house and jumped into his car, squealing off to meet "Dynamite Bob." Excited at the possibility of getting information on the case, Jones followed closely enough that they could see Blanton continuously checking his rearview mirror. The FBI and the bombing suspects had played cat-and-mouse for years, and Klan members (rightly) suspected the feds bugged their homes and meeting places.

Without warning, right in front of Blanton, a car ran through the intersection. He slammed on the brakes, jostling the transmitter under his seat, and it tumbled out into plain view. Lankford and Jones heard Blanton's muttered, "Damn!" Unsurprisingly, he aborted the meeting with Chambliss.

About a week later, Detective Jones approached Blanton as the Klansman pulled up outside the city hall parking lot. Jones demanded the return of his expensive bug and transmitter. Without a word, Blanton reached inside his car, took out a sack containing the devices, and handed it to the detective.[590]

WHILE MOMENTOUS CHANGES WERE occurring in Birmingham, many were small, perhaps trivial, but their cumulative ripples resulted in a change of culture. One such change occurred in Karl Friedman's law office, which at that time was comprised of four Jewish men who had worked their way through law school while supporting their families.

"It was time," Friedman said, "for us to make a stamp of who we were. The first thing I did was to hire a young black lady, [Maple Fikes]. She was eighteen; she'd graduated from the black high school here with excellent grades. I told her what the job description was. I told her if she would work hard at it, she would overcome this problem, the racial problem. She was courageous and ready."

Friedman had Fikes make the coffee, something he had been doing himself, and bring it to clients, as well as the secretaries, who were taking thirty to forty-five minutes to get coffee for themselves. That morning, three of the secretaries asked him, "Mr. Freidman, we understand what you're doing, but is she gonna use our bathroom?"

"Yes," he replied, turned around, and walked out.

Friedman had Fikes take mortgages to the courthouse to record them. "She would wait and then bring them back. We didn't have any noise from the courthouse either. Finally, she began opening the mail, and did it well. She did some bookkeeping. She stayed about three or four years, and [then] she wanted to move on to something else. She was a success. Stayed in touch with me the rest of her life."[591]

One of the elderly Black women Wayne Flynt had taken to register to vote the previous year was ready to vote for the first time in 1966. "First ballot, she was so proud. She was dressed up like she was going to Sunday worship: the hat, the finest dress she had. It would just bring tears to your eyes even remembering it." Flynt took her to the Homewood precinct. After giving her name, she was directed to the electronic voting machine and told to pull the levers for the candidates. At that point, she revealed she couldn't read and asked how she would know which lever to pull. The voting monitor told her if she couldn't read, she couldn't vote.

"'Yes, ma'am, she can really vote.'" Flynt told the monitor. "'She does not have to read,'"

"'Well, how is she gonna vote if she can't read?'

"'The Voting Rights Act of 1965 says that if she can't read, someone can go in with her and they can pull the lever.'

"'You can't go into a voting booth with somebody.'

"'Yes, ma'am, you can.'"

The argument grew heated. Everyone stopped to listen. The monitor threatened to call the police. Flynt, knowing the law, replied that would be fine. "'And since the federal voting registrars are all over Birmingham today monitoring this election, you call the Homewood Police, and I'm going to call the Department of Justice, and I'm going to have you arrested, and I'm going to have everybody who is denying this woman the right to vote here arrested.'"

Backing down, the woman grumbled, "'You can go in there and do it. But I want you to know that I don't like this.'"[592]

A more public first occurred in 1966 when the Birmingham Police Department hired Leroy Stover as the first Black officer. Karl Friedman and the Anti-Defamation League of B'nai B'rith played a little-known role behind the scenes. The ADL had established a one-man office in Birmingham. The director and Friedman persuaded city government leaders to work on hiring Black officers and offered to screen the applicants. One was Stover, an Alabama native and Korean War veteran.

Stover had never considered being a police officer, but Cordis Sorelle, his White employer, encouraged him to take the test. Stover's firsthand encounters with corrupt, racist officers informed his perspective of the police department. His experiences of mistreatment or even criminal behavior were similar to other police interactions under Bull Connor. Those experiences by Blacks understandably stained the perception of all Birmingham police officers and eroded trust. Despite his past experiences and the hostility and resentment he encountered as the first Black officer, Stover acknowledged, "All of the guys weren't obnoxious and hateful. Some were very helpful."[593]

At one point, he was moved to the West Precinct, long considered a home for pariahs in the department. When Stover was not permitted to borrow study material for promotional exams, other officers helped him. His transfer to the West Precinct "was like throwing a rabbit in the briar patch. I thrived out here because the white officers looked on me as an outcast, so I fit right in, and they did all they could to help me. They borrowed the books and materials in their own names and let me use them."

Moore was "a bright spot," telling Stover he was glad to have him on the force. "He wanted to see me make it."[594] In his memoir, *Leroy Stover, Birmingham's First Black Policeman*, Stover said, "Despite his gruff exterior, Chief Jamie Moore was truly a good friend, who was always looking out for my welfare. He would ride out on the beat I was working on to ensure that the white officers I was assigned with were treating me fairly." Stover also named chiefs that followed Moore—Jack Warren and Bill Myers—as being supportive. "There were others too numerous to mention that assisted me in my development as an officer with the Birmingham Police Department."[595] Stover's career covered thirty-two years. He retired from the department as a deputy chief.

Johnnie Johnson was the second Black hired in the Birmingham Police Department. As a youth, he ran when he saw a police car, but one day an officer in a patrol car stopped and offered him a ride to school. Not sure what to do, he took a chance and got in the car. On the way to school, the officer encouraged him to do well in school. It was a small moment but opened his eyes to the possibility that not all White police officers were bad and fed into his strong belief in the power of community policing, something he advocated many years later as the first Black police chief in Birmingham.[596]

In the mid-1960s, Karl Friedman was president of the Jewish Community Center board, and "the Community Chest (which became the United Way) and was urging integration on all social levels. The Jewish Community Center solicited [members] through Black organizations' memberships." When the first Black couple was approved for JCC membership "a mob of us came to the swimming pool that Sunday morning. . . . When I got there, the two little Black children were playing in the baby pool. . . . The husband and wife found themselves under an umbrella with two other couples, chatting and coming to know each other. After that, and we were very proud, there was a general trickle [membership] of Black people."

Besides his work on getting Black police hired, Friedman, along with members of the Jewish Committee, acted behind the scenes as agents for other social change, persuading the Downtown Club, one of the city's most influential social organizations, to take one Jewish member and one Black member. "There was no noise made about it," Friedman said, "and the Black member invited his friends to come, so that issue was almost dead." The group quietly challenged Indian Springs School, a prestigious private boys' school, to lift the rigid race restrictions of the founder's will and take a Black candidate, allowing director Louis "Doc" Armstrong to set a progressive path for the school.

Despite their prominence in the financial life of the city, Jews were scarce in executive positions on the boards of banks, insurance, and real estate companies, and Black representatives were pretty much nonexistent. The Jewish Committee created a task force, internally called the "Executive Suite," that used its leverage to get members on important boards that had excluded them. For the first time, the tightly sealed boardroom doors cracked open, "albeit at a slow pace," and Black membership slowly followed.[597]

37

Two Steps Forward, One Step Back

In August 1966, Wallace's state school superintendent "defended segregated schools as part of God's natural order."[598] Several Birmingham women, including Florence Siegel, Anny Kraus, and Janet Griffin made trips to the local board of education and to the state board of education to protest the state's fourth-grade history textbook, *Know Alabama*, which was "filled with romanticized, *Gone with the Wind* versions of how blacks were treated."[599] Their efforts would be in vain until 1970, when a new edition was printed. Griffin recalled learning that Wallace's secretary had an ownership interest in the publication.[600]

Other forces were at work in the state. Along with the hiring of the first Black Birmingham police officer, changes rippled through Birmingham's legal community. Karl Friedman, Abe Berkowitz, Edward Friend, and Charles Cleveland were among those supporting admitting Black attorneys to the Birmingham Bar Association. Civil rights attorney Oscar Adams was the first Black to join the Birmingham Bar in 1966 (later he would be the first Black on the Alabama Supreme Court). His admittance to Bar membership, which had been stymied three years before, passed "by an overwhelming vote."

Adams's law firm became the first integrated practice in the state. His partner was Birmingham Jewish attorney Harvey Burg, whose passion was civil rights cases. While still in law school, Burg had spent his summers in Birmingham and sometimes in Tuscaloosa, where he learned that a certain drugstore was selling mustard oil to burn people who were peacefully demonstrating. Outraged, he put a big Jewish star around his neck, walked up the main street into the drugstore and said, "I'm looking for mustard oil." Cars followed Burg when he left the store, but he knew the back roads and evaded them. In 1963, to prepare for the March on Washington for Jobs and Freedom, young Burg answered a call for volunteer marshals trained to intervene between the marchers and the police if necessary. It was the beginning of his involvement in civil rights and connection to Birmingham, where he would settle to make a career after graduating.

As a civil rights attorney in Birmingham, Burg went undercover as a journalist at Birmingham's University Hospital and discovered the unequal treatment given pregnant Black women and Black burn victims. His firm negotiated a settlement with the hospital that forever changed care in the state's largest medical system.[601]

On a more personal scale, desegregation haltingly spread even into the all-White suburbs. Myra E. Horne attended Shades Valley High School in Homewood. Walking into her homeroom on her first day as a senior, she saw a Black girl sitting alone in the middle of the room. White students were lined up, backs against the walls, unwilling to be the first person to sit next to her. Myra's father had always provided a role model of equality and acceptance. When Martin Luther King Jr. came to Birmingham, he would often hang out at Horne's Baptist bookstore, much to the consternation of the White employees. Horne's father told them that was the way things were going to be and to leave if they couldn't handle it.

Myra sat down beside the isolated Black girl in her classroom and introduced herself to Cynthia Ann Jackson. They became lifelong friends and often visited each other's homes. As Myra left after the first visit to the Jacksons' house, Black neighbors stood in their front yards and driveways to watch.[602]

IN APRIL 1967, UNIVERSITY of Alabama student government association president Don Siegelman (a future Alabama governor) joined Miles College's Black student government president in a statewide effort to protest Governor Lurleen Wallace's attempt to delay further desegregation in Alabama. The first resolution of the Alabama Association of Student Body Presidents criticized the "futile and irresponsible acts of resistance [to integration] on the part of our leaders."[603]

Other efforts focused on the local level. During the summer of 1967, members of the Reverend Joseph Ellwanger's Lutheran church, along with volunteers from other parts of the country, started the "Head Start on High School" project led by Mary Lynn Buss. They tutored Black ninth-graders who would integrate White schools in the fall.[604]

That same year Shelley Stewart, the Black radio announcer who had rallied children to march in 1963, became a silent partner with his Jewish friend Cy Steiner in the Steiner Bressler Zimmerman advertising agency (later o2ideas). Lest racism cost the agency clients, Stewart stayed a silent partner until Steiner's death in 1992. The first client he and Zimmerman approached with the revelation was Donald Hess with Parisian clothing store. Despite Stewart's trepidation, Hess "was delighted, congratulating Stewart heartily and telling him how much he looked forward to continue working with him." Ronnie Bruno of Bruno's grocery chain was "equally enthusiastic."[605]

Other first-efforts to cross the racial gulf occurred in the religious communities. A native of South Carolina, Paul Hardin had come to downtown Birmingham's First Methodist Church in 1941. He rejected the concept of racial superiority, believing that the church should "wage successful combat" against social ills, including racism. In the mid-sixties, he, organized a small youth meeting at the Methodist Church's Camp Sumatanga. Bill Thomason attended with some fifty other teenagers. He recalled that Hardin presented arguments discouraging them from following the lead of their elders and encouraging them to recognize the human rights of black people.[606]

In 1957, when Klansmen randomly kidnapped and then castrated Judge Edward Aaron and left him to die in the woods, Hardin "called the 'so-called defenders of the 'Southern way of life' Birmingham's worst enemies.'" In response, threatening phone callers told "the 'nigger-loving' preacher to get out of town or he was dead." The threats continued for a month, culminating in a cross being burned in his yard. By 1960, Bishop Hardin oversaw a broader conference, but he left a legacy that included instructing his church ushers, "I'm counting on you . . . to see that no one will be turned away because of their skin color."[607]

When Bishop Hardin ordered the Black and White members of the Methodist conference to meet together for the first time, the tension was palpable. Blacks and Whites sat on separate sides of the room, while Hardin sat before them answering questions. "When a white delegate asked how long it would be before the bishop assigned a black preacher to a white church, a hushed silence fell over the room. With a wide grin, Hardin answered: 'Brother, I . . . can't hardly get you to take a white one.' The auditorium exploded in laughter, and the delegate [who had asked the question] pulled a white handkerchief from his back pocket and waved it in the air, surrendering."[608]

At First Presbyterian Church, only two years after Black activists integrated the church, elders pondered what to do should Negroes wish to enter the church again on Easter. After much discussion, an elder moved that should any Negroes visit on Easter Sunday, the ushers should quietly seat them in any convenient pew. The minutes from that meeting reflect the motion carried, but with one change—a line was drawn through the words "on Easter Sunday."[609]

Sheila Blair, a northern transplant who lived in the genteel suburb of Mountain Brook, developed a friendship with the Black woman who cleaned her house, Louvenia (Beanie) Murphy. When Murphy opened up and shared her thoughts, frustrations, and anger about the constrictions and unfairness of her world, it opened Blair's eyes. In 1967, she joined two White women from Mountain Brook—Ann Edwards and Jeannette Hancock—and a Black staff member, Mildred Johnson, to start a Girl Scout leadership training in the poverty-stricken Black area of north Birmingham known as Collegeville.[610]

That same year, at age thirty, Harvard College dean John Usher Monro left his prestigious position to move to Birmingham and become a professor and director of freshman studies at Miles College. Three previous summers' work at the HBCU had convinced him it was the place where he could offer "useful, significant contributions." The school had lost its accreditation because of substandard libraries and a lack of teachers with doctorates. It could only pay its faculty half what White institutions paid. Monro never sought to rise in the administrative ranks, only to teach and contribute. Opening his mail, he would find vicious threats of murder against him and his wife, but he ignored them. Educating "thousands of students and mentoring dozens of teachers," he also bore with equanimity rebuff by Blacks "who could warm up to no white person."[611]

Support from the White community encouraged Monro. Irene Russakoff and Mary Prichard Forman formed the Friends of Miles College, "a predominantly white group of Birmingham citizens who [supplied funds and sought] . . . areas for cooperation between Miles and the Birmingham community."[612] From 1963–1965, the Reverend Edward Harris led a campaign to supply Miles' new library with books. In December 1969, through the dedication and hard work of Black and White faculty and its students, Miles College earned its accreditation from the Southern Association of Colleges and Schools.

For several years prior to taking a position at Miles, Monro had brought Harvard College students to Miles to work at Head Start programs. Miles College and the Unitarian Church were the only places willing to take a racial mix of children, a requirement of the federally funded program. When Black children registered at the Unitarian Church, White parents withdrew their children. The Reverend Lawrence McGinty walked door to door, talking and listening to the White families, addressing their concerns and prejudices; they returned their children to the program.[613]

David Walbert, who had marched in Selma with the Concerned White Citizens of Alabama, was a student volunteer at the Miles Head Start program. In 1967, he opened a coffeehouse he named Society's Child in downtown Birmingham that would become a haven for youth and an irritant for some local police who considered the attendees "communist hippies." Society's Child was, according to Walbert, the first legally integrated music venue and band in the city.[614]

For many years before, however, White teens had been fans of Black music. Music drew the races together. Shelley Stewart estimated 40 percent of his 1960s radio audience was White, and many White and Black youths came to his and "Tall Paul" Dudley White's platter parties and sock hops and danced together at different Black venues, despite Jim Crow laws. And Black and White adults had frequented Gip's Place in Bessemer to hear local musicians since the 1950s.

APRIL 1968 SAW THE tragic assassination of Martin Luther King. Not everyone considered it a tragedy. Appalled when some in their church applauded at the news, Janet and Gene Griffin sought a new church home.

In the immediate aftermath of Dr. King's murder, riots broke out in 125 cities. In Birmingham, there was anguish, but no violence. Three days after his death, "nearly 4,000 citizens, both Black and White, gathered outside the 16th Street Baptist Church and marched silently . . . to the courthouse for a memorial service. Birmingham's new mayor, George Seibels . . . pledged to serve all of the city's residents, regardless of race."[615] David Vann later reflected, "no buildings were burned, no riots were held" in Birmingham, unlike most of the major cities in the United States.[616]

On June 6, 1968, three months after the funeral for King, an assassin killed presidential candidate Senator Robert Kennedy. Once again, the shocked nation tried to come to terms with the violence that stole its leaders.

IN BIRMINGHAM, A HISTORIC first occurred when sitting City Councilman R. W. Douglas died while in office. Several council members met at Councilman Alan Drennen's home and decided to appoint attorney Arthur Shores to serve in his place—making Shores the first Black to sit on the council. In a citywide vote the following year, Shores won election to a full term in 1969 and reelection in 1973; fellow council members elected him president pro tem.

Attorney Robert "Bob" S. Vance Sr. gave notice of his progressive views when he decided Black jurors would serve the interest of one of his civil cases (*Norton Company v. Harrelson*). He was the first Birmingham attorney to ignore the "gentleman's agreement" among White lawyers to strike Black jurors and continued that practice throughout his law career. In 1966, he was elected chairman of the Alabama Democratic Party. Vance, a future federal judge, and Vann, a future Birmingham mayor, worked to put Blacks on the State Democratic Party's executive committee and defeat George Wallace's attempts to control the party. Wallace was running for president as an Independent candidate, but the Alabama Democratic Party was supporting him rather than the national party's candidate. The rebels formed the Alabama Independent Democratic Party (also known as National Democratic Party of Alabama) as a vehicle to run presidential electors.

In August 1968, at the Democratic National Convention in Chicago, Alabama Democrats, led by Vance, seated their first biracial delegation in history. Bob Vance Jr. recalled being told by his father that there was a secret deal with at least a couple of the White delegates to drop out "at the eleventh hour," allowing Vance to appoint more Blacks as delegates. J. Mason Davis confirmed the tale and said there also was a deal with the party's credentials committee "to seat the 'Vance delegation' at the expense of the regular delegation that supported George Wallace." In fact, by August 29, Vance notified the chair of the national committee that due to changes by "illness, absence, etc." or members "who declined to execute the pledge as required by the Credentials Committee," the previous alternates, J. Mason Davis, Rufus Lewis, Peter A. Hall, and Isom Clemon were now regular delegates, joining the original two Black delegates, Joe L. Reed and Arthur

Shores.[617] The accomplishment escaped the country's notice due to the Chicago convention's heavily televised anti-war demonstrations and violent clashes between police and protesters.[618]

IN SEARCH OF A better world, the women of the interracial Friendship and Action group pursued an exciting, but intimidating idea. In 1968, the Birmingham group became a chapter of the national Panel of American Women. The local group formed a diverse panel and sought speaking engagements at schools, churches, libraries, and any venue that would have them. "We talked about ourselves and our families and tried to show how prejudice affected us on a personal level, how it hurts," recalled Virginia Sparks Volker. The Birmingham panel consisted of a Catholic, a Jew, a White Protestant, a Japanese American, and a Black woman. The panel members rotated, but one group presented together many times: "Gertrude Goldstein (Jewish), Betty O'Brien (Catholic), Virginia Volker (WASP), Deenie Drew (Negro), and Martha Dagg (Japanese American)."[619]

Questions put to the panel were tough: "'Why don't you successful Negroes stay in the ghetto and help your own kind?' 'Why are Negroes so hostile when I go through a black neighborhood?' 'How do you feel about interracial marriage?' or more bluntly, 'Would you want your child to marry one?'"

Threats accompanied the women's participation on the Panel of American Women. In neighboring St. Clair County, Black Muslims had bought farmland. The Alabama Commission to Preserve the Peace pounced, resulting in misdemeanor arrests, and the Black Muslims found their cows poisoned.[620]

Not long after, unknown persons threw a rock through the window of White activists Janet and Gene Griffin's home. The rock bore a note that read, "What's Good for Cows Is Even Better For Negro Lovers. —Klan." They found firecrackers in the engine of their car. When the Griffins' children left for school on their bikes, phone calls to their parents began, threatening the lives of their children. "We lived in Central Park in a blue collar neighborhood," Gene Griffin said. "Our neighbors disagreed with our politics but protected us and came to our defense when we felt threatened."[621]

Barbara Butts, a White Protestant panelist, was asked why she gave her time and energy to such a potentially unpopular project as the Panel of American Women. She responded that she was, at first, afraid. "Not for myself, but for fear that someone might take it out on my children." But then "a time came when I just had to speak out, no matter what. Perhaps I lost some friends, but I think my children gained a mother who can live with herself."[622]

"Over the years," Virginia Volker said, "we did see a difference. It got easier, and the questions got less ridiculous. I think we did have an impact."[623]

INTEGRATION DID NOT MEAN equal opportunity. Well aware of this, a group of "black and white, women and men, clergy and laity" founded a private organization in 1969. Greater Birmingham Ministries committed to social justice and to address the "decades-weight of racial oppression," including issues of poverty and need. The organization's three original churches—Methodist, Episcopal and Presbyterian—worked together, adding seventeen other faith communities representing Christianity, Judaism, and Islam.[624]

Recruiting Black faculty at the university was almost as thorny an issue as hiring Black police officers. Despite the pressure to move forward, several factors complicated hiring qualified Black faculty: the expanding rate of higher education across the country, which made demand for Black teachers strain the limited supply; the relatively low salaries paid to Alabama professors; the lure of more prestigious schools in the North and West; the tarnished reputation of the South; and the specter of George Wallace as governor and presidential candidate.

When medical facilities expanded to include obstetrics care, Dr. Charles Flowers headed that department. He worked to integrate it and provide equal obstetrics' care to all women giving birth there. It was 1969 before Arthur C. Segal, a Jewish math professor and acting chairman of the math department, was able to recruit and hire Thomas Lamar Alexander as the school's first tenure-track, full-time non-medical Black faculty. While Alexander was an instructor, he worked on and completed his doctorate at the University of Alabama and was promoted to assistant professor of mathematics at UAB.[625]

By the end of the 1960s, "some five thousand black children were attending formerly all-white schools. . . . The number of registered [Black] voters had increased dramatically, and blacks held important positions on the planning committees, the Chamber of Commerce, the board of education, and all the major civic organizations."[626] Underlying racial tensions, however, still festered, and White flight to the suburbs continued, but the city doggedly progressed and rapidly exchanged the smog of steel production for the powerhouse economic engine of UAB, which, as both a university and medical center, became the state's largest employer.

Meanwhile, the Vietnam War was tearing the country apart. Birmingham native Bill Terry was twenty when he died there. He had requested to be buried in Elmwood Cemetery, because it was near his home in a small Black community of Birmingham called Titusville. When his body was brought home in 1969, the privately owned cemetery refused to bury him because of his race.

Black and White members of the community, including Janet Griffin, her husband, their children, and her mother, marched in protest down Sixth Avenue South, past the jail where Dr. King wrote his famous letter, to the cemetery. The Department of Defense and President Richard Nixon received hundreds of letters supporting Terry's right to be buried where he wished. His mother and wife sued. In 1970, the court found in their favor. He was the first Black buried in Elmwood Cemetery. "Twelve hundred marchers followed Terry's body from Our Lady of Fatima Church to Elmwood Cemetery, where Josephite Friar Eugene J. Farrell told the marchers: 'We are rejoicing, not mourning. This is not really a funeral march. This is a victory march for Billy and for truth and right.'"[627]

38

Justice, Finally

The chief suspect in the 1958 Temple Beth-El attempted bombing had never been identified. Almost two decades later (1977) Bob Eddy, an investigator for the state attorney general, discovered the suspect's identify while he was digging through files in the Birmingham FBI field office looking for evidence in another bombing case. His boss had instructed him not to get sidetracked, but he was stunned when Birmingham Police Detective Tom Cook contacted him. Cook had been Bull Connor's man more than a decade before and had once confessed to Lankford he had set up an attempted assassination of Fred Shuttlesworth. Cook said he and Connor had suspected that NSRP attorney J. B. Stoner was responsible for the dynamite at the synagogue. Later that year (1958), with Connor's blessing, Cook had sought to expose Stoner in an undercover sting after the attempted bombing,

Cook told Eddy he had posed as an out-of-town businessman and put out the word that he was looking for the bombers with a lucrative job offer in mind. Stoner contacted him. Cook showed Stoner a list of targets to bomb and told him to wait for his call on which one to hit. But Stoner acted before Cook made the call and could set up surveillance. Stoner threw out dynamite at Shuttlesworth's residence, which was attached to Bethel Baptist Church. A volunteer church guard, sixty-two-year-old Will Hall, grabbed the paint can full of dynamite and set it on the street. About a minute later, it exploded. At the time, the local district attorney refused to prosecute, fearing the entrapment aspects had damaged the case.

Eddy sent Cook's information to his boss, Attorney General Bill Baxley, who opened the case. Stoner was indicted but skipped town prior to arrest and was not brought to trial until 1980. Then for three years after his conviction, Stoner dodged capture. When his appeals ran out, he was a fugitive for four months and then prison time until 1986. Without Stoner's leadership, the NSRP unraveled and by 1987 had dissolved into obscurity. Stoner died in 2005.

In 1977, while the Stoner case was being pursued, Eddy continued to dig into files at the Birmingham's FBI office. He was there because Baxley, acting on a promise made to himself as a law student to bring justice to the four dead girls, had reopened the unsolved 1963 16th Street Baptist Church bombing case.

Retired Birmingham Chief Jamie Moore had worked for Baxley as an early investigator on the case. Not long after Moore began interviews, unknown persons shot into his car outside his home.

Baxley himself received personal threats about opening the investigation but was undeterred. He had been hindered by J. Edgar Hoover's refusal to share information and the clock was ticking in 1977 on his last year as state attorney general. He finally got access to the Bureau's records and sent Eddy to Birmingham to work with a reluctant FBI office. That was how and why Eddy stumbled on the Stoner case, but his primary focus was on the 1963 church bombing. Working long hours trying to get a handle on the fourteen-year-old cold case, Eddy discovered information that led him, with help from Birmingham police captain Jack LeGrand, to Elizabeth Cobbs, the niece of "Dynamite Bob" Chambliss.

In 1977, with encouragement and support from Eddy and Baxley, a fearful Cobbs faced her uncle in court with testimony that was a key factor in bringing Chambliss to justice. He died in prison in 1985.

As THE YEARS PASSED, other suspects in the church bombing eluded justice until Rob Langford arrived in Birmingham. Langford, a graduate of Auburn University, had served a tour in Vietnam before joining the FBI in 1968. He served for years in Detroit and Washington, D.C., before returning to Alabama as the special agent in charge of the Birmingham office. Struck by the distrust between law enforcement and the Black community, he held a meeting in his office with several Black ministers to open a dialogue. The Reverend Abraham Woods commented bitterly on the open wound of the church bombing and stated that the FBI had never really tried to investigate it. Langford promised he would, and in 1995 he decided to reopen the case but keep the investigation secret for as long as possible.[628]

No physical evidence existed. Many potential witnesses and one of the main suspects, Herman Cash, had died. The investigators had no leads. Finding evidence three decades after the bombing seemed impossible. Conviction of the Klan suspects hinged on Special Agent Bill Fleming's discovery of missing tape recordings. One critical tape had been dubbed the "Kitchen Tapes."

In 1965, the FBI had noticed there was a vacancy in the duplex apartment adjacent to that occupied by one of the Cahaba River Boys, Thomas Blanton. An FBI agent posed as a traveling truck driver and rented the apartment. With authorization under national security provisions by Attorney General Robert Kennedy, the FBI bugged the apartment. To get that authorization, the FBI presented evidence about the social unrest and violence of the time, the grave concern over communist influence, the church bombing and subsequent riots, and the assassination of President Kennedy.

Bureau employees drilled a small hole in the wall, which turned out to be right under Blanton's kitchen sink. Because the recordings were not authorized for criminal case purposes, only national security intelligence, the FBI filed away the tape of a conversation between Blanton, his wife, and an unknown third party and other tapes recorded during that time. The tapes were lost, along with the 1965 reel-to-reel recordings from the trunk of Mitch Burns's car when Burns had ridden around town with Thomas Blanton. By dogged determination and some luck, Agent Fleming found all the tapes in a dusty box in the corner of the FBI's Birmingham evidence room.

The other major factor in the ultimate convictions of Klansmen Blanton and Bobby Frank Cherry were White witnesses who stepped forward to testify, including a dying man who came in a wheelchair with his oxygen tank and his doctor; elderly FBI agents, Cherry's ex-wife and stepdaughter; and the aging informant Burns, who took the stand to testify about riding alone night after night with Blanton to secretly record conversations for the FBI.

After a five-year investigation by FBI Special Agent Fleming and Birmingham Police Sergeant Ben Herren, U.S. Attorney Doug Jones and his team prosecuted and convicted the two still-living Klansmen responsible for the 1963 church bombing—Thomas Blanton and Bobby Frank Cherry. Cherry died in prison in 2004. Blanton died in prison in 2020.[629]

39

The Way Forward

In 1978, Whites were still a majority in Birmingham when council member Richard Arrington was elected as Birmingham's first Black mayor. He served for twenty years. In 1992, Johnnie Johnson become the city's first Black police chief, and the Birmingham Civil Rights Institute opened, "strongly supported by the City of Birmingham, by almost every major business in the city and hundreds of committed individuals of all races."[630]

Vincent Townsend Sr., the former *Birmingham News* potentate and behind-the-scenes influencer, has been criticized for his paper's coverage of civil rights, for trying to shape the city's image as always positive—even down to what photos were printed—and for failing to portray the concerns and issues of the Black community. Businessman Richard "Dick" Pizitz, whose downtown business was caught in the middle of the protests, perceived the biggest impediment to a quicker resolution of Birmingham's woes had been the lack of editorial leadership in the *Birmingham News*.

That view has been echoed by others who have pointed out that many stories about the early boycotts and demonstrations deserved far more play than they received. Gene Roberts and Hank Klibanoff examined the era's newspapers reporting in their book *The Race Beat* and concluded that both Birmingham daily newspapers "missed the evolution of the movement." They used their second pages to give "short, straight, stenographic renderings of the previous day's activities, with no explanation of why they were happening." The authors conceded, however, that the afternoon *Birmingham News*, editorially, took the protests more seriously than had the morning *Birmingham Post-Herald*. The *News* said that "the Negro leaders 'are often brilliant strategists' and refrained from calling King or Shuttlesworth anything more incendiary than 'more pressing, more activist, than older more established leadership.'"[631] Roberts and Klibanoff also credited the Birmingham papers for honoring "the separation between news and opinion. Reporters weren't expected to reflect their publisher's interests the way the reporters . . . [for other Southern papers] were."[632]

The local papers were not alone in underplaying events. Outside reporters covering the change-of-government election of 1963 treated the demonstrations as "a sidebar" until the explosion of the children's marches. Even the Black-owned *Birmingham World* was torn between the demonstrators and the Black businessmen who "wanted to give the newly elected Boutwell administration a chance to perform."[633] Although many of the early protests were not considered front page material at the time, many major civil rights happenings were headlined across the top of the front page, resulting in several journalism awards for Tom Lankford in the early 1960s.

Despite the criticism of him, there is no doubt that Townsend loved his city. Over his lifetime he was recognized with several prestigious personal awards, but it is doubtful that any meant as much to him as Birmingham's All-America City designation in 1970, due, in large part, to his efforts and the work of Chamber of Commerce Chairman Dick Pizitz.

A 2014 editorial in the weekly newspaper *Weld for Birmingham* reflected, "In many ways, [Townsend] embodied the reluctant evolution of Birmingham's white power structure during the years of the civil rights movement. He—and the city's newspaper of record—went from benignly ignoring glaring issues, to viewing the demonstrations in Birmingham as purely a public relations problem, to understanding that the city had to change or die."[634] Buddy Cooper reflected that Townsend "stepped on a lot of backs to get up the ladder, but he used his power to aid this community to be a better place."[635]

Jesse Lewis Sr. offered a more personal perspective. As a young man, Lewis had dreamed of starting his own newspaper and went to the horse's mouth for advice. He arrived at the *Birmingham News* seeking an audience with Townsend to relate his desire to found a news publication for the Black community. At the time, the person of color in the *News* building, outside of the janitors, was Geraldine Moore, who wrote a Townsend-created column called "What Negroes Are Doing." Townsend took Lewis under his wing, advising him and critiquing his writing, and the younger Black man became a familiar sight at the *News*.[636]

Lewis founded the *Birmingham Times* newspaper in 1964. He attested that Townsend was "totally against segregation and discrimination" and did "more to help the civil rights movement than anyone. . . . He was responsible for going to the merchants and telling them they had to let black people drink out of the fountains, use the bathrooms, ride the elevators and try on clothes. During the heat of the [civil rights] movement, we often talked two or three times a day. He was not the type of person that did anything openly, for recognition or publicity; he just did it out of the goodness of his heart."[637]

Asked why historians have not recognized Townsend's work on civil rights, Lewis said, "He never took credit. He went to meetings and would tell people what they should do, how to make sure government would react the way they wanted. He went to those meetings, and he stood up, but he didn't go back and write about it. He and [Emory O.] Jackson [publisher of the *Birmingham World*] would dialogue all the time. [Sometimes] they had heated debates. . . . Townsend worked with [Mayor] Boutwell [to move the city forward]. He stayed on him."[638]

Townsend's enduring legacy came not from an award or recognition for his city, but from his work on the Downtown Improvement Association (DIA), which Townsend founded with other civic leaders. In 1966 the DIA folded into one of its committees, Operation New Birmingham (ONB), an organization which had a profound effect on stimulating the city's center.[639] The original biracial Community Affairs Committee established by Mayor Boutwell after the 1963 accord had only lasted a short time. But five years later, Townsend invited twenty-seven leaders—Black and White—to serve on a new community relations committee, "a private biracial citizens panel organized to discuss community problems and work to solve them."[640] Townsend died in 1978. His legacy, the biracial CAC, continues to meet every Monday morning and address community race-related problems.

Another legacy that grew from Townsend's ONB was the Police Athletic Team, a bold attempt to bridge the divide between the police and the Black community, particularly the low-income neighborhoods, through the medium of youth baseball. The idea was not originally popular in the police department. Many viewed it as a waste of time and not "real" policing. But White officer Bobby Hayes took up the challenge as the first director, along with officers Kurt Zassoda and Gary Ervin. Hayes soon recruited the third Black hired to the Birmingham department, Robert Boswell, who was to spend many years of his life associated with the police athletic teams. Boswell recalled that the teams were created near the Black housing projects. Uniformed officers worked with local coaches. He watched as the "joy that playing ball brought to those kids won over the white officers."[641]

According to Boswell, Chief Jamie Moore would come out to the neighborhood fields to make sure the youth were safe, and he often stayed and had his lunch with them. On Saturdays, the different teams met at Rickwood Field, which remains the oldest intact professional baseball field in the country. Built in 1910, it was the original home of the (White) Birmingham Barons and the Birmingham Black Barons.

When Boswell inherited the directorship of the program, he realized that ball playing was more than a community relations tool; it was a singular opportunity for many talented youths. "Most of those kids had never been over the state line," he said. "In order to get them noticed [by college coaches], we had to get them out of Alabama, give them a chance to be exposed." But traveling took money. Boswell donated from his own pocket, but he also found donors and raised money. He recalled that Birmingham's Jewish community generously contributed funds for equipment and the maintenance of the ball fields, naming in particular Rabbi Milton Grafman and Ferd Weil, who owned the Parliament House Hotel. By 1980, Birmingham's youth program had become a national model and continues to be one.[642]

As described by Karl Friedman, Jim Head was a fierce debater with a powerful physical presence, never losing his temper, chastising no one, but declaring with passion his position that people needed to treat each other with respect and dignity, regardless of the color of their skin. Friedman recalled that Head took this principle as such a given, "he was thoroughly surprised by the negative responses he got from most of his friends."

When Head sold his supply store and opened a furniture store, he quickly donated furniture for the Legal Aid Society. Traveling across the state, he sold furniture to libraries. "In each community he visited, he also sought out the community leaders—mayors, sheriffs, council members, and prominent businessmen—and tried to convince them that even though there might not be outward [racial] conflict in their town, they were holding themselves back by not recognizing the wrongs of segregation. Needless to say, he did not meet with much agreement, but he never stopped trying."[643]

Edward Harris worked for Head and called him a mentor who lost business because of his stances, but it never stopped him. He raised money for Miles College, finally persuading other business associations to match payroll contributions from their Black employees for the college.[644]

Jeff Drew recalled that Head, like Abe Berkowitz, often visited in the Drews' home. Head donated bond money to the movement, "probably out of his own pocket."[645]

As president of the prestigious Birmingham Rotary Club and the Birmingham Chamber of Commerce, Head was active and outspoken in the business community. As early as 1955, he initiated biracial meetings and dialogues at the Chamber; other members objected to them as inappropriate, considering the city's ordinances, and they halted the meetings.[646]

Among Head's achievements was the rescue of Howard College. In partnership with Mervyn Sterne, their efforts to raise funds to support the failed school resulted in the establishment of Samford University. Similar efforts supported the founding of two local hospitals as well as Miles College. Head was a member of the Civil Rights Commission, the Chamber of Commerce, and the progressive Young Men's Business Club (YMBC).

Head's values of mutual respect for all persons led to his role as a founder, along with Rabbi Morris Newfield, William P. Engel, and other civic leaders of the local chapter of the National Conference of Christians and Jews (later renamed the National Conference of Community and Justice) whose mission was to "fight bias, bigotry and racism and promote understanding and respect among all people."[647] That organization birthed ongoing programs (later continued by the YWCA of Central Alabama) such as Peace Birmingham, a monthly dialogue that "allows teens from different cultures and faiths to learn about each other"; Anytown Alabama, a diverse youth camp; and the Heritage Panel, which trains youth how to discourage "bullying, harassment and discrimination at their schools."[648] Head died in 2010 at the age of 106.

JEROME "BUDDY" COOPER'S LIFE work as a labor attorney and outspoken proponent of freedom and equality left a mark on Birmingham and the nation. Cooper's work and progressive values took him across the entire Southeastern region. He encouraged the unions to maintain unity between the races, despite the pressure from the mine and steel factory owners and their proxies. This work improved the lives of hundreds of Black and White laborers. U. W. Clemon, state senator and the first Black federal judge in Birmingham, observed that "desegregation came about at the union's insistence that black workers who work the same job as whites in a particular bargaining unit be paid the same pay as the whites. If you look back at it, it [the union] was responsible to a great extent for the success of the [civil rights] movement."

Cooper, in a speech at a state university, pointed out the hypocrisy of devout churchgoers who were staunch segregationists. He said, "If our freedom is to be truly enriched and enlarged—more than tolerance, or acceptance, or even obedience to basic law" is needed. We need "faith in the indivisible character of freedom. That means there must be voices here, as elsewhere in the land, to say, unafraid and with conviction: Ours is a society of government and hope for all men. We limit no one's potential; we draw no public or governmental lines of distinction—because of color or race or creed. Discrimination based on such considerations is wrong—morally wrong—and wrong by the standards of our Judeo-Christian ethic."[649]

Prominent Black attorney Demetrius Newton recalled that the "black community . . . felt they could always trust Buddy Cooper." Two of Birmingham's Black institutions, Union Baptist Seminary and Daniel Payne College, gave Cooper and Harold E. Katz honorary degrees recognizing their humanitarian service.[650] Former Alabama Attorney General Bill Baxley noted that the majority of Cooper's clients probably didn't agree with his stances. "Buddy not only jeopardized his life, as [progressives in Birmingham] all did, but he ran the risk of making his clients locally very unhappy with him. He didn't flinch though."[651]

SID SMYER STATED IN an interview, "I'm still a segregationist, but I hope I'm not a damn fool."[652] In a later interview with journalist Howell Raines, he said his actions in the 1960s were "a dollar and cents thing," that the city was in a depression and that he knew "if we're going to have a good business in Birmingham, we'd better change our way of living." He claimed economics were his sole intent, but to Raines, Smyer confided, "Listen, I came up the hard way, and I knew what it was to be on the low-down side."[653]

Smyer's record leaves no doubt he had been a staunch segregationist. His reputation for conservatism gave him credibility among the business community. Did he purposefully continue to espouse that stance to maintain his influence among his peers?

Jim Head said, "Smyer was the only person who could have done what he did in Birmingham at that time." The Reverend Edward Harris recalls returning to Birmingham for an awards ceremony where Sid Smyer introduced Dr. Lucius Pitts. "We changed," he recalled Smyer saying. "Not because we were forced but because it was the right thing to do." Harris's reaction at the time was negative, but in later reflection he said, "Sid Smyer and lots of other white men were trying to do what was right even though forced. They just understood it differently from me."[654]

Was Smyer's desire to maintain and grow business in Birmingham the entirety of his position regarding civil rights? Smyer, like many others, resented the "agitation" of outsiders, but pushed and supported discussion with local Black leaders. Journalist and author Mark Kelly observed that Smyer should be credited with a "willing journey of evolution and enlightenment by a man who possessed two qualities rarely seen in conservative men who accumulate considerable power—the ability to confront his own flaws and the willingness to place his own status and reputation on the line for the greater good of the community."[655]

SEVERAL ARTICLES HAVE NOTED that the little-known Birmingham Police Chief Jamie Moore "often clashed with Bull Connor." Leon Moore "remembered his father as 'a man of stability and fairness' and one who had few fans among local racists."[656] He was advocating Black police officers in 1963 and possibly as early as 1956.[657] Lankford, who knew him well, gave him this tribute: "Moore was a true, decent, cautious professional who did his job exceptionally well with dignity and without prejudice." Moore served as police chief in Birmingham from 1956 to 1972 and died in 2002.

NEAR THE END OF 1963 David Vann, J. Vernon Patrick Jr., and Erskine Smith—all YMBC members who had worked on civil rights issues—were fired or convinced they had to leave their law firms. As Alabama author Chervis Isom wrote, "It was Abe Berkowitz, their elder guru, who gathered them in like a mother hen and gave them a home [making them partners in his firm]. . . .

Joining them was Charles F. Zukoski Jr., the sixty-five-year-old head of the Trust Department of the First National Bank of Birmingham who had been pushed into retirement because of his civil rights activities."[658] Five years later, Berkowitz would also welcome Don Siegal, who had been the president-elect of student affairs in 1963 at the University of Alabama and worked to make certain the campus integrated peacefully.

JEFFERSON COUNTY SHERIFF MEL Bailey integrated his department. In 1971, his work with the Alabama Sheriffs Boys Ranch led to the legislature recognizing him as Alabama Law Enforcement Officer of the Year. Throughout his career, both Black and White members of the community supported him. Jesse Lewis Sr. of the *Birmingham Times* recalled that "Mel Bailey, even during the height of segregation, was fair. He did not believe in segregation."[659]

When asked about the stance of law enforcement in those days, Bailey admitted that many of his deputies were "highly prejudiced," but "we were like a referee, no matter who it is, if he's safe, call it. If he's out, call it. It don't matter who he is or what color he is or she. And this is what we strived desperately, daily, to do, and it went on seven days and nights around the clock for weeks and weeks here." Bailey served the county from 1963 to 1996 and died in 1997 at age seventy-two.

WHEN RABBI MILTON GRAFMAN spoke from his broken heart after the 16th Street Baptist Church bombing, his final words reflected hope for his city. He related a conversation with Black friends the Reverend J. L. Ware and Dr. Lucius Pitts whom he told, "'Some day we are going to work out an accommodation [between the races] and it is going to be a far superior accommodation than anything north of the Mason-Dixon Line,' and both of them said, 'You are so right. Once we get to understand each other, this is going to be the greatest area in the country.'" Grafman challenged his congregation: "'You have got a stake and a share in that area in this city. You could make it possible.'"

When Grafman died in 1995, the Reverend Abraham Woods, local president of the Southern Christian Leadership Conference, noted that the community had lost "one of our great assets." Orzell Billingsley, a leading civil rights attorney who had been among those representing Martin Luther King, showed his respect by attending Grafman's funeral.[660]

Karl Friedman credited Grafman with pushing to integrate the Greater Birmingham Ministerial Council. (The Reverend Alfred Hobart of the Unitarian Church also labored toward that end and established an integrated ministers' group.) Friedman reflected, "I am still angry about how some people reacted [to King's "Letter from Birmingham Jail"] who had no idea what the facts were, but I can positively declare that Rabbi Milton Grafman was the greatest single force in guiding the community and helping [move] toward [racial harmony and desegregation]."

THIRTY-FIVE YEARS AFTER THE 16th Street Baptist Church bombing and the same-day murder of young Virgil Ware, Detective Dan Jordan got in touch with the victim's brother, James. The two had lunch at Niki's West Restaurant and later met at the spot where young Virgil died. James Ware told Jordan he didn't believe in hating people. "'I have forgiven those boys.'" Jordan asked him if anyone had stopped to help. That night on the road with his dead brother, Ware recalled, a green car occupied by White people Ware did not know, stopped, got out and asked if there was anything they could do to help. Ware asked them to find his mother and bring her to the scene, which they did. "'I would like to thank the white people in the green car—whoever they are, for helping me and my family that night.'"[661]

TEN YEARS AFTER THE 1963 arrival of the rabbis at the Birmingham airport on a rainy night in the middle of the tense negotiations, Rabbi Rubenstein, the group's leader, came to speak in person to the Birmingham Jewish Community. Karl Friedman was present. "He [Rubenstein] said, 'I've come here to apologize,' and he hung his head. He said, 'I was young, and I was reckless, and I thought it was something that would be a credit for me.'"

"I was in attendance when he made his apology," Friedman recalled, "it was standing-room only, and I had been charged with the responsibility of appropriately chastising him. I did not. . . . The community has forgiven him."

In a letter penned years later, Rubenstein admitted he realized his error almost immediately upon his arrival in Birmingham. "Although many regarded us as heroes when we returned home, the real heroes were the local Jewish leadership. . . . Without revealing confidential information, I can honestly write that the leadership of the Jewish community proceeded to act with great dignity and in a way that no Jew could be ashamed of."[662]

Karl Friedman worked at his law firm, Sirote & Permutt, in Birmingham into his nineties and had lunch daily with law partners Jack Held and J. Mason Davis. Friedman's life was recognized with a multitude of accolades, but he counted his many deep friendships and the quiet work he did to forward civil rights as far more important milestones. Friedman died in 2018.

LOOKING BACK ON HIS career as a journalist and his close relationship with law enforcement, Tom Lankford expressed pride in having "no other media come close to beating us on any story," but it was mixed with the awareness he had lost some professional objectiveness in the process. "Obviously, I crossed the line in becoming so close to police, even joining in their work. News reporters just shouldn't do that."

Bob Eddy—the career law enforcement professional who took on the investigation that brought "Dynamite Bob" Chambliss to justice—had a different perspective. "Tom put his career in danger to help law enforcement on several occasions, and it cost him. His enemies went after him with everything they could find or make up. Tom could accomplish more because of his total devotion to his friends. . . . He knew when to tell a friend he was wrong and do it in a way that never hurt their relationship. He has done that for me. His reputation as a writer and his work with law enforcement during a time this state needed leadership was outstanding. He never backed down from writing the truth, and it caused him to develop enemies in high political offices. I am fortunate to have him as a friend."[663]

Lankford believed he had, for the most part, been on the side of the "good guys." Despite realizing that he had not adhered to the "by the book" principles he had learned at his professor's knee in journalism school, he had no regrets. If he had done otherwise, he would never have had the access, the stories, and the relationships he would treasure all his life. Lankford—whose award-winning journalism/photography career took him from reporter and then night city editor at the *Birmingham News* to editor and general manager of the *Huntsville News* and to the Middle East as a media consultant—lived in retirement with his beloved wife, Tan, in his hometown of Hokes Bluff, Alabama. He died in 2021.

Postscript

The loudest, most radical voices, the violence of the Klan, and the stories of Black movement leaders have dominated the headlines and historical reflection, obscuring the contributions of those in the White community who—quietly and moderately or openly and boldly—worked to further understanding and bridge the gulf between the races. This book has named only a few of those forgotten voices.

Jeffery Zorn, who worked as a White teacher at Miles College from the late 1960s, observed that "Birmingham's white liberals walked the walk. Around Harvard and M.I.T. it was easy to talk the talk, strike revolutionary poses, and feel really good about yourself."[664] Martin Luther King Jr. acknowledged that "white liberals or moderates" made it possible to have "cooperation between the races."[665] Civil rights attorney Fred D. Gray Sr., whose legal strategy broke the back of school segregation in Alabama, reflected that "any number of white persons helped in many ways."[666] In *Bus Ride to Justice*, his autobiography, Gray added, "The white lawyer upon whom I depended most was Clifford Durr." Durr practiced law in Birmingham and later moved back to his hometown of Montgomery where he mentored Gray. "Durr was a great behind-the-scenes lawyer throughout the Montgomery Bus protest. . . . He, more than any other person, taught me how to practice law." Though he helped behind the scenes, Durr and his wife, Virginia Foster Durr, "endured public scorn and social ostracism from prominent whites in the city for their sympathetic support and involvement."[667] Judge Houston Brown said, "There have always been white folks who did the right thing."[668]

The "right thing" was an evolving thing. Tennant McWilliams, historian and UAB dean of social sciences, said that "a 1930s liberal would have been someone who strongly opposed the Klan, who strongly advocated for black education and the development of black professional life, but my family, like most Southern white liberals of the '30s, certainly did not turn the corner to advocate total racial equality. So, there was a strong strain of benign but nevertheless paternalistic racial superiority that was there."[669] From that beginning, however, Southern society did evolve, though progress was often slow, resentful, and conflicted.

In part, the positive growth was built from everyday relationships that existed during segregation, despite the constraints of Jim Crow. The 1961 summer before his senior year in college, Chervis Isom, who had been brought up believing in segregation and the White superiority, developed a deep respect and friendship for a fifty-year-old Black man he knew only as Arizona. Isom witnessed all the indignities the man stoically endured at the hands of White supervisors in a Birmingham pipe foundry yard where they both worked. Arizona once saved his life, warning him just before a load of pipes broke free. On the last day of his job there, Isom struggled to find a way to express his feelings. Jim Crow laws forbade a Black man and a White man to sit down together for a beer in a public place, so they sat in Isom's car after work, sharing a bottle of whiskey and talking about their families. It was a small moment, not one for history books, but it profoundly impacted Isom's life.[670] Many years later, Isom played a significant role in bringing about a memorial statue dedicated to the children who died the day of the 16th Street church bombing.

Rebecca Allison, a White woman who grew up in segregated Birmingham said of that time, "There was [often] a genuine affection between the races. But it was almost a schizophrenic thing because, on the one hand, you could love them if you were right there living next to them [as domestic help] but, on the other hand, don't you dare marry Mamie's son. It just wasn't done. So, it was an odd, a very odd way to grow up." Asked how to move toward a more true equality, she replied, "We just have to keep talking, get to know each other. In the South, we've got a leg up on knowing each other. At one time someone made the comment that up North they love the race but hate the individual. Down South, we love the individual but hate the race."[671]

Some have claimed that friendships between Blacks and Whites were only true friendships in the eyes of the Whites, and there might be some truth in that, but others recall a more nuanced and complex picture, possibly an aspect of the contradictory intimacy between the races dating from slavery days[672] and why, as Rabbi Grafman and Black minister J. L. Ware and Miles president

Lucius Pitts agreed, that "some day we [in the South] are going to work out an accommodation and it is going to be a far superior accommodation than anything north of the Mason-Dixon Line."[673]

"Whites and blacks in the South had a strange relationship," Black activist Frank Dukes explained:

> Many white people were reared up by black women. On Saturdays, black kids would work for white people, cut their grass, etc. Black women would take white kids to the park. They had the authority to discipline the white kids. . . . My mother worked for Mary Coretta. Her husband was a foreman for U.S. Steel. We all sat at the same table and ate together.[674]

Ruth Barefield-Pendleton recalled that she and others called on White members of the Friendship and Action to help raise money for bail during the marches and demonstrations and to pick up people at the airport. She said she could count on Carolyn McCoy and Peggy Fuller to make themselves available for "whatever was needed."[675]

Dukes agreed that during the civil rights movement days, many White people helped behind the scenes:

> The movement got good information from many liberal (White) people. They got money for bail and opened doors that were closed to us. . . . There were white folks who were supporting us that I didn't even know. Some donated money. Deenie Drew had a white friend who would go to the [White] Citizens Council meetings and tell Deenie what was happening. Those [White] people kept us informed. We've always had some help from white folks, but never had enough white folks with us.[676]

Those that were "with them" deserve to be remembered. Many risked their lives; across the South, a few gave their lives. Countless people followed their principles in quieter ways. Some refused to do business with racists or opened the door of their homes or dared intense peer pressure to give a kind word. Many treated Black workers with respect and established genuine friendships across racial lines, despite the social ostracizing and possible violent retribution that incurred. Dukes recalled, "Some of the best friends in my life have been white, and they helped me when I needed it the most." It is worthwhile to ponder that most such acts and relationships occurred without witnesses or without notice by any recorder of history.

AND WHAT DID THOSE who reached out from the White "side" gain? One woman's response to an audience member at a presentation by the Panel of American Women might provide a piece of an answer. The man said he had come prepared to dislike the panel members and find them ugly, but as the women spoke, they all grew more and more beautiful in his eyes. One housewife on the panel, reflecting on that, said, "In growing to understand each other . . . perhaps we have each been able to remove our own masks of distrust for people different from ourselves. Perhaps in trying to help solve problems in our community, we've stumbled on the best cosmetic of all—a mutual compassion."[677]

Martin Luther King Jr. described 1963 as "the year of Birmingham," the year that brought the issue of civil rights to the nation, paving the way for progress, and that was true for the nation. For Birmingham, however, as historian Jonathan Bass noted, "it was the citizens of the Magic City, both black and white, not Martin Luther King and the SCLC, that brought about real transformation of the city. . . . Moderation and the push for change had been in process several months before King arrived on the scene in Birmingham. The Freedom Rides, the park controversy, and the excesses of Bull Connor and the city commission had rallied the reform forces in the white community."[678] The Reverend Lawrence McGinty observed, "'There is a time and place for demonstrations, but, after the crowds and the reporters have gone home, the work of racial understanding, reconciliation, and the accomplishment of practical projects must go on.'"[679]

Birmingham's journey is far from over. In the August 1971 issue of *Ebony*, Vincent Townsend wrote, "Birmingham, Alabama, is a city where the phrase 'status quo' is a bad word. Because of bad images—some deserved, and some not deserved—this Southern city has begun to live together and work together. Birmingham—that is, the total Birmingham—knows well that it is only beginning to solve its problems." Almost four decades later, in a tribute to attorney Chuck Morgan, Pulitzer Prize-winning journalist John Archibald wrote, "Perhaps—we hope—we have moved beyond issues of hatred and racial violence. The things that confront Birmingham today are harder to see. They are issues of intolerance and ignorance, a pervasive sense of civic doom, the malaise of self-interest, and, of course, that silence of the powerful."[680]

OTHER ISSUES ARE NOT hard to see; they confront the entire country—challenges of urban and rural poverty; lack of widespread quality education and the growing cost of higher education; the availability and accessibility of health, drug rehabilitation, and mental health services; and the need for social and justice reform. These problems often affect the Black community more intensely. Birmingham has created an additional challenge to solving these problems by fighting its history. Many tried to cover the city's dark image with a shiny new one. *Why dwell on the ugly past? That's not who we are.* At the other extreme, voices have said, *That's all we have to define ourselves.*

In 2013, the fiftieth anniversary of Project C in Birmingham, the city underwent a profound change in how it saw itself. Tentatively, at first, many citizens of the Magic City realized they needed to embrace their history, pull back the curtain. It is human nature to turn from horror and scars. Many Jewish families would not speak to their children about the Holocaust, as black families didn't speak of the 1921 massacre in Tulsa or the Birmingham church bombing in 1963. Pulling scabs from those wounds was (and is) painful and met with resistance. But the way forward, Birmingham is learning, is by acknowledging the past and that its story has been profound and far reaching. As Odessa Woolfolk, one of the founders of the Birmingham Civil Rights Institute remarked, "People around the world—in Poland, China, South Africa, Central America, began singing 'We Shall Overcome' as they overthrew their oppressors."[681]

In the city's acknowledging its role in changing the world, it is taking the leadership in telling Birmingham's story. And in doing so, to the surprise of many, it has discovered the hues hiding under that two-color paint, some subtle, some brilliant, and has opened itself to the lessons a truthful, broader look at the past can teach, lessons of courage, truth, and emotional intelligence—the best of what makes us human.

> *It is from numerous, diverse acts of courage and belief that human*
> *history is shaped each time a man stands up for an ideal or acts to*

improve the lot of others, or strikes out against injustice. He sends a tiny ripple of hope, and crossing each other from a million different centers of energy and daring, these ripples build a current that can sweep down the mightiest walls of oppression and resistance.

—ROBERT KENNEDY

Appendix

BIRMINGHAM MINISTERS' LETTER OF JANUARY 16, 1963

In these times of tremendous tensions and change in cherished patterns of life in our beloved Southland, it is essential that men who occupy places of responsibility and leadership shall speak concerning their honest convictions.

We the undersigned clergymen have been chosen to carry heavy responsibility in our religious groups. We speak in a spirit of humility, and only for ourselves. We do not pretend to know all the answers, for the issues are not simple. Nevertheless, we believe our people expect and deserve leadership from us, and we speak with firm conviction for we do know the ultimate spirit in which all problems of human relations must be solved.

It is clear that a series of court decisions will soon bring about desegregation of certain schools and colleges in Alabama. Many sincere people oppose this change and are deeply troubled by it. As southerners, we understand this. We nevertheless feel that defiance is never the right answer nor the solution. And we feel that inflammatory and rebellious statements can lead only to violence, discord, confusion and disgrace for our beloved state.

We therefore affirm and comment to our people:

1. That hatred and violence have no sanction in our religious and political traditions.

2. That there may be disagreement concerning laws and social change without advocating defiance, anarchy and subversion.

3. That laws may be tested in courts or changed by legislatures, but not ignored by whims of individuals.

4. That constitutions may be amended, or judges impeached by proper action, but our American way of life depends upon obedience to the decisions of courts of competent jurisdiction in the meantime.

5. That no person's freedom is safe unless every person's freedom is equally protected.

6. That freedom of speech must at all costs be preserved and exercised without fear of recrimination or harassment.

7. That every human being is created in the image of God and is entitled to respect as a fellow human being with all basic rights, privileges, and responsibilities which belong to humanity.

We respectfully urge those who strongly oppose desegregation to pursue their convictions in the courts, and in the meantime peacefully to abide by the decisions of those same courts.

We recognize that our problems cannot be solved in our strength nor on the basis of human wisdom alone. The situation which confronts us calls for earnest prayer, for clear thought, for understanding love, and for courageous action. Thus, we call on all people of good will to join us in seeking divine guidance as we make our appeal for law and order and common sense.

Signed by: Bishop Nolan B. Harmon, Bishop of the North Alabama Conference of the Methodist Church; Bishop Paul Hardin, Bishop of the Alabama-West Florida Conference of the Methodist Church; C. C. J. Carpenter, D.D., LL.D., Bishop of Alabama; Joseph A. Durick, D.D., Auxiliary bishop, Diocese of Mobile-Birmingham; Earl Stallings, Pastor, First Baptist Church, Birmingham, Alabama; George M. Murray, D.D., LL.D., Bishop Coadjutor, Episcopal Diocese of Alabama; Rabbi Milton Grafman, Temple Emanu-El, Birmingham, Alabama; Edward V. Ramage, D.D., Moderator, Synod of the Alabama Presbyterian Church in the United States; Revs. Soterios D. Gouvellis, Priest, Holy Trinity, Holy Cross Greek Orthodox Church; Rabbi Eugene Blackschleger, Temple Beth-Or, Montgomery, Alabama; J. T. Beale, Secretary-Director, Christian Churches of Alabama.

Birmingham Ministers' Letter of April 12, 1963

We the undersigned clergymen are among those who, in January, issued "An Appeal for Law and Order and Common Sense," dealing with racial problems in Alabama. We expressed understanding that honest convictions in racial matters could properly be pursued in the courts but urged that decisions of those courts should in the meantime be peacefully obeyed.

Since that time there has been some evidence of increased forbearance and a willingness to face facts. Responsible citizens have undertaken to work on various problems which cause racial friction and unrest. In Birmingham recent public events have given indication that we all have an opportunity for a new constructive and realistic approach to racial problems.

However, we are now confronted by a series of demonstrations by some of our negro citizens, directed and led in part by outsiders. We recognize the natural impatience of people who feel that their hopes are slow in being realized. But we are convinced that these demonstrations are unwise and untimely.

We agree rather with certain local negro leadership which has called for honest and open negotiations of racial issues in our area. And we believe this kind of facing of issues can best be accomplished by citizens of our own metropolitan area, white and negro, meeting with their knowledge and experience of the local situation.

Just as we formerly pointed out that "hatred and violence have no sanction in our religious and political traditions," we also point out that such actions as incite to hatred and violence, however technically peaceful these actions may be, have not contributed to the resolution of our local problems. We do not believe that these days of new hope are days when extreme measures are justified in Birmingham.

We commend the community as a whole, and the local news media and law enforcement officials in particular, on the calm manner in which these demonstrations have been handled. We urge the public to continue to show restraint should the demonstrations continue, and the law enforcement officials to remain calm and continue to protect our city from violence.

We further strongly urge our own negro community to withdraw support from these demonstrations, and to unite locally in working peacefully for a better Birmingham. When rights are consistently denied, a cause should be pressed in the courts and in negotiations among local leaders, and not in the streets. We appeal to both our white and negro citizenry to observe the principles of law and order and common sense.

The document was signed by Bishop Nolan B. Harmon, Bishop of the North Alabama Conference of the Methodist Church; Bishop Paul Hardin, Bishop of the Alabama-West Florida Conference of the Methodist Church; C. C. J. Carpenter, D.D., LL.D., Bishop of Alabama; Joseph A. Durick, D.D., Auxiliary bishop, Diocese of Mobile-Birmingham; Rabbi Milton Grafman, Temple Emanu-El, Birmingham, Alabama; George M. Murray, D.D., LL.D., Bishop Coadjutor, Episcopal Diocese of Alabama; Edward V. Ramage, D.D.,

Moderator, Synod of the Alabama Presbyterian Church in the United States; Earl Stallings, Pastor, First Baptist Church, Birmingham, Alabama.

PARTICIPANTS IN CONCERNED WHITE CITIZENS MARCH
Selma, Alabama March 6, 1965
List from Peggy Fuller's notebook

BIRMINGHAM: Miss Lois Almon, Maurice (Max) Baer*, Helen Baer*, Monana Cheney, Rene Chetelat, Bob Dillo, Joseph Ellwanger, Joyce Ellwanger, Gertrude Goldstein, Mary Gonzalez, Kathy Gonzalez, Nina Gonzalez, Marcia Herman-Giddens, Helen Knox, Frederick W. Kraus, Anny W. Kraus, Marjorie Linn, Carolyn McCoy, the Reverend Lawrence E McGinty, Helen Morin, Richard D. Morin, Scott Morin, James Olmsted, Peggy Rupp, Donald Rupp, Dr. R. C. Sailer, Mrs. Louise Sailer, Florence Siegel, Dr. Abraham Siegel, Elizabeth Spiegel, Lee Spiegel, Edward Steinberg, Margit Tinglum, Ottmar Tinglum, David Walbert, Mrs. Eileen Walbert, Burton Zell

TUSCALOOSA: Edward H. Carlson, Louise D. Carlson, Willita S. Goodson, Margaret Klitzke, Dr. Theodore Klitzke

HUNTSVILLE: Otto Borgmaier, Margaret G. Clements, Myra Copeland, R. Cordray, Ellen Day, Frank J. Holm, Don Newroth, Dale Schmiet, Ernie Sylvester, Jane Tucker

TUSKEGEE AND AUBURN: Tom Milliken, Frank Schulz

SELMA: Father Maurice F. Ouelette

FAIRHOPE: Mrs. William Hill

MOBILE: Rev. Marin Nichols, Rev. Jack Thompson

SHEFFIELD: Rev. Furman C. Stough

* These names were not included on Fuller's handwritten list but came from other sources (See Baer in Bibliography).

LETTER FROM CONCERNED WHITE CITIZENS PRESENTED IN SELMA
March 6, 1965

We, as white citizens of Alabama have come to Selma today to tell the nation that there are white people in Alabama who will speak out against the events which have recently occurred in this and neighboring counties and towns. We deem it a tragic retreat from the American principle of 'no taxation without representation' when citizens of Alabama, Negro and white, must undergo a college level examination to be able to exercise their right as a responsible, law-abiding, taxpaying citizen to vote.

We are horrified at the brutal way in which the police at times have attempted to break up American citizens who are exercising their constitutional right to protest injustice. And we are shocked at the inhumane way American citizens of Dallas and other counties in Alabama have been treated when taken prisoner in the recent demonstrations.

We are sickened by the totalitarian atmosphere of intimidation and fear officials have purposefully created and maintained to discourage lawful assembly and peaceful expression of grievances against the existing conditions.

THEREFORE, as citizens of the United States of America and of this state of Alabama, we do by our presence here affirm our faith in the abiding principles upon which our nation and our state our founded and for which our forefathers died. We are immoveable in our determination that this be a 'nation under God for liberty and justice for all.'

We urge that the governor of our state and all elected officials, state and local, use their power and prestige to see that all open and subtle intimidation of persons seeking to be registered to vote be removed.

We request that, since many citizens have for so long been given the clear picture that they are not wanted in the registrar's office, the state and local officials owe it to these citizens systematically to inform them that they are welcome and that they are encouraged to register and vote. We ask that not only the federal government, but our own state legislature go on record against the 'college test' type of a registration form in favor of a simple informational blank and that assistance be made available to fully understand or fill out the form.

We finally plead for federal help in terms of laws and registrars if these injustices are not removed forthrightly.[682]

Notes

1 Jimerson, Randall C. *Shattered Glass in Birmingham: My Family's Fight for Civil Rights, 1961–1964*. Louisiana State University Press, 2014, 65.

2 "Current of compromise flows through tension here," *Birmingham News*, April 14, 1963, A-2.

3 Gossom, Jr., Thom. *Walk-On*. Best Gurl, Inc., 2013.

4 Bass, Jonathan. *Blessed Are the Peacemakers: Martin Luther King, Eight White Religious Leaders, and the "Letter from Birmingham Jail,"* Louisiana State Press, 2001, 225.

5 Brook, Larry. *Southern Jewish Life*, March 2015.

6 Jimerson, *Shattered Glass in Birmingham,*162. Prologue

7 Lankford, Tom, multiple emails and personal memoir notes to author, 2009–2017.

8 LaMonte, Edward Shannon. *Politics & Welfare in Birmingham, 1900–1975*. University of Alabama Press, 1995, 165.

9 Lankford, Tom, personal notes.

10 Bagley, Joseph Mark, "School Desegregation, Law and Order, and Litigating Social Justice in Alabama," 1954–1973, PhD diss., Georgia State University, 2014.

11 Tilford, Earl H., *Turning the Tide*, University of Alabama Press, 2014, 16.

12 Greenhaw, Wayne, *Fighting the Devil in Dixie*. Lawrence Books, 2011, 71.

13 "Student paper banned from political views," *Birmingham News*, June 12, 1958, 1.

14 Tilford, *Turning the Tide*, 116.

15 Isom, Chervis, interviewed by Horace Huntley, Birmingham Civil Rights Institute. Oral History Project, March 22, 2007; Isom, Chervis, interviewed by Tammi Sharpe, Birmingham Civil Rights Institute. Oral History Project, October 17, 2014.

16 Chilcoat, Mathew, author interview.

17 Keith, Don, *Mattie C's Boy*. NewSouth Books, 2013, 102.

18 Dukes, Frank, author interview.

19 Brown, Houston, YMBC speech. Birmingham, Alabama. May 16, 2016.

20 Ibid.

21 Bass, *Blessed Are the Peacemakers*, 93.

22 LaMonte, *Politics & Welfare in Birmingham*, 170.

23 Underwood, Paul, "A Progressive History of the Young Men's Business Club of Birmingham, Alabama," 1946–1970, Samford University, 1980, 71.

24 McWilliams, Tennant S., *New Lights in the Valley: The Emergence of UAB*," University of Alabama Press, 2007, 152.

25 Sullivan, Patricia, "Charles Morgan Jr.: Lawyer Championed Civil, Voting Rights." *Washington Post*, January 9, 2009.

26 Drake, Jack, emails with author, June 8, 2020.

27 Stewart, Shelley, author interview, Birmingham, Alabama, May 10, 2017 and May 24, 2017.

28 LaMonte, *Politics & Welfare in Birmingham*, 154.

29 Nail, Kay Cochran, "Birmingham's Jewish Women and Social Reform 1880–1980," University of Alabama in Birmingham, 2010. Master's thesis, 23.

30 Harris, W. Edward, interviewed by Horace Huntley, Birmingham Civil Rights Institute, Oral History Project, February 18, 1998, transcript.

31 LaMonte, *Politics & Welfare in Birmingham*, 156.

32 Eskew, Glenn T., *But for Birmingham: The Local and National Movements in the Civil Rights Struggle*, The University of North Carolina Press, 1997, 113.

33 Garrison, Greg, "Friend to MLK and Enemy of the Klan, Liberal Minister Confronted Injustice," Life Stories: Jack Zylman," *al.com*,

November 15, 2013.

34   Ibid, Stewart, Shelly, author interview.

35   Keith, *Mattie C's Boy*, 222–23.

36   Sullivan, Patricia, "Charles Morgan Jr.: Lawyer Championed Civil, Voting Rights," *Washington Post*, January 9, 2009.

37   Nunnelley, William A., *Bull Connor*, University of Alabama Press, 1991, 93; ibid, footnote, 37.

38   Morgan, Charles, Jr., *A Time to Speak*, Holt, Rinehart and Winston, 1964, 95–6.

39   Eskew, *But for Birmingham*, 167.

40   Morgan, *A Time to Speak*, 95–6.

41   Lankford, Tom, personal notes.

42   Brown, Donald, interview by Tammi Sharpe, Birmingham Civil Rights Institute, Oral History Project, transcript, October 30, 2014.

43   Bass, *Blessed are the Peacemakers*, 95.

44   Gray, Jeremy, "In 1938 Birmingham, Eleanor Roosevelt faced Bull Connor's wraith," *al.com*, April 24, 2019.

45   Kelly, Robin D.G., Hammer And Hoe: Alabama Communists During The Great Depression, The University of North Carolina Press, 2015.

46   Woodham, Rebecca. "Southern Conference for Human Welfare (SCHW)," Encyclopedia of Alabama, July 7, 2008, updated April 21, 2015.

47   Nunnelley, *Bull Connor*, 93; ibid, footnote, 40.

48   "The 3,000 pages of FBI letters, memos and teletypes clearly show that the FBI knew that Sgt. Thomas Cook, of the BPD intelligence branch, was passing information on the activities of the civil rights workers directly to the top leadership of the Klan." Magnusson, Paul "FBI Knew Policeman Was Leak to Klan on Freedom Riders." *Washington Post*, August 20, 1978.

49   Halberstam, David, *The Children*, Fawcett Books, Ballantine Publishing Group, 1998, 263.

50   Magnusson, Paul, "FBI Knew Policeman Was Leak to Klan on Freedom Riders." *Washington Post*, August 20, 1978.

51   Lankford, Tom, "Mob terror hits city on Mother's Day," *Birmingham News*, May 15, 1961, 1, 8.

52   "National States Rights Party, Monographs and Attorney General's Letter," Federal Bureau of Investigations, Freedom of Information archives, August 1966.

53   Newton, Michael, *White Robes and Burning Crosses: A History of the Klan from 1866*, Macfarland, 2014, 135.

54   Arsenault, Raymond, *Freedom Riders: 1961 and the Struggle for Racial Justice*, Oxford University Press, 2011, 105.

55   Nunnelley, *Bull Connor*, 107.

56   Ibid, 99.

57   Lewis, John, and Michael D'Orso, *Walking with the Wind: A Memoir of the Movement*, Simon & Schuster, reissue edition, 2015, 147.

58   Eskew, *But for Birmingham*, 156. Note: Bergman suffered a stroke ten days after the incident and was confined to a wheelchair the rest of his life. Bergman sued the FBI, after FBI informant Gary Thomas Rowe testified in Congress that he had given the FBI information about the pending attack. Bergman eventually won a small settlement of $35,000 in 1983. He died in 1998.

59   Lewis, *Walking with the Wind*, 142.

60   Arsenault, *Freedom Riders*, 150.

61   Nunnelley, *Bull Connor*, 97.

62   Lankford, Tom, "Mob terror hits city on Mother's Day," *Birmingham News*, May 15, 1961, 1.

63   Benn, Alvin, Reporter: Covering Civil Rights . . . And Wrongs In Dixie, AuthorHouse, 2006, 32.

64   Lankford, personal notes and emails with author.

65   Eskew, *But for Birmingham*, 158–59.

66   Lewis, *Walking with the Wind*, 145.

67   Nunnelley, *Bull Connor*, 92.

68   Lankford, *Birmingham News*, May 15, 1961, 1,8.

69   Nunnelley, *Bull Connor*, 101.

70   Lewis, *Walking with the Wind*, 148.

71   Ibid, 149.

72   Lankford, Tom and Bud Gordon, "Integrators send another group to city," *Birmingham News*, May 19, 1961, 1.

73   "Liberated at State Line, Negro Agitators Return," *Selma Times-Journal*, May 19, 1961, 2.

74   Ibid.

75   Lewis, *Walking with the Wind*, 152.

76   Bright, Taylor, "Bull Connors Police Chief recalls turbulent civil rights movement," *Gadsden Times*, May 22, 2002.

77   Lankford, Tom, "Women Join with Men

in savage scene," May 20, 1961, 1; Lankford, Tom, "Two rescued by Floyd Man," *Birmingham News*, May 20, 1961, 1, 2.

78 *Eyes on the Prize: American Civil Rights Movement 1954–1985*. PBS, Judith Vecchione, dir., 2012. Blackside, Inc., American Experience, PBS, 1987, 1990, 2012, DVD.

79 Vann, David, interviewed by Horace Huntley, Birmingham Civil Rights Institute, Oral History Project, transcript, February 2, 1995 and March 25, 1999.

80 Bass, *Blessed are the Peacemakers*, 62.

81 Eskew, *But for Birmingham*, 171.

82 Kimerling, Solomon, author interview.

83 Schaffer, Sheldon, "Birmingham Notations on the Civil Rights Era—Personal Views," Unpublished paper, Harriet Schaffer, personal files, April 22, 2002, updated April 20, 2003.

84 Kimerling, Solomon, "Unmasking the Klan: Late 1940s Coalition Against Racial Violence," *Weld for Birmingham*, July 18, 2012.

85 Ibid.

86 For less serious military justice incidents in the pre-Viet Nam era, it was not uncommon for a non-attorney to act as trial prosecutor or defense council. Jim Sturdivant, author interview, March 2021.

87 Friedman, Karl, Multiple interviews, Birmingham, Alabama, 2013–2016.

88 Kelly, Mark, *A Powerful Presence, the Birmingham Regional Chamber of Commerce*, 2008, 110.

89 Smyer, S.W. Jr., "Need for Local Negro Leaders," *Birmingham News*, May 13, 1963, 5.

90 Morgan, A Time to Speak, 56.

91 King, Pamela, "The Revolt of the Moderates," *Weld for Birmingham*, April 17, 2013.

92 Ellwanger, Joseph, *Strength for the Struggle*, Mavenmark Books, 2014, iv.

93 Hillman Hospital merged in 1945 with the county's Jefferson Hospital to become University Hospital (University of Alabama Hospitals and Clinics), which was the teaching hospital for the University of Alabama's School of Medicine. In 1966 they merged into the University of Alabama in Birmingham. In 1969 the latter became an autonomous university and in 1984 changed its name to the University of Alabama at Birmingham.

94 Nail, "Birmingham's Jewish Women," 8–12.

95 Ibid, 15–16.

96 Ibid, 31.

97 Dr. Nathan Edgar Miles, in addition to giving time and services to those who could not afford it, was a community philanthropist. The Jewish N. E. Miles Day School is named for him, as well as a chair at the UAB School of Ophthalmology.

98 Nail, "Birmingham's Jewish Women, 2, 26.

99 Eskew, *But for Birmingham*, 144.

100 White, Bradley, Arant, and Rose.

101 Jimerson, *Shattered Glass in Birmingham*, 11.

102 Drake, interview.

103 Rupp, Peggy, author interview.

104 Fuller, John, interviewed by Horace Huntley, Birmingham Civil Rights Institute, Oral History Project, transcript, March 25, 1998.

105 Vann, David, interviewed by Horace Huntley.

106 Rupp, author interview.

107 Nail, "Birmingham's Jewish Women," 30–1.

108 Knowlton, Sam, author interview.

109 Jimerson, *Shattered Glass in Birmingham*, 43, 83.

110 Lankford, email correspondence.

111 Harris, W. Edward, *Miracle in Birmingham: A Civil Rights Memoir 1954–1965*, Stonework Press, 2004, 167.

112 McWilliams, Tennant, interview by Tammi Sharpe, Birmingham Civil Rights Institute, Oral History Project, transcript, September 5, 2014.

113 Mazzara, Jackie, interview with Pamela Powell, mp3 file, unknown date,

114 Weaver, Jeanne Moore, "A History of the Unitarian Universalist Church of Birmingham, Alabama 1952–2016," Unpublished, Jeanne Weaver, personal collection, 8.

115 Weaver, "History of the Unitarian Church," 16.

116 Mazzara, Jackie, interview with Pamela Powell.

117 Gibson, Gordon Davis, *Southern Witness: Unitarians and Universalists in the Civil Rights Era*, Skinner House Books, 2015, 158.

118 Weaver, "History of the Unitarian Church," 15.

119 Lankford, Tom, personal notes.

120 Vann, David, interviewed by Horace Huntley.

121 Brown, Houston, speech to YMBC.

122 Eskew, *But for Birmingham*, 104.

123 Harris, *Miracle in Birmingham*, 58.

124 Lankford, Tom, personal notes.

125 Nunnelley, *Bull Connor*, 66.

126 Jimerson, *Shattered Glass in Birmingham*, 75.

127 Weaver, Lamar, interview by Horace Huntley, Birmingham Civil Rights Institute, Oral History Project, transcript, March 16, 1995.

128 Weaver, "History of the Unitarian Church," xxii.

129 Friedman, Karl, personal notes.

130 Webb, Clive, *Fight Against Fear: Southern Jews and Black Civil Rights*, The University of Georgia Press, 2003, 46.

131 Stanton, Mary, *The Hand of Esau*, River City Publishing, Montgomery, Alabama, 2006, 104–05,

132 Harris, *Miracle in Birmingham*, 30.

133 Friendly, Fred W, "CBS Reports: Who Speaks for Birmingham," Smith, Howard K, narrator, CBS, 1961.

134 Bagley, "School Desegregation," 143–44.

135 Friedman, Karl, "Birmingham Civil Rights, A Jewish Perspective," videoed speech at the Birmingham Public Library, Birmingham, Alabama, Birmingham Holocaust Education Center, prod., March 13, 2013; Friedman, author interview.

136 Schaffer, Sheldon, "Birmingham Notations on the Civil Rights Era—Personal Views," Unpublished paper, Harriet Schaffer, personal files, April 22, 2002, updated April 20, 2003.

137 Kimerling, author interview.

138 Brook, Larry, "Rabbi Grafman, Dr. King, and the Letter from the Birmingham Jail," April 4, 2013.

139 Nail, "Birmingham's Jewish Women," 29.

140 "Bearing witness: A controversial 1963 trip to Birmingham by 19 rabbis," *Southern Jewish Life*, Friday, May 3, 2013.

141 "Bombing Matters," Federal Bureau of Investigations, office memorandum, File 62–1922, SAC, Birmingham, July 24, 1958.

142 Friedman said it was a subcommittee of the Jewish Federation, but possibly he meant the Jewish Community Council, which had a board consisting of all the Jewish organizations. The Birmingham Jewish Federation didn't exist as such until 1970. Elovitz in *A Century of Jewish Life in Dixie* (1974), 179–80, referenced a "a committee of the Jewish Community Council established to concern themselves with anti-defamation and civil liberties." In an advisory to members of the Jewish Community Council it was mentioned that "appropriate Council committees were preparing . . . a campaign to . . . safeguard its [the Jewish community's] interests and welfare."

143 Friedman, author interview.

144 Ibid, Friedman speech, "Birmingham Civil Rights."

145 Ibid, Boswell, author interview, circa 2015.

146 Friedman, author interview.

147 Lankford, Tom, personal notes.

148 Corley, Robert Gaines, "The Quest for Racial Harmony: Race Relations in Birmingham, Alabama, 1947–1963," University of Virginia, 1979. PhD diss., 219.

149 Nunnelley, *Bull Connor*, 116.

150 Friedman, Paul, Sr. Letter to Robin Gotlieb, June 6, 1995, Birmingham Public Library, Grafman files.

151 "Jaycees take stand against parks closing," *Birmingham News*, December 12, 1961.

152 Kimerling, Solomon, "Transforming Birmingham," *Weld for Birmingham*, November 21, 2012.

153 Hanes, Art, Jr, speech at YMBC, March 6, 2017,

154 Vann, David. interview by Horace Huntley.

155 Harris, *Miracle in Birmingham*, 184.

156 Ibid, 106; Thornton, J. Mills, III, *Dividing Lines: Municipal Politics and the Struggle for Civil Rights in Montgomery, Birmingham, and Selma*, University of Alabama Press, 2002, 254.

157 Jimerson, *Shattered Glass in Birmingham*, 75–6.

158 Berkowitz, Abraham, letter to editor, *Birmingham News*, December 22, 1961, Chervis Isom, personal collection; Griffin, Janet, personal scrapbook on 1960s.

159 Kimerling, Solomon, "Transforming Birmingham," *Weld for Birmingham*, November 21, 2012.

160 Sales, Amy L. and Tobin, Gary A., Church

and Synagogue Affiliation: Theory, Research, and Practice (Contributions to The Study of Religion), Greenwood Publishing Group, 1995, 164.

161 Bass, *Blessed are the Peacemakers*, 52.

162 Eskew, *But for Birmingham*, 180.

163 Corley, "Quest for Racial Harmony," 213–14.

164 Lankford, Tom. "Integration techniques at stake as Albany program bogs down." *Birmingham News*, July 29, 1962, A-25.

165 Roberts, Gene, and Hank Klibanoff, *The Race Beat: The Press, the Civil Rights Struggle, and the Awakening Of A Nation*, Vintage Books, 2007, 256.

166 Lankford, Tom, personal notes.

167 Lewis, *Walking with the Wind*, 159.

168 Pritchett, Laurie, unknown interviewer, Blackside, Inc., Eyes on the Prize: America's Civil Rights Years 1954–1965, Washington University Libraries Film and Media Archive, Henry Hampton Collection, video, November 7, 1985.

169 McWhorter, Diane, *Carry Me Home: Birmingham, Alabama, the Climactic Battle of the Civil Rights Revolution*, Touchstone, 2001, p 341.

170 Heldman, Alan W., interview transcript by Willoughby Anderson, Carolina Digital Repository, UNC University Libraries, May 26, 2003.

171 Cleveland, Charles, author interview.

172 Jimerson, *Shattered Glass in Birmingham*, 97.

173 Friedman, author interview.

174 Jimerson, *Shattered Glass in Birmingham*, 98–9.

175 Baer, Helen, Mary Y. Gonzalez, and Eileen Walbert, "The Concerned White Citizens of Alabama and their Appearance in Selma, March 6, 1965," interview by Max Baer. UAB Digital Collection. Oral interviews, Mervyn Sterne Library, transcript, October 27, 1975.

176 Walbert, Eileen, Birmingham, Alabama, author interview.

177 Davis, J. Mason, author interview.

178 Dukes, Donna, author interview.

179 *STAND! Untold Stories of the Civil Rights Movement*, Donna Dukes, exec. prod./dir., Birmingham, Alabama, 3D Productions, DVD, 2018; Dukes, Frank, author interview.

180 Ibid.

181 Dukes, Frank., author interview.

182 Nunnelley, *Bull Connor*, 136.

183 McWilliams, *New Lights in the Valley*, 156.

184 Nunnelley, *Bull Connor*, 122.

185 *STAND!*

186 Ibid.

187 Roberts, Gene, and Hank Klibanoff, *The Race Beat*, Vintage Books, 2007, 309.

188 Lankford, Tom, "Mayola says boy killed in his sleep," *Birmingham News*, August 13, 1962; Lankford, *Birmingham News*, August 13, 1962, 1,4; Lankford, Tom, "Crackdown on sex perverts ordered for city by Connor," *Birmingham News*, August 8, 1962, 30.

189 Lankford, Tom, "Negroes link own race in dynamitings," January 23, 1962, 1, 2.

190 Jimerson, *Shattered Glass in Birmingham*, 146.

191 LaMonte, *Politics & Welfare in Birmingham*,166.

192 Harris, *Miracle in Birmingham*, 31.

193 "Birmingham Yields to Court Order: Prepares to Integrate High Schools," *New Castle News*, August 20, 1963, 1.

194 Miller, Elaine Hobson, author interview.

195 Eskew, *But for Birmingham*, 187; Vann, David, interviewed by Horace Huntley; Rumore, Samuel, author interview.

196 Kelly, Mark, *A Powerful Presence*, 142–44.

197 Vann, David, interview by Horace Huntley.

198 Cleveland, Charles personal notes.

199 Swift, Ivan, "Petition Response Amazing," *Birmingham News*, August 29, 1962, 1.

200 "Judge Meeks checks petition seeking change in city," *Birmingham News*, September 6, 1962, 55.

201 Eskew, *But for Birmingham*, 182.

202 Nunnelley, *Bull Connor*, 126–27; Vann, David, interview by Horace Huntley,

203 Swift, Ivan, "Vann explains three forms of government." *Birmingham News*, September 12, 1962.

204 Jimerson, *Shattered Glass in Birmingham*, 143–46.

205 Eskew, *But for Birmingham*, 203.

206 Elovitz, Mark H., *A Century of Jewish Life in Dixie: The Birmingham Experience*, University of Alabama Press, 1974, 27–28.

207 Raines, Howell, *My Soul Is Rested*, Putnam Publishing, 1977, 157.

208 Nunnelley, *Bull Connor*, 132.

209 Pizitz, Richard, Birmingham, Alabama, author interview.

210 Lankford, Tom, "Firefighters told vote key to raise," *Birmingham News*, October 18, 1962, 10; Lankford, Tom, personal notes.

211 Harris, *Miracle in Birmingham*, 120.

212 Vann, David, interview by Horace Huntley.

213 Friedman, Karl, personal notes.

214 Lankford, email to author.

215 *The Thunderbolt*, Birmingham Alabama, Issue 46. *The Thunderbolt* described itself as "the official White Racial Organ of the National States Rights Party."

216 Vann, David, interview by Horace Huntley.

217 Davis, author interview.

218 Vann, David, interview by Horace Huntley.

219 Isaccson, Lou, "Commissioners may call mass meeting of citizens," *Birmingham News*, October 19, 1962, 26.

220 Connor, Eugene, "We Ask David Vann," *Birmingham News* (advertisement), November 2, 1962, 31.

221 "City vote called victory for all," *Birmingham News*, November 7, 1962, 4.

222 Bagley, "School Desegregation," 184.

223 Barefield-Pendleton, Ruth and Walbert, Eileen, author interviews.

224 Brown, Houston, speech to YMBC.

225 Rosenbaum, Alvin, *Birmingham News*, "Letter to the Editor," January 18, 1963, 14

226 Bass, *Blessed are the Peacemakers*, 16.

227 Ibid, 21–2.

228 Powell, Robert, interviewed by Tammi Sharpe, Birmingham Civil Rights Institute, Oral History Project, transcript, September 24, 2014.

229 Ewing, Joel, "The Arms of Safety: Al Lingo and the Strategy of Massive Interference 1963–1965," University of Alabama at Birmingham, August 2008, master's thesis, 10, 11.

230 Harris, *Miracle in Birmingham*, 91.

231 Sparrow, Hugh, "Public Safety Files Being Amassed On 'Subversives' Now," *Birmingham News*, B-4, February 9, 1964.

232 Harris, *Miracle in Birmingham*, 90.

233 Rupp, Peggy, author interview.

234 Young, Andrew, *An Easy Burden: The Civil Rights Movement and the Transformation of America*, Baylor University Press, 2008, 203.

235 Dukes, Frank, author interview.

236 "Mel Bailey, longtime sheriff in Alabama, 72," *Atlanta Journal*, August 30, 1997, C-9.

237 Orange, David, Birmingham, Alabama, author interview.

238 Lankford, Tom, personal notes.

239 Federal Communications Act of 1938.

240 *Olmstead v. U.S.* and *Nardone v. U.S.* See also Boucher, Sarah, Edward Cotler, and Stephen Larson, "Internet Wiretapping and Carnivore," student paper, May 17, 2001.

241 Orange, David Wayne, *From Segregation to Civil Rights and Beyond: A Story of the Southland*, PublishAmerica, 2004, 150.

242 Lankford, Tom, personal notes. According to Lankford, the surveillance equipment was used primarily during the civil rights unrest. The Unit members did, however, use these tools for other investigations. "Over an eight-year period, when not needed for racial matters, the Unit tapped telephone lines, homes, and cars of gambling kingpins, drug pushers, safe burglars, car thieves, and any other persons suspected of a criminal act. But the line was not drawn at criminals. Bir*mingham News* and its publisher were assisted in investigations, including use of wiretaps and room transmitters against its labor union, a 'bought off' news editor and dozens of politicians . . . and at one time, the governor of the State."

243 "Interview with Sheriff Mel Bailey," *Eyes on the Prize*, video, Blackside, Inc., Birmingham, Alabama, November 2, 1985.

244 Ibid.

245 Morin, Relman, "Are City Chimes Saying Hour Late for Old South?" *Birmingham News*, May 11, 1963, A-4.

246 Lankford, Tom, "Barnett admits he knew Marshals were en route," *Birmingham News*, May 9, 1963, 24.

247 Ibid, personal notes; "AP honors News for story cooperation," *Birmingham News*, November 13, 1962, 18.

248 Bagley, "School Desegregation," 159.

249 "Extremist Organizations Part II, National States Rights Party," Federal Bureau of Investigations, Birmingham Field Office Bureau File *t 105–66233, March 4, 1963 Freedom of Information archives.

250 Lankford, Tom, personal notes.

251 Probably Office of Strategic Services, which was the predecessor of the Central

Intelligence Agency.

252 Ibid, email.

253 Orange, *From Segregation to Civil Rights*, 158.

254 Lankford, Tom, personal notes.

255 Greer, Peter, "Martin Luther King and John F. Kennedy: Civil Rights' Wary Allies," Christian Science Monitor, January 20, 2014.

256 Lankford, Tom, personal notes.

257 Nunnelley, *Bull Connor*, 135.

258 "Decent responsible people must resume leadership Birmingham businessman asserts," *Birmingham News*, March 5, 1963, 1,2,5.

259 Nunnelley, *Bull Connor*, 136.

260 Corley, "Quest for Racial Harmony," 245–47.

261 Nunnelley, *Bull Connor*, 137.

262 "Birmingham and Bull Connor," *Atlanta Constitution*, March 7, 1963, 4.

263 Bartlett, Charles, "King Crisis Needed to Sustain His Image," *Boston Globe*, May 14, 1963, 8.

264 Jimerson, *Shattered Glass in Birmingham*, 165.

265 Dukes, author interview.

266 Jimerson, *Shattered Glass in Birmingham*, 165.

267 Lankford, Tom, personal notes.

268 Ibid. The police's Uher recorder could be operated at 15/16 inches per second, adequate for speech.

269 Bass, *Blessed are the Peacemakers*, 130.

270 "10 more Negroes arrested in sit-ins," *Birmingham News*, April 5, 1963, 2.

271 Nunnelley, Bull Connor, 139.

272 Orange, From Segregation to Civil Rights, 146.

273 Secretary to the Birmingham movement, Ruth Barefield-Pendleton said she met with leaders at 9:00 am in Room 30 or, if there was a march that day, they met at the A. G. Gaston Hall in the afternoon. It appears this, however, may have been a special meeting that included the community.

274 Friedman, Karl, personal notes.

275 Barr, Terry, "Rabbi Grafman and Birmingham's Civil Rights Era," *The Quiet Voices: Southern Rabbis and Black Civil Rights, 1880s to 1990s*, Bauman, Mark K. and Kalin, Berekley, editors, University of Alabama Press, 1997, 172.

276 Brook, Larry, "Rabbi Grafman, Dr. King, and the Letter from Birmingham, Jail,"

Southern Jewish Life, April 2013.

277 Friedman, Karl, personal notes. The timing of this reported encounter is uncertain; it might have been before the negotiations conclude or afterward in preparing for implementing the agreed on terms.

278 Friedman, author interview and speech.

279 Harris, *Miracle in Birmingham*, 82.

280 Jimerson, *Shattered Glass in Birmingham*, 167.

281 LaMonte, *Politics & Welfare in Birmingham*, 113.

282 Garrow, David J. "The FBI and Martin Luther King." *The Atlantic*, July/August 2002..

283 Barr, Rabbi Grafman, 181; Bass, *Blessed are the Peacemakers*, 11, 203.

284 Carpenter, Douglas M., *A Powerful Blessing, The Life of Charles Colcock Jones Carpenter Sr., 1899-1969 Sixth Episcopal Bishop of Alabama*, TransAmerica Printing, 2012, 334.

285 Rose, Stephen C., "Test for Nonviolence," Christian Century, May 14, 1963.

286 "Negroes Attend Two White Churches," *Birmingham News*, April 15, 1963, Shannon Webster, personal collection.

287 "Negroes Attend Two White Churches," *Birmingham News*, April 15, 1963, Shannon Webster, personal collection.

288 Ramage, Katherine, "Easter Sunday, 1963," KidsinBirmingham1963.org.

289 Bass, *Blessed are the Peacemakers*, 85.

290 West, Peggy, author interview.

291 Bass, *Blessed are the Peacemakers*, 3.

292 *Preserving Justice: The Birmingham Civil Rights Movement*, Birmingham Bar Foundation, producers in partnership with The University of Alabama Center for Public Television and Radio, The Magic City Bar Association and the Birmingham Bar Association, film, 2013.

293 "Ministers Manifesto: A Declaration of Equality," Regional Council of Churches of Atlanta (RCCAtl) January 24, 2008. (Originally published in *Atlanta Constitution*, November 3, 1957).

294 Bass, *Blessed are the Peacemakers*, 5.

295 Barr, "Rabbi Grafman," 179.

296 "Bishop Raps Methodist unit stand on King." *Birmingham News*, August 27, 1963, 1.

297 Barr, "Rabbi Grafman," 181, 183.

298 Ibid, 179.

299 Ibid, 182.
300 Bass, *Blessed are the Peacemakers*, 151.
301 Bailey, *Eyes on the Prize*.
302 Friedman and Davis, author interviews.
303 Lankford, Tom, "Change to enhance police chief's role," *Birmingham News*, April 4, 1963, 9.
304 Krulak, Charles C, "Young Birmingham-Southern student was a trailblazer for civil rights," *al.com*.
305 Raines, Howell, "Why was Marti so Alone?" KidsinBirmingham1963.org. Rosenbaum, Alvin, phone interview by Judith Michaelson, March 16, 2008.
306 Kraus, Ingrid, "Strength to pursue our ideals," KidsinBirmingham1963.org.
307 McWilliams, Tennant video interview by Tammi Sharpe.
308 Friedman, Karl, personal notes. Again, it is not certain whether these meetings took place prior to the May 10, 1963 accord or afterward in trying to work out details of what was agreed upon.
309 Keith, *Mattie C's Boy*, 239.
310 Eskew, *But for Birmingham*, 265.
311 Ibid.
312 Ibid, 266.
313 Ibid, 269.
314 Nunnelley, *Bull Connor*, 148.
315 Barefield-Pendleton, Ruth, author interview.
316 Young, *An Easy Burden*, 244.
317 Nunnelley, *Bull Connor*, 148.
318 "Fire hoses, police dogs used to halt downtown Negro demonstrations," *Birmingham News*, May 3, 1963, 2.
319 Ibid.
320 Ibid.
321 Nunnelley, *Bull Connor*, 152.
322 Lankford, Tom, personal notes.
323 Ibid.
324 McWhorter, Diane, *Carry Me Home*, 375.
325 Snow, Louis correspondence.
326 Nunnelley, *Bull Connor*, 152.
327 Vann, David, interviewed by Horace Huntley.
328 Hampton, Henry and Steve Fayer, Voices of Freedom: An Oral History of the Civil Rights Movement from the 1950s through the 1980s, Random House Publishing, 1991, 133.
329 Friedman, Karl, personal notes.
330 Morgan, Camille, author interview.
331 Shiland, Arnold, author interview.
332 Eskew, *But for Birmingham*, 270.
333 Ibid, 271.
334 "Legends in the Law: Louis F. Oberdorfer," DCBar Report, December/January 1997.
335 Eskew, *But for Birmingham*, 272.
336 "Hundreds of hooky-playing demonstrators arrested here along with Negro comedian." *Birmingham News*, May 6, 1963, 2.
337 Marshall, Burke, Oral History interview by Anthony Lewis, John F. Kennedy Library Archives, June 10, 1964.
338 Drennen, Alan, interview by Mary Boehm, produced by University of Alabama at Birmingham for StoryCorps, January 15, 2011.
339 "Hundreds of hooky-playing demonstrators arrested here along with Negro comedian," *Birmingham News*, May 6, 1963, 2.
340 Bailey, *Eyes on the Prize*.
341 Jordan, E. Dan, *No More Hiding Under the Bed*, Xlibris Corp., 2010, 167–69.
342 Drew, Jefferson "Jeff," Birmingham, Alabama, January 13, 2017.
343 *Preserving Justice*, film, Birmingham Bar Association.
344 Nunnelley, *Bull Connor*, 154.
345 Eskew, *But for Birmingham*, 278.
346 Stein, Judith, *Running Steel, Running America : Race, Economic Policy, and the Decline of Liberalism*, The University of North Carolina Press, 1998, 37.
347 Ibid, 38.
348 "Preserving Justice Profile: Jerome 'Buddy' Cooper," The Center for Public Television, April 30, 2013, video.
349 Eskew, *But for Birmingham*, 278.
350 Marshall, Burke, Oral History, interviewed by Anthony Lewis, John F. Kennedy Library Archives, June 10, 1964.
351 Eskew, *But for Birmingham*, 279.
352 Raines, *My Soul Is Rested*, 162.
353 Marshall, Burke, oral interview, JFK library, 101.
354 Eskew, *But for Birmingham*, 282.
355 Ibid, 281.
356 Ibid, 282.
357 Bailey, *Eyes on the Prize*.
358 Eskew, *But for Birmingham*, 295.
359 Gray, Jeremy. " Shuttlesworth Injured by Fire," *al.com*, May 2015.
360 Drew, Jeff, author interview. King had

called on John Drew during the Montgomery bus boycott (1955) to provide insurance for Black church buses, so they could legally be considered public transport.

361 Eskew, *But for Birmingham*, 284; Young, *An Easy Burden*, 244.
362 Young, *An Easy Burden*, 244.
363 Eskew, *But for Birmingham*, 284.
364 Friedman, Karl, personal notes.
365 Kimerling, Solomon author interview.
366 Elovitz, *A Century of Jewish Life*, 170–72.
367 Friedman, Karl, personal notes.
368 Young, *An Easy Burden*, 247.
369 Eskew, *But for Birmingham*, 288–89.
370 Bass, *Blessed are the Peacemakers*, 178.
371 Friedman, Karl, personal notes.
372 *The Thunderbolt*, Issue 45.
373 See Chapter "Justice"
374 "National States Rights Party, Monographs and Attorney General's Letter," Federal Bureau of Investigations, Freedom of Information archives, August 1966.
375 Stewart, Shelley, author interview.
376 Friedman, author interview and speech.
377 Young, *An Easy Burden*, 245; Cooper, Jerome, interviewed by Horace Huntley, Birmingham Civil Rights Institute Oral History Project, video, September 20, 1995.
378 "Harvard Jew appointed by Hugo Black to be law clerk," The Harvard Crimson, October 5, 1937.
379 Erdreich, Ben, Birmingham, Alabama, May 2, 2016.
380 Erdreich, Ben, author interview.
381 Cooper, J., interviewed by Horace Huntley.
382 Erdreich, Ben, author interview; Wilson, Bobby, M., *Race and Place in Birmingham: The Civil Rights and Neighborhood Movements*, Rowman & Littlefield Publishers, 2000, 98; Eskew, But for Birmingham, 291.
383 Brinkley, Douglas, "The Man Who Kept King's Secrets," Vanity Fair, January 19, 2014.
384 Eskew, *But for Birmingham*, 292.
385 Ibid, 293–94.
386 Ibid, 295.
387 "Only five juveniles remain in custody of 1,500 arrested," *Birmingham News*, October 13, 1963.
388 ""Court rules states can't bar mixing," *Birmingham News*, May 20, 1963, 1.
389 Raines, My Soul Is Rested, 177.
390 Sitton, Claude, "50 Hurt in Negro Rioting After Birmingham Blasts," *New York Times*, May 13, 1963, 1, 28.
391 "At least three reported hurt," *Birmingham News*, May 12, 1963, 1.
392 Schaffer, Sheldon, "Birmingham Notations on the Civil Rights Era—Personal Views," unpublished paper, Harriet Schaffer, personal files, April 22, 2002, updated April 20, 2003.
393 Schaffer, Harriet, email exchange, June 28, 2017.
394 "U.S. Feels Troopers Were Too Heavy Handed Says Riots Fault of Ala Cops," *Boston Globe*, May 13, 1963, 8.
395 Eskew, *But for Birmingham*, 301.
396 Jordan, *No More Hiding*, 170–73.
397 Bailey, *Eyes on the Prize*.
398 Vann, David, interviewed by Horace Huntley.
399 Eskew, *But for Birmingham*, 301.
400 Ibid, 302.
401 "U.S. Feels Troopers were Too Heavy Handed says Riots Fault of Ala Cops," *Boston Globe*, May 13, 1963, 3.
402 "Troops Not Needed Boutwell Declares," *Birmingham News*, May 13, 1963, 22.
403 Eskew, *But for Birmingham*, 308.
404 Ibid, 306.
405 Bailey, *Eyes on the Prize*.
406 Lankford, Tom, personal notes.
407 Ibid.
408 Bagley, "School Desegregation," 210, 220, 221.
409 "New YMBC president calls for plan to mix city schools," *Birmingham News*, June 2, 1963.
410 Lankford, Tom, personal notes.
411 Sitton, Claude, "Alabama Admits Negro Students; Wallace Bows to Federal Force; Kennedy Sees 'Moral Crisis' in U.S." *New York Times*, June 12, 1963. General Graham had been in charge of the National Guard in Montgomery to put down the white supremacists' rioting against the Freedom Riders,
412 Bagley, "School Desegregation," 205.
413 Eskew, *But for Birmingham*, 311.
414 Bass, *Blessed are the Peacemakers*, 165.
415 Young, *An Easy Burden*, 248,
416 Rosenberg, Jonathan, and Zachary Karabell, *Kennedy, Johnson, and the Quest for Justice: The Civil Rights Tapes*, W. W. Norton & Company, 2003, 149.

417 Eskew, *But for Birmingham*, 312–13.

418 Vann, David, video interview.

419 Fields, Edward, bulletin, David Vann collection, Birmingham Public Library, July 26, 1963.

420 Vann, David, interview by Horace Huntley.

421 Cleveland, Charles, interviewed by Pam Powell, video, May 31, 2016.

422 Jimerson, *Shattered Glass in Birmingham*, 195.

423 Cleveland, video interview by Pam Powell.

424 Mazzara, Jackie, interview with Pamela Powell.

425 Harris, video interview by Horace Huntley.

426 "Jack Greenberg 1961–1984." NAACP Legal Defense and Educational Fund, Inc., www.naacpldf.org/about-us/history/jack-greenberg/.

427 Volker, Virginia (Sparks), Birmingham, Alabama, author interview.

428 McWilliams, *New Lights in the Valley*, 150.

429 BCRI Harris, interview by Harris Huntley; Stewart, Shelley, author interview.

430 "Owner of Alabama backyard juke joint Gip's Place dies," *Chattanooga Times Free Press*, October 9, 2019.

431 Weaver, "A History of the Unitarian Universalist Church," 18.

432 Huebner, Michael, "Birmingham's Laura Toffel Knox, Advocate for Arts, Civil Rights Dies at 85," *al.com*, April 4, 2011.

433 Friedman, author interview and speech.

434 Pizitz, Richard, author interview.

435 Harris, *Miracle in Birmingham*, 138.

436 Friedman, Karl, personal notes.

437 Eskew, *But for Birmingham*, 317.

438 Cooper, E., author interview; Pizitz, R., author interview.

439 Orange, David, author interview.

440 LaMonte, *Politics & Welfare in Birmingham*, 192–3.

441 Lankford, Tom, "City Council acts in crisis," *Birmingham News*, August 21, 1963, 1.

442 Biggers, George C., III, "'False Charges' brought attack on police," *Birmingham News*, August 21, 1963, 1.

443 Eskew, *But for Birmingham*, 299.

444 "Schools Must Stay Open, Strife Avoided, Women Told," *Birmingham News*, August 9, 1963, 18.

445 "Amidst Crisis—Ministers of all denominations call for order," *Birmingham News*, September 2, 1963, 1–2

446 "Jaycees condemn any interference," *Birmingham News*, September 3, 1963, 2.

447 Parker, Alton, author interview.

448 Weaver, Jeanne, "Unitarian Universalist Church in Birmingham: History." Accessed on March 20, 2017, http://www.uucbham.org/history/.

449 "Motorcade urged at big 'white rally," *Birmingham News*, September 4, 1963, 48.

450 Carter, Dan, *The Politics of Rage: George Wallace, the Origins of the New Conservatism*, Simon & Schuster, 1995, 167–69.

451 Bagley, "School Desegregation," 256.

452 Lankford, Tom, "Yelling whites set off melee at Graymont," *Birmingham News*, September 4, 1963, 1.

453 Bagley, "School Desegregation," 256, 257.

454 Self, Tom, "Witnesses see rage erupt at Ramsay," *Birmingham News*, September 4, 1963, 1.

455 *Spartanburg Herald*, Thursday, September 5, 1963, Photo.

456 Garrison, Greg, "From Sgt. Joe to 'Joe Cool,' First Birmingham Police Chaplain Changed with the Times," Life Stories: Joe Rhodes, *al.com*, October 20, 2013.

457 Faulk, Kent, "'You're going to have to shoot me in the back' retiring judge says he once told officer," *al.com*, June 26, 2015.

458 Lankford, Tom and Joe Campbell, "Negroes attack policemen with bricks, bottles, rocks," *Birmingham News*, September 5, 1963, 1, and "Coroner says stray bullets killed Negro," September 6, 1963, 1.

459 Ibid.

460 Harris, *Miracle in Birmingham*, 182–83.

461 Gibson, Gordon, interviewed by Pam Powell, May 29, 2016, personal video files of Pam Powell; Gibson, Gordon Davis, *Southern Witness: Unitarians and Universalists in the Civil Rights Era*, Skinner House Books, 2015.

462 Harris, *A Miracle in Birmingham*, 183.

463 Fuller, John, interviewed by Horace Huntley,

464 Campbell, Joe, "1,000 skip classes; nine adults arrested," *Birmingham News*, September 10, 1963, 1.

465 "Demonstrators get heavy fines, terms," *Birmingham News*, September 13, 1963, 2.

466 Wilson, Joseph, "Racist Center Abandoned in Birmingham," *Southern Courier*, August 28–29, 1965.

467 Lankford, Tom, personal notes and email.

468 Bagley, "School Desegregation," 272–73.

469 Crawson, John Noel, interviewed by Tammi Sharpe, Birmingham Civil Rights Institute, Oral History Project, transcript, December 19, 2014.

470 Harris, *Miracle in Birmingham*, 181.

471 Ibid.

472 Weaver, "Unitarian Universalist Church," 13.

473 Bagley, "School Desegregation," 273.

474 Lankford, Tom and Irving Beiman, "The day a church became a tomb," *Birmingham News*, September 16, 1963, 1.

475 Dunnam, Charlie, Facebook messenger exchange, 2020.

476 "Six Dead After Church Bombing," United Press International, *Washington Post*, September 16, 1963, 1.

477 Jordan, *No More Hiding*, 181.

478 Harris, video interview by Horace Huntley.

479 Alabama allowed deadly force to stop a "fleeing felon" but, unless an officer was seriously wounded from the rocks, it is unclear what felony may have been committed. That law was ruled unconstitutional in 1985 in Tennessee v. Garner.

480 Jordan, No More Hiding, 183.

481 Bright, Taylor, "Bull Connors Police Chief recalls turbulent civil rights movement," *Gadsden Times*, May 22, 2002; "On the Death of Jamie Moore," Tuscaloosa News, December 29, 2002.

482 "Shock, Disbelief, and Tears, Mayor Boutwell's Reaction," The Montgomery Advertiser, September 16, 1963, 1.

483 Drennen, Alan, interviewed by Mary Boehm, produced by University of Alabama at Birmingham for StoryCorps, January 15, 2011.

484 Weaver, J., "Unitarian Universalist Church," 13.

485 Harris, *Miracle in Birmingham*, 181; Weaver, "Unitarian Universalist Church," 13.

486 Ibid, 129.

487 Biggers, George C., "Jurors told lawbreakers must be halted," *Birmingham News*, September 16, 1963, 1, 5.

488 "Chambliss Group," Federal Bureau of Investigations, part 15 of 51, October 18, 1963. https://vault.fbi.gov.

489 Lankford, Tom, personal notes.

490 Sparks, author interview.

491 Tilford, Earl, Multiple emails to author, 2017.

492 Morgan, Charles III, speech to YMBC, February 22, 2021

493 Morgan, C., author interview.

494 Barr, "Rabbi Grafman," 185.

495 "Sermon by Rabbi Milton Grafman, September 19, 1963." Jewish Women's Archive, jwa.org/media.

496 Bagley, "School Desegregation," 284.

497 Nail, "Birmingham's Jewish Women," 37–8.

498 Flynt, Wayne, interviewed by Tammi Sharpe, Birmingham Civil Rights Institute, Oral History Project, transcript, December 4, 2014.

499 Jimerson, *Shattered Glass in Birmingham*, 221.

500 May, Gary, "40 Years for Justice: Did the FBI Cover for the Birmingham Bombers?" *Daily Beast*, September 13, 2015 (updated July 11, 2017).

501 Thorne, T.K. *Last Chance for Justice: How Relentless Investigators Uncovered New Evidence Convicting the Birmingham Church Bombers*, Lawrence Books, 2013, 152–53.

502 Brown, Donald, interview by Tammi Sharpe.

503 McWilliams, *New Lights in the Valley*, 150–1.

504 "What's racial situation in Birmingham?" *Birmingham News*, October 13, 1963, 1, 4.

505 STAND!

506 "Negro declined police officer job here," *Birmingham News*, December 20, 1963, 38.

507 Kessler, Bryan Scott, "White, Black, and Blue: The Battle Over Black Police, Professionalization, and Police Brutality in Birmingham, Alabama 1963–1979," thesis for Virginia Commonwealth University, 2012.

508 Ibid, 9,10.

509 "What's racial situation in Birmingham?" *Birmingham News*, October 13, 1963, 1, 4.

510 McWilliams, *New Lights in The Valley*, 151.

511 "Dr. Abraham Hyman Russakoff," Find A Grave, Essex, December 27, 2013; Pittman, James, *Tinsley Harrison, M.D.: Teacher of Medicine*, NewSouth Books, 2014, 83.

512 Loftin, Mack, J. Jr. *Healing Hands: An Alabama Medical Mosaic*, University of Alabama Press, 1995, 91–3.

513 McWilliams, *New Lights in The Valley*, 151–52.

514 Ibid, 152.

515 Ibid, 153.

516 Raviv, Lynn Weinstein, interview and notes with author and Dr. Leon Weinstein, Oral Histories, UAB Archives.

517 Cooper, Priscilla Hancock, interview by Deborah R. Layman, director and producer of film *Phyllis Weinstein: The Art of Leadership*, 2012. Phyllis Weinstein was a founder of the N.E. Miles Jewish Day School and the Birmingham Holocaust Education Center.

518 Ellwanger, *Strength for the Struggle*, 128–130.

519 Harris, *A Miracle in Birmingham*, 184.

520 McPhillips, Julian, Jr., *Civil Rights in My Bones*, New South Books, 2016; Vaughn, J. Barry, Bishops, Bourbons, and Big Mules: The History of the Episcopal Church in Alabama, University of Alabama Press, 2013, 140.

521 Villet, Grey, "Up to Her Ears in Good Works," Life, December 28, 1959.

522 Katopodis, John (April 24, 2015) "Cecil Roberts and the Statue from Hell," The Path Well Traveled weblog, https://johnkatopodis.wordpress.com.

523 Barefield-Pendleton, Ruth, author interview, June 26, 2020.

524 Ibid.

525 Jimerson, *Shattered Glass in Birmingham*, 105.

526 Ibid.

527 Weaver, Unitarian Universalist Church, 13; Griffin, personal scrapbook.

528 Jimerson, *Shattered Glass in Birmingham*, 106.

529 Walbert, Eileen, interviewed by Horace Huntley, Birmingham Civil Rights Institute, Oral History Project, transcript, February 3, 1995 and January 21, 1999.

530 Goldstein, Gertrude, interviewed by Horace Huntley, Birmingham Civil Rights Institute, Oral History Project, transcript, January 21, 1999. Weaver, "Unitarian Universalist Church," 16.

531 Kimerling, author interview and personal documents.

532 Jimerson, *Shattered Glass in Birmingham*, 246.

533 Harris, interview by Horace Huntley.

534 Barr, "Rabbi Grafman," 172.

535 Harris, *Miracle in Birmingham*, 136, 196; Harris, interview by Horace Huntley; Cleveland, Charles, personal notes, unknown date; Fiquette, Larry, "The Day My Wife Got Fired for Drinking Beer," unpublished essay from the private papers of Charles Cleveland, unknown date.

536 Friedman, Karl, personal notes.

537 Ibid, author interview.

538 Nail, "Birmingham's Jewish Women," 40.

539 Walbert, Eileen, interview by Pam Powell, June 2, 2016, Pam Powell, personal files, video; Walbert, author interview.

540 Baer, "Concerned White Citizens."

541 Ibid. See list in Appendix.

542 Nail, "Birmingham's Jewish Women," 41.

543 Baer, "Concerned White Citizens."

544 Harris, *A Miracle in Birmingham*, 185.

545 Nail, "Birmingham's Jewish Women," 41.

546 Rupp, author interview. Baer, "Concerned White Citizens.

547 Robinson, Amelia B., Bridge Across Jordan, Schiller Inst., 1991, 101.

548 Ellwanger, *Strength for the Struggle*, 106–7.

549 Nail, "Birmingham's Jewish Women," 43.

550 Walbert, Eileen, author interview, January 20, 2016.

551 Griffin scrapbook.

552 Goldstein, Gertrude, interviewed by Horace Huntley.

553 Harris, *Miracle in Birmingham*, 164.

554 Macnab, Rowena, Internet interview from Springville, Alabama, May 28, 2020. Volker, Virginia Sparks, interviewed by Pam Powell, May 31, 2016.

555 Harris, *Miracle in Birmingham*, 164.

556 Johnson, Lyndon B., "Letter to Birmingham Mayor Boutwell," April 3, 1965, www.presidency.ucsb.edu; "Five Bombs Found in Negro Neighborhood of Birmingham," *Chicago Tribune*, March 22, 1965, 2.

557 Eskew, But for Birmingham, 394.

558 Cleveland, interviewed by Pam Powell; Cleveland, author interview.

559 Rumore, Samuel Jr., "The Bomb That Did Not Explode: The Civil Rights Story of Nina Miglionico of Birmingham," Speech at the Alabama Historical Association, April 2012, transcript courtesy of Samuel Rumore, personal collection.

560 Ibid.

561 Ibid.

562 Cleveland, interviewed by Pam Powell.

563 Walbert, interviewed by Pam Powell.

564 Cromwell, Sydney, "Learning How to Be Brave," *Homewood Star*, October 30, 2014; Walbert, Eileen, author interview.

565 Musselman, Clay, "Rights Group Plans For 1966 School Integration," *Southern Courier*, September 25–26, 1965.

566 Nail, "Birmingham's Jewish Women," 38.

567 Wilson, Joseph, "Racist Center Abandoned in Birmingham," *Southern Courier*, August 28–29, 1965.

568 The 1964 Civil Rights Act required equal application of poll taxes. The 24th Amendment in 1964 prohibited the requirement of poll taxes to vote in national elections. Based on the 1965 Civil Rights Act, the Supreme Court in United States v. State of Alabama in 1966 prohibited poll taxes in the state.

569 Flynt, interview by Tammi Sharpe.

570 Ibid.

571 Franklin, Denson N., to Robin Gotlieb, June 7, 1995, Birmingham Public Library, Grafman files.

572 Clemon, U. W., "Negroes, Whites Make Progress in Birmingham," *Southern Courier*, July 16, 1965.

573 Harris interview by Horace Huntley.

574 Orange, *From Segregation to Civil Rights*, 151.

575 "Lingo Blames Trammel For Incident At Selma," *Montgomery Advertiser*, April 14, 1966.

576 "Lingo Bids for Negro Vote," *Alabama Journal*, April 13, 1966, 1.

577 Lankford, Tom, "Lingo Blames Wallace for Selma Bridge," *Birmingham News*, April 13, 1966, 1.

578 Lankford, Tom, personal notes.

579 Greenhaw, Wayne, Fighting the Devil in Dixie, Lawrence Books, 2011, 187, 189.

580 Harris, interview by Horace Huntley.

581 Harris, *Miracle in Birmingham*, 144–47, Author's note: Harris says the event and award of "Man of the Year," was given to Dr.

Lucius Pitts as the first African American to receive that award. Dr. Pitts does not appear on the list of those awards given by YMBC 1946–1996. Possibly it was another civic award.

582 Lankford, Tom, personal notes.

583 Lankford, Tom and Dave Langford, "None hurt as homes ripped," *Birmingham News*, September 25, 1963, 1.

584 Brown, Houston, Birmingham, Alabama, author interview.

585 LaMonte, *Politics & Welfare in Birmingham*, 207–9.

586 Schaffer, Harriet, email to author June 28, 2017.

587 Ibid, 211.

588 Brown, Houston, author interview and speech to YMBC.

589 Thorne, *Last Chance for Justice*, 56–7.

590 Lankford, Tom, personal notes.

591 Friedman, Karl, personal notes.

592 Flynt, interview by Tammi Sharpe.

593 Robinson, Carol, "Birmingham's 1st black police officer shares struggles and successes in new book," *al.com*, November 22, 2013.

594 Robinson, Carol, "Long-awaited police West Precinct opens; dedicated to first black officer," *al.com*, March 16, 2015.

595 Stover, Leroy, Leroy Stover, *First Birmingham Black in Blue, An Inspirational Story*, Xulon Press, 2013, EPUB e-book.

596 Isom, Lanier, "Policing the Community—Johnnie Johnson Jr., —Birmingham's First Black Police Chief," *Bitter Southerner*, unknown date, https://bittersoutherner.com.

597 Friedman, Karl, personal notes.

598 Tilford, *Turning the Tide*, 111.

599 Nail, "Birmingham's Jewish Women," 35–6.

600 Griffin, Janet author interview.

601 Burg, Shana, "On Being a Civil Rights Lawyer in the 1960s," unknown date. http://shanaburg.com.

602 Horn, Myra E., "My twin sister and I hoped our small efforts made a difference," KidsofBirmingham1963.org.

603 Gail, Mary Ellen, "No Delay in Desegregation; School District File Plans," *Southern Courier*, April 22–23, 1967.

604 Gail, Mary Ellen, "No Delay in Desegregation; School District File Plans," *Southern Courier*, April 22–23, 1967.

605 Keith, Mattie C's Boy, 288.

606 Thomason, Bill, email to author, 2014.

607 Bass, *Blessed are the Peacemakers*, 66–8.

608 Ibid, 207.

609 Session Minutes of the First Presbyterian Church of Birmingham, Alabama, archives of the Birmingham Public Library's Henley Building, April 15, 1965, Shannon Webster, personal collection; Drew, Henry, Sermon at First Presbyterian Church of Birmingham, Alabama, March 9, 2008.

610 Blair, Sheila, author interview, 2016.

611 Zorn, Jeffery, "Miles College Memories," unpublished manuscript, 2017.

612 Russakoff, Dale S., "Miles from Harvard: The Black College," The Harvard Crimson, February 7, 1973. "Mary Prichard Forman," *al.com*, obituaries.

613 Harris, *Miracle in Birmingham*, 184.

614 Walbert, David, author interview by telephone from Birmingham, Alabama, January 24, 2017.

615 Bass, *Blessed are the Peacemakers*, 231.

616 Vann, David, interviewed by Horace Huntley.

617 Vance, Robert S., Letter to John Bailey, Chairman of Democratic National Party, August 29, 1968, From the personal files of Robert Vance, Jr.

618 Davis, author interview; Vance, Robert, Jr., interview by author, Birmingham, Alabama, April 28, 2017; Vance, Robert Smith, from Robert Smith Vance, Jr., private collection.

619 Griffin scrapbook.

620 Footnote: Chuck Morgan, Orzell Billingsley, Jack Drake et al filed and won a lawsuit in 1970, Wallace v. Brewer, that found the Commission to be unconstitutional, and a later injunction forced its dissolution.

621 Griffin scrapbook, Pockstaller, Pockstaller, Ben, "Alabama civil-rights-era 'Peace Commission' spied on people who opposed segregation, had leftist views," *Saint Clair Times*, August 5, 2017.

622 Stalvey, Lois Mark, "How Women Answer The 10 Hardest Race Questions," *Woman's Day*, June 1969.

623 Volker, Virginia, author interview.

624 Greater Birmingham Ministries (GBM), "History," GreaterBirminghamMinistries.org, unknown date, accessed June 16, 2017.

625 Segal, Arthur, author interview from Springville, Alabama.

626 Bass, *Blessed are the Peacemakers*, 231.

627 Farrell, Eugene, Current Comment, 122(2) America, January 17, 1970, Dr. Jonathan Bass Collection, Box 7, Special Collections, Samford University Library, Birmingham, Alabama.

628 Langford, "Rob," author interview, circa 2012

629 See T.K. Thorne's *Last Chance for Justice* for the story of the 16th Street Church bombing case.

630 Pijeaux, Lawrence Jr., "The Birmingham Civil Rights Institute: A Brief History," BlackPast.org, no date given, accessed June 19, 2017.

631 Roberts, Gene, and Hank Klibanoff, *The Race Beat*, 309.

632 Ibid, 306.

633 Ibid, 309.

634 "Five Who Shaped Birmingham Like No One Else," editorial, *Weld for Birmingham*, February 11, 2014.

635 Cooper, J., interviewed by Horace Huntley.

636 Lewis, Jesse, Sr., author interview, Birmingham, Alabama. 2016.

637 "Four Communication, Information Leaders to be Inducted into UA CIS Hall of Fame," UA News, September 23, 2009, http://uanews.ua.edu.

638 Lewis, J., author interview.

639 ONB (Operation New Birmingham) merged with Main Street into REV Birmingham in 2012.

640 LaMonte, *Politics & Welfare in Birmingham*, 194.

641 Boswell, author interview.

642 Ibid.

643 Friedman, Karl, personal notes.

644 Harris, *Miracle in Birmingham*, 184

645 Drew, author interview.

646 Kelly, *A Powerful Presence*, 111.

647 Spencer, Thomas, "James A. Head, businessman, advocate for racial equality, dies at 106," *Birmingham News*, December 22, 2010,

648 YWCA Central Alabama, www.ywcabham,org,

649 Cooper, Jerome, "To Seek and Enrich Our Future," speech at Troy State University, February 15, 1965, Transcript courtesy of Ben Erdreich, personal collection.

650 Elovitz, *A Century of Jewish Life*, 181.

651 "Preserving Justice Profile: Jerome "Buddy" Cooper." Center for Public Television, University of Alabama, Tuscaloosa, Alabama, unknown date, Video, https://vimeo.com/65144750.

652 "Demonstrations thwarted mixing plan, says Smyer," *Birmingham News*, May 17, 1963.

653 Raines, *My Soul Is Rested*, 165.

654 Harris, *Miracle in Birmingham*, 196, Author's note: Harris says the event and award of "Man of the Year," was given to Dr. Lucius Pitts as the first African American to receive that award. Dr. Pitts does not appear on the list of those awards given by YMBC 1946–1996. Possibly another civic award.

655 Kelly, *A Powerful Presence*, 110, 136–46.

656 "On the Death of Jamie Moore," *Tuscaloosa News*, December 29, 2002.

657 Rosenberg, Jonathan, and Zachary Karabell, Kennedy, Johnson, and the Quest for Justice: The Civil Rights Tapes, W. W. Norton & Company, 2003.

658 Isom, Chervis H., "Birmingham Office Born from Civil Rights Movement," Diversity Matters Newsletter, January 4, 2013.

659 Lewis, Jessie, Sr., author interview.

660 Solomon, Jon, "Stephen Grafman: How Martin Luther King's 'Letter from Birmingham Jail' hurt one rabbi," *al.com*, February 21, 2013.

661 Jordan, *No More Hiding*, 222.

662 Rubenstein, Richard, email to Larry Brook, May 18, 2014.

663 Eddy, Bob, Email to author. February 2, 2015.

Postscript

664 Zorn, Jeffery, "Miles College Memories," unpublished manuscript, 2017.

665 King, Martin Luther, *Where Do We Go from Here: Chaos or Community?* Harper & Row, 1967.

666 Gray, Fred D., speech at Highlands Methodist Church, "Faith+Action+Justice" Series, Birmingham, Alabama, November 4, 2015.

667 Gray, Fred D., *Bus Ride to Justice: The Life and Works of Fred D. Gray*, NewSouth Books, 1995, 44–5.

668 Brown, Houston, speech to YMBC.

669 McWilliams, Tennant, interview by Tammi Sharpe, Birmingham Civil Rights Institute, Oral History Project, transcript, September 5, 2014.

670 Isom, Chervis, *The Newspaper Boy: Coming of Age in Birmingham, Alabama During the Civil Rights Era*, The Working Writer Discovery Group, 2013, 271–78.

671 Allison, Rebecca, interviewed by Tammi Sharpe, Birmingham Civil Rights Institute, Birmingham, Alabama, Oral History Project, July 21, 2014, transcript. Allison's remembered quote about the individual and the race is a reference to W. J. Cash's *The Mind of the South*.

672 Woodward, C. Vann, *The Strange Career of Jim Crow*, 11–60

673 "Sermon by Rabbi Milton Grafman, September 19, 1963." Jewish Women's Archive.

674 Dukes, Frank, author interview.

675 Barefield-Pendleton, Ruth, author interview.

676 Dukes, Frank., author interview.

677 Stalvey, Lois Mark, "When Women Speak Their Minds About Prejudice," *Woman's Day*, June 1969.

678 Bass, *Blessed are the Peacemakers*, 226.

679 Harris, W. Edward, "Our Church in Birmingham: It Has Not Kept Silent," Unitarian Universalist Register-Leader, November 1964.

680 Archibald, John, "Morgan's Conscious Still Speaks," *al.com*, January 15, 2009.

681 Taylor, Andrea, "Birmingham, We Can Change the World," Comeback Town. *al.com*, September 4, 2016.

682 Ellwanger, *Strength for the Struggle*, 106–7.

Bibliography

"10 more Negroes arrested in sit-ins." *Birmingham News*, April 5, 1963.

50 U.S.C.A. § 841.

"Alan Drennen," January 14, 2015, www.bhamwiki.com/w/Alan_Drennen.

"Amidst Crisis—Ministers of all denominations call for order." *Birmingham News*, September 2, 1963.

"AP honors News for story cooperation." *Birmingham News,* November 13, 1962.

Archibald, John. "Morgan's Conscious Still Speaks," *al.com*, January 15, 2009.

Armbrester, Margaret England. *Samuel Ullman and "Youth,"* University of Alabama Press, 1993.

Arsenault, Raymond. *Freedom Riders: 1961 and the Struggle for Racial Justice*, Oxford University Press, 2011.

"At least three reported hurt." *Birmingham News*, May 12, 1963.

Bagley, Joseph Mark. "School Desegregation, Law and Order, and Litigating Social Justice in Alabama," 1954-1973, PhD diss., Georgia State University, 2014.

Barr, Terry. "Rabbi Grafman and Birmingham's Civil Rights Era," *The Quiet Voices: Southern Rabbis and Black Civil Rights*, 1880s to 1990s, Bauman, Mark K. and Kalin, Berekley, editors, University of Alabama Press, 1997.

Barra, Allen. "The Integration of College Football Didn't Happen in One Game," The Atlantic, November 15, 2013.

Bartlett, Charles, "King Crisis Needed to Sustain His Image." The Boston Globe, May 14, 1963.

Bass, Jonathan. *Blessed Are the Peacemakers: Martin Luther King, Eight White Religious Leaders, and the "Letter from Birmingham Jail,"* Louisiana State Press, 2001.

"Bearing witness: A controversial 1963 trip to Birmingham by 19 rabbis," *Southern Jewish Life*, Friday, May 3, 2013.

Benn, Alvin. *Reporter: Covering Civil Rights . . . And Wrongs In Dixie*. AuthorHouse, 2006.

Berkowitz, Abraham. Letter to Editor, *Birmingham News*, December 22, 1961, Chervis Isom, personal collection.

Bernstein, Adam. "Ala. Sheriff James Clark; Embodied Violent Bigotry," *The Washington Post*, June 7, 2007.

Biggers, George C., III. "'False charges' brought attack on police." *Birmingham News*, August 21, 1963.

_____, "Jurors told lawbreakers must be halted." *Birmingham News*, September 16, 1963.

"Birmingham and Bull Connor," *Atlanta Constitution*, March 7, 1963.

Birmingham Downtown Improvement Association, "Property Owners Workshop," Downtown Club, December 3, 1963.

"Birmingham Yields to Court Order: Prepares to Integrate High Schools," *New Castle News*, August 20, 1963.

"Bishop Raps Methodist unit stand on King." *Birmingham News*, August 27, 1963.

"Bombing Matters." Federal Bureau of Investigations, Office Memorandum, File 62-1922, SAC, Birmingham, July 24, 1958.

Boucher, Sarah, Edward Cotler, and Stephen Larson. "Internet Wiretapping and Carnivore," student paper, May 17, 2001.

"Boutwell, council lauds two Negroes." *Birmingham News*, September 30, 1963.

Bright, Taylor. "Bull Connors police chief recalls turbulent civil rights movement." *The Gadsden Times*, May 22, 2002. https://www.gadsdentimes.com/article/DA/20020522/News/603218014/GT.

Bright, Taylor. *The Gadsden Times*, May 22, 2002.

Brinkley, Douglas. "The Man Who Kept King's Secrets," *Vanity Fair*, January 19, 2014..

Brook, Larry, "Rabbi Grafman, Dr. King, and the Letter from Birmingham Jail," *Southern Jewish Life*, April 4, 2013.

_____. *Southern Jewish Life*, March 2015.

Brown, Houston. Speech to YMBC, May 16, 2016.

Bryant, Paul Bear and John Underwood. *Bear: The Hard Life And Good Times of Alabama's Coach Bryant*, Little Brown, 1975.

Burg, Shana. "On Being a Civil Rights Lawyer in the 1960s," unknown date. http://shanaburg.com/educators/a-thousand-never-evers/the-making-of/on-being-a-civil-rights-lawyer-in-the-1960s/.

Callahan, Nancy. *The Freedom Quilting Bee*, University of Alabama Press, 2005.

Campbell, Joe. "1,000 skip classes; nine adults arrested." Birmingham News, September 10, 1963.

Carpenter, Douglas M., *A Powerful Blessing, The Life of Charles Colcock Jones Carpenter, Sr.* 1899-1969 Sixth Episcopal Bishop of Alabama, TransAmerica Printing, 2012.

Carter, Dan. *The Politics of Rage: George Wallace, the Origins of the New Conservatism*, Simon & Schuster, 1995.

"Chamblis Group." Federal Bureau of Investigations, part 15 of 51, October 18, 1963. https://vault.fbi.gov/16th%20Street%20Church%20Bombing%20/16th%20Street%20Church%20Bombing%20Part%2015%20of%2051/view.

"City vote called victory for all." *Birmingham News*, November 7, 1962.

"Civic leaders solidly back bad image war." *Birmingham News*, March 5, 1963.

Clark, Cullpepper, E. *The Schoolhouse Door: Segregation's Last Stand at the University of Alabama*, Fire Ant Books, 2007.

Clemon, U. W. "Negroes, Whites Make Progress in Birmingham." *The Southern Courier*, July 16, 1965.

Cleveland, Charles. Personal notes. Unknown date.

Congressional Record, V. 148, Pt. 1, January 23, 2002 to February 13, 2002, United States Government Printing Office, 2002.

Connerly, Charles E. *The Most Segregated City in America City Planning and Civil Rights in Birmingham, 1920-1980.*" University of Virginia Press, 2005.

Connor, Eugene. "We Ask David Vann." *Birmingham News* (advertisement), November 2, 1962.

Cooper, Jerome. Interviewed by Horace Huntley, Birmingham Civil Rights Institute Oral History Project, September 20, 1995. Video.

Cooper, Jerome. "To Seek and Enrich Our Future." Speech at Troy State University, February 15, 1965, courtesy of Ben Erdreich. Transcript.

Corley, Robert Gaines. "The Quest for Racial Harmony: Race Relations in Birmingham, Alabama, 1947-1963." University of Virginia, 1979. PhD diss.

"Court rules states can't bar mixing." *Birmingham News*, May 20, 1963.

"Covering and Making News in the 1960's." Office of Student Media Alumni, University of Alabama, unknown date. http://osmalumni.ua.edu/2013/07/26/covering-and-making-news-in-the-1960s/.

Cromwell, Sydney. "Learning How to Be Brave." *The Homewood Star*, October 30, 2014. http://thehomewoodstar.com/peopleplaces/%E2%80%98learning-how---to-be-brave%E2%80%99/.

"Current of compromise flows through tension here," *Birmingham News*, April 14, 1963.

Danaher, William J. "Dare We Be Disciples." Day1 Radio, June 19, 2005. Sermon transcript about Francis Walters. http://day1.org/943-dare_we_be_disciples.

"Decent responsible people must resume leadership Birmingham businessman asserts." *Birmingham News,* March 5, 1963.

Dees, Morris, with Steve Fifer. *A Lawyer's Journey: The Morris Dees Story*, ABA Publishing, 2001.

"Demonstrations thwarted mixing plan, says Smyer." *Birmingham News*, May 17, 1963.

"Demonstrators get heavy fines, terms." *Birmingham News*, September 13, 1963

Diener, Sam. "When White Firemen Refused to Attack Civil Rights Demonstrators." *Daily Kos*, May 5, 2012, www.dailykos.com.

"Dr. Abraham Hyman Russakoff." Find A Grave, Essex, December 27, 2013.

Dreier, Peter. *The 100 Greatest Americans of the 20th Century: A Social Justice Hall of Fame*, Nation Books, 2012.

Drew, Henry. Sermon at First Presbyterian Church of Birmingham, Alabama, March 9, 2008.

Edmondson, Stephen. *To Live and Die in Alabama*, Blue Rooster Press, 2016.

Ellwanger, Joseph. *Strength for the Struggle*, Mavenmark Books, 2014.

Elovitz, Mark H. *A Century of Jewish Life in Dixie: The Birmingham Experience*, University of Alabama Press, 1974.

The Episcopal Diocese of Alabama, "The Jonathan Daniels Story," ESPN, 2010.

Erdreich, Ellen Cooper. "My Father's Legacy." Speech at Temple Emanu-el, January 13, 2017.

Eskew, Glenn T. *But for Birmingham: The Local and National Movements in the Civil Rights Struggle*. University of North Carolina Press, 1997.

Ewing, Joel. "The Arms of Safety: Al Lingo and the Strategy of Massive Interference

1963-1965." University of Alabama at Birmingham, August 2008. Master's thesis.

"Extremist Organizations Part II, National States Rights Party." Federal Bureau of Investigations, Birmingham Field Office Bureau File *t 105-66233, March 4, 1963 Freedom of Information archives.

"Failure to play race news in headlines draws ire from Wallace, Shuttlesworth," *Birmingham News*, April 5.

Farrell, Eugene. Current Comment, 122(2) America, Jan. 17, 1970. Document contained in the Dr. Jonathan Bass Collection, Box 7, Special Collections, Samford University Library. Birmingham, Alabama.

Faulk, Kent. "'You're going to have to shoot me in the back' retiring judge says he once told officer," June 26, 2015, www.al.com/news.

Feldman, Glenn. *Politics and Religion in the White South.* University Press of Kentucky, 2005.

Ferris, Marcie Cohen & Mark I. Greenberg. *Jewish Roots in Southern Soil, A New History.* Brandeis University Press, University Press of New England, 2006.

Fields, Edward. *Birmingham Daily Bulletin*, July 26, 1963. Birmingham Public Library archival files, David Vann.

Fields, Edward. Bulletin. David Vann collection, Birmingham Public Library, July 26, 1963.

"Fire hoses, police dogs used to halt downtown Negro demonstrations," *Birmingham News*, May 3, 1963.

"Five Bombs Found in Negro Neighborhood of Birmingham." *Chicago Tribune*, March 22, 1965.

"Five Who Shaped Birmingham Like No One Else," editorial, *Weld for Birmingham*, February 11, 2014. http://weldbham.com/blog/2011/10/07/rev-fred-shuttlesworth-the-greatest-american/.

"Former Birmingham Chief Known for Making Integration Work," *Birmingham Post-Herald*, January 1, 2003.

"Former Police Chief Dead at 96," *The New York Times*, AP, December 27, 2002.

"Four Communication, Information Leaders to be Inducted into UA CIS Hall of Fame," *UA News*, September 23, 2009. http://uanews.ua.edu/2009/09/four-communication-information-leaders-to-be-inducted-into-ua-cis-hall-of-fame/.

Fiquette, Larry. "The Day My Wife Got Fired for Drinking Beer." Unpublished essay from the private papers of Charles Cleveland. Unknown date.

Franklin, V. P. and Nancy L. Grant. *African Americans and Jews in the Twentieth Century: Studies in Convergence*, University of Missouri, 1999.

Friendly, Fred W. "CBS Reports: Who Speaks for Birmingham." Smith, Howard K, narrator, CBS, 1961.

Gail, Mary Ellen. "No Delay in Desegregation; School District File Plans." *Southern Courier*, April 22-23, 1967.

Gaillard, Frye. *Cradle of Freedom: Alabama and The Movement That Changed America.* University of Alabama Press, 2004.

Garrison, Greg. "From Sgt. Joe to 'Joe Cool,' First Birmingham Police Chaplain Changed with the Times." Life Stories: Joe Rhodes, *al.com*, October 20, 2013. http://

www.al.com/living/index.ssf/2013/10/from_sgt_joe_to_joe_cool_first.html.

Garrison, Greg. "Friend to MLK and Enemy of the Klan, Liberal Minister Confronted Injustice." Life Stories: Jack Zylman," *al.com*, November 15, 2013. http://blog. al.com/spotnews/2013/11/friend_to_mlk_and_enemy_of_the.html.

Garrow, David J. "The FBI and Martin Luther King." *The Atlantic*, July/ August 2002. http://www.theatlantic.com/magazine/archive/2002/07/ the-fbi-and-martin-luther-king/302537/.

Garrow, David J. *MLK: An American Legacy: Bearing the Cross, Protest at Selma, and The FBI and Martin Luther King*. Open Road Media, 2016.

Gibson, Gordon Davis. *Southern Witness: Unitarians and Universalists in the Civil Rights Era*. Skinner House Books, 2015.

Gibson, Gordon. "Unitarian Universalist Ministers in the Deep South—Brief Introductory Notes." http://www.mit.edu/people/fuller/unitarian.htm#carolyn.

Goldstein, Gertrude. Interview by Horace Huntley. Birmingham Civil Rights Institute. Oral History Project, January 21, 1999. Transcript.

Gossom, Jr., Thom. *Walk-On*. Best Gurl, Inc., 2013.

Graetz, Robert S. *Montgomery: A White Preacher's Memoir*. Fortress Press1991.

Graetz, Robert S. Jr. *A White Preacher's Message on Race and Reconciliation*. NewSouth Books, 2006.

Gray, Fred D. Speech at Highlands Methodist Church, "Faith+Action+Justice" Series, Birmingham, Alabama, November 4, 2015.

Gray, Fred D. *Bus Ride to Justice: The Life and Works of Fred D. Gray*. NewSouth Books, 1995.

Gray, Jeremy. "In 1938 Birmingham, Elanor Roosevelt faced Bull Connor's wraith." Al.com, April 24, 2019. https://www.al.com/news/2019/04/in-1938-birmingham-eBleanor-roosevelt-defied-bull-connor.html.

Gray, Jeremy. " Shuttlesworth Injured by Fire." *al.com*, May 2015. http://blog.al.com/ birmingham-news-stories/2013/05/shuttlesworth_injured_by_fire.html.

Greater Birmingham Ministries (GBM). History, Unknown date, accessed June 16, 2017. https://gbm.org/about/history/.

Greenberg, Ben. "From the Delmar Archive to Bombingham, Alabama (Part 4), Searching the life and times of my father, Paul Greenberg." April 27, 2004. http:// minorjive.typepad.com/hungryblues/2004/04/from_the_delmar.html.

Greenberg, Jack. *Crusaders in the Courts: How a Dedicated Band of Lawyers Fought for the Civil Rights Revolution*. Basic Books, New York, 1994.

Greenhaw, Wayne. *Fighting the Devil in Dixie*. Lawrence Books, 2011.

Greer, Peter. "Martin Luther King and John F. Kennedy: Civil Rights' Wary Allies." Christian Science Monitor, January 20, 2014.

Griffin, Janet. Personal Scrapbook on 1960s.

Halberstam, David. *The Children*. Fawcett Books, Ballantine Publishing Group, 1998.

Hampton, Henry and Steve Fayer. *Voices of Freedom: An Oral History of the Civil Rights Movement from the 1950s through the 1980s*. Random House Publishing, 1991.

Hanes, Art, Jr. Speech at YMBC, March 6, 2017.

Harris, W. Edward. *Miracle in Birmingham: A Civil Rights Memoir 1954-1965*.

Stonework Press, 2004.

_____. "Our Church in Birmingham: It Has Not Kept Silent." Unitarian Universalist Register-Leader, November 1964.

Hartford, Bruce. "We'll Never Turn Back History & Timeline of the Southern Freedom Movement 1951-1968." Unknown date. http://www.crmvet.org/tim/timhome.htm.

"Harvard Jew appointed by Hugo Black to be law clerk." *The Harvard Crimson*, October 5, 1937.

Harvey, Gordon. "Public Education in Alabama After Desegregation," Encyclopedia of Alabama, Encyclopedia of Alabama, March 8, 2013, updated February 12, 2015. http://www.encyclopediaofalabama.org/article/h-3421.

Hearth, Amy Hill. *The Delany Sisters Book of Everyday Wisdom*. Kodansha America, Inc., New York, 1994.

Heldman, Alan W., interview transcript by Willoughby Anderson, cdr.lib.unc.edu U0081_Transcript.pdf, May 26, 2003.

Hollars, B.J. *Opening The Doors of Desegregation of the University of Alabama and the Fight for Civil Rights in Tuscaloosa*. University of Alabama Press, 2013.

Huebner, Michael. "Birmingham's Laura Toffel Knox, Advocate for Arts, Civil Rights Dies at 85." April 4, 2011, http://blog.al.com.

"Hundreds of hooky-playing demonstrators arrested here along with Negro comedian." *Birmingham News*, May 6, 1963.

"Interview with Sheriff Mel Bailey." *Eyes on The Prize*, Production Team C, Blackside, Inc. Birmingham, Alabama, November 2, 1985. Video.

Isaccson, Lou. "Commissioners may call mass meeting of citizens." *Birmingham News*, October 19, 1962.

Isom, Chervis H. "Birmingham Office Born from Civil Rights Movement." *Diversity Matters Newsletter*, January 4, 2013.

Isom, Chervis. *The Newspaper Boy: Coming of Age in Birmingham*, Alabama During the Civil Rights Era. The Working Writer Discovery Group, 2013.

Isom, Lanier, "Policing the Community—Johnnie Johnson, Jr., —Birmingham's First Black Police Chief," unknown date, bittersoutherner.com.

Jarvis, Gail. "Birmingham: The Rest of the Story." November 25, 2003. https://www.lewrockwell.com.

"Jaycees condemn any interference." *Birmingham News*, September 3, 1963.

"Jaycees take stand against parks closing." *Birmingham News*, December 12, 1961.

Jenkins, Carol, and Elizabeth Gardner Hines. *Black Titan: A.G. Gaston and The Making of A Black American Millionaire*. One World, 2004.

Jerome, Fred. *The Einstein File: J. Edgar Hoover's Secret War Against the World's Most Famous Scientist*. St. Martin's Press, 2002.

Jimerson, Randall C. *Shattered Glass in Birmingham: My Family's Fight for Civil Rights, 1961-1964*. Louisiana State University Press, 2014.

Johnson, Carrie. "Johnny's Death: The Untold Tragedy in Birmingham." NPR Around the Nation, September 15, 2010.

Johnson, Gerald. "Amendment 4 Violates States Responsibility to Public Education,"

October 31, 2012, http://blog.al.com.

Johnson, Lyndon B. "Letter to Birmingham Mayor Boutwell." April 3, 1965, www.presidency.ucsb.edu.

Jordan, E. Dan. *No More Hiding Under the Bed.* Xlibris Corp., 2010.

"Judge Meeks checks petition seeking change in city." *Birmingham News*, September 6, 1962.

Katopodis, John (April 24, 2015) "Cecil Roberts and the Statue from Hell." *The Path Well Traveled* weblog, https://johnkatopodis.wordpress.com.

Keith, Don. *Mattie C's Boy.* NewSouth Books, 2013.

Kelly, Mark. *A Powerful Presence.* The Birmingham Regional Chamber of Commerce, 2008.

Kelly, Robin D.G. *Hammer And Hoe: Alabama Communists During The Great Depression.* University of North Carolina Press, 2015.

Kessler, Ronald. *The Secrets of the FBI.* Crown Publishing, 2011.

Kimerling, Solomon. "Unmasking the Klan: Late 1940s Coalition Against Racial Violence." *Weld for Birmingham*, July 18, 2012.

Kimerling, Solomon. "Transforming Birmingham." *Weld for Birmingham*. November 21, 2012.

King, Martin Luther. *Where Do We Go from Here: Chaos or Community?* Harper & Row, 1967.

King, Martin Luther. "A Message from Jail." July 21, 1962, www.thekingcenter.org.

King, Pamela. "From Albany to Birmingham." *Weld for Birmingham*, Dec. 19, 2012.

King, Pamela. "The Revolt of the Moderates." *Weld for Birmingham*, April 17, 2013.

Kraus, Ingrid, "Strength to pursue our ideals." KidsinBirmingham1963.org.

Krulak, Charles C. "Young Birmingham-Southern student was a trailblazer for civil rights." Al.com.

LaMonte, Edward Shannon. *Politics & Welfare in Birmingham, 1900-1975.* University of Alabama Press, 1995.

Langston, Scott M. "Rabbi Morris Newfield: Ambassador to the Gentiles, a Balancing Act." American Jewish Archives, January 2, 2007.

Lankford, Tom. "Barnett admits he knew Marshalls were en route." *Birmingham News*, May 9, 1963.

_____. "Change to enhance police chief's role." *Birmingham News*, April 4, 1963.

_____. "City Council acts in crisis." *Birmingham News*, August 21, 1963.

_____. "Crackdown on sex perverts ordered for city by Connor." *Birmingham News*, August 8, 1962.

_____ and Irving Beiman. "The day a church became a tomb." *Birmingham News*, September 16, 1963.

_____. "Firefighters told vote key to raise." *Birmingham News*, October 18, 1962.

_____. "Integration techniques at stake as Albany program bogs down." *Birmingham News*, July 29, 1962.

_____ and Bud Gordon. "Integrators send another group to city." *Birmingham News*, May 19, 1961.

_____. "Lingo blames Wallace for Selma bridge." *Birmingham News*, April 13, 1966.

_____. "Mayola says boy killed in his sleep." *Birmingham News,* August 13, 1962.

_____. "Mob terror hits city on Mother's Day." *Birmingham News*, May 15, 1961.

_____ and Joe Campbell. "Negroes attack policemen with bricks, bottles, rocks." *Birmingham News*, September 5, 1963.

_____. "Negroes link own race in dynamitings." January 23, 1962.

_____. "Police quiz Negro in King bombing." *Birmingham News*, August 24, 1963.

_____ and Joe Campbell. "Negroes attack policemen with bricks, bottles, rocks." *Birmingham News*, September 5, 1963.

_____ and Dave Langford. "None hurt as homes ripped." *Birmingham News*, September 25, 1963.

_____. "Women join with men in savage scene." May 20, 1963.

_____. "Yelling whites set off melee at Graymont." September 4, 1963.

_____. "Women join with men in savage scene." May 20, 1961, 1, 2.

Layman, Deborah R., director and producer. *Phyllis Weinstein: The Art of Leadership*, film, 2021.

Lee, Helen Shores and Barbara S. Shores. *The Gentle Giant of Dynamite Hill.* Zondervan, 2012.

"Legends in the Law: Louis F. Oberdorfer." DCBar Report, December/January 1997. http://www.dcbar.org.

Leighton, George. "Birmingham, Alabama The City of Perpetual Promise." *Harper's Magazine*, Volume 175, August 1937.

"Leroy Stover," March 17, 2015, www.bhamwiki.com.

Lesher, Stephan. *George Wallace: American Populist.* Addison Wesley Publishing, 1994.

Leventhal, Willy S., and Ranall Williams, editors. *The Children Coming On . . .*, Black Belt Press, 1998.

Lewis, John, and Michael D'Orso. *Walking with the Wind: A Memoir of the Movement.* Simon & Schuster; Reissue edition, 2015.

"Liberated at State Line, Negro Agitators Return." *The Selma Times-Journal*, May 19, 1961.

"Lingo Bids for Negro Vote." *Alabama Journal*, April 13, 1966.

"Lingo Blames Trammel For Incident At Selma," *The Montgomery Advertiser*, April 14, 1966.

Loftin, Mack, J. Jr. *Healing Hands: An Alabama Medical Mosaic.* University of Alabama Press, 1995.

Lubin, Samuel. "Report of Field Trip, Birmingham and Montgomery, Alabama." February 7, 1957, Sol Kimerling, personal collection.

Magnusson, Paul "FBI Knew Policeman Was Leak to Klan on Freedom Riders." *Washington Post*, August 20, 1978.

Malone, E.T. "Jonathan Daniels and Other Civil Rights Martyrs Honored at Alabama Event." Episcopal News Service, www.episcopalarchives.org.

Manis, Andrew M. *A Fire You Can't Put Out: The Civil Rights Life of Birmingham's Reverend Fred Shuttlesworth.* Tuscaloosa: University of Alabama Press, 1999.

Marsh, Dave. "Shelley Stewart, Radio and the Birmingham Civil Rights Movement." June 12, 2002, www.counterpunch.org.

"Mary Prichard Forman," obituaries, http://obits.al.com.

May, Gary. "40 Years for Justice: Did the FBI Cover for the Birmingham Bombers?" September 13, 2015 (updated July 11, 2017), https://www.thedailybeast.com.

McKean, Andrew, J. "Preston Learns to Talk, and Sara Uses a Fork." *The Southern Courier*, January 6-7, 1968.

McPhillips, Julian, Jr. *Civil Rights in My Bones*. New South Books, 2016.

McWhorter, Diane. *Carry Me Home: Birmingham, Alabama The Climactic Battle of the Civil Rights Revolution*. Touchstone, 2001.

McWilliams, Tennant S. *New Lights in The Valley: The Emergence of UAB*." University of Alabama Press, 2007.

"Mel Bailey, longtime sheriff in Alabama, 72." *Atlanta Journal*, August 30, 1997.

"Ministers Manifesto: A Declaration of Equality." Regional Council of Churches of Atlanta (RCCAtl) January 24, 2008. (Originally published in *Atlanta Constitution* on November 3, 1957).

Morgan, Charles, Jr. *A Time to Speak*. Holt, Rinehart and Winston, 1964.

Morin, Relman. "Are city chimes saying hour late for Old South?" *Birmingham News*, May 11, 1963.

Morris, Mary. "Rare Civil Rights-Era Newsletter Now Available Online." University Record, University of Michigan, January 23, 2014, https://record.umich.edu.

"Motorcade urged at big 'white rally." Birmingham News, September 4, 1963.

Musselman, Clay. "Rights Group Plans For 1966 School Integration." *The Southern Courier*, September 25-26, 1965.

Nail, Kay Cochran. "Birmingham's Jewish Women and Social Reform 1880-1980." University of Alabama in Birmingham, 2010. Master's thesis.

"National States Rights Party, Monographs and Attorney General's Letter." Federal Bureau of Investigations, Freedom of Information archives, August 1966.

"Negro declined police officer job here." *Birmingham News*, December 20, 1963.

"Negroes attend two white churches." *Birmingham News,* April 15, 1963.

"Nelson v. The Honorable H. H. Grooms." *Race Relations Law Reporter* 7.3, Fall, 1962.

Newton, Michael. *White Robes and Burning Crosses: A History of the Klan from 1866*. Macfarland, 2014.

"New YMBC president calls for plan to mix city schools." *Birmingham News*, June 2, 1963.

Norris, Michelle. *The Grace of Silence, A Family Memoir*. Vintage Books, 2011.

Nunnelley, William A. *Bull Connor*. University of Alabama Press, 1991.

"On the death of Jamie Moore." *Tuscaloosa News*, December 29, 2002. https://www.tuscaloosanews.com/news/20021229/on-the-death-of-jamie-moore.

"Only five juveniles remain in custody of 1,500 arrested." *Birmingham News*, October 13, 1963.

Orange, David Wayne. *From Segregation to Civil Rights and Beyond: A Story of the Southland*. PublishAmerica, 2004.

Oshinsky, David M. "Freedom Riders, David Halberstam's Account of the Civil Rights Movement, from the Sit-ins to the Buses, and Those who Led it." Book review, *The New York Times*, March 15, 1998. http://www.nytimes.com/books/98/03/15/

reviews/980315.15oshinst.html.

"Owner of Alabama backyard juke joint Gip's Place dies." *Chattanooga Times Free Press*. October 9, 2019.

Pace, Eric. "David E. Feller, 86; Lawyer Who Argued Key Labor Cases." February 17, 2003. http://www.nytimes.com/2003/02/17/us/david-e-feller-86-lawyer-who-argued-key-labor-cases.html.

Palmer, Mary. *George Wallace: An Enigma*. Intellect Publishing, 2016.

Pennycuff, Tim L. "Hillman Hospital." Encyclopedia of Alabama, July 7, 2008, up-dated October 31, 2012. http://www.encyclopediaofalabama.org/article/h-1592.

"People are asking: Where were the police?" *Birmingham News*, May 15, 1961.

Pijeaux, Lawrence, Jr. "The Birmingham Civil Rights Institute: A Brief History." BlackPast.org, no date given, accessed June 19, 2017. http://www.blackpast.org/perspectives/birmingham-civil-rights-institute-brief-history.

Pittman, James. *Tinsley Harrison, M.D.: Teacher of Medicine*. NewSouth Books, 2014.

Pockstaller, Ben. "Alabama civil-rights-era 'Peace Commission' spied on people who opposed segregation, had leftist views." Saint Clair Times, August 5, 2017. https://www.annistonstar.com/the_st_clair_times/alabama-s-civil-rights-era-peace-commission-spied-on-people/article_883ccc1c-7a44-11e7-8f81-cb6470cb8a57.html.

Pratt, Minnie Bruce. "Lowndes County Alabama 'The Original Black Panther Party.'" March 30, 2016. http://www.workers.org/2016/03/30/lowndes-county-alabama-the-original-black-panther-party/#.WKhywBA9LW1.

"Preserving Justice Profile: Abe Berkowitz." Center for Public Television, University of Alabama, Tuscaloosa, Alabama on Vimeo.com, unknown date. Video. https://vimeo.com/64924047.

"Preserving Justice Profile: Harvey Burg. Center for Public Television, University of Alabama, Tuscaloosa, Alabama on Vimeo.com, unknown date. Video. https://vimeo.com/65144749

"Preserving Justice Profile: Jerome "Buddy" Cooper." Center for Public Television, University of Alabama, Tuscaloosa, Alabama on Vimeo.com, unknown date. Video. https://vimeo.com/65144750.

"Rabbi Milton Grafman Sermon, September 19, 1963." Living the Legacy. Jewish Women's Archive. Podcast. https://jwa.org/teach/livingthelegacy/documentstudies/rabbi-milton-grafman-sermon.

Raines, Howell. *My Soul Is Rested*. Putnam Publishing, 1977.

_____. "Why was Marti so Alone?" KidsinBirmingham1963.org. http://kidsinbirmingham1963.org/why-was-marti-so-alone/#more-255.

Ramage, Katherine. "Easter Sunday, 1963." KidsinBirmingham1963.org. http://kidsinbirmingham1963.org/easter-sunday-1963/#more-97.

Reed, Jon. "Scholarship fund in honor of 4 girls killed in 16th Street Baptist Church bombing seeks donations." *al.com*, September 15, 2014. http://www.al.com/news/birmingham/index.ssf/2014/09/scholarship_fund_in_honor_of_4.html.

Reisig, Robin. "Birmingham Kids Prepare for Integrated High School." *The Southern Courier*, September 2-3, 1967. http://www.southerncourier.org/low-res/Vol3_No36_1967_09_02.pdf.

"Report on a Study of Negro Police." Jefferson County Coordinating Council. From the Mr. Mervyn Hayden Sterne Collection, Mervyn Sterne Library. Spring, 1953. http://contentdm.mhsl.uab.edu/cdm/singleitem/collection/mhs/id/73/rec/89.

"Rev. Fred Shuttlesworth: The Greatest American," editorial, Red Dirt, *Weld for Birmingham*, October 7, 2011. http://weldbham.com/blog/2011/10/07/rev-fred-shuttlesworth-the-greatest-american/.

Roberts, Gene, and Hank Klibanoff. *The Race Beat: The Press, The Civil Rights Struggle, and the Awakening of a Nation*. Vintage Books, 2007.

Robinson, Amelia B. *Bridge Across Jordan*. Schiller Inst., 1991.

Robinson, Carol. "Birmingham's 1st black police officer shares struggles and successes in new book." *al.com*, November 22, 2013. http://blog.al.com/spotnews/2013/11/birminghams_first_black_police.html.

Robinson, Carol. "Long-awaited police West Precinct opens; dedicated to first black officer." *al.com*, March 16, 2015. https://www.al.com/news/birmingham/2015/03/long-awaited_police_west_preci.html.

Robinson, Carol. "Fifty years later, Birmingham police have made great strides since days of dogs, firehoses, segregation." *al.com*, March 1, 2013. http://blog.al.com/spotnews/2013/03/fifty_years_later_birmingham_p.html.

Rose, Stephen C. "Test for Nonviolence." Christian Century, May 14, 1963. http://www.crmvet.org/info/bham-mlk.htm.

Rosenberg, Jonathan, and Zachary Karabell. "Kennedy, Johnson, and the Quest for Justice: The Civil Rights Tapes." W. W. Norton & Company, 2003.

Rudd, Edward M. "Tense Lowndes Erupts as Minister is Slain." *The Southern Courier*, August 28-29, 1965. http://www.southerncourier.org/low-res/Vol1_No07_1965_08_28.pdf.

Rumore, Samuel, Jr. "The Bomb That Did Not Explode: The Civil Rights Story of Nina Miglionico of Birmingham." Speech at the Alabama Historical Association, April 2012. Transcript from Samuel Rumore, personal collection.

Russakoff, Dale S. "Miles from Harvard: The Black College." February 7, 1973. http://www.thecrimson.com/article/1973/2/7/miles-from-harvard-the-black-college/?page=1.

Ryskind, Allen H. "JFK and RFK Were Right to Wiretap MLK." Human Events, Powerful Conservative Voices, Feb 24, 2006. http://humanevents.com/2006/02/24/jfk-and-rfk-were-right-to-wiretap-mlk/.

Sales, Amy L. and Tobin, Gary A. *Church and Synagogue Affiliation: Theory, Research, and Practice (Contributions to The Study Of Religion)*. Greenwood Publishing Group, 1995.

Schaffer, Shelton. "Birmingham Notations on the Civil Rights Era—Personal Views." Unpublished paper, Harriet Schaffer, personal files. April 22, 2002, updated April 20, 2003.

"Schools must stay open, strife avoided, women told," *Birmingham News*, August 9, 1963.

Schlesinger, Arthur. M. *Robert Kennedy and His Times*. Houghton Mifflin Harcourt, 2002.

Self, Tom. "Witnesses see rage erupt at Ramsay." *Birmingham News*, September 4. 1963.

Serwer, Adam. "Lyndon Johnson Was a Civil Rights Hero. But also a Racist." MSNBC: 20 Years, April 11, 2014. http://www.msnbc.com/msnbc/lyndon-johnson-civil-rights-racism.

Session Minutes of the First Presbyterian Church of Birmingham, Alabama, archives of the Birmingham Public Library's Henley Building. April 15, 1965. Shannon Webster, personal collection.

Siegal, Bobbie and Don Siegal. Speech, The Women's Network, Birmingham, Alabama, July 23, 2015.

Sitton, Claude. "50 Hurt in Negro Rioting After Birmingham Blasts." *The New York Times*, May 13, 1963.

Sitton, Claude. "Alabama Admits Negro Students; Wallace Bows to Federal Force; Kennedy Sees 'Moral Crisis' in U.S." *New York Times*, June 12, 1963. https://partners.nytimes.com/library/national/race/061263race-ra.html.

"Six Dead After Church Bombing." United Press International, *The Washington Post*, September 16, 1963.

Smyer, S.W., Jr. "Need for local Negro leaders." *Birmingham News*, May 13, 1963, 5.

Solomon, Jon. "Stephen Grafman: How Martin Luther King's 'Letter from Birmingham Jail' hurt one rabbi." *al.com*, February 21, 2013. http://blog.al.com/spotnews/2013/02/steven_grafman_how_martin_luth.html.

Sparrow, Hugh. "Public Safety files being amassed on 'subversives' now." *Birmingham News*, B-4, February 9, 1964.

Spencer, Thomas. "James A. Head, businessman, advocate for racial equality, dies at 106." *Birmingham News*, December 22, 2010. http://blog.al.com/spotnews/2010/12/james_a_head_businessman_advoc.html.

Stalvey, Lois Mark. "How Women Answer The 10 Hardest Race Questions." *Woman's Day*, June 1969.

Stalvey, Lois Mark. "When Women Speak Their Minds About Prejudice." *Woman's Day*, June 1969.

Stanton, Mary. *The Hand of Esau*. River City Publishing, Montgomery, Alabama, 2006.

Staples, Brent. "How the Swastika Became a Confederate Flag." *New York Times*, May 22, 2017. https://www.nytimes.com/2017/05/22/opinion/white-supremacist-confederate-monuments-nazi.html?emc=edit_th_20170522&nl=todaysheadlines&nlid=53508566&_r=0.

Stein, Judith. *Running Steel, Running America : Race, Economic Policy, and the Decline of Liberalism.* University of North Carolina Press, 1998.

Stover, Leroy. *Leroy Stover, First Birmingham Black in Blue, An Inspirational Story.* Xulon Press, 2013. EPUB e-book.

"Student paper banned from political views." *Birmingham News*, June 12, 1958.

Sullivan, Patricia. "Charles Morgan Jr.: Lawyer Championed Civil, Voting Rights." *The Washington Post*, January 9, 2009.

Sutton, Marie. *The A.G. Gaston Motel in Birmingham*. The History Press, 2014.

Swift, Ivan. "Petition response amazing." *Birmingham News*, August 29, 1962, 1.

Swift, Ivan. "Vann explains three forms of government." *Birmingham News*, September 12, 1962.

Taylor, Andrea. "Birmingham, We Can Change the World." Comeback Town, *al.com*, September 4, 2016. blog.al.com/comebacktown/2016/09/birmingham_we_can_change_the_w.html.

Thompson, Wright. "Ghosts of Mississippi," ESPN 2010, http://sports.espn.go.com/espn/eticket/story?page=mississippi62, ESPN, Outside the Lines.

Thorne, T.K. *Last Chance for Justice: How Relentless Investigators Uncovered New Evidence Convicting the Birmingham Church Bombers*. Lawrence Books, 2013.

Thornton, J. Mills, III. *Dividing Lines: Municipal Politics and the Struggle for Civil Rights in Montgomery, Birmingham, and Selma*. University of Alabama Press, 2002.

Tilford, Earl H. *Turning the Tide*. University of Alabama Press, 2014.

Toffel, Miriam Abigail, editor, *A Collection of Biographies of Women Who Made a Difference In Alabama*. The League of Women Voters of Alabama, 1995.

"Troops not needed Boutwell declares." *Birmingham News*, May 13, 1963.

"Two rescued by Floyd Mann." *Birmingham News*, May 20, 1961.

Underwood, Paul. "A Progressive History of the Young Men's Business Club of Birmingham, Alabama." 1946-1970, Samford University, 1980.

"U.S. feels troopers were too heavy handed says riots fault of Ala cops." *The Boston Globe,* May 13, 1963.

Vance, Robert Smith. Documents from Robert Smith Vance, Jr., private collection.

Vaughn, J. Barry. *Bishops, Bourbons, and Big Mules: The History of the Episcopal Church in Alabama*. University of Alabama Press, 2013.

Villet, Grey. "Up to Her Ears in Good Works." *Life*, December 28, 1959. https://books.google.com/books?id=e1UEAAAAMBAJ&lpg=PA134&ots=8CBVdd5Zw8&pg=PA133&hl=en#v=onepage&q&f=false.

"Viola Liuzzo Murder." Federal Bureau of Investigations, part 9 of 14, File Numbers: 44-28601.

https://archive.org/stream/Viola-Liuzzo-FBI/liuzzo9_djvu.txt.

Walter, Francis X. "Selma Inter-Religious Project." December 6, 1965, Archives Selma Inter-religious Project. Newsletter.

The Washington Post, Morgan Obituary, Jan. 9, 2009.

Weaver, Jeanne Moore. "A History of The Unitarian Universalist Church of Birmingham, Alabama 1952-2016." Unpublished, Jeanne Weaver, personal collection.

Weaver, Jeanne. "Unitarian Universalist Church in Birmingham: History." Accessed on March 20, 2017. http://www.uucbham.org/history/.

Weaver, Lamar, and Rueben Jackson. *Bury My Heart in Birmingham, The Lamar Weaver Story*. Writers Club Press, 2001.

Webb, Clive. "A Tangled Web: Black-Jewish Relations in the 20th Cent. South." *Jewish Roots in Southern Soil*, Ferris, Marcie Cohen and Mark I. Greenberg, editors, 2006.

Webb, Clive. *Fight Against Fear: Southern Jews and Black Civil Rights*. University of Georgia Press, 2003.

"What's racial situation in Birmingham?" *Birmingham News*, October 13, 1963.

Widell, Robert W., Jr. *Birmingham and The Long Freedom Struggle*. Palgrave Macmillan, 2013.

Wilson, Bobby M. *Race and Place in Birmingham: The Civil Rights and Neighborhood*

Movements. Rowman & Littlefield Publishers, 2000.

Wilson, Doris E. Hobson. 1962-1963 Change in Government, personal scrapbook, courtesy of Elaine Hobson Miller.

Wilson, Joseph. "Racist Center Abandoned in Birmingham." *The Southern Courier,* August 28-29, 1965. http://www.southerncourier.org/low-res/Vol1_No07_1965_08_28.pdf.

Woodham, Rebecca. "Southern Conference for Human Welfare (SCHW)." Encyclopedia of Alabama, July 7, 2008, updated April 21, 2015. http://www.encyclopediaofalabama.org/article/h-1593.

Woodward, C. Vann. *The Strange Career of Jim Crow.* Oxford University Press, 2002.

Wright, Barnett. *1963: How the Birmingham Civil Rights Movement Changed America and the World. Birmingham News,* 2013.

Yaeger, Don, and Sam Cunningham. *Turning of the Tide: How One Game Changed the South.* Center Street, 2006.

Young, Andrew. *An Easy Burden: The Civil Rights Movement and the Transformation of America.* Baylor University Press, 2008.

Young, Andrew. Speech, Birmingham Rotary Club, May 3, 2014.

VIDEO/AUDIO INTERVIEWS/FILMS:

Cleveland, Charles. Interview by Pam Powell, video, May 31, 2016.

Drennen, Alan. Interview by Mary Boehm, produced by University of Alabama at Birmingham for StoryCorps, January 15, 2011.

Eyes on The Prize: American Civil Rights Movement 1954-1985. Directed by Judith Vecchione. 2012. Blackside, Inc., American Experience, PBS, 1987, 1990, 2012, DVD.

Eyes on The Prize: America's Civil Rights Years 1954-1965. Directed by Judith Vecchione. 1985. Blackside, Inc., November 2, 1985.

Eyes on The Prize: The Limits Of Nonviolence 1962. Directed by Judith Vecchione.

Friedman, Karl. "Birmingham Civil Rights, A Jewish Perspective." Videoed speech at the Birmingham Public Library, Birmingham, Alabama. Produced by the Birmingham Holocaust Education Center. March 13, 2013.

Friedman, Karl. Interview by Mark Kelly and Jason Ruha. Unknown date. From personal collection of Mark Kelly, video file.

Gibson, Gordon. Interview by Pam Powell. May 29, 2016. From personal files of Pam Powell. Video File.

Horn, Myra E. "My twin sister and I hoped our small efforts made a difference." KidsofBirmingham1963.org. http://kidsinbirmingham1963.org/category/myra-horn/.

Loeb, Betty. Interview by Mark Kelly and Jason Ruha. Unknown date. From personal files of Mark Kelly. Video File.

Preserving Justice: The Birmingham Civil Rights Movement," Birmingham Bar Foundation, producers in partnership with University of Alabama Center for Public Television and Radio, The Magic City Bar Association and the Birmingham Bar Association, film, 2013.

"Preserving Justice Profile: Abe Berkowitz." The Center for Public Television. April

30, 2013. Video file. https://vimeo.com/64924047.

"Preserving Justice Profile: Jerome 'Buddy' Cooper." The Center for Public Television. April 30, 2013. Video File. https://vimeo.com/65144750.

"President Johnson to George Wallace, 18 March 1965." 4:33 p.m. Tape WH6503.09, Citation #7094, Recordings of Telephone Conversations, White House Series, Recordings and Transcripts of Conversations and Meetings, Lyndon B. Johnson Library. Audio file.

Pritchett, Laurie. Unknown interviewer. Blackside, Inc. 1985. Filmed for *Eyes on the Prize: America's Civil Rights Years 1954-1965.* Washington University Libraries Film and Media Archive, Henry Hampton Collection, online video. November 7, 1985. http://repository.wustl.edu/concern/videos/w9505204d.

Stand! Untold Stories of the Civil Rights Movement. Directed by Donna Dukes. 2018. Birmingham, Alabama: 3D Productions, DVD.

Volker, Virginia Sparks. Interview by Pam Powell. May 31, 2016.

Walbert, Eileen, interview by Pam Powell, June 2, 2016. From personal files of Pam Powell. Video File.

VIDEO INTERVIEW TRANSCRIPTS:

Allison, Rebecca. Interview by Tammi Sharpe. Birmingham Civil Rights Institute, Birmingham, Alabama. Oral History Project. July 21, 2014, transcript.

Baer, Helen, Mary Y. Gonzalez, and Eileen Walbert. "The Concerned White Citizens of Alabama and Their Appearance in Selma, March 6, 1965." Interview by Max Baer. October 27, 1975. UAB Digital Collection. Oral Interviews, Mervyn Sterne Library, transcript. http://contentdm.mhsl.uab.edu/cdm/compoundobject/collection/oralhistory/id/629/rec/2.

Brown, Donald. Interview by Tammi Sharpe. Birmingham Civil Rights Institute, Oral History Project. October 30, 2014. Transcript.

Cousins, John. Interview by Tammi Sharpe. Birmingham Civil Rights Institute, Oral History Project March 12, 2015. Transcript.

Crawson, John Noel. Interview by Tammi Sharpe. Birmingham Civil Rights Institute, Oral History Project, December 19, 2014. Transcript.

Drake, Jack. Interview by Kimberly Hill, June 19, 2007. Transcript. http://dc.lib.unc.edu/cgi-bin/showfile.exe?CISOROOT=/sohp&CISOPTR=4199&filename=4221.pdf.

Flynt, Wayne. Interviewed by Tammi Sharpe. Birmingham Civil Rights Institute, Oral History Project December 4, 2014. Transcript.

Friedman, Karl. Personal collection of Mark Kelly. Unknown date. Transcript.

Fuller, John. Interview by Horace Huntley. Birmingham Civil Rights Institute. Oral History Project, March 25, 1998. Transcript.

Harris, W. Edward. Interview by Horace Huntley. Birmingham Civil Rights Institute. Oral History Project, February 18, 1998. Transcript.

Isom, Chervis. Interview by Horace Huntley, Birmingham Civil Rights Institute. Oral History Project, March 22, 2007. Transcript.

Isom, Chervis. Interview by Tammi Sharpe. Birmingham Civil Rights Institute. Oral

History Project, October 17, 2014. Transcript.

Kessler, Bryan Scott. "White, Black, and Blue: The Battle Over Black Police, Professionalization, and Police Brutality in Birmingham, Alabama 1963-1979." Thesis for Virginia Commonwealth University, 2012. https://scholarscompass.vcu.edu/cgi/viewcontent.cgi?referer=&httpsredir=1&article=3833&context=etd.

Loeb, Betty. Personal collection of Mark Kelly. Unknown date. Transcript.

Marshall, Burke. Oral History Interview by Anthony Lewis. John F. Kennedy Library Archives, June 10, 1964. Transcript. https://archive1.jfklibrary.org/JFKOH/Marshall,%20Burke/JFKOH-BM-05/JFKOH-BM-05-TR.pdf.

McWilliams, Tennant. Interview by Tammi Sharpe. Birmingham Civil Rights Institute. Oral History Project. September 5, 2014. Transcript.

Powell, Robert. Interview by Tammi Sharpe. Birmingham Civil Rights Institute. Oral History Project, September 24, 2014. Transcript.

"President Johnson to George Wallace." Citation #7124, Recordings of Telephone Conversations – White House Series, Recordings and Transcripts of Conversations and Meetings, Lyndon B. Johnson Library. March 18, 1965, 9:13 p.m. Tape WH6503.10. Transcript.

Vann, David. Interview by Horace Huntley. Birmingham Civil Rights Institute. Oral History Project. February 2, 1995 and March 25, 1999. Transcript.

Walbert, Eileen. Interview by Horace Huntley. Birmingham Civil Rights Institute. Oral History Project, February 3, 1995 and January 21, 1999. Transcript.

Weaver, Lamar. Interview by Horace Huntley. Birmingham Civil Rights Institute. Oral History Project, March 16, 1995. Transcript.

Zorn, Jeffery. "Miles College Memories," unpublished manuscript, 2017.

LETTERS, NOTES, AND EMAIL:

Berkowitz, Richard. Email to Frank James. August 4, 2009.

Eddy, Bob. Email to author. February 2, 2015.

Franklin, Denson N., to Robin Gotlieb, June 7, 1995, Birmingham Public Library, Grafman files.

Friedman, Karl. Multiple emails to author 2009-2016.

Friedman, Paul, Sr. Letter to Robin Gotlieb, June 6, 1995, Birmingham Public Library, Grafman files.

_____. Multiple emails and personal memoir notes to author, 2009-2018.

Rubenstein, Richard. Email to Larry Brook, May 18, 2014.

Schaffer, Harriet, email to author, June 28, 2017.

Snow, Louis, Face Book Messenger, July 16, 2019.

Tilford, Earl. Multiple emails to author. 2017.

Tofel, Richard. "Not Shutting Up." August 29, 2019.

Vance, Robert S. Letter to John Bailey, Chairman of Democratic National Party, August 29, 1968. From the personal files of Robert Vance, Jr.

PERSONAL INTERVIEWS BY THE AUTHOR:

Barefield-Pendleton, Ruth. Phone interview, Springville, Alabama, June 26, 2020.

Blair, Sheila. 2016.

Boswell, Robert. Circa 2015.

Brown, Houston. YMBC speech, Birmingham, Alabama, May 16, 2016.

Brown, Houston. Birmingham, Alabama. June 21, 2017.

Carlton, Aaron. Birmingham, Alabama. October 5, 2015.

Chilcoat, Matthew. Birmingham, Alabama. July 15, 2017.

Davis, J. Mason. Birmingham, Alabama. December 30, 2015.

Drake, Jack, email correspondence. June 8, 2020.

Drew, Jefferson (Jeff). Birmingham, Alabama. January 13, 2017.

Dukes, Frank. Birmingham, Alabama. September 18, 2015.

Edmondson, Stephen. Birmingham, Alabama. 2015.

Erdreich, Ben. Birmingham, Alabama. May 2, 2016.

Friedman, Karl. Multiple interviews. Birmingham, Alabama. 2013-2016.

Graetz, Robert and Jeannie. Birmingham, Alabama. April 20-23, 2016.

Glaze, Robert. Birmingham, Alabama. December 2, 2013.

Green, Thomas C. Birmingham, Alabama. 2015.

Griffin, Janet. Birmingham, Alabama. November 1, 2015 and January 28, 2016.

Hartline, Anne. Birmingham, Alabama. January 13, 2017.

Huffman, Charles. Birmingham, circa 2016.

Huntley, Horace. Telephone interview. Birmingham, Alabama. May 3, 2017.

Kimerling, Solomon. Birmingham, Alabama. December 19, 2013.

Knowlton, Sam and Gwen. Springville, Alabama. April 28, 2017.

LaMonte, Edward Shannon. Telephone interview, Fairhope, Alabama, March 2014.

Langford, "Rob," circa 2012.

Lankford, Thomas. Multiple interviews, 2009-2017.

Lewis, Jesse, Sr. Birmingham, Alabama, 2016.

Macnab, Rowena, Internet interview from Springville, Alabama, May 28, 2020.

McPhillips, Julian, Jr. Montgomery, Alabama. April 23, 2106.

Miller, Elaine Hobson. Springville, Alabama. April 25, 2018.

Morgan, Camille, telephone interview from Birmingham, Alabama. September 27, 2015.

Orange, David. Birmingham, Alabama. January 13, 2015.

Parker, Alton. Birmingham, Alabama. September 14, 2015.

Patton, Martha Jane, Birmingham, Alabama. November 19, 2016.

Pizitz, Richard. Birmingham, Alabama. February 5, 2016.

Raviv, Lynn, telephone interview from Birmingham, Alabama. November 23, 2020.

Rumore, Samuel, Birmingham, Alabama. April 11, 2017.

Rupp, Peggy Horne. Birmingham, Alabama. January 4, 2016.

Russakoff, Dale. Telephone interview from Birmingham, Alabama. July 5, 2017.

Shiland, Arnold. Telephone interview from Birmingham, Alabama. September 27, 2015.

Siegal, Bobbie. Telephone interview from Springville, Alabama. May 11, 2017.

Siegal, Don. Telephone interview from Springville, Alabama. May 11, 2017.

Segal, Arthur. Telephone interview from Springville, Alabama. June 23, 2020.

Stewart, Shelley Birmingham, Alabama. May 10, 2017 and May 24, 2017.
Sturdivant, Jim. March 2021.
Tilford, Earl. Tuscaloosa, Alabama. January 2, 2016.
Vance, Robert, Jr. Birmingham, Alabama. April 28, 2017.
Volker, Virginia (Sparks). Birmingham, Alabama. April 4, 2014.
Walbert, David. Telephone interview from Birmingham, Alabama. January 24, 2017.
Walbert, Eileen. Birmingham, Alabama. January 28, 2016.
Webster, Shannon. Birmingham, Alabama. August 18, 2009.
Weinstein, Phyllis G., email exchange, August 13, 2020.
West, Peggy. Birmingham, Alabama. August 21, 2017.

Index